THE CONVENTION AND THE KINGDOM

How and why did the European Convention turn from a neglected legal tool into one of the most important human rights documents in legal practice? This book argues this remarkable development was not merely the result of a top-down movement initiated by the European Court but of a far more dynamic process in which the national and European spheres engaged in constant co-creation. Focusing on the Netherlands and uncovering little known archival sources, it lays bare how the Convention was received over time throughout the entire Kingdom. In doing so, it incorporates insight into how European human rights were perceived in Europe and beyond. A much more varied story comes to light in which contingency and interaction take centre stage and which uncovers the choices that continue to shape the character of the Convention as we know it today.

Wiebe Hommes is Assistant Professor in European Law and Legal History at the University of Amsterdam. His research revolves around the history of human rights and European integration, as well as the role of individuals in the creation of (international) law.

LAW IN CONTEXT

Since 1970, the Law in Context series has been at the forefront of a movement to broaden the study of law. The series is a vehicle for the publication of innovative monographs and texts that treat law and legal phenomena critically in their cultural, social, political, technological, environmental and economic contexts. A contextual approach involves treating legal subjects broadly, using materials from other humanities and social sciences, and from any other discipline that helps to explain the operation in practice of the particular legal field or legal phenomena under investigation. It is intended that this orientation is at once more stimulating and more revealing than the bare exposition of legal rules. The series includes original research monographs, coursebooks and textbooks that foreground contextual approaches and methods. The series includes and welcomes books on the study of law in all its contexts, including domestic legal systems, European and international law, transnational and global legal processes, and comparative law.

Books in the Series

Acosta: *The National versus the Foreigner in South America: 200 Years of Migration and Citizenship Law*

Alaattinoğlu: *Grievance Formation, Rights and Remedies*

Ali: *Modern Challenges to Islamic Law*

Alyagon Darr: *Plausible Crime Stories: The Legal History of Sexual Offences in Mandate Palestine*

Anderson, Schum & Twining: *Analysis of Evidence, 2nd Edition*

Ashworth: *Sentencing and Criminal Justice, 6th Edition*
Barton & Douglas: *Law and Parenthood*
Baxi, McCrudden & Paliwala: *Law's Ethical, Global and Theoretical Contexts: Essays in Honour of William Twining*
Beecher-Monas: *Evaluating Scientific Evidence: An Interdisciplinary Framework for Intellectual Due Process*
Bell: *French Legal Cultures*
Bercusson: *European Labour Law, 2nd Edition*
Birkinshaw: *European Public Law*
Birkinshaw: *Freedom of Information: The Law, the Practice and the Ideal, 4th Edition*
Blick: *Electrified Democracy*: *The Internet and the United Kingdom Parliament in History*
Broderick & Ferri: *International and European Disability Law and Policy: Text, Cases and Materials*
Brownsword & Goodwin: *Law and the Technologies of the Twenty-First Century: Text and Materials*
Cane & Goudkamp: *Atiyah's Accidents, Compensation and the Law, 9th Edition*
Clarke: *Principles of Property Law*
Clarke & Kohler: *Property Law: Commentary and Materials*
Collins: *The Law of Contract, 4th Edition*
Collins, Ewing & McColgan: *Labour Law, 3rd Edition*
Corrias, Law and Inhumanity: *Dehumanization, Silent Claims and Atrocity Crimes*
Cowan: *Housing Law and Policy*
Cranston: *Making Commercial Law Through Practice 1830–1970*
Cranston: *Legal Foundations of the Welfare State*
Darian-Smith: *Laws and Societies in Global Contexts: Contemporary Approaches*
Dauvergne: *Making People Illegal: What Globalisation Means for Immigration and Law*
David: *Kinship, Law and Politics: An Anatomy of Belonging*
Davies: *Perspectives on Labour Law, 2nd Edition*
Dembour: *Who Believes in Human Rights?: Reflections on the European Convention*
de Sousa Santos: *Toward a New Legal Common Sense: Law, Globalization, and Emancipation*
Diduck: *Law's Families*
Douglas-Scott: *Brexit, Union, and Disunion: The Evolution of British Constitutional Unsettlement*
Dowdle: *Transnational Law: A Framework for Analysis*
Dupret: *Positive Law from the Muslim World: Jurisprudence, History, Practices*
Emon: *Jurisdictional Exceptionalisms: Islamic Law, International Law, and Parental Child Abduction*
Estella: *Legal Foundations of EU Economic Governance*
Fortin: *Children's Rights and the Developing Law, 3rd Edition*
Garnsey: *The Justice of Visual Art: Creative State-Building in Times of Political Transition*
Garton, Probert & Bean: *Moffat's Trusts Law: Text and Materials, 7th Edition*
Ghai & Woodman: *Practising Self-Government: A Comparative Study of Autonomous Regions*

Glover-Thomas: *Reconstructing Mental Health Law and Policy*
Gobert & Punch: *Rethinking Corporate Crime*
Goldman: *Globalisation and the Western Legal Tradition: Recurring Patterns of Law and Authority*
Haack: *Evidence Matters: Science, Proof, and Truth in the Law*
Harlow & Rawlings: *Law and Administration, 4th Edition*
Harris: *An Introduction to Law, 8th Edition*
Harris, Campbell & Halson: *Remedies in Contract and Tort, 2nd Edition*
Harvey: *Seeking Asylum in the UK: Problems and Prospects*
Herring: *Law and the Relational Self*
Hervey & McHale: *European Union Health Law: Themes and Implications*
Hervey & McHale: *Health Law and the European Union*
Holder & Lee: *Environmental Protection, Law and Policy: Text and Materials, 2nd Edition*
Jackson & Summers: *The Internationalisation of Criminal Evidence: Beyond the Common Law and Civil Law Traditions*
Jeutner: *The Reasonable Person: A Legal Biography*
Kennedy: *Inducing Intimacy: Deception, Consent and the Law*
Kostakopoulou: *The Future Governance of Citizenship*
Kreiczer-Levy: *Destabilized Property: Property Law in the Sharing Economy*
Kubal: *Immigration and Refugee Law in Russia: Socio-Legal Perspectives*
Lewis: *Choice and the Legal Order: Rising above Politics*
Likosky: *Law, Infrastructure and Human Rights*
Likosky: *Transnational Legal Processes: Globalisation and Power Disparities*
Lixinski: *Legalized Identities: Cultural Heritage Law and the Shaping of Transitional Justice*
Loughnan: *Self, Others and the State: Relations of Criminal Responsibility*
Lunney: *A History of Australian Tort Law 1901-1945: England's Obedient Servant?*
Maughan & Webb: *Lawyering Skills and the Legal Process, 2nd Edition*
McGaughey: *Principles of Enterprise Law*
McGlynn: *Families and the European Union: Law, Politics and Pluralism*
Mertens: *A Philosophical Introduction to Human Rights*
Miller: *An Introduction to German Law and Legal Culture: Text and Materials*
Moffat: *Trusts Law: Text and Materials*
Monti: *EC Competition Law*
Morgan: *Contract Law Minimalism: A Formalist Restatement of Commercial Contract Law*
Morgan & Yeung: *An Introduction to Law and Regulation: Text and Materials*
Nash: *British Islam and English Law: A Classical Pluralist Perspective*
Ng: *Political Censorship in British Hong Kong: Freedom of Expression and the Law (1842–1997)*
Nicola & Davies: *EU Law Stories: Contextual and Critical Histories of European Jurisprudence*
Norrie: *Crime, Reason and History: A Critical Introduction to Criminal Law, 3rd Edition*
Norrie: *Rethinking Criminal Justice: Punishment, Abolition and Moral Psychology*
O'Dair: *Legal Ethics: Text and Materials*

Oliver: *Common Values and the Public–Private Divide*
Oliver & Drewry: *The Law and Parliament*
Palmer & Roberts: *Dispute Processes: ADR and the Primary Forms of Decision-Making, 1st Edition*
Palmer & Roberts: *Dispute Processes: ADR and the Primary Forms of Decision-Making, 3rd Edition*
Picciotto: *International Business Taxation*
Pieraccini: *Regulating the Sea: A Socio-Legal Analysis of English Marine Protected Areas*
Probert: *The Changing Legal Regulation of Cohabitation, 1600-2010: From Fornicators to Family, 1600-2010*
Qiao: *The Authoritarian Commons: Neighborhood Democratization in Urban China*
Radi: *Rules and Practices of International Investment Law and Arbitration*
Reed: *Internet Law: Text and Materials*
Richardson: *Law, Process and Custody*
Roberts & Palmer: *Dispute Processes: ADR and the Primary Forms of Decision-Making, 2nd Edition*
Rowbottom: *Democracy Distorted: Wealth, Influence and Democratic Politics*
Sauter: *Public Services in EU Law*
Scott & Black: *Cranston's Consumers and the Law*
Seneviratne: *Ombudsmen: Public Services and Administrative Justice*
Seppänen: *Ideological Conflict and the Rule of Law in Contemporary China: Useful Paradoxes*
Siems: *Comparative Law, 3rd Edition*
Stapleton: *Product Liability*
Stewart: *Gender, Law and Justice in a Global Market*
Tamanaha: *Law as a Means to an End: Threat to the Rule of Law*
Taylor: *Fortin's Children's Rights and the Developing Law, 4th Edition*
Tuori: *Properties of Law: Modern Law and After*
Turpin & Tomkins: *British Government and the Constitution: Text and Materials, 7th Edition*
Twining: *General Jurisprudence: Understanding Law from a Global Perspective*
Twining: *Globalisation and Legal Theory*
Twining: *Human Rights, Southern Voices: Francis Deng, Abdullahi An-Na'im, Yash Ghai and Upendra Baxi*
Twining: *Jurist in Context: A Memoir*
Twining: *Karl Llewellyn and the Realist Movement, 2nd Edition*
Twining: *Rethinking Evidence: Exploratory Essays, 2nd Edition*
Twining & Miers: *How to Do Things with Rules, 5th Edition*
Varney: *Disability, Human Rights and Contract Law*
Wan: *Film and Constitutional Controversy: Visualizing Hong Kong Identity in the Age of 'One Country, Two Systems'*
Ward: *A Critical Introduction to European Law, 3rd Edition*
Ward: *Law, Text, Terror*

Ward: *Shakespeare and Legal Imagination*

Watt: *The Making Sense of Politics, Media, and Law: Rhetorical Performance as Invention, Creation, Production*

Wells & Quick: *Lacey, Wells and Quick: Reconstructing Criminal Law: Text and Materials, 4th Edition*

Woodhead: *Caring for Cultural Heritage: An Integrated Approach to Legal and Ethical Initiatives in the United Kingdom*

Yeung and Ranchordás: *An Introduction to Law and Regulation: Text and Materials, 2nd Edition*

Young: *Turpin and Tomkins' British Government and the Constitution: Text and Materials, 8th Edition*

Zander: *Cases and Materials on the English Legal System, 10th Edition*

Zander: *The Law-Making Process, 6th Edition*

International Journal of Law in Context: A Global Forum for Interdisciplinary Legal Studies

The *International Journal of Law in Context* is the companion journal to the Law in Context book series and provides a forum for interdisciplinary legal studies and offers intellectual space for ground-breaking critical research. It publishes contextual work about law and its relationship with other disciplines including but not limited to science, literature, humanities, philosophy, sociology, psychology, ethics, history and geography. More information about the journal and how to submit an article can be found at http://journals.cambridge.org/ijc

THE CONVENTION AND THE KINGDOM

How the Netherlands Received the European Convention on Human Rights

Wiebe Hommes

University of Amsterdam

CAMBRIDGE
UNIVERSITY PRESS

CAMBRIDGE
UNIVERSITY PRESS

Shaftesbury Road, Cambridge CB2 8EA, United Kingdom

One Liberty Plaza, 20th Floor, New York, NY 10006, USA

477 Williamstown Road, Port Melbourne, VIC 3207, Australia

314–321, 3rd Floor, Plot 3, Splendor Forum, Jasola District Centre,
New Delhi – 110025, India

103 Penang Road, #05–06/07, Visioncrest Commercial, Singapore 238467

Cambridge University Press is part of Cambridge University Press & Assessment,
a department of the University of Cambridge.

We share the University's mission to contribute to society through the pursuit of education, learning and research at the highest international levels of excellence.

www.cambridge.org
Information on this title: www.cambridge.org/9781009676816

DOI: 10.1017/9781009676809

When citing this work, please include a reference to the
DOI 10.1017/9781009676809

First published 2025

Cover image: *Misty Sea,* Jan Toorop (1858-1928), oil on canvas, 1899, on loan from the Triton Collection Foundation, https://id.rijksmuseum.nl/200100988

A catalogue record for this publication is available from the British Library

A Cataloging-in-Publication data record for this book is available from the Library of Congress

ISBN 978-1-009-67681-6 Hardback

To my parents

Contents

Acknowledgements

This book is a revised version of a PhD conducted at the University of Amsterdam. I was often warned that doing a PhD would be a lonely, lonesome process, yet little did I know that the process I embarked on would in fact be an extremely enjoyable journey. Most thanks in that regard go to my supervisors, Christina Eckes and Marc de Wilde. Both have served as mentors and sources of inspiration throughout the process, and I couldn't have wished for a better set of people in moving the project forward.

Christina, the way you do and see research, critically and engaged, has not only taught me more than I could imagine but has also been a source of academic and personal inspiration throughout the years. Marc, your genuine intellectual curiosity and capability to engage with a wide variety of disciplines is something I aspire to.

I would wish to express my gratitude to the members of my doctorate committee, Yvonne Donders, Barbara Oomen, Leonard Besselink, Ronald Janse, Carla Zoethout and Antoine Vauchez who took the time of reading a rather extensive study and providing constructive takes and critique, which were instrumental in moving the project forward.

At the University of Amsterdam, I joined a vibrant research community, not just intellectually, but also socially. Special thanks to Teresa, Jackson and Wim, who made the entire trajectory a joy to follow alongside. I cherish the time spent with Marta, Sophie, Debadatta and Filipe in 'our' room. I am grateful for Filipe for not just being an academic powerhouse but also – with Mariana – a great host and cook. Marta, your ability of being equal amounts busy and attentive continues to amaze. In the Graduate Studies Committee and Central PhD Council I was happy to work alongside people who shared the ambition of making the university a better place. Small parts of this book have appeared in other form elsewhere: Section 3.4 on the importance of the Greek case has been based on a chapter in the edited volume *The 1969 Greek Case in the Council of Europe*. Section 4.2 builds on work put forward in the *European Law Open*.

My gratitude goes further to Ingo Venzke, who showed me it was actually possible to work on the history of international law using archival research and pointed out the opportunity for a PhD position when I was still wondering where to go next. Anniek de Ruijter was of great help when I needed insight into how 'doing a PhD' actually worked, even though she had to put up with my own stubbornness plenty of times. All the other colleagues on the tenth, and by now also the eight floor, thank you for having been of great help throughout the process. With Karin van Leeuwen I share an avid interest in the proper 'history' of law: I am looking forward to more interactions on the topic in the future. The group which is emerging around this direction in Oslo, with Brigitte Leucht, Morten Rasmussen, Mala Loth and Magnus Esmark is a source of fundamental intellectual stimulation. León Castellanos-Jankiewicz is to me an example of how to be an academic and simply a wonderful and generous person.

I look back with particular fondness at my stay at iCourts in Copenhagen, where the reception could not have been more welcoming and where the comments pushed me to explore new directions. All the people at Dutch Research Council made the Covid-months I spent there a pleasure, even though they were mostly spent behind a screen. I owe a distinct gratitude to Harold Zee from the Ministry of Foreign Affairs, whose help on accessing even the more recent files, tucked away in a small reading room in The Hague, was unwavering.

To my friends, you made this PhD possible in more ways than you know.

Ciska, thanks for being a constant factor of positivity: thank you Kick for all the small moments of self-evident understanding.

I owe everything to my parents. Pap, mam, the way you have always and continuously expressed interest and support, wherever I went, has been invaluable.

Introduction

FOR A GREAT PERIOD OF TIME, the European Convention on Human Rights (the Convention) was barely known. Inactive on the European level and shunned at the domestic level, it would seem European human rights offered very little promise. To lawyers, European human rights seemed irrelevant to legal practice and unable to provide any meaningful impact for individuals. In the 1960s, it was common for domestic lawyers to be accused by the presiding judge of 'defaming the government' by invoking the Convention, whereas to the states signing up to the Convention in 1950 in the Palazzo Barberini in Rome, the idea that one day they would routinely be judged by an international court for human rights violations was considered nothing less than absurd. When Paul-Henri Spaak, president of the Consultative Assembly of the Council of Europe, quipped on that occasion that it was 'a lovely palace but not a very good Convention', he voiced a sentiment which would carry on for decades.[1]

Fast forward to the present-day, the situation is drastically different. The European Court of Human Rights (the Court) is frequently described as a victim of its own success, and the Convention serves as a key instrument of human rights protection for individuals ranging from the U.K. to Azerbaijan. This striking development, of a document once considered irrelevant to a key tool in legal practice, has not gone unnoticed. In recent years, the Convention and its accompanying Court find themselves under increasing political pressure. They are perceived by

[1] Quoted in Jonas Christofferson and Mikael Rask Madsen (eds.), *The European Court between Law and Politics* (Oxford: Oxford University Press, 2011), p. 6.

politicians to be overly intrusive in domestic legal orders and seen as constraining a country's freedom to legislate or take action. In the last decade, an open backlash against the Court has emerged, prompting multiple initiatives to enhance the principle of subsidiarity, reflect critically on the direction of the case law of the Court or even resulting in calls to abandon the system altogether.[2]

In order to illustrate this development, this book takes a specific context as its focus: the Kingdom of the Netherlands.[3] One may ask what the added value of a focus on one particular single state is in this story, yet in this book, I argue that the Netherlands forms a particular fascinating case study, as it allows for an in depth, detailed study into the very microlevel of engagement with the Convention and yields insights which are of relevance to entire system.

First, with the remarkable constitutional openness of the Netherlands, where Articles 94 and 120 of the Dutch Constitution entail that judges cannot review legislation against the Constitution but can do so against directly applicable international law, the Convention occupies an, on paper at least, tremendously important position. Over the years it has indeed come to serve as a surrogate 'Constitutional document' and prime legal tool for fundamental rights protection.[4] These provisions ensure that from very early on, there was already great potential for an active engagement with European human rights.[5]

[2] Lize Glas, 'From Interlaken to Copenhagen: What Has Become of the Proposals Aiming to Reform the Functioning of the European Court of Human Rights?' *Human Rights Law Review* Vol. 20 Nr. 1 (2020), pp. 121–151; Mikael Rask Madsen, 'From Boom to Backlash? The European Court of Human Rights and the Transformation of Europe' in H. Aust and D. Esra (eds.), *The European Court of Human Rights: Current Challenges in Historical and Comparative Perspective* (Cheltenham: Edward Elgar, 2021), pp. 21–42.

[3] The Kingdom entails not just the 'European' Netherlands but also the islands in the Caribbean: Aruba, Curaçao, Sint Maarten and Bonaire, Saba and St. Eustatius. In this work, also the former parts of the Kingdom, such as New Guinea and Suriname, will be considered.

[4] Janneke Gerards and Carla Sieburgh (eds.), *De invloed van Fundamentele rechten op het materiele recht* (Deventer: Kluwer, 2013), pp. 543–544.

[5] There is currently no such study on the Netherlands: The leading socio-legal inquiry on human rights in the Netherlands is Barbara Oomen, *Rights for Others: The Slow Home-Coming of Human Rights in the Netherlands* (Cambridge: Cambridge University Press, 2014).

Moreover, one of the original signatory states, the Netherlands was involved from the beginning of the Convention and a quite active participant in Strasbourg. Over the years, it acquired a reputation as a strong human rights proponent. Yet in recent years it was also one of the states vocal in pushing back against what was perceived to be an overreach of the European Court, with calls to simply withdraw from the treaty altogether increasing in prominence on the national level. The case of the Netherlands can hence shed light on this pushback and illustrate how recent critique is in fact far from new. Rather than a distinct break from an otherwise golden age of human rights protection, recent discussions are a continuation of an open and ongoing legal and political debate over both the Convention as well as the Dutch identity.

For, in addition, a study into the Netherlands brings another key element into the picture, which often remains sidelined and has only recently entered the history of European law and of the Convention, namely the colonial dimension. This book shows how European human rights functioned in relation to the imperial states of which it became a part. After the signing of the Convention in 1950, the Netherlands had to balance the interests of its empire with the demands of European human rights. It was not alone in that position: France, Belgium and the U.K. faced the same challenge. However, the Netherlands took a unique route by extending the Convention, *including* the right of individual petition, to these 'overseas territories' quite early on, making European human rights a relevant factor beyond Europe as well.[6]

Such a focus on the colonial dimension matters greatly, as far too often the Convention has been presented as a story which only affects the 'European' part of the world. However, European human rights were and are not confined to Europe. They function as legal tools in the Caribbean islands and formed part of the law of the land in Suriname. Moreover, continuing elements of colonial thinking were crucial in determining the value and meaning of the Convention, as the colonial

[6] France would not even ratify the Convention out of concern for the impact it could have on its war in Algeria, whereas the U.K. would extend the Convention, but not the right of individual petition and often immediately suspend the Convention with an appeal of the state of emergency.

element was a constant factor in the minds of those drafting and interpreting the meaning of European human rights. But again, this was never merely a 'European' issue. In this book, also the relevant actors from the 'overseas territories' are incorporated in their engagement with the Convention, thereby restoring the agency of these often sidelined actors in the history of European human rights.[7]

As such this book illustrates how and why the European Convention turned from a barely used instrument, with an inactive Court tucked away in Strasbourg, into the primary means of legal protection for individuals seeking to protect their fundamental rights in the Kingdom of the Netherlands. Moreover, they did so in front of a Court which became increasingly considered by some as invasive and excessively powerful, as European human rights were made to matter in areas previously considered immune to human rights.

THE MANY HISTORIES OF THE CONVENTION

In doing so, this study builds on a wealth of previous research. The question of how the Convention 'turned active' is a question which has puzzled scholars for quite some time now. The most pervasive explanation for this change is the one in which the law itself, and in particular the actions of the European Court, have taken up a central role: after its decision in *Tyrer* v. *UK* to establish the Convention as a living instrument, the road was open to a progressive interpretation of the treaty which has continued until today.[8] It's a story of the 'rise and rise' of the European Convention which, after a slow start, took off to become the most important regional human rights system in the world. The image conjured in this narrative is that of the Convention as 'Sleeping Beauty': passive and quiet until Prince Charming (the Court) steps in to wake her up, and living happily ever after.

[7] It takes inspiration from other studies in the field of EU-law in this regard, most notably Megan Brown, *The Seventh Member State: Algeria, France and the European Community* (Cambridge: Harvard University Press, 2022).

[8] Ed Bates, *The Evolution of the European Convention on Human Rights: From Its Inception to the Creation of a Permanent Court of Human Rights* (Oxford: Oxford University Press, 2010); Stephen Greer, *The European Convention on Human Rights: Achievements, Problems and Prospects* (Cambridge: Cambridge University Press, 2006).

Yet that classical narrative is slowly shifting. (Legal) historians have in recent years, for instance, shed light on the early years of the Convention and convincingly shown the limits of the traditional humanitarian liberalist narrative of the early history of the Convention.[9] Instead, they have shown how the drafters of the document were, alongside the impact of the Cold War, far more concerned with maintaining a conservative image of European civilization than with creating a liberal humanitarian template.[10]

However, these accounts tend to focus primarily on the drafting history of the Convention, or the first decade of the existence of the Convention. Yet the drafting of any kind of human rights treaty is only the beginning of the history of that particular instrument. What is subsequently missing from these studies, therefore, is insight into the ensuing legal practice of European human rights.

A different discipline, namely socio-legal scholarship, has been at the forefront of those narratives.[11] Studies in this tradition have stepped away from the focus on the Court and instead highlighted the vital role of the relation between the national and European spheres[12], they have shed the light on key actors, such as individual lawyers[13], and have set out how the European Court first had to gain sufficient authority in the eyes of the relevant stakeholders before it could launch its interpretative revolution.[14]

This book builds on these crucial insights in order to unsettle the image of the Convention as a Sleeping Beauty, but adds three broad

[9] Samuel Moyn, *The Last Utopia: Human Rights in History* (Cambridge: Harvard University Press, 2010); A. W. B. Simpson, *Human Rights and the End of Empire: Britain and the Genesis of the European Convention* (Oxford: Oxford University Press, 2004).

[10] Marco Duranti, *The Conservative Human Rights Revolution: European Identity, Transnational Politics, and the Origins of the European Convention* (Oxford: Oxford University Press, 2017).

[11] Mikael Rask Madsen, *La Genèse de l'Europe des droits de l'homme: enjeux juridiques et stratégies d'état (France, Grande-Bretagne et pays scandinaves, 1945-1970)* (Strasbourg: Presse Universitaires de Strasbourg, 2010).

[12] Helen Keller and Alec Stone Sweet (eds.), *A Europe of Rights: The Impact of the ECHR on National Legal Systems* (Oxford: Oxford University Press, 2008).

[13] Vauchez, *Brokering Europe: Euro-Lawyers and the Making of a Transnational Polity* (Cambridge: Cambridge University Press, 2015); Laurens Lavrysen, 'Strasbourg was Something New, It was an Adventure: A History of the Belgian Cases before the European Court of Human Rights in the 1960s, 1970s and 1980s' *TVRG* Vol. 86. Nr. 3–4 (2018), pp. 482–527.

[14] Jonas Christofferson and Mikael Rask Madsen (eds.), *The European Court between Law and Politics* (Oxford: Oxford University Press, 2011).

points. First, it adds historical sensitivity to the legal and socio-legal scholarship by using a historical methodology to analyse extensive archival sources of governmental and non-governmental actors. This allows for a more diverse source of material to draw conclusions from, test the sociological theories against historical facts, and to shed light on forgotten or secret discussions and initiatives. Second, it adds new actors – such as diplomats, lawyers, and scholars themselves – to both the legal and historical narratives by shifting the focus from European institutional developments to the wider national legal practice and its interaction with the European context. Finally, it adds a much wider time frame to the historical studies. The book focuses on the period from 1945 to 2022 in order to show the subtle changes in how the Convention has been perceived and how its meaning was constructed. In doing so, this work not only brings these narratives together, but also provides a more nuanced and complete answer as to the changing status of European human rights.

Ultimately, this book presents a new narrative on the history and development of the Convention. It steps away from a top-down development by the Court and sets out, on the basis of extensive archival research, a contingent and open history in which the shifting meanings of the Convention over the decades, driven by the actions of a variety of actors in constant interaction between the European and national levels, are laid bare.

WRITING A RECEPTION HISTORY: APPROACH, ACTORS AND CHOICES

A RECEPTION HISTORY. This narrative is put forward by means of a 'reception history' of the Convention in the Kingdom of the Netherlands. This approach requires some explanation of the choices made in this regard, primarily begging the question of what is in fact meant by the 'reception' of law and, closely related, who actually are the recipients.

First, it is evident that law 'by itself' does not do anything: it needs individual actors to mobilize it.[15] This basic fact entails consequences

[15] In particular, I draw upon 'practice theory'. Clearly, that is no clear-cut theory in itself, but it revolves around a similar insight in how the law is made in a constant daily usage. As Rajkjovic, Aalberts and Gammeltoft-Hansen note 'law emerges not in and out of

for how, for instance, international or European law find their way into national legal orders.[16] Ultimately, this also depends on the engagement of individuals with that particular law. As such, the focus of how law moves is shifted from top-down narratives to 'bottom up, where definitions, concepts and categories are studied as they are produced by the relevant actors in/of the field'.[17]

This serves as starting point of the idea of 'reception' used in this book, which is the process with which actors in a certain jurisdiction engage, and thereby interpret and give meaning to the Convention. In doing so, these actors exhibit a broader agency than merely accepting or resisting a rule.[18] Indeed, the engagement and interpretations of these actors have an impact on the law which is received. Reception, hence is distinctively not a passive state of affairs in which the receiving jurisdiction meekly accepts 'top down' developments, important as they may be.[19] Rather, it is an incredibly productive process in which these actors, by engaging with the law in practice, also shape and give meaning to the 'received' law.[20] Law is, after all, to use the words of Sheila Jasanoff, embedded in 'social practices, identities, norms, conventions, discourses, instruments and institutions', which fundamentally shape

itself, but out of the way it is used in daily practice by a wide variety of actors'; Rajkovic, N., Aalberts, T., and Gammeltoft-Hansen, T. (eds.), *The Power of Legality: Practices of International Law and their Politics* (Cambridge: Cambridge University Press, 2016).

16 For the Netherlands, see Wibo Van Rossum, 'The Roots of Dutch Strategic Human Rights Litigation: Comparing "Engel" to "SGP"' in: M. van den Brink, S. Burri and J. Goldschmidt (eds.), *Equality and Human Rights: Nothing but Trouble? Liber amicorum Titia Loenen* (Utrecht: SIM, 2015) pp. 387–401.

17 Rajkovic, Aalberts and Hansen, *The Power of Legality*, p. 12.

18 This is close but broader than the definition used by Keller and Stone Sweet, namely 'how – that is, through what mechanisms – national officials confront, make use of, and resist or give agency to Convention rights'. However, the focus on national officials is relatively limited. Instead, legal philosopher Denis Gallagan offers a somewhat broader framework: 'how groups of citizens and officials handle the law, use the law, take care of its demands, or push this to the sidelines'. This has an additional benefit of including groups of citizens. The usage of the law is also broader: leaving aside is, after all, *one* of the ways in which law can be used. Denis Galligan, *Law in Modern Society* (Oxford: Oxford University Press, 2007), p. 121.

19 Thomas Duve, *Entanglements in Legal History: Conceptual Approaches* (Frankfurt: Max Planck Institute, 2014), pp. 29–66.

20 See for a similar strategy in EU law. Tomasso Pavone, *The Ghostwriters: Lawyers and the Politics behind the Judicial Construction of Europe* (Cambridge: Cambridge University, Press 2022).

the understanding of law.[21] This entails that in order to understand the law, and in particular the knowledge and practice of that law, one needs to take those elements into account.

What emerges if one applies this lens to the Convention is a process of continuous co-creation of European human rights. The Convention is not merely the creation of courts but the result of the engagement of a myriad of actors. This is not an isolated domestic process. Far from it even: the national and European spheres are not separated, with the national reception feeding back into the European context and vice versa.[22] Indeed, the transnational opportunities which the Convention offers transform both the international through national actors *and* the national through the impact of the international.[23] In the context of the Convention, this holds that a firm and constant reflective entanglement between the international and the national contexts takes place.[24]

ACTORS AND ARCHIVES. Such an approach foregrounds the individual actors who are active in this co-creation, which begs the question of who these people actually are. Here, the book draws on 'practice theory' to define the key groups within society that are engaged in this process. For if we understand the law to be the result of legal practice, these actors involved in its creation are not solely the courts or individual judges or lawyers. Rather, using this more holistic idea of legal engagement, the perspective opens up to include a much wider group of relevant actors.

[21] Sheila Jasanoff, 'The Idiom of Co-Production' in Jasanoff (ed.), *States of Knowledge: The Co-Production of Science and the Social Order* (London: Routledge, 2004), p. 3.

[22] Mikael Rask Madsen, 'The Protracted Institutionalization of the Strasbourg Court: From Legal Diplomacy to Integrationist Jurisprudence' in J. Christoffersen and M. R. Madsen (eds.), *The European Court of Human Rights between Law and Politics* (Oxford: Oxford University Press, 2011), pp. 43–60.

[23] Yves Dezalay and Bryant G. Garth, *Dealing in Virtue: International Commercial Arbitration and the Construction of a Transnational Legal Order* (Chicago: University of Chicago, Press, 1996), p. 4.

[24] As socio-legal scholarship sets out, the development of international courts is closely tied to its authority, which subsequently is tied to its domestic (national) audiences. See in that regard, most prominently, Karen Alter, Mikael Rask Madsen and Laurence Helfer (eds.), *International Court Authority* (Oxford: Oxford University Press, 2018); see also S. Hennette-Vauchez, 'Constitutional v International? When Unified Reformatory Rationales Mismatch the Plural Paths of Legitimacy of ECHR Law', in Christoffersen and Madsen (eds.), *The European Court of Human Rights between Law and Politics*, pp. 144–163.

Following the flexible definition of Rajkovic, Aalberts, and Gammeltoft-Hansen, at least four groups can be defined. First, the institutional actors, being the national courts and the European Court/Commission. Second, there are the political actors, broadly understood as being governmental actors, Parliamentarians, diplomats, NGOs, and individual activists or plaintiffs. Third, scholars – academics and other interpreters – play a distinctive role. Far from being mere commentators, scholars put forward their own conceptions of what the law could, and often should, be.[25] Finally, also the media play a distinctive role, as they shed light on what the broader public knows, hears, or reads about the Convention.[26]

A vital point here is that these actors do not remain isolated in their siloed area or national jurisdiction. After all, these are not monolithic fields that exist in splendid isolation from each other. Rather, actors often cross over from one field to another, forming an integral part of several instances and competing over the correct interpretations within their own fields and with other fields. Moreover, they constantly interact with the European level: by receiving the Convention, they in turn have an impact on the European context. Relating to the specific history of the Convention, these 'travelling' individuals have indeed played a vital role in its history. For instance, those actors moving between the national and European levels served (and serve) as key translators between the two spheres. The 'double hat' of the first members of the Commission, being both politicians as well as lawyers or legal officials, ensured they had a vital impact on the functioning of the Commission *and* on domestic politics, whereas academics writing about the Convention played defining roles – as 'Euro-human rights-lawyers' – in bringing cases to Strasbourg in order to 'prime the pump' of the European human rights system.

This book thus embraces a broad conception of who 'received' and subsequently shaped the Convention in order to uncover those choices.[27]

[25] Rajkovic, Aalberts and Hansen, *The Power of Legality*, p. 18.

[26] See in this vein also the approach of Oomen, 'A Serious Case of Strasbourg-bashing?' *The International Journal of Human Rights* Vol. 20 Nr. 3 (2016), pp. 407–425. Media is broadly understood: it pertains to newspapers, cartoons, advertisements and other forms of expression.

[27] It is in that regard broader than Bill Davies' seminal work: Bill Davies, *Resisting the European Court of Justice: West Germany's Confrontation with European Law, 1949–1979* (Cambridge: Cambridge University Press, 2012).

It follows governmental diplomats as they attempt to curtail the Court, Ministers who for their part seek to energize the Court, judges who cry out in anguish in the face of appeals on the Convention, activists who are accused of building 'castles in the sky', and scholars who write case notes on cases they themselves brought to the Court. In doing so, the narrative moves beyond a Court-centered approach to include a host of other actors in the story, being part of government, Parliament, media, academia or 'civil society'. These are the actors who also created the European Convention.

A final element to consider when it comes to these actors is that most of them could be found in leading echelons of government, judiciary and academia. In particular in the early days of the Convention, one group was distinctively absent from these venues: women.[28] Even though women played influential roles in, for instance, the local Dutch European movement, it would take time for European human rights to truly become a shared venue of engagement. In this regard it is important to keep in mind how from the very beginning the Convention was set up based on traditional values, excluding the right of non-discrimination on grounds of sex, for instance. Even when the feminist movement emerged in the sixties and seventies, the Convention was not necessarily the strongest or most obvious choice for legal engagement, something which only started to change roughly in the nineties, during which the Convention increasingly figured in women's rights movements.[29]

Through the actions of all these actors, the meaning of the Convention was ultimately defined. In their engagement with European human rights, they engaged in a struggle over the perceived meaning of the law at hand. As this was and remains in constant flux, there is no distinct 'correct' version of the Convention. Legal change therefore forms the result of a continuous search for possible interpretations and outcomes in light of other possibilities. Interpretation therefore ultimately comes down to a power struggle: which vision prevails and who has the power

[28] On this mechanism, see Janne Nijman, 'Marked Absences: Locating Gender and Race in International Legal History' *European Journal of International Law* Vol. 31 Nr. 3 (2020), pp. 1025–1050.

[29] Renée Römkens, 'Bestemd Voor Binnenlands Gebruik: De Invloed van de Vrouwen- En Mensenrechtenbeweging Op Het Debat En de Aanpak van Gendergerelateerd Geweld' *Tijdschrift Sociologie* Vol. 12 Nr. 3 (2016), pp. 295–319, 310.

to define the meaning of the law at hand?[30] In this process, choices were and are being made in a 'battle for law'. It also entails how not all actors had similar impact or power, or that these remained constant throughout time. The impact of domestic courts, for instance, was rather minimal in the sixties, but extremely important in the eighties: precisely a historical study can show these shifts in engagement.

This lets the historian face the distinctive task of uncovering these choices and moments: who put forward which option and when? Which visions prevailed and why? And who was not thought of, or was absent in these decisions? As this book sheds light on those moments, the resulting story is one of fundamental openness: the Convention could have been different. As a result, many of the initiatives discussed in the next chapters are, in fact, the history of failures. One remarkable element of the Convention, the conspicuous absence of socio-economic rights, for instance, was debated, considered and rejected on several occasions. It is precisely insights into those failures which matter in providing a sense of historical contingency, as they show how other paths were considered, probed, tried, and ultimately not taken.

There are several ways to go about taking on such a broad approach. One option is to present the reception of law thematically, describing how it was received and shaped in distinct subfields such as parliamentary debate, media, or academia.[31] However, doing so would neglect precisely the porous boundaries between those fields, whereas this book seeks to emphasize those moving in between: the journalist writing about the Convention today was yesterday's academic integrating it in his teaching, just as the politician promoting the Convention today was yesterday's legal officer deciding cases in the European Commission. Hence, it opts for an integrated approach, instead describing the reception process chronologically, describing how it took place in a distinct set of periods.

A second problem relates to historical sources. If reception is such a broad societal phenomenon which entails several groups of actors, how

[30] In this vein, Ingo Venzke, *How Interpretation Makes International Law: On Semantic Change and Normative Twists* (Oxford: Oxford University Press, 2016).

[31] See for an example of this approach Davies, *Resisting the European Court of Justice.*

does one study the precise historical context in which these actors were engaged? This is different for every sector, but archives form the bulk of the answer. Archives relating to actors in each of the fields involved allow us to step into the story behind what is publicly available and gain insight into the deliberations, tensions, and context in which decisions were taken. The character of the available archives concerning the variety of actors differs, however, and occasionally requires a different approach in 'reading' them.[32]

When it comes to the main political actors, namely governmental actors, the archives of the Ministries of Foreign Affairs, Justice and Internal Affairs, as well as these archives relating to intra-Kingdom relations and the governance of Suriname and the Antilles situated in the National Archives in The Hague, provide a wealth of previously unexplored sources. They shed light on the internal discussions in governmental circles, set out the reasons for actions in Strasbourg and for the shifting attitudes with regard to the Convention and the Court. For Parliament, records of parliamentary debates have been used. These sources allow us to 'pierce the veil' of the state and shed light on the internal deliberations, power struggles and reasons for external actions.[33] They also provide a window into the discussions in Strasbourg itself: even if these are focused through the Dutch lens, the materials found in the archives of Foreign Affairs concerning notes of meetings, discussions with other delegations, or one-on-ones in the hallways of the Committee of Ministers shed light on the broader European context in which these decisions and choices took place.[34]

[32] As the sources are mostly in Dutch or French, translations into English were made, which are all mine.

[33] For a similar approach see Eyal Benvenisti, Doreen Lustig, 'Monopolizing War: Codifying the Laws of War to Reassert Governmental Authority, 1856–1874' *European Journal of International Law* Vol. 31 Nr. 1 (2020), pp. 127–169.

[34] This cannot compensate entirely for the fact that many archives of the Council of Europe, of the Court and Commission most prominently, are still closed and confidential, but it does help to understand the discussions in the Committee of Ministers, albeit from a Dutch perspective. Clearly, other archives of the Council of Europe are accessible. However, they often lack the insights 'behind the screens' which are vital to understand the ultimate decision-making, something which is at the core of the national archives. One additional element is that usually, these governmental sources only become available after thirty years. The Ministry of Foreign Affairs has graciously

A study based solely on data from governmental archives would risk a high amount of institutional bias.[35] In order to broaden the view to those working 'on the ground', archives of the most prominent NGOs and activist movements which dealt with human rights were consulted to gain insights into how the Convention was perceived by plaintiffs, promoters of European integration, and human rights activists themselves, substantiated with secondary literature.[36]

As for the study of key individuals, their personal archives offer crucial insights into either the inner workings of the European institutions and/or into their human rights activism and legal engagement. Of those archives, there are fewer available. Where possible, the personal archives of leading diplomats, scholars and lawyers have also been studied.[37] Alternatively, contributions of or about actors in secondary literature, such as opinion pieces, reflections on their work and (auto) biographies, provided additional insight into their motivations and experiences.[38]

A different kind of 'archive' can also be found in academic contributions themselves. In particular, the early scholarly engagement with the Convention was largely confined to the realm of universities. These

allowed insight into its files until the present-day: hence, I was able to also include the more recent controversies in this research

[35] David Bederman, 'Foreign Office International Legal History' in Matthew Craven, Malgosia Fitzmaurice and Maria Vogiatzi (eds.), *Time, History and International Law* (Leiden: Brill, 2007), pp. 43–63.

[36] I have selected these NGOs by noting which of them were most prominently connected to the European Convention by either their actions or by their statutory mission. This entails the archives of the Dutch European movement and its predecessors, as therein the earliest engagement can be found. When it comes to human rights groups, the archives of the NJCM, Amnesty International Netherlands, the CoorhertLiga, the solidarity movement with Greece, the Liga voor de Rechten van de Mens and the VVDM have been studied.

[37] The personal archives of key individuals F. M. van Asbeck, Bas de Gaay Fortman, Bert Röling, Peter Baehr and Willem van Bellekom have been visited. In two cases, semi-structured interviews were conducted, one with a former academic and one with a former civil servant, to further expand on these actors' own personal experiences: these serve as illustrations of the archival materials and provide additional background information. These were semi-structured interviews, held in informal setting.

[38] For instance, published interviews with key actors on their work provide insight in their perception of what was going on.

scholarly works have a distinct value as a historical source. Academic interventions in the form of articles in journals, just like Court decisions, play a distinctive historical role in the sense that they create the narrative of what could be seen as relevant or redundant. Yet as such, these sources also need to be approached in a slightly different way. Where the study of the governmental and activist actions is more in line with traditional political and social history, to read and evaluate judgements and academic pieces is more in line with intellectual history.[39] Understanding how certain arguments in these pieces relate to what came before, or to what should be done, requires awareness regarding what these authors in fact are responding to. Academic journals and scholarly debates are therefore put forward as distinctive historical sites of intellectual contestation.[40]

Finally, a range of different source materials has been used, such as the leading newspapers' coverage of the Convention, or defining cases, in order to shed light on the broader discussion of certain judgements or developments and how these were presented to the wider public.[41]

FOCUS AND SCOPE. This is a study on the ECHR. As such, it doesn't deal in detail with other international human rights instruments, or only in passing. Moreover, it means that instead of focusing on distinct articles or themes, such as the emergence of a 'reasonable time' requirement in Article 6, or the impact of Article 8 on family law, the document as a whole will be taken into account. This does pose certain challenges, particularly in the more recent time period, during which the ECHR has expanded

[39] It is hence no surprise the study of the history of (international) law has so far been primarily the domain of intellectual historians or of historians looking at the politics of international law. This research aims to bring those together.

[40] Clearly, one cannot cover *all* Court cases or academic contributions. A selection into these has been made by limiting the coverage of the Convention, or cases involving the Convention, in the leading legal journals in the Netherlands: the NJB, Ars Aequi, RM Themis and SEW. After the late seventies, human rights started to acquire a place of their own in the academic study, which allowed for a study into the more general NJB and the specialized NJCM Bulletin. When it comes to court cases, precisely those which were taken up in the societal or academic debate stand out and are, where necessary, treated in more detail.

[41] These newspapers are available via Delpher, the online newspaper database.

massively. European human rights as enshrined in the Convention now touch upon nearly every aspect of life. Still, the Convention does so also as a source in itself. For many years, the question was not necessarily what the value of Article 6 would be, but rather what the value of the Convention would be.

Those questions still remain: the present-day pushback focuses more on the broad implications of the European system as such than on distinct case law concerning the right to a fair trial or the right to property of the first protocol. An additional benefit is how a focus on the Convention as a whole keeps the perspective as open as possible. A narrow focus on a distinct articles would provide a very limited view on the development of European human rights, simply because it would miss out on key moments which occurred in a different field. By also taking those into account, it becomes possible to sketch a much more complete image of the trajectory of the Convention.

BEYOND SLEEPING BEAUTY: WHY HISTORY MATTERS

All in all, this work thus puts forward a new and distinct narrative as to how the Convention developed as it moves beyond the main narrative of a Convention turning from passive to active by the actions of the European Court and presents a much more intricate story of interaction. Such an endeavour is more than an antiquarian enterprise. Historical narratives are fundamental in shaping and defining our present understanding of reality. They serve as benchmarks which shape ideas of who 'we' are, where we come from, and how we relate to a particular object, and therefore, any work of history is simultaneously a work connected to the present. This particular intervention is no different, but has gained acute relevance as the current flawed narrative is being employed in present-day debates.

To return to the image of the Sleeping Beauty, it's a clear image with a promise of a bright future. However, a metaphor describing a passive state of affairs which suddenly changed due to an electrifying encounter with Prince Charming, may not be very instructive if we want to understand what actually happened. It presents an idealized version of the past, meaning that those who subscribe to the story may be unaware of pitfalls, critical junctures, or past debates, and conversely, may approach present-day conditions with a distorted vision of how we ended up here in the first place.

This becomes acute in light of the present debate on the role and impact of the Convention. The Court in particular has found itself in the spotlight and has been accused of stretching the Convention far beyond what was acceptable to the signatory states, with serious threats of leaving or dismantling the system as a result.

Yet it is interesting to note that both sides in this debate have turned to history to substantiate their respective positions. For critics, the story of the history of the Convention is that of a rude awakening. To stick to the image of a Sleeping Beauty, their critique revolves very much around the prince overstepping the boundaries by kissing awake the princess via a line of progressive case law. In doing so, it turned the Convention into something the drafters never meant it to be, at the expense of democratic legislation. The kiss, in other words, was not consensual.

Coming out in defence of the Court, proponents have also turned to the fairy tale: from this perspective, the Court and Convention are the most tangible remnants of a post-war consensus to protect individual human rights against governmental intrusion. As a 'beauty', it is inherently worth defending. After a slow beginning, the prince breathed life into the Convention and the princess and prince began their joyful time together as they brought civilization to the states of Europe, in particular after the end of the Cold War. Despite some backlog, according to this version, the Court fulfils an almost historical calling as the most tangible answer to the horrors of the Second World War in its defence of individual rights. This story *embraces* the kiss of the prince, as such an action was a necessary and logical prerequisite for the princess to shine. Yet this story too eagerly accepts the Court as prime actor, or the Convention as a beauty, leaving other actors out of the picture.

Telling a more varied story matters greatly in this debate. Not merely because, as a history, this approach may hold a better claim to understanding how things came to be, but also in response to the challenges the Convention faces today. If we understand the twists and turns, the debates and choices which accompanied the Convention as it 'came to matter', we can better understand where the present-day concerns come from (albeit these are far from new), but also present a better, more nuanced story in its defence. The book does not deny the importance of the European Court in bringing about change and providing meaning to the Convention. However, it does not leave it at that. If one shows how – again and again – the actions of the courts were met with reactions from a range of actors, it becomes clear how the construction of the Convention was just as much a product of societal and political (understood in a broad sense) processes. Yes, governments rejected certain judgements, but they also had an active role in furthering the Convention, just as academics, judges and activists played a myriad of different roles.

This new story also entails a message for the future. The fairy tale offers a false sense of stability: the courts have, and will continue to, protect individual rights or conversely, will subvert democratically legitimized policies irrespective of political initiatives. Yet what this book shows is how courts were only *part* of the story. Rather, the 'success or failure' of the Convention has depended on scholars, activists, lawyers, judges, diplomats, and politicians. And just as there have been multiple paths in the past which could have been taken, multiple paths lie open for the Convention in the future, to be determined also in those venues.

ON PERIODIZATION

The final choices relate to the way in which this story is told, in particular when it comes to periodization. The book starts in 1945, directly after the Second World War, as the first formal engagements with what would turn out to become the Convention kicked off shortly thereafter. Yet certain ideas and dispositions were transposed into those engagements from the pre-war era. Where relevant, these continuities will be pointed out, but not as a topic of extensive research. Another element is the simple fact the research ends relatively late, namely in 2022.[42] For a historical study, that is an unusual choice. Historians are, after all, dependent on their sources, which tend to run out or are not yet available for more recent periods. However, with the availability of many key documents

[42] Developments after 2022 have, where possible, been included, yet are not part of the main bulk of (archival) research.

and due to the relevance of the recent period, the research into the very near past became not just possible, but also important. This also allows for a more conclusive evaluation of the developments in the nineties since those choices have only truly brought forward their consequences in the last decade.

The second element pertains to the choices made in demarcating the periods between 1945 and 2022. As this book employs a chronological narrative, a question emerges of how to delineate the different chapters. In this book, they revolve around key moments which relate to shifts in meaning. As in all manners of periodization, these are not clear-cut. Sometimes, ideas carried on through distinct chapters but in different fields, whereas at other times a certain development had been set in some years before. However, by and large, the sketched periods revolve around key elements which bind them together, to be ended by events which altered those constellations.

Such an approach focused on subtle changes over time has an additional benefit in that it allows for an addition to what occasionally is done within the history of human rights, namely the search for a 'beginning' or 'breakthrough': a distinctive moment when human rights acquired its modern day position, be it the forties, seventies or nineties.[43] Yet such a search for any kind of defining period would blind us to the more nuanced and incremental shifts. Rather than focus on a distinct time period, a more protracted view adds the benefit of how a distinct human rights treaty in fact changed its character, and the periodization chosen seeks to illuminate just that.

The book proceeds as follows. Chapter 1, 'constructing the moral basis of European integration', focuses on the early history of European human rights in the Netherlands before they were, in fact, part of any legally binding constellation in the period 1945–1954. It sheds light on how they were constructed, drafted and ratified, and in particular, how they were conceived by the key players defining their meaning. European human rights were closely related to the broader desire for European integration. Via that intersection emerged a peculiar connection to what

[43] Jan Eckel and Samuel Moyn (eds.), *The Breakthrough: Human Rights in the 1970s* (Philadelphia: University of Pennsylvania Press, 2015).

it meant to be 'European'. From the outset, European human rights were not for everybody. As the legacy of empire was not easily dismissed, the resulting Convention was a peculiar limited conscience of Europe, to which the Netherlands had rather not subscribed to at all.

Chapter 2, 'The open beginning of the Convention', turns to the period directly after ratification, from 1954 to 1962. It has been often argued that the Convention did not matter in this period, but I seek to contest that understanding. Instead, the Convention was immediately tried and tested and entered the domestic context in a flurry of heated activity, as litigants and other players set out their campaigns to define what the Convention would mean, now that it was legally binding. The chapter ends in 1962 with failure on both the domestic and the European levels to make the Convention into something more than a distant document. These failures set the stage for the Convention's perceived legal meaning in the decades to come in the Kingdom.

Chapter 3, 'From European rights to human rights', covers the period from 1962 to 1968, as in those years a subtle, but lasting shift took place in Dutch society and government with regard to the approach of the Convention. In particular, decolonization made its impact. With the 'loss' of New Guinea, a new foreign policy could emerge based more on right than on might. Moreover, as Suriname and the Antilles became part of the active protection of human rights, the Convention began to turn from a document built around conservative European ideals and integration ever more into a document based on the need to protect individual human rights claims. One catalyst in this development was the interstate complaint procedure of 1967 against Greece. This not only forced the Dutch government to make a distinct choice as to what the Convention entailed, but also served as 'boomerang' to galvanize human rights activism as such.

Chapter 4 relates to human rights as they were transformed in 'the age of activism', 1968–1979. In this decade, human rights went through an interpretative revolution. Even though the courts remained wary, in the grassroots a fundamental shift occurred regarding what human rights should be. From there, the Dutch government itself set out to energize the Court, which was suddenly put forward as a solution to problems, rather than a threatening institution of which one should steer clear.

A more active European Court was the result. Crucially, these grassroots developments predated the legal revolution and formed a necessary precondition for the legal changes which followed later.

Chapter 5, 'The defining decade', ranges from 1979 to 1989 and sheds light on the distinctive legal revolution and societal mainstreaming of human rights as it took place in the Dutch context. After decades of hesitation, the courts, both domestic and European, sprang into action and unleashed a veritable legal avalanche of activity. They were supported by the recently formed professional academic study of human rights, and on occasion, went further than had previously been considered possible. But simultaneously, the governmental support began to waver. Although it had been crucial in the activation of the system, a certain caution surrounding the activities of the European Court began to seep in during the eighties, and the European activities which seemed to be continuously expanding the reach of European human rights were consistently met with brakes from the states.

Finally, Chapter 6, 'From permissive consensus to persistent critique', turns to the most recent past of the Convention. After the end of the Cold War, engagement with European human rights tied into the general human rights hosanna of the nineties, but the member states' caution had not suddenly disappeared. Instead, it resurfaced, first in an initiative behind the screens to curtail the expansion of the Convention, but in the past decade that caution was put much more out in the open. What was new was how the Convention also became a topic of public debate: in order for that debate to flourish, a fundamental change in the previous, rather self-evident acceptance of human rights as inherently desirable was brokered as the Court got caught up in wider debates surrounding national identity and, above all, migration. This was an area where the Convention was distinctly made to matter by a wide variety of actors, but which invited strong pushback along the way.

CHAPTER 1

1945–1954

Constructing the Moral Basis for European Integration

IN 1946, WITH THE SECOND WORLD WAR ONLY JUST OVER, a small booklet was handed over in The Hague to the Minister of Foreign Affairs.[1] Written by leading names in Dutch academia, it put forward new ideas for the restructuring of the (international) post-war society. The most burning issues to be tackled, according to the professors, were the position of Germany and the closely connected topic of the broader reconstruction of Europe. With the European countries in shambles, the academics included in their solutions one common element: the need for European integration. Professor of international law in Leiden, Baron F. M. van Asbeck made a forceful plea for a new sense of morality, based on a European tradition:

> Europe knew – before the renaissance and the reformation – as Corpus Christianum a common moral connection to a common moral heritage. That connection loosened in the more recent history, and is nowadays almost gone within our industrialized and secular mass-society. The world has [...] no common 'moral purpose' anymore. It lacks, following Max Huber, a 'common ethos', which is so vital as a base for the international law. The awareness of being bound to common, supra-human ethics, has broken down. The spiritual rapprochement of Germany and the West is only one aspect of the colossal moral reform the world needs, and which she craves ...[2]

[1] F. M. Baron van Asbeck, J. Tinbergen, and J. H. W. Verzijl (eds.), *Bouwstof voor de oplossing van Na-Oorlogsche Vraagstukken* (Den Haag: Nijhoff, 1946).

[2] van Asbeck, *Bouwstof*, p. 18.

van Asbeck embodied this zeal for a moral renewal. Initially active in the establishment of the World Council of Churches, he would soon become part of the most eye-catching attempt to give Europe 'a moral purpose' when he became the first Dutch judge in the European Court of Human Rights. This Court, supreme guardian of the European Convention on Human Rights, formed the crown jewel of the Council of Europe, set up to put forward the idea of European integration. It was the direct outcome of this campaign for a new world – or at least European – order, and combined the desire for European integration with that of a common morality: European human rights.

But van Asbeck also embodied the *limits* of this reform. In parallel with his search for moral reconstruction and pleas for the protection of the individual in international law, van Asbeck wrote to his close friend, Hubert van Mook, the Lieutenant-Governor-General of the Dutch colony of Indonesia. Van Asbeck, having heard of the contentious situation in Indonesia, put himself at the Governor-General's disposal. Should his friend have need of assistance in the governing of the colony, van Asbeck would not hesitate to come over. Holding to his word, van Asbeck joined the colonial governance as Van Mook's assistant in November 1945 and attempted, despite his idea that Indonesia should be 'led to independence', to maintain Dutch imperial rule in an increasingly violent war of recolonisation.[3] The curious intersection of roles as a colonial official and a human rights judge serves as a reminder of the fact that human rights were not quite solely the project of progressive liberals, as they are occasionally presented, but existed alongside and within longstanding European imperial traditions, the limits of which were not easily transcended.[4]

This peculiar connection between human rights and the concept of Europe was forged primarily by transnational non-governmental activists, in particular European Federalists.[5] With the Dutch state wary of

[3] A fact van Asbeck was keenly aware of; Anne-Lot Hoek, *De Strijd om Bali: Imperialisme, Verzet en Onafhankelijkheid 1846–1950* (Amsterdam: De Bezige Bij, 2021), pp. 335–347.

[4] Cf. Duranti, *The Conservative Human Rights Revolution.*

[5] 'The usual focus on the role of the government has to do – apart from the obvious statement that ultimately, governments draw up the treaty' with the fact that most historical accounts rely heavily on the official traveux préparatoires for their historical sketch: see,

human rights, these activists were the ones who turned human rights from moral and cultural claims into parts of European legal integration. As they established these early meanings of the Convention, they drew the slate upon which the states would later act. Yet in linking the concepts of Europe and human rights, they did not create rights as universal values available to all humans, or merely echoed of the Universal Declaration on Human Rights.[6] Instead, they built upon distinct conceptions of 'Europeanness' which were based around a very peculiar cultural and moral ideas of what that entailed. European human rights were thus from the beginning restrained by pervasive civilisational, colonial and racial considerations. Above all, European human rights were perfectly compatible with the idea and practice of Empire.

Finally, when the governments took over and turned European human rights into law by signing the Convention in 1950, the ideals of the non-governmental activists were distinctly hampered. For the Netherlands, the aim was to keep European human rights at bay. Little was expected of the document, and the most innovative elements, such as the right of individual petition, were regarded with firm distrust. Crucially, the 'European' character of these human rights did not fit easily with the notion that the Kingdom of the Netherlands was not solely a European country. As discussions emerged on the role and place of European

for example, the historical chapters in Y. S. Klerk, *Het ECRM Toezicht-Mechanisme; Verleden, Heden, Toekomst* (Nijmegen: Ars Aequi Libri, 1995), the work of Ed Bates, *The Evolution of the European Convention on Human Rights: From Its Inception to the Creation of a Permanent Court of Human Rights* (Oxford: Oxford University Press, 2010), or Mikael Rask Madsen, 'The Protracted Institutionalization of the Strasbourg Court: From Legal Diplomacy to Integrationist Jurisprudence' in J. Cristoffersen and Mikael Rask Madsen (eds.), *The European Court of Human Rights between Law and Politics* (Oxford: Oxford University Press, 2011), pp. 43–61; for the Governmental perspective of Netherlands and European integration in general, see Matthieu Segers, *Reis naar het Continent: Nederland en de Europese Integratie, 1950 tot heden* (Amsterdam: Bert Bakker, 2013). The leading political science work also has very little to say about the influence of non-governmental actors: Andrew Moravcsik, 'The Origins of Human Rights Regimes: Democratic Delegation in Postwar Europe' *International Organization* Vol. 54 Nr. 2 (2000), pp. 217–252. A welcome addition has been made by Duranti; Duranti, *The Conservative Human Rights Revolution.*

6 This in contrast to, for instance, Segers, who presents human rights in Europe as directly linked to the project of the Universal Declaration through Cassin. See Mathieu Segers, *The Origins of European Integration: The Pre-History of Today's European Union, 1937–1951* (Cambridge: Cambridge University Press, 2024), pp. 54–60.

human rights in Indonesia, Suriname, the Dutch Antilles and Papua New Guinea, a distinctive exclusionary meaning of the Convention emerged.

1.1 LINKING HUMAN RIGHTS AND EUROPEAN INTEGRATION

Contrary to popular belief, the early post-war period was by no means one in which states rushed to 'lock themselves in' by ratifying fundamental rights treaties.[7] The Dutch government had its reasons for this hesitance. The Netherlands lay in tatters after the Second World War. Human suffering had been widespread during the war and circumstances would remain harsh for some years to come. People, houses, roads and parts of cities had been destroyed. Moreover, after the War, peace was only relative in the Kingdom. Indonesia, the largest colony, had declared its independence in 1945, provoking a violent Dutch war of recolonisation, meaning that almost immediately after the end of fighting in Europe, the Netherlands found itself embroiled in a colonial war.[8]

As a result, human rights were not embraced as governmental priorities. In the context of the United Nations, the Dutch delegation did not actively participate in the drafting of the Universal Declaration, for instance, and when it did its engagement was 'declaratory' and 'chaotic'.[9] The Dutch addition to the debates, voiced by its delegate Leo Beaufort who was a priest alongside a diplomate, consisted of pushing for the divine foundation of human rights.[10] Also a governmental advisory committee on human rights, set up at the request of the Economic and Social Council of the UN (ECOSOC) in 1946 is illustrative of this lack of attention. The committee lasted only two years, during which it produced few results

[7] Moravcsik, 'The Origins of Human Rights Regimes', p. 220.

[8] See in general Tony Judt, *Postwar: A History of Europe since 1945* (New York: Vintage, 2006); Keith Lowe, *The Fear and the Freedom: How the Second World War Changed Us* (New York: Picador, 2017). For the Netherlands, see also Ruud van Dijk, Samuel Kruizinga, Vincent Kuitenbrouwer and Rimko van der Maar (eds.), *Shaping the International Relations of the Netherlands 1815–2000: A Small Country on the Global Scene* (Oxford: Routledge, 2018), pp. 1–17.

[9] Monique Castermans-Holleman, *Het Nederlandse mensenrechtenbeleid in de Verenigde Naties* (Den Haag: TMC Asser Instituut, 1992), pp. 169–181.

[10] Mooij, 'Nederland en het nieuwe mensenrechtenstelsel' *Tijdschrift voor Geschiedenis*, p. 451.

before falling silent on the topic altogether in 1948.[11] Governmental participation with the Universal Declaration, or international human rights in general, was therefore passive and very minimal.

There were simply more pressing matters which required the Dutch government's attention. Decolonisation and security were deemed vastly more important than an active occupation with human rights. Moreover, international human rights did not sit easily alongside another aim of the immediate post-war period: the restoration of the nation state. Directly after independence, the reaffirmation of the nation state took centre ground in political discussions. Having been occupied for five years, a new sense of the 'national community' was installed, resulting in a self-image of victimhood. As collaboration was conveniently forgotten, victimhood and heroism became the prime themes within the communal memory, thereby installing a theme of national innocence which would last well into the sixties. Wartime suffering was taken as a collective aspect: the importance of individual and indeed the notion of specific Jewish suffering were neglected in this early post-war era. Memory culture was placed firmly in the service of *restoring* the nation state, harking back to an idealized communal image.[12] Within this context, very little room could be foreseen for limitations on state power via the means of human rights. The nation would continue to serve as the building block for the new world, also as an answer to the new threats of the post-war moment.

The main threat to that newly reconstructed nation state was believed to be found in what had supposedly caused the war: the position of the 'masses'. This was a key issue in the immediate post-war era which dominated the intellectual analysis, illustrated by the fact the work *The revolt of the Masses* by the Spanish conservative philosopher José Ortega y Gasset was the best-selling philosophical book throughout Europe for years after the war had ended.[13] A main takeaway from Ortega y Gasset's work was how mass poverty and ensuing frustration had built on the basis of

[11] Castermans-Holleman, *Het Nederlandse mensenrechtenbeleid*, pp. 101–102.

[12] Frank van Vree, *In de Schaduw van Auschwitz: Herinneringen beelden, geschiedenis* (Groningen: Historische Uitgeverij, 1995), pp. 16–27.

[13] Jan Werner Müller, *Contesting Democracy: Political Ideas in Twentieth Century Europe* (New Haven: Yale University Press, 2013), p. 141. Also in the Netherlands, this stream of thinking was very much present, with Prime Minister Schermerhorn even writing an

the political mass movements: fascism and communism and the ensuing totalitarianism threatening national and individual liberty.

Solutions on the political level were primarily sought in planning and social security, which became a key element in preventing future authoritarian temptations. Inspired by the Beveridge report in the UK, noting how social safety would have to be one of the key post-war elements, in the Netherlands the report Van Rhijn argued along similar lines for the introduction of a social welfare state. Not necessarily a touch of altruism, social security was an attempt to prevent the next war by keeping the masses above a critical level of poverty.[14] This was a national affair however: these were not framed in terms of human rights but rather as element of the newly re-established national community.[15]

From the national government, active support for human rights was thus not to be expected in these early post-war years. The movement towards European human rights hence began elsewhere, namely in the non-governmental activist groups of European federalists, which turned to the concept to provide a moral basis for European integration.

1.1.1 CREATING A EUROPEAN FREEDOM. Those persons pushing the creation of European human rights warrant attention not solely because it was on their preparatory work the governments would later act but also because through them one can better understand the perceived meaning of the Convention in its early days. After all, many of these individuals later emerged in positions from which they influenced the further developments of the Convention, be it in Europe or in the Netherlands, while others became key authoritative interpreters, succesful in pushing their vision of what the Convention meant.

Their particular strand of activism, European federalism, was one of many non-governmental movements that popped up directly after the war, in the search for societal and political renewal. Religious movements

introduction to the 'Dutch' version of Gasset's work; S. H. Stoffel, *De Massa-mensch en zijn toekomst* (Amsterdam: Uitgeverij Vrij Nederland, 1946).

14 See Abraham de Swaan, *Zorg en Staat: Welzijn, onderwijs en Gezondheidszorg in Europa en de Verenigde Staten in de Nieuwe tijd* (Amsterdam: Bert Bakker, 1989).

15 In this vein, Samuel Moyn, *Not Enough: Human Rights in an Unequal World* (Cambridge: Harvard University Press, 2018).

were another popular option.[16] Not only did people flock to the local churches but also broader international movements such as the 'Moral Re-Armament' and the ecumenical movement became very popular.[17] There were also calls for an all-encompassing 'world government', as in the case of the world federalist movement,[18] which focused its hopes mostly on the newly founded United Nations. Yet it was soon clear to this particular strand of idealism that the UN would not overcome the strict political limits of the international political reality. The United Nations got locked in Cold War tensions and swiftly diminished in importance.[19]

This left another, and soon more popular, route, which was to adhere to a regional approach: 'Europe'. Much more than the global international solution, European integration and European human rights became seen as the ideal solution to both political and moral fears and insecurities. Part of its attractiveness lay in the vagueness of the concepts in question: 'Europe' could function as a 'screen' on which every possible meaning could be projected.[20]

It was precisely when it came to European human rights that non-governmental actors made their mark. It was in those groups that the idea of a Court first emerged and finalized. Yet what these actors put forward was a particular connection. In understanding the Convention, it is crucial to realise how European human rights, from the outset, were not just more stringently guarded universal values. They were rights of Europeans. This resulted in a particular interpretation of how human rights should be seen.[21]

[16] Nationaal Archief, Den Haag, Europese Beweging in Nederland en Voorgangers, number access 2.19.109, Inventory Number 1, 'first documents European Action'.

[17] Lowe, *The Fear and the Freedom*, 175; Bastiaan Bouwman, 'From Religious Freedom to Social Justice: The Human Rights Engagement of the Ecumenical Movement from the 1940s to the 1970s' *Journal of Global History* Vol. 13 Nr. 2 (2018), pp. 252–273. To be clear, there was quite some overlap between these movements.

[18] See also Mark Mazower, *Governing the World: the History of an Idea* (London: Penguin Press, 2012).

[19] Roger Normand and Sarah Zaidi, *Human Rights at the UN: The Political History of Universal Justice* (New York: Indiana University Press, 2008), pp. 139–143.

[20] Robin de Bruin, *Elastisch Europa: De integratie van Europa en de Nederlandse Politiek, 1947–1968* (Amsterdam: Wereldbibliotheek, 2014), p. 41.

[21] This in contrast to, for instance, Segers, who presents human rights in Europe as directly linked to the project of the Universal Declaration through Cassin. See Mathieu Segers,

For what was meant by this 'Europeanness' was primarily informed by the philosophical tradition of 'personalism', in particular the ideas of Denis de Rougemont and Jacques Maritain.[22] Of the many blueprints for European integration after the War, the European Convention was carried forward predominantly by thinkers who brought together ideas on individual rights and the need for cultural and political European integration.[23] This movement was most prominent on the European level, where personalism became closely connected to European integration due to the heightened impact of key 'agents of internationalism' who were instrumental in putting forward their ideas.[24] Yet their ideas in turn greatly influenced key Dutch actors, where personalist approaches brought together socialists and Christian democrats.

Central to their vision of personalism was the position that the individual had, as a 'person', his own freedom, but was at the same time part of larger communities. In doing so, personalists drew upon Christian thought, putting the person in their context as being both an individual before God and a member of their community at the same time.[25] Personalism embraced a focus on individual rights or freedoms yet presented freedom as far from absolute. Rather, it had to be reached within the confines of the broader societies to which the person had distinct responsibilities.[26] Notions of the 'freedom of the person', or the more humanitarian loaded concept of 'human dignity', therefore did not have the secular connotation they might seem to have today but were rooted in a Christian tradition.[27]

The Origins of European Integration: The Pre-History of Today's European Union, 1937–1951 (Cambridge: Cambridge University Press, 2024), pp. 54–60.

[22] Segers, *The Origins of European Integration,* p. 84.

[23] Mats Andrén and Ettore Costa, 'Transnationalism in the 1950s Europe: Ideas, Debates and Politics' *History of European Ideas* Vol. 46 Nr. 1 (2020), pp. 1–12.

[24] Jessica Reinisch, 'Introduction: Agents of Internationalism' *Contemporary European History* Vol. 25 Nr. 2 (2016), pp. 195–205.

[25] See for the spiritual element of personalism also Dries Deweer and Steven van Hecke (eds.), *De Mens Centraal; Essays over het Personalisme vandaag en morgen* (Kalmthout: Pelckmans Pro, 2017), p. 14.

[26] Samuel Moyn, *Christian Human Rights* (Philadelphia: University of Pennsylvania Press, 2015), p. 67.

[27] Samuel Moyn, *Human Rights and the Uses of History* (New York: Verso Books, 2014), pp. 19–35.

This vision on human rights received a distinct political element when it became connected to European integration and the call for a European federation. This was shaped most prominently by De Rougemont, a Swiss philosopher, who was an important voice in a group of predominantly French thinkers. In particular after the Second World War, a European federal state would – according to the Rougemont – be the only way to safeguard the special character of the person against the impact of the mass movements. This added a clear political direction to what had hitherto been a primarily cultural philosophy. Following De Rougemont, only a federation would be able to both maintain the peace and the diversity of societies in which the person could exist. As threats to peace grew, in particular in light of the – nuclear – war Europe was seemingly facing between the USA and the Soviet Union, a European federal structure would help achieve stability and ensure internal national diversity.

Moreover, within that federation, the special *European* character of the person could be defended against the masses. In light of the threats posed to 'the European man', structures had to be in place to 'save the liberty of the European person'.[28] For this European person was quite frankly *different* from the American or Russian individual. In those societies, the 'common man' was celebrated, whereas in Europe, the freedom of the individual to excel, to be different – the European 'genius' – had to be protected from the temptations of atomistic liberalism or the passion of the masses.[29]

As such, it offered a moral and political 'third way' between American liberalism and Soviet collectivism. Embracing the person within these communities, personalism was a rejection of both the large 'organist' movements where persons were never more than a simple part of the whole mass (such as in fascism or communism) and also of the perceived 'atomistic' liberal, American stance of thinking on individual freedom.[30]

[28] Denis de Rougemont, *L'Europe en Jeu: Unie ou Colonisée* (Boudry: Editions de la Baconnieère, 1948), p. 23.

[29] De Rougemont, *l'Europe en Jeu*, p. 30.

[30] To be clear, the distinctive 'European' approach can be traced back in many venues of integration. German inspired ordoliberalism stood at the basis of the economic rationale behind the early initiatives for the single market. On this, see also Kiran Klaus Patel, *Project Europe: A History* (Cambridge: Cambridge University Press, 2020), p. 110.

Such a European approach had consequences for which kind of rights could be envisioned. Personalism did not exclude social or economic rights, for instance. Since a person could only reach freedom within the social context, according to a personalist way of thinking it was perfectly possible to provide the individual with social rights in order to thrive.[31] It also made personalism a very flexible way of thinking: its focus on individual freedom with corresponding duties to society could appeal to confessionals, liberals and socialists alike.[32] But it was no limitless freedom: De Rougemont envisioned European personal freedom as always requiring a careful balance between interest of society and individual: a key characteristic of the European human rights framework to this day.[33]

1.1.2 PERSONALISM ON THE NATIONAL LEVEL. The ideas of De Rougemont and Maritain were swiftly taken up in the national context. In the Netherlands, personalist thinking enjoyed a moment of significant popularity after 1945. This Dutch so-called 'socialistic personalism' has been described as having the character of a 'straw fire': bright but brief.[34] Its thinking stood at the basis of the foundation of a new political movement, the Nationale Volksbeweging (N. V. B.), supported by the first Dutch Prime Minister after the Second World War, Wim Schermerhorn. It had close connections to the Labour party (the PvDA) where personalistic language was used to present a socialist worldview.[35] Yet it also faded out swiftly: as the N. V. B. had no ambition to form

[31] See, for example, L. J. C. M. Beaufort, *Van anarchie naar Rechtsgemeenschap: Rede uitgesproken bij de aanvaarding van buitengewoon hoogleraar in het volkenrecht aan de R.K. Universiteit te Nijmegen op maandag 15 maart 1948* (Dekker & Van de Vegt: Nijmegen, 1948). In this piece, Beaufort explicitly makes the claim for socio-economic rights based on personal freedom.

[32] On the many ways in which personalist thinking was taken up, see Rachel Johnston-White, 'A Moral Language for Our Time? Human Rights and Christianity in Historical Perspective' *Contemporary European History* Vol. 31 Nr. 1 (2022), pp. 155–166.

[33] With the exception of the prohibition on torture.

[34] Hendrik Brugmans, 'Het Personalisme Leeft Voort', *De Gids* Vol. 154 Nr. 8 (1991), pp. 607–614, 607.

[35] Prime Minister Willem Drees, for instance would claim the need for a protection of the 'person' as opposed to the overtly individualistic liberties in the constitution: Karin van Leeuwen, *Uit het spoor van Thorbecke: Grondwetsherziening en Staatsvernieuwing in Naoorlogs Nederland (1945–1983)* (Amsterdam: Boom, 2013), p. 68.

its own permanent political party, its intellectual ideas did not as such become institutionalized in domestic politics. Its impact was more lasting in the realm of individual activism, in particular in the Dutch European Movement. There, personalist ideas formed key points of reference for leading Dutch federalists such as Hendrik Brugmans, Maan Sassen or Hans Nord, who were avid supporters of the ideas of De Rougemont.[36]

What emerges from this Dutch engagement with these ideas is the notion that European human rights and the federative framework which they should support were not a break with Empire. Firmly rejecting the power of the masses had been part of the popularity of personalism, yet the 'teeming masses' of the colonial empires were perceived to be *just as* threatening to the precarious European freedoms. Personalism, in particular as it revolved around the European person, was not colour-blind. Schermerhorn made the racialized connotation explicit when he noted in 1946 how personalism could offer a way out 'of the marsh, in which the white part of humanity now threatens to sink'.[37]

This racialized fear was, in fact, a part of the Dutch urge for European integration. When the 'Nederlandse Actie Europa', one of the first movements on behalf of European integration and a predecessor of the broader Dutch European Movement, called for a first national meeting in 1946, it drew its inspiration from the South African leader Jan Smuts.[38] Smuts, later responsible for drafting the preamble of the UN Charter and himself an avid proponent of the dignity of the human personality, was a living example that one could support both the language of human rights and human dignity without disavowing an imperialist racialized world order.[39] The South African Marshal had been celebrated in the

[36] Annemarie van Heerikhuizen, *Pioniers van een Verenigd Europa: Bovennationaal denken in het Nederlandse Parlement (1946–1951)* (Dissertation, University of Amsterdam, 1998), p. 207. Sassen was one of the politicians who strongly pushed for the 'second police action' in Indonesia: another example of how European idealism could go hand in hand with imperial preferences.

[37] Willem Schermerhorn, voorwoord, p. 3 in S. H. Stoffel, *De Massa-Mensch en zijn toekomst Proeve van een analyse onzer samenleving* (Amsterdam, 1946).

[38] NL-HaNA, Europese Beweging Nederland, 2.19.109, inv. nr. 1, '25 October 1946, invitation to first meeting'.

[39] Mark Mazower, *No Enchanted Palace: The End of Empire and the Ideological Origins of the United Nations* (Princeton: Princeton University Press, 2009), pp. 28–65; Saul Dubow,

Netherlands due to his achievements in the Boer War, and in October 1946 he gave a speech to the Dutch Parliament in which he hailed the strength of Europe as the 'most developed group of the entire human race', which was now struggling due to the legacy of the devastating war. But – according to Smuts – Europe should not look to other continents for its salvation: only Europe and the Europeans themselves could fulfil its destiny.[40]

This call to action was enthusiastically taken up by the early proponents of European unity, with the 'Europese Actie' noting the necessity for Europe to rise again. This was no disavowal of imperialism, but instead, European integration was necessary to prevent becoming a colony oneself. Robbed by the new powers of 'almost all its monopolies and means of power', De Rougemont himself presented European integration explicitly as the choice between 'unie ou colonisée'.[41]

The fear of 'losing Europe' was echoed in the early actions in support of European unity in the Netherlands. As the 'Europese actie' noted in its programme, 'the atmosphere is suffocating, and dangers loom that Europe will become either a protectorate of the one, or a colonial area of the other. Once turned into plaything in the political power struggle between East and West, the states of Europe, yes, Europe in its entirety, will be lost'.[42] Personalism again formed the key moral basis for this endeavour, as Europe's calling was described as 'recognizing the value of the person, who knows itself in light of the separate communities it forms part of…'.[43]

Initially, the link between human rights and European integration remained moral and cultural, and also Dutch actors didn't actively seek to make the rights of persons into binding law.[44] Yet the crucial step

'Smuts, the United Nations and the Rhetoric of Race and Rights' *Journal of Contemporary History* Vol. 43 Nr. 1 (2008), pp. 45–74.

40 The speech of Smuts can be partially reviewed through www.openbeelden.nl/media/1195413/MAARSCHALK_SMUTS_IN_DE_VERENIGDE_VERGADERING_DER_STATEN__GENERAAL (last accessed 18 October 2024).

41 De Rougemont, *L'Europe en Jeu*, p. 28.

42 NL-HaNA, Europese Beweging Nederland, 2.19.109, inv. nr. 3, 'statutes'.

43 Ibid.

44 Although the Dutch European movement aimed at closer European integration, the terminology of legally binding human rights remains absent from their works until later, after the Congress of Europe.

towards legalisation of European human rights would come in 1948, at the Congress of Europe. There, leading personalist thinkers such as De Rougemont himself and Alexandre Marc were highly prominent voices in the discussions, and they went to great lengths to shape the final outcomes of the Congress.[45] As such, the distinctive personalist conception of human rights would form the basis for what would become the draft European Convention. Two years after van Asbeck had urged Europe to find its own way, based on a common ethos, it was again at The Hague that Europe and human rights were truly connected for the first time.

1.2 DRAFTING: CREATING THE EUROPEAN CONVENTION

In the spring of 1948, The Hague found itself in the centre of European attention for a couple of days. The International European Movement had arrived: before the eyes of hundreds of journalists and thousands of interested civilians, a group of prominent thinkers, activists and politicians would set out provisions for a common European future. The Congress formed the foundation of what was to become the European Convention: it was here that European human rights would transform from moral claims to legally enforceable concepts. At the same time, the Congress had a very specific conservative character, which had its impact on the final result of the Congress.

The Congress was the result of a coordinated effort of the 'Joint International Committee of the Movements for European Unity' (a mixed bag of movements for European unity under supervision of the UK's Duncan Sandys) in order to give a powerful impulse to the campaign throughout Europe.[46] The city of The Hague gladly functioned as forum for such a prestigious event. The Dutch government provided the Hall of Knights as venue for deliberation, although it could not offer any substantial financial subsidies: it was thanks to the contribution of major industrial companies that the Congress was also financially feasible.[47]

[45] Duranti, *The Conservative Human Rights Revolution*, p. 281.

[46] Felix Klos, *Winston Churchill, Vader van Europa* (Amsterdam: Hollands Diep, 2016), p. 195.

[47] Klos, *Churchill*, pp. 206–207.

Guest of honour was Winston Churchill. In fact, it never was the Congress itself which attracted the massive crowds: most of the people came to catch a glimpse of the cigar- and cane-wielding 'saviour of Europe'. Churchill would not personally participate in the actual debates, yet his thoughts resonated loudly throughout the Congress, if only because his lines to Sandys (his son-in-law) were remarkably short.[48] In three respects, this was a very special kind of gathering. First of all, one particular important group was not invited: communists. With the coup in Prague of early 1948 fresh in people's memory, communists were perceived as the prime threat to European unity, and what it meant to be European would soon be defined in opposition to the developments in Eastern Europe.[49]

Second, Germans were invited, with Konrad Adenauer himself participating actively in the meetings. One of the main aims of the Congress was explicitly to reinstate Germany in the 'European Family', both politically and morally. This aim was not commonly accepted. For a large part of the Dutch audience, Germans were still regarded as the enemy, and providing hotel rooms to Germans was a sensitive issue.[50] However, a Europe without some kind of role for Germany was hard to fathom, and with the unrelenting support for German re-integration from Churchill himself, their participation had been secured. Their reintegration was aided by Anthony Eden, close aide to Churchill, who – noting the deplorable state of the shoes of the German participants – started collecting money in order for the Germans to buy some new ones. Walter Hallstein, later head of the European Commission, would keep this pair of shoes as a memory on his bookshelf until he died.[51]

Third, and most important, it was a predominantly conservative, Christian-influenced Congress.[52] That is not to say there were no other

[48] Duranti, *The Conservative Human Rights Revolution*, pp. 161–164.

[49] Jean-Michel Guieu and Christophe Le Dreu (eds.), *Le Congrès de l'Europe à La Haye (1948–2008)* (Brussels: Peter Lang, 2009), pp. 15–45.

[50] Klos, *Churchill*, p. 210.

[51] W. H. Weenink, 'Den Haag was in mei 1948 het centrum van Europa', *NRC Handelsblad* 15 May 1988.

[52] Conservative is meant here not as it stands opposed to progressive, but more as it stands against revolutionary. On the Christian origins of European cooperation, see Wolfram Kaiser, *Christian Democracy and the Origins of European Union* (Cambridge: Cambridge University Press, 2007).

lines of thought present – a large amount of secularist thinkers participated, as well as socialists, humanists, functionalists and others. Indeed, this intellectual variety sometimes led to clashes on certain issues and served also to 'secularize' certain notions, especially in the cultural committee.[53] Yet, both in organization (which foresaw in centrally planned religious activities on the Sunday) as well as in terms of sheer numbers, Christian-democrats shaped the character of the Congress.[54]

The relation between the Christian democrats and the second-largest group, the socialists, was tricky from the beginning. Socialists suspected the majority of an attempt to reinstate an old legacy of capitalism and feudalism, disguised in a new jacket of European unification.[55] The fact that the Congress was sponsored by major industrial parties did not help in this regard. Before the start of the Congress, the British Labour party boycotted the Congress, and it took a lot of pressure for individual members of that party to participate in a personal capacity.

Also, while in The Hague, the European socialists had already decided to host their own congress in Paris, where the issue of a European federation would be the first point on the agenda.[56] The Dutch organisation, concerned about this possible rift in the Congress, reached out to its 'own' socialist, Marinus Van der Goes van Naters, who subsequently assured them that the Paris meeting was by no means meant to counter the Congress at The Hague, as it would be an internal socialist affair and every European socialist would remain free to engage fully within the Hague Congress.[57] Nonetheless, it was a sign of how the Congress in The Hague was one particular gathering, subscribing to a distinct vision on European unity. With the socialist summit ahead, this alternative European project never truly disappeared from the setting and

53 For an exhaustive treatment of all different ambitions and programmes at the Congress, see Jean-Michel Guieu and Christophe Le Dreu (eds.), *Le Congrès de l'Europe à La Haye.*

54 NL-HaNa, Europese Beweging Nederland, 2.19.209, inv. nr. 93, 'programme Congress of Europe'; Duranti, *The Conservative Human Rights Revolution*, pp. 148–150.

55 Duranti, *The Conservative Human Rights Revolution*, p. 391.

56 Anne-Isabelle Richard, 'The Limits of Solidarity: Europeanism, Anti-colonialism and Socialism at the Congress of the Peoples of Europe, Asia and Africa in Puteaux, 1948' *European Review of History: Revue européenne d'histoire* Vol. 21 Nr. 4 (2014), pp. 519–537.

57 Nl-HaNa, Europese Beweging Nederland, 2.19.209, inv. nr. 93, 'letter to Goes van der Naters, 30 March 1948'.

provided socialists with an alternative. For the socialists, the Congress of Europe was simply one of the options for European integration. As passions rose high, particular in the economic committee, the French and Belgian socialists at one point left the room declaring 'clearly, this is a reactionary Congress!'.[58]

As a result, the conservative-oriented Christian parties were most active in bringing about a successful congress. This specific character of the Congress also found its way into the link between European thinking and human rights. The most anticipated speech, and the one which most clearly linked the two, was that of Winston Churchill. In an oft-cited passage, Churchill declared:

> The movement for European Unity must be a positive force, deriving its strength from our common sense of spiritual values. It is a dynamic expression of democratic faith based upon moral conceptions and inspired by a sense of mission. In the centre of our movement stands a charter of human rights, guarded by freedom and sustained by law.[59]

With Churchill as a champion for human rights, one would not receive support for inalienable universal human rights. Rather, Churchill was an ardent imperialist, whose insistence on human rights as shared moral values of European integration was couched in referrals to 'the great design' – reminiscent of the 'holy league', the Christian collaboration between states of the 1600's. Alongside his explicit rejection of communism, this made human rights into a conservative, Christian product. If European human rights were to be defined against communism, which promoted secularism, egalitarianism and a new world order, European human rights were to promote its antithesis: religion, freedom and the imperial past.[60]

This line of thinking was reflected in the opening speech of the Congress as well. Welcoming participants to the congress on behalf of the local Dutch European Movement was Hendrik Brugmans, later rector at the College of Europe. European unity would be politically

[58] *Trouw*, 11 May 1948.
[59] Nl-HaNa, Europese Beweging Nederland, 2.19.209, inv. nr. 95 'speech Churchill'.
[60] Duranti, *The Conservative Human Rights Revolution*, pp. 96–164.

inevitable, according to Brugmans, in order to prevent economic collapse and further conflict. European integration, however, could not *only* be political in nature. 'There also are moral issues', he stated, continuing:

> the magic word 'Europe' means not only a region of the globe, it means also a way of life for both groups and individuals. The European has never accepted for any length the supremacy of a master-group. He will never accept leaders unless they guarantee to him the rights of man. Europe has an instinct for liberty, of which the greater proportion of men have never dreamed either the excitements or the sweetness. Europe is Mozart; Europe is Charles Peguy; Shakespeare is its epitome.[61]

Brugman's invocation here of the rights of man in this moral-cultural context celebrating the 'European Genius' was no coincidence. After all, human rights *were* part of larger moral issues at the start of the Congress, not necessarily legal ones.[62] Although, following De Rougemont, it was necessary to establish a federation to protect the freedom of the European person, the respect for individual rights was just as much a moral and cultural claim as it was a legal one.

De Rougemont himself was ecstatic during the Congress. His work there, being a rapporteur for the cultural committee, was a dream come true, and his firm belief was the Congress, where socialists, conservatives and the 'Mad Hatter of Alice in Wonderland' (Bertrand Russell was present as well), would see his vision come to fruition.[63]

1.2.1 CULTURAL OR POLITICAL? THE DEBATE IN THE DIFFERENT SECTIONS. Debates at the Congress would take place within three committees. A political committee would set out ideas for political integration in a European Union, an economic one sought to establish a template for the kind of economic cooperation, and finally a

[61] Nl-HaNa, Europese Beweging Nederland 2.19.209, inv. nr. 95 'Speech Brugmans "the vital issue"'.

[62] Although the distinction is always hard to make: see also Adam Etinson (ed.), *Human Rights: Moral or Political* (Oxford: Oxford University Press, 2018).

[63] De Rougemont, *L'Europe en Jeu*, p. 125–128.

cultural committee would provide a resolution on the shared moral and cultural basis upon which this integration would take place.

Human rights originally formed part of precisely the *cultural* committee of the Congress. In order to establish the common cultural heritage, the committee had turned to human rights as elements of what it meant to be 'European'. With the firm involvement of De Rougemont, the notion of European human rights would be squared to the need of a European cultural centre.[64]

What followed was a wide-ranging and sometimes fierce discussion on the specific character of this moral basis as well as on the European conception of 'man'. Was it Christian, humanist, secular, or Christian-humanist? Here too the personalist federalists made their influence felt, via the introduction of an extensive rapport on human rights from French thinker Alexandre Marc and Dutch federalist Hans Nord. They proposed to accompany these rights by a distinct European Court which could safeguard their core.[65]

However, after the first day, notice was given of a remarkable shift. It was proposed to move the topic of human rights, along with an idea of a Court ruling over these rights, over to the political Committee. This was a decision of the central organisation of the Congress. Especially the idea of a Court was considered too politically sensitive to be left to the 'cultural' committee. Some disappointment in the cultural committee ensued, although in the end the move would not prevent them from including human rights in their final proposal. Still, the British chair, Kenneth Lindsay, noted:

> I regret very much that the question of human rights and the supreme court has gone to the political committee. All the speeches this morning showed that we are agreed that a civilized society cannot be maintained solely by political and economic arrangements. Men are not like ants: they do not cooperate by instinct but they need capital of transcendental ideas on which they can draw at all times. Now the other two committees are making practical proposals for merging sovereignty, but you cannot

[64] Congress of Europe, *Verbatim Report 4: Cultural Committee* (The Hague, 1949), p. 3.
[65] See further Duranti, *The Conservative Human Rights Revolution*, p. 113.

> merge sovereignty unless the two parties have a common cultural and ethical code behind them...[66]

This move to the political committee had to do with two factors: the turn taken at the Congress to use human rights as 'entry ticket' for political participation in European integration, and the issue of a Supranational Court, which could rule on sovereign member states. With an eye on the latter, the European Court was closely connected to the agenda of the federalist members of the Congress. This made it all the more relevant for the political committee. If freedom of the individual person was the prerequisite of European cooperation, a European Court had to be its guardian. In this sense, it was perceived as some kind of Constitutional Court, guarding a European bill of rights. Additionally, the Court should be open to individual citizens: not only in order to effectively safeguard their rights, but also to enhance European integration through a shared European citizenship.[67]

As regards the first issue, one of the burning questions at the Congress was which countries could actually join the European integration project. Dissidents from Eastern Europe and Spanish exiles pleaded frantically to be taken seriously, yet could their countries even remotely be conceived as part of the new Europe? Early cold war tendencies made this an even more pressing issue. As a response to these questions, it was decided that only 'democratic governments' which respected a charter of human rights could join.[68] The dynamic of exclusion this was aimed to achieve was primarily aimed at the communists: the violent Greek civil war, where concentration camps popped up and communists were themselves detained, was no topic of debate.[69] Neither was decolonisation or the relation to empire. The colonial wars waged outside Europe to maintain the former empires were never mentioned. As the speakers attempted to draw up the cultural and ethical code of Europeanness, violence reigned in Indonesia in the name of European civilisation.

66 Congress of Europe, *Verbatim Report 4*, p. 57.

67 Congress of Europe, *Verbatim Report 2*, p. 90.

68 Congress of Europe, *Verbatim Report 2*, p. 42.

69 Duranti, *The Conservative Human Rights Revolution*, p. 107.

Another group not immediately thought of when defining who formed part of the 'European person' were women. Even though there were several women's organisations active in The Hague, assuring the men that they were 'pas des féministes revendicatrices', in their attempts to make their voices heard, their overall influence remained limited.[70] This limited impact goes to explain the absence of any substantial article of equal treatment between men and women in the Convention, leaving only a general provision on non-discrimination which is dependent on other rights in the Convention. From the outset, European human rights were very male-orientated.

The Congress ended with a specific conception of human rights emerging as a key concept for further European integration. Both the cultural and political committees urged the drafting of a European human rights charter and the creation of a European Human Rights Court.[71] From the political committee, the follow up was ensued. Noting the need for a Charter of Human Rights, it decided to set up a Commission in order to draft such a Charter. A Supreme Court should then be set up to rule on violations of that Charter. It was therefore this political committee which cemented human rights as one of the core issues of future European – legal – integration. By tying the two concepts together, something new could emerge: a notion of distinctly legal European human rights. The Congress' main result in the field of human rights was thus twofold. On the one hand, it had combined the moral agenda of rights of the person with a political and legally binding European project.[72] On the other hand, it called upon the European movement to come up with a concept of a European Convention of Human Rights in order to make this project – and the dream of De Rougemont – a reality.

In the follow up, a special committee was appointed to draw up the Convention, under the leadership of the French politician Pierre-Henri Teitgen and British lawyer Sir David Maxwell Fyfe. Particularly Maxwell

[70] Congress of Europe, *Verbatim Report*, p. 23. See in particular Barbara Oomen and Alexandra Timmer, 'Four Or Fewer Freedoms: Justice Contested and Codified between 1941 And 1957' in T. Knijn and D. Lepianka (eds.), *Justice and Vulnerability in Europe: An Interdisciplinary Approach* (Cheltenham: Edward Elgar 2020), pp. 73–89.

[71] The resolutions are available at www.cvce.eu/.

[72] This clearly was not a binary option; rather it was a combination of the two.

Fyfe, former prosecutor at the Nuremberg trials and conservative free market idealist, would become very influential in the finalisation of the draft charter.[73] With the creation of the Council of Europe as first truly 'European' forum, human rights had become more than declaratory moral claims or cultural statements: they now were beginning to form part of the organising legal principles of this new European cooperation.

1.2.2 THE NATIONAL INPUT AND THE END OF SOCIO-ECONOMIC RIGHTS AS EUROPEAN HUMAN RIGHTS. From there, a new dynamic unfolded. In the interaction between the central committee of Teitgen and national committees, the first Dutch legal engagement with European human rights emerged. Although the Dutch Europeanists had been somewhat absent during the initial process of linking the two, now they had to engage with them.[74] In doing so, they put forward a much more ambitious programme which would have seen European human rights contain a wide selection of social and economic rights as well. Even though these ambitions were kept at bay by Teitgen himself, the Dutch proposition served as beginning of a more durable interest in the Convention, in which actors such as Beaufort and Willem Riphagen formed their position on what the Convention entailed, which they would maintain for decades to come.

As the drafting process took off, the committee of Teitgen and Fyfe sent out requests for input into the national sections of the European movement, although the final word came from the European level. This request led to the formation of a 'judicial section' of the European Movement in the Netherlands, which would concern itself with the further development of a European Court, European human rights and what these two things ideally should entail.[75]

[73] Duranti, *The Conservative Human Rights Revolution*, pp. 219–221.

[74] Annemarie van Heerikhuizen, 'Europe: a "Common Interest?" The Netherlands at the Congress of Europe, May 1948' in Jean-Michel Guieu and Christophe Le Dreu (eds.), *Le Congrès de l'Europe à La Haye*, pp. 199–211.

[75] Nl-HaNa, Europese Beweging Nederland, 2.19.109, inv. nr. 228, 'Setting up judicial section European Movement'.

The members were: L. J. C. Beaufort, J. A. W. Burger, G. J. van Heuven, prof. G. van der Leeuw, Prof. Th. Keulemans, M. Klompé. H. R. Nord, C. Van Rij, J. J. R. Schmal, and W. Verkade.

This Dutch judicial section of the European Movement laid the groundwork for Dutch involvement with the ECHR: before the government had any notion of its position, it was this small group of people who aimed to shape European human rights. The judicial committee included not only lawyers but also academics and politicians with a broad interest in the direction of European integration, resulting in a committee with a mixed character, ranging from Catholics to socialists and liberals. There were the same faces already known in the European movement, such as the Parliamentarians Marga Klompé and Jan Schmal, who would later pressure the Dutch government from the Consultative Assembly in the Council of Europe.[76] Also present was Hans Nord, the personalist who had worked with Alexandre Marc on the report on human rights for the Congress of Europe.[77]

From this group of people, in particular the influential professor in international law 'Le Père' Beaufort stood out. Beaufort was a remarkable figure: he combined his Catholic faith with an active diplomatic and academic career, and in the immediate post-war period, he was the 'Dutch face' when it came to human rights. As we have seen, he had been the Dutch delegate at the drafting of the Universal Declaration and hence already had quite some experience on the issue of human rights when he became involved with the European Convention. As far as his European activities were concerned, however, not only would Beaufort be part of this non-governmental drafting committee, he subsequently advised the government, became the Dutch member of the European Commission for human rights, *and* was an influential senator for the Catholic party. Combining these positions, he formed a crucial actor in the early years of shaping Dutch engagement with the Convention.

But at this stage, he supported the drafting of a Dutch proposal on human rights. The idea that European human rights were something more than just a new legal tool was prominent from the start: the conception of human rights as moral foundations for European integration did not suddenly disappear.[78] The section made two strong claims

[76] Nowadays the Consultative Assembly is named the parliamentary assembly.

[77] Duranti, *Conservative Human Rights*, p. 275.

[78] Nl-HaNa, Europese Beweging Nederland, 2.19.109, inv. nr. 228, 'Memo from the European Movement setting up a legal section, 24 April 1949'.

in its interaction with the European judicial section. First, the Dutch section pressed for the creation of an independent Attorney General Department. If there was to be a Court, the Dutch stated, this should be linked to a strong enforcement mechanism as well. Here, the strong federalist framework within which the judicial committee saw the European Court was evident. The Court should be supranational, with powers to investigate threats against human rights, even against the will of the member states.[79] Fully in line with this thinking, the Dutch section expressed a firm distrust of political engagement in the field of human rights. In particular, the enforcement of human rights protection was seen as being too sensitive to be left to the states. 'These disputes', the section noted, 'definitely have to be removed from the political sphere'.[80]

Second, the section pushed for a broad conception of human rights. As social standards now were a source of governmental concern on the national level, it was proposed to expand those to the European domain, and hence, social-economic rights had to be included in the notion of European human rights as well. In a draft proposal, the section claimed that 'any person has the right to work [...] and such economic and social rights, that his personality can flourish in freedom, and to protection against financial consequences arising from unemployment, disease, handicap and old age...'[81] This was an example of the socialist personalistic thinking so prevalent in the Netherlands in this period, shared by both Christian and social-democratic participants, which left its mark on these early engagements with European human rights. Beaufort himself, in his inaugural lecture in 1948, had pleaded for strong national socio-economic protection in order to maintain human dignity for all and to prevent 'unchristian fear-psychoses'.[82]

However, both proposals met with a cold reception at the European level. From the start, these claims were supported neither by Teitgen nor Fyfe. From their point of view, precisely because enforcement was a

[79] Nl-HaNa, Europese Beweging Nederland, 2.19.109 inv. nr. 228, 'draft proposal Dutch judicial section'.

[80] Nl-HaNa Europese Beweging Nederland, 2.19.109 inv. nr. 228, 'proposal Dutch judicial section'. Underlining in the original text.

[81] Ibid.

[82] Beaufort, *Van Anarchie naar Rechtsgemeenschap*, p. 18.

sensitive topic, it was best left to the member states, while the Convention should rather consist solely of classical conservative freedoms.[83] Especially Maxwell Fyfe, a conservative free market ideologist, had grave concerns about these 'socialist' rights. For him, the Convention was not as much a tool to guard Western democracies against totalitarian temptations, as a way to keep the British Labour government in check when it came to overtly zealous legislation. 'Étatisme' was something to be frowned upon, Teitgen also noted. Yet, as the state clearly was the actor responsible for providing these socio-economic rights, this was inherently dangerous: if anything, Maxwell Fyfe and Teitgen agreed, the Convention had to be a safeguard *against* governmental intrusion.[84]

In the draft proposal of the international European Movement of a European Convention, there would, therefore, not be a single word about social or economic rights, nor about the idea of an attorney-general. Much to the dismay of the Dutch section, the draft was a somewhat skeletal set-up, far from the supranational Bill of Rights they had hoped for. The Dutch response to the draft noted that the section had hoped for a more ambitious proposal before expressing disappointment over the absence of socio-economic rights. 'Also collective rights are at stake here', the committee noted. 'We should like to insert a clause on social rights. It is clear that these can only be defined later, but by mentioning them here we make sure that [...] Governments will have to tackle them'.[85] However, the Dutch found themselves isolated. No other national section offered comparable support for socio-economic rights, which left the Dutch claims easily dismissed.[86]

What took place here was a clash of conceptions of what European human rights should all be about. For the Dutch section, socio-economic rights were a perfectly valid issue to be Europeanized. Moreover, incorporating these rights into the draft proposal was part of a legal tactic in order to force European governments to engage with the problems of mass unemployment and malnutrition. A Europe of human rights would

[83] Duranti, *The Conservative Human Rights Revolution*, p. 240.

[84] Ibid, pp. 230–240.

[85] Nl-HaNa, Europese Beweging Nederland 2.19.109, inv. nr. 228, 'note by the Dutch judicial section on Draft Proposal, 27 June 1949'.

[86] Duranti, *The Conservative Human Rights Revolution*, p. 242.

by no means be different from a social Europe. Yet, the other European actors, in particular those responsible for drafting the final proposal, saw things differently. Teitgen personally intervened and vetoed the inclusion of social-economic rights in the proposal, claiming it would be 'inapplicable in the present circumstances' and 'the resulting guarantee would be theoretical and illusory'.[87] As a result social rights were never put forward to the national governments in a European context, which, as a consequence, had no incentive to adopt them. From the outset, the European Convention would therefore be focused on a particular set of freedoms keeping the state at bay, rather than Europeanising the requirements of states to act.

The final proposal of the European Movement 'to preserve the moral values and democratic principles which are their common heritage' would thus include freedom from arbitrary deprivation of property, but not any safeguard from poverty. Faced with this opposition on the European level and clearly outvoted, the Dutch section could do very little but set out its ambition to 'continue to try and influence events in the desired direction, as soon as practical possibilities will present themselves'.[88]

These possibilities would arrive soon enough. As the final draft of the European movement was presented to the Committee of Ministers in the newly founded Council of Europe on 12 July 1949, the Convention entered a new stage: whereas earlier it had been a project carried out entirely by non-governmental actors, now the governments took over.

1.2.3 GOVERNMENTAL LIMITS ON FEDERALIST IDEALS: THE CAUTIOUS BEGINNING OF THE COUNCIL OF EUROPE. In the wider context of the Council of Europe, the institutional setting in which the Convention would be placed, the federalist ideals which had been put forward from the Congress of Europe onwards were swiftly dismantled. This international body, to the great dismay of some of its members in the Consultative Assembly, its democratic institution which could offer

[87] Ibid.

[88] Nl-HaNa, Europese Beweging Nederland 2.19.109, inv. nr. 228, 'note by the Dutch judicial section on Draft Proposal'.

non-binding recommendations, was firmly intergovernmental in nature due to the strong British resistance to any supranational European integration. Also, the Dutch government was no proponent of the Council. There existed doubts as to its added value, and there were fears in The Hague that it would soon become redundant. As the Dutch noted, 'French and Italians are always prone to create international organs, expecting task and work will automatically appear afterwards'.[89] Its existence was ultimately condoned by the aim to 'maintain the spirit which had led to its creation'.[90]

Much in line with the general hesitation about the Council of Europe, the Dutch government initially adopted a highly sceptical position towards the proposed draft for the European Convention on Human Rights. The statement of Dutch civil servant Connie Patijn of how 'we Dutchmen, have very little interest in Conventions such as these, as we in our country won't need them in the slightest' was an adequate summary of the position of the Dutch government.[91] Aside from general disinterest, the Convention also raised a number of concerns. First of all, the Dutch government feared that a Supranational Court and Commission to which individuals could file complaints, would turn political and become involved in sensitive internal affairs. Prime amongst these sensitivities were 'religious education or the ban on processions in this country'.[92] These were salient points indeed in the predominantly Protestant Netherlands. The so-called 'procession-ban' was a constitutional provision which forbade Catholic processions to be held in areas where it had not already been allowed in 1848. As such, it had been a contentious and heavily debated issue for over a century in a country where Catholics and Protestants were to a degree 'living apart together'.[93]

[89] Nationaal Archief, Den Haag, Ministerie van Buitenlandse Zaken: Code-archief 1945–1954, number access 2.05.117, inventory number 20414, '8 juli 1950, memo from Patijn to Boon'.

[90] NL-HaNA, Buitenlandse Zaken/Code-Archief 45–54, 2.05.117, inv. nr. 20414, 'standpoint with regard to the Council of Europe'.

[91] NL-HaNa, Buitenlandse Zaken/Code-Archief 45–54, 2.05.117, inv. nr. 7399, 'Memo 8 July 1950 from Patijn to Boon'.

[92] Ibid.

[93] Although this underlines the main findings of the Conservative Human Rights revolution as described by Marco Duranti, it is also an important nuance: this Catholic

In addition, Article 14 of the draft proposal contained the principle of 'nulla poena sine lege' which brought up distinct problems relating to the ending of the Second World War. In a draft memo, the Netherlands proposed dropping the principle altogether, as it would be hypocritical to sign up to such a principle whilst still in the process of administering post-war justice. This was directly connected to the punishment of Dutch collaborators with Nazi Germany on grounds which, on face value, were in conflict with this principle: it was feared the Convention could interfere with their punishment. The Dutch proposal immediately drew warnings from the Dutch civil servant in service of the Council, Arnold Struycken. Struycken had been put forward as a proposed member of the new institution and was involved in these early discussions surrounding the Convention. Telegraphing to The Hague, he warned of how this proposal would make the Netherlands the first state which proposed watering down the system: wary of that position, the Dutch put their critique on hold.[94]

Finally, the idea of a new International Court was seen as unwelcome competition for the International Court of Justice in the Hague, thereby diminishing the importance of the Dutch position in international law. In its line of reasoning, the Ministry was much influenced by its chief advisor on international law, Professor J. P. A. François. François, an ardent internationalist who had spent the last years of the war living in the garden house of the Peace Palace, had a clear preference for traditional international law. As such, he was – unlike Beaufort – sceptical of political European integration: if there had to be cooperation, this had to be on the global level and intergovernmental.[95]

character was not just the reason for the success of the convention, but also of its little legal importance in the early years. As a Dutch judge would later describe his dismissal of an appeal to the 'Treaty of Rome', as it came to be called in the Netherlands, 'Madam, better leave Rome to the Catholics', Egbert Myjer, *Bij een Vijftigste Verjaardag: aantekeningen over het Europees Verdrag tot bescherming van de rechten van de mens en de fundamentele vrijheden en de Nederlandse strafrechtspleging* (Oration: Amsterdam, 2000), p. 9.

94 NL-HaNA, Buitenlandse Zaken/Code-Archief 45–54, 2.05.117, inv. nr. 7399 'Memorandum 13 January 1950, from Struycken to the Hague'.

95 R. J. A. Alfaro, F. M. van Asbeck and L. Beaufort (eds.), *Varia juris Gentium: Liber Amicorum aangeboden aan Jean Pierre Francois ter gelegenheid van zijn 70ste verjaardag* (Leiden: Slijthoff, 1959), p. 16. His attachment to the international sphere is maybe best illustrated by his

This was also the message that François transmitted to the Dutch judicial section of the European Movement when he was invited to give an indication on the position of the government concerning the proposed Court and Convention. Any talk of a European Court would be premature, François stated. With the developments surrounding human rights going on at the United Nations and with perceived opposition from European states on the issue of the Court, the government could not be expected to be in favour of such an effort. Rather, the international option had to be explored before alternatives would be pursued.[96]

However, in the Council of Europe, it soon became clear this Dutch preference for a proper international route would not resonate with other delegations. It was noted by the Dutch delegate in Strasbourg that such an argument made little to no impact in what emerged was a distinctive European environment.[97] Therefore, cooperation within the European sphere became necessary.

Politically speaking, the Ministry of Foreign Affairs even noted some positive aspects: as the European project had just started (at the time it was still believed the Council of Europe could fulfil the political, moral and economic promises of European integration) the Convention could play a role in showing at least 'something had been set in motion'.[98] Moreover, setting out the benefits of the European Convention, the Ministry noted that 'European unity would miss its most basic foundations, if not the spiritual and moral values are clearly articulated, which are common to all European peoples'.[99]

Legally speaking, however, the government remained wary of a binding human rights covenant. As the draft of Teitgen was received and debated by the governments, it was sent to a committee of governmental experts to deal with the more technical questions: would the rights

residence during the war: as he was forced to leave his private house, he spent the final years of the war in the garden house of the Peace Palace.

96 NL-HaNA, Buitenlandse Zaken/Code-Archief 45–54, 2.05.117, inv. nr. 7398, 'Memo Francois, 1 August 1949'.

97 Ibid, 'Memo 26 August 1949'.

98 Ibid, 'Memo 22 October 1949'.

99 Ibid.

mentioned be posed in general or specific wording, and what would the position of the Court be? The Netherlands asked Beaufort to this meeting as their delegate. Although he was a member of the European Movement, the government appreciated his earlier work in the context of the UN and his 'moderate' opinions in general.[100] Yet as Beaufort fell ill, he was replaced by a young civil servant, Willem Riphagen, who had a keen eye for the political interests of the states involved.[101]

Riphagen faced several problems in the drafting process. The first was the question whether the Convention would be merely an expansion upon the already established statute of the Council of Europe, which asked its members to respect human rights (as such making the Convention nothing more than an intergovernmental treaty), or whether it would be the nucleus of a European federation, which would grant individual European citizens the right of appeal (as the European movement had proposed).[102] Second, there was the issue of territorial scope: would the Convention also apply in the overseas territories, for instance, or would there be a 'colonial clause' restricting access to human rights?

In answering these questions, the Netherlands found itself again on the conservative side of the states. When it came to the status of the Convention, the first option was most appealing for the Dutch: individual recourse to a Human Rights Court was seen as the final step in integration, definitely not as the first.[103] It did not stand alone: alongside the Scandinavian countries and the UK (its labour government wary of this pet project of Churchill's), the Netherlands found itself in a 'coalition of the unwilling'.[104] If human rights were to be included, this would have

100 NL-HaNA, Buitenlandse Zaken /Code-Archief 45–54, 2.05.117, inv. nr. 7399, 'Memo 4 January 1950'.

101 On Riphagen, see P. Jansen, *Willem Riphagen 1919–1994* (TMC Asser Instituut – The Hague 1998).

102 Ibid. See also the analysis of Ed Bates, who delves into the – mainly English conception of this tension.

103 Ibid. See also Klerk and Van Poelgeest, 'ratificatie a contre coeur', p. 226.

104 The British position has arguably been most extensively researched, among others by Simpson and Bates. For the Norwegian position, see Kjersti Brathagen, 'Competition or Complement to Universal Human Rights? The Norwegian Position on a European Convention on Human Rights, 1949–51' in Rasmus Mariager, Karl Molin and Kjersti

to be in an intergovernmental context. Consequently, the Dutch initially opposed both the installation of the Commission and the Court.

Second, attempts to make the Convention into a document which would protect all inhabitants of the European empires were swiftly dismantled. Even though the Consultative Assembly had declared itself a strong proponent of removing the colonial clause, which, in the words of Léopold Senghor would turn the declaration from a document protecting human rights into one protecting solely 'European human rights', the states had different ideas.[105] The Netherlands supported a British proposal which introduced a colonial clause and noted it would only be able to ratify if the clause was accepted as well. This was a distinctive step back from the draft of the European movement whereby the Convention would apply to all territories, but the political rights were to be limited to the metropole.

Instead, the newly inserted colonial clause left it up to the states to decide whether or not to apply the Convention to its overseas territories. The final wording amounted to a double safeguard for the imperial states. Even if the signatory state in question would allow the Convention to apply in a territory of its choice, it still would need to take into account the local circumstances, amounting in practice to lower standards of protection.[106] From the outset, human rights for Europeans were thus of a different order than those for their colonial counterparts.

This left the question of what to do with the two most innovative elements of the Convention, the right of individual petition and the permanent European Court. Deliberations on these topics were contentious: for the legal experts, these were political matters, for the politicians, there were constant twists. Ultimately, a compromise was found by accepting the right of individual petition and the jurisdiction of a European Court, but leaving the states free to decide whether they wished to sign up to those provisions or not. The same went for the colonial clause: the Committee of Ministers

Brathagen (eds.), *Human Rights in Europe during the Cold War* (New York: Routledge, 2014), pp. 15–26.

105 Jens Theilen, 'Locating Progress in the European Convention on Human Rights' *Völkerrechtsblog*, 19.09.2023, doi: 10.17176/20230919-223736-0.

106 As set out in article 63 of the Convention. See Anne-Isabelle Richard: *The European Convention of Human Rights' Colonial Clause and the End of Empire*, *VerfBlog*, 2022/1/26, doi: 10.17176/20220127-060144-0; Brian Simpson, *Human Rights and the End of Empire*, p. 694.

accepted the restriction of the Convention to geographical Europe and left it up to the states themselves to see if its application would be expanded.

This might give the impression the input from the Consultative Assembly, and with it the domestic European Movement, was consequently sidelined throughout the drafting process. Sometimes this was indeed the case: quite some ambitious proposals were left aside as the Ministers watered down the proposals substantively. Some members grew increasingly frustrated as the governments narrowed down the original federalist ideals and wanted the Council of Europe to be much more ambitious.

Still, their impact can be found when it comes to some specific contents of the Convention. As the Consultative Assembly of the Council of Europe was filled with national parliamentarians who, in the Dutch context, were almost all involved with the European Movement, opportunities were sometimes taken to pressure governmental policies from both fora. It was an alternative route to influence the government, not via the Assembly, but through the national Parliament. One example of this influence can be found in the right to education. Set in the first protocol of the European Convention next to the protection of property and the right to free elections, this right was of great importance to the Dutch parliamentarians, in particular those from the Christian parties. They saw it as vital to protect the specific Dutch context of educational policy whereby everyone had the constitutional right to provide education on any grounds possible, be they religious, secular, or anything in between.[107] The Assembly had proposed that a broad definition of the right be included, but it was feared the governments would try and narrow it further down.

Here, the parliamentarians actively used their influence. In pushing for an extensive protection, in particular of the rights of parents to pick their own religious or philosophical education for their children, they did not shy away from making threats. As the government noted:

> The Dutch members of the Assembly have made it very clear that the Tweede Kamer would reject the additional protocol, and maybe even the Convention of Rome itself, if the right of parents to choose the education

[107] These rights, particularly the protection of property, were too contentious to be included in the original Convention but were instead included in the first protocol, signed two years later in 1952.

> of their children would not be safeguarded in conformity with the text proposed by the Assembly [...] Under these circumstances, the position of the government cannot waiver...[108]

Subsequently, the Dutch government indeed pressed for the acceptance of the broad formulation of the right as proposed by the Assembly, which would ultimately end up in the Convention.[109] In this way, Dutch peculiarities not only led to an urge to minimize the impact of the Convention in order to safeguard them from European interference, but could also lead to a drive to actively 'Europeanise' these notions.

All this meant that when the Convention was signed in Rome in 1950, the original idea of a Federal Court for every European citizen had – much to the disappointment of those in the European Movement and the Consultative Assembly – been firmly dismantled by the governments of the signatory states. Rather, the Convention had to be seen as a tool to prevent states from slipping into authoritarian excesses: the liberties it entailed were the liberties as they stood at that particular time, and should serve as a warning bell against rising authoritarianism.[110]

1.3 RATIFYING: BRINGING THE CONVENTION INTO THE KINGDOM

This now brought the discussion back to the domestic context. There, in the lead-up to ratification, the Dutch government had to decide on three key points before it proposed a law to the Parliament. First, what would be the legal value of the Convention? Second, would the facultative options of the right of individual petition and jurisdiction of the Court be accepted? And finally, there was the struggle with Empire: where in the Kingdom would European human rights apply?

As to the first question, the government had to answer whether or not individuals would be able to claim rights under the Convention before

[108] NL-HaNA, Buitenlandse Zaken /Code-Archief 45–54, 2.05.117, inv. nr. 2811, 'Memo 17 January 1952 to Council of Ministers'.

[109] Nationaal Archief, Den Haag, Ministerie van Justitie: Afdeling Wetgeving m.b.t. de Internationale Organisaties, number access 2.09.84, inv. nr. 171, 'Memo 22 juni 1951, van directie Europa, to Ministry of Justice'.

[110] Simpson, *Human Rights and the End of Empire*, pp. 711–754.

the national judge. This question became even more pressing as in 1952 the Dutch Parliament had adopted an amendment to the constitution which would allow judges to test laws against treaty provisions which were directly applicable: if followed, this would mean the Convention would supersede domestic laws and arguably become a more important document than the Constitution.[111] On this issue, opinions were divided: Foreign Affairs stated that the Convention did indeed have a direct effect. However, according to the Minister of Justice, this was not the case. The Convention was – in the view of the Ministry – not directly applicable, as it was primarily aimed at states: a special provision would have to be made stating that such was the case.[112]

It was a topic of fierce internal debate, where the expertise of Beaufort – who made a plea for direct applicability – was put forward as authoritative argument. After all, he had been involved in the drafting process itself. Ultimately, it was decided that there could be no other option than to accept this direct effect: a meeting with legal experts of the departments confirmed that the only possible reading of the Convention was that it was directly applicable.[113] This was eased first by the idea that Dutch legislation was believed to be fully in conformity with the Convention, even though 'no Dutch lawyer can be completely sure about that, because of the width of the matter and the vagueness of the articles of the Treaty', the experts noted.[114]

Second, even if judges went on to apply the Convention to circumvent domestic legislation, the government had faith in the Netherlands' judiciary and leading Court, the Hoge Raad, to act cautiously. As the memorandum of the experts set out the issue in detail: 'Although the application of the Treaty by the lower judiciary perhaps cannot be thought to be safe all the time, one may expect the highest court – also

111 Klerk and Van Poelgeest, 'Ratificactie a contre coeur', p. 232.

112 NL-HaNa, Justitie/Wetgeving/International Organisaties, 2.09.84, inv. nr. 171, 'Memo Eijssen, 11 december 1952'.

113 The meeting was held between Mr Eijssen from the Ministry of Justice and Mr François of the Ministry of Foreign affairs. Beaufort was asked to comment on the issue as expert, and made a strong case for the direct applicability of the Convention. NL-HaNA, Justitie/Wetgeving/Internationale Organisaties, 2.09.84, inv. nr. 171, 'memo 28 January 1953'.

114 Ibid.

taking into account the experience of recent years – to take all relevant factual circumstances into account, and will not find easily a tool in this treaty to block Dutch legislation'.[115] Such behaviour was a constitutional tradition: as the Dutch constitution entrusted Parliament with the power to review the quality of legislation over the courts, who were (and are) famously barred from constitutional review, the judiciary had always left great room for manoeuvre to the legislature.

As a result of these two reasons, the potential impact of the Convention was expected to be very minimal. Human rights violations were deemed to happen solely in totalitarian countries, whereas the judiciary was known to be conservative in its application of international treaties.[116]

1.3.1 DEALING WITH THE FACULTATIVE CHOICES: THE COURT AND THE RIGHT OF INDIVIDUAL PETITION. This left three issues to be decided. The right of individual petition, the jurisdiction of the Court and the scope of application. On the issue of the right of individual petition, the government made itself clear: as the Netherlands did not need supranational human rights protection, it was also deemed undesirable if an individual would be able to go to an International Court concerning human rights related issues. This was 'chefsache'. Prime Minister Drees personally felt very strongly about this issue. He saw the individual complaint procedure as too expensive, as a threat to the national legal order, and a way for 'querulants' and communists to obstruct domestic justice.[117] In his almost categorical denial of the desirability of this right, Drees' concerns became the foundational governmental position. As complaints of individuals first had to go past the European Commission on Human Rights, the key lay with this institution. With no sense of how the Commission would act or how intrusive its practices would be, the governmental position was to wait and see if the Commission could be 'trusted' in these affairs.

The Parliament accepted the reasoning, albeit by a very slim margin. In particular, the vocal group of pro-European Members was

[115] NL-HaNA, Justitie/Wetgeving/Internationale Organisaties, 2.09.84, inv. nr. 171, 'memo 28 January 1953'.

[116] Van Leeuwen, *Uit het spoor van Thorbecke*, p. 60.

[117] Klerk and Van Poelgeest, 'Ratificactie a contre coeur', p. 232.

disappointed on how the government 'missed out' on an opportunity to show its dedication to the cause.[118] A motion to force the government to accept the right of individual complaint was only narrowly defeated by three votes: despite pressure from the social-democrats and liberal foreman Pieter Oud to accept the right (as it was the only tool which would provide the Convention with actual meaning), the government's insistence on its undesirability swayed the majority.[119] However, it was a prelude to the continuous pressure from Parliament on the government to accept this particular element of the Convention.

The individual plaintiff would thus not be able to take a 'European' route in the Netherlands after ratification. On the issue of jurisdiction of the Court, the government was more lenient, but not out of genuine support. Only because Belgium, a close ally in the context of European policy, had declared itself a proponent of the Court (Benelux countries mostly took similar positions in European affairs), the Dutch government was persuaded to accept its jurisdiction. Nonetheless, this acceptance was conditional: jurisdiction was accepted only for a period of five years, after which it had to be renewed. This 'temporary' acceptance of the jurisdiction of the Court was not unusual. Other European countries did so as well, placing a strain on the authority and arguably on the potential of the Strasbourg institutions to be truly 'free' in their judgements from the beginning.[120] With the rejection of the access of individuals to this Court, however, the move was more of a symbolic gesture rather than the embracing of a supranational institute.[121]

[118] These were not necessarily bound to one party, but very much the result of personal convictions. The labor party embodied both sceptics (Drees) and proponents of the European idea (Goes van Der Naters), whereas the Catholics were inclined to euro-friendly positions but voted against the right of individual complaint. The liberals, on their part, voted to accept the right.

[119] The amendment introduced to accept the right of individual complaint was defeated 32–35. Klerk and Van Poelgeest, 'Ratificatie a contre coeur', pp. 240–241.

[120] Both Belgium and the United Kingdom would threaten to not extend their acceptance of the Court on occasion, and this particular circumstance has been invoked to explain the early hesitancy of the Court: see the Belgium Linguistics case as an example; Bates, *The Evolution of the European Convention*, p. 176.

[121] NL-HaNA, Buitenlandse Zaken/Code-Archief 45–54, 2.05.117, inv. nr. 7399, 'Memo 4 April 1950'.

1.3.2 A CONVENTION FOR EUROPEANS. The last matter of debate which the Convention presented to the government was its scope of applicability. As the government had to decide whether or not the Convention would be extended to the overseas territories for whose international affairs it was responsible, the question emerged if the Convention would apply solely on European soil or throughout the Dutch Empire.[122] There were three territories in question. In the 'east' there was Dutch New Guinea, a last piece of the empire in the Indonesian archipelago which had been kept out of the transfer of sovereignty to Indonesia. In the 'west', there were the Dutch Antilles and Suriname, where there had been no broad demands for independence, and which were still part of the Empire.

The question of who would be protected by European human rights coincided with broader questions surrounding the relation between European integration and Empire. Directly after the ceremonial signing of the Convention, on 4 November 1950 in Rome, Dutch representatives of the Consultative Assembly, asked the governmental representative about a resolution of the Assembly. For the Assembly had launched an initiative to – informally – involve Parliaments of overseas territories in the work of the Council of Europe as well, in order to better convey their interests. The British had noted there was high interest in Canada and Australia for such a move. In response, the Dutch Parliamentarians asked the government whether the Netherlands would send representatives from Suriname and the Antilles.[123]

This was shut down by the Ministry of Foreign Affairs, which deemed it unnecessary to invite the 'States' – the local Parliaments – of Suriname and the Antilles. The other states to which the proposal of the Consultative Assembly related, notably those from the Commonwealth, such as Canada, in fact conducted their own foreign policy. Since this

[122] Nationaal Archief, Den Haag, Ministeries voor Algemeene Oorlogvoering van het Koninkrijk (AOK) en van Algemene Zaken (AZ): Kabinet van de Minister-President (KMP), nummer toegang 2.03.01, inventarisnummer 2811, 'verslag tweede zitting'; NL-HaNA, Buitenlandse Zaken/Code-Archief 45–54, 2.05.117, inv. nr. 7400, 'Memo 2 May 1952'.

[123] Civil servants Van de Kieft and Serrarens. NL-HaNA, Buitenlandse Zaken/Code-Archief 45–54, 2.05.117, inv. nr. 20524 'Memo 9 November 1950 from Scheltema to Minister'.

was not the case for the areas within the Dutch Kingdom, there was – according to the Ministry – no need to involve them in the process. Indeed, no invites would be sent, with the result that when it came to the Kingdom, the political involvement in the Assembly would be limited to Dutch Parliamentarians.

Second, and this was a sensitive issue, the question emerged if they should also send representatives from Indonesia, which did conduct its own foreign policy.[124] Indonesia, after all had just gained its sovereignty in December 1949 but was still constitutionally connected to the Netherlands. Independence was achieved, but the country maintained a link with the Netherlands via the so-called Dutch-Indonesian Union, a constitutional set up which provided for a confederation of two equal partners, the Kingdom of the Netherlands and Indonesia. Yet would Indonesians in that context also have a say when it came to European integration?

The Minister immediately warned against this idea. The constitutional connection could exist, but inviting Indonesian representatives was politically undesirable. The initial stance was to simply ignore the request. However, this became increasingly hard when Arnold Struycken, the Dutch civil servant in the Council of Europe, had informally put the Dutch government on notice of recent developments which spelt trouble. The British had responded to the resolution of the Assembly by inviting all members of its Commonwealth, whereas the French announced they would invite members from Laos and Cambodia, even though these areas did not – yet – possess a Parliament. In order not to fall behind, the Dutch had to act. Struycken carefully inquired if, and if so *how*, such an invitation would be phrased and be received by the Indonesians.[125]

Driven by the urge not to fall behind these other states, the Dutch ultimately *did* extend an invitation to the Indonesian Parliament but abstained from traditional diplomatic niceties. As the first draft of the invite, noting how the Dutch would receive the Indonesian presence in Strasbourg 'with the greatest pleasure', was deemed too positive, ultimately a very neutral invitation to the Indonesian parliament.[126]

124 Ibid.

125 NL-HaNA, Buitenlandse Zaken/Code-Archief 45–54, 2.05.117, inv. nr. 20524 'Memo 14 December 1950'.

126 Ibid, 'Invitation to Indonesia, 6 July 1950'.

The question now was whether Indonesia would heed the invitation and send envoys to the Council of Europe. If they accepted, it would mean European integration, envisioned as a tool to preserve 'Europeanness', would actively include voices from the Dutch imperial sphere. However, precisely the idea of involvement was, as such undesirable for the recently independent states. The Indonesian parliament voted against the move – albeit by a slim majority – as it was seen as hampering the desire for independence. First of all, a presence in the Council of Europe could be seen as an act in the Cold War. As the European bloc was distinctly anti-communist, joining the Council would threaten the neutral position of Indonesia. Second, the idea of a Dutch delegation joined by an Indonesian group of envoys could be perceived as Indonesian cooperation in the context of the Dutch-Indonesian Union. That was undesirable: independence, rather than collaboration or continued ties with the previous occupier, was the aim of the new Indonesian government.[127] Ultimately, the Council of Europe would therefore remain solely the realm of Dutch Parliamentarians, proceeding without input from other areas within the Kingdom.

The episode sheds light on two reinforcing trends. First, even though some states were very keen on politically involving the – former – colonies in the project of European integration, the Netherlands distinctly did not express an interest in those initiatives. Ideally, those states or territories would be kept voiceless. Second, when asked, those states or territories themselves were highly distrustful of joining European integration, as it would hamper their own freedoms.

Both trends can be observed in the further debates surrounding the Convention and its applicability in the Kingdom. The Dutch government was by no means willing to provide strong human rights protection to everyone in the Empire. Conversely, there was also distrust in, for example, Suriname of the implications on being dragged into a European project.

1.3.3 THE CONVENTION IN THE KINGDOM. Faced with the question of where the Convention would apply, the Dutch government swiftly decided *not* to extend it to Dutch New Guinea. This was the result

[127] Ibid, 'Memo 1 August 1951, from Jakarta to The Hague'.

of old colonial thinking. The main reason for excluding New Guinea from the Convention was the perceived lack of development of the area: 'In the present stadium of development, it is doubtful whether it would be responsible to expand the working of the Treaty to that area', the Ministry of Overseas Territories noted.[128] 'Full application of the articles of Treaty and Protocol presupposes with the population a certain level of development, which the population of New Guinea does not yet possess'.[129] European human rights, in other words, were only valid if one had achieved a certain level of civilisation.

Regarding the right to individual petition, this option was even considered dangerous for the colonial mission. The Dutch supervision required, or so it was believed, an image of the Dutch as infallible: after all, they were the ones educating the population to an appropriate level of development. To allow an opportunity for international revision of that process could, in the eyes of the Dutch government, undermine the trust of the 'still underdeveloped' population in the responsible government.[130] For the Dutch, the possibility that Papuans could invoke the Convention in front of a judge was considered most undesirable.[131] As reassurance, it was noted that under Article 73e of the UN Charter, the Dutch had a duty to report on – inter alia – the human rights situation in New Guinea.[132] This was deemed enough to satisfy the human rights commitment.

This echo of colonialism was not necessarily in line with the approach of other European colonial powers: as the United Kingdom extended the application of the Convention to basically all its dependencies (albeit without acceptance of the Court or any right of individual complaint), the Dutch, regarding New Guinea, flat out rejected it.[133] Aware

[128] NL-HaNA, Buitenlandse Zaken/Code-Archief 45–54, 2.05.117, inv. nr. 7400, 'Memo of ministry of overseas territories, 29 July 1952'.

[129] Ibid.

[130] Ibid.

[131] Nationaal Archief, Den Haag, Digitaal Duplicaat: Gouverneur van Suriname, Kabinet, nummer toegang 2.10.26, inventarisnummer 918, 'Memo to Suriname, 29 December 1953'.

[132] Ibid.

[133] For the British case, see Simpson, *Human Rights and the End of Empire*, pp. 711–754. Put briefly, the British simply did not expect the Convention to have any impact. The Dutch were slightly more cautious in that regard.

of these diverging approaches, Foreign Affairs noted how it would set the Netherlands apart: 'in the present time, those territories with overseas dependencies should avoid any appearance they would have other principles as regards their colonial policies than which would apply to the mother country'.[134] Legal advice from Prof. François would seal the deal, however. In response to these concerns voiced by Foreign Affairs, he stated that such an approach would be too academic: 'how this international engagement with a matter, which until this moment was part of the domestic jurisdiction plays out, remains to be seen. One needs to take into account, that the entire treaty and its supervision are being carried by a European mentality and lies completely in the European sphere'.[135] Legally speaking, François therefore concluded, it would be wise to keep the Convention to those it was meant to protect: Europeans.

This refusal to extend the Convention to New Guinea remained in place even when the Dutch became aware of their precarious position. The Permanent Representation in Strasbourg reported with concern on the British extensions of the Convention. When British Northern Borneo, an area relatively comparable to Dutch New Guinea, got included in this extension, notice was given with strong advice to reconsider the Dutch refusal, only to be met with the cold shoulder from The Hague. There was no interest in changing the previous course of actions.[136]

The case was somewhat different in the western dependencies, Suriname and the Antilles. There, the idea to first educate the local population was not deemed desirable to use as a legitimation for presence in these territories.[137] The civilising argument did not fly: a governing

[134] NL-HaNA, Buitenlandse Zaken/Code-Archief 45–54, 2.05.117, inv. nr. 7400, 'Memo Foreign Affairs 24 October 1952'.

[135] NL-HaNA, Buitenlandse Zaken/Code-Archief 45–54, 2.05.117, inv. nr. 7400, 'Memo François 28 October 1952'. Despite (or because of) his sceptical attitude on European integration, the distinctive European character of the Convention did not escape François.

[136] N NL-HaNA, Buitenlandse Zaken/Code-Archief 45–54, 2.05.117, inv. nr. 16582, 'Memo 10 November 1953'.

[137] Gert Oostiendie and Inge Klinkers, *Knellende Koninkrijksbanden: Het Nederlandse dekolonisatiebeleid in de Caraiben, 1940–2000 – deel 1, 1940–1954* (Amsterdam: Amsterdam University Press, 2001), pp. 132–133.

structure was already present, and in the constitutional framework, Suriname and the Antilles had autonomy to co-decide upon these issues. This changed the setting, as local politicians could express their voices. Here, it was not just a matter of extending a colonial policy from 'centre to periphery'. Rather, the dependencies were indeed allowed their own say in the matters, thereby opening up the possibility for a 'non-European' input into this European Convention.

When consulted upon the question of whether or not to expand the application of the ECHR to these areas, the specific danger, as it was perceived by local and Dutch authorities, lay in the right of individual complaint. It was feared that inhabitants of the dependencies would take an international route to challenge local authorities. Although the application of the Convention in general was met with little concern (again, the expected impact was limited), any right of individual complaint was deemed extremely undesirable. 'One has to take into account the possibility that the right of individual complaint shall be more often used in the West than in the Netherlands', the Ministry of Overseas Territories warned, hinting at possible 'abuse' by local inhabitants of the individual complaint.[138] The local governments also expressed such opinions: the Antilles noted that 'under no circumstance […] an investigation such as that can be tolerated in the Dutch Antilles'.[139]

Surinamese representatives took the opportunity to raise a different question, however. They went to the heart of the tension between the protection of human rights on the one hand and the European character of the Convention on the other. Suriname had no problem with participating in a document which sought to protect human rights, the local government stated. It perceived the Convention as little more than an international document stating the same rights already present in its own domestic 'landsregeling'. However, the representation of Suriname in the Netherlands, Mr Henri Pos, noted

[138] The 'West' refers to the western dependencies, being Suriname and the Dutch Antilles. These stood in contrast to the 'East', namely Indonesia. NL-HaNA, Buitenlandse Zaken/Code-Archief 45–54, 2.05.117, inv. nr. 7400, 'Memo of ministry of overseas territories, 29 July 1952'.

[139] NL-HaNA, Buitenlandse Zaken/Code-Archief 45–54, 2.05.117, inv. nr. 16582, 'Memo from Antilles to the Hague, 15 December 1953'.

something peculiar: 'this Convention does not primarily deal with human rights, but with the integration of Europe'.[140]

To Pos, this was a crucial point. After all, the preamble of the Convention specifically mentioned 'European states' and was adopted in the larger framework of the Council of Europe, under pressure from the European movement, which altogether aimed to achieve a larger unity between European states. But where did Suriname fit in that story?[141] The recent establishment of the European internal market for coal and steel made the question even more pressing: European integration seemed to be here to stay. When it came to the Convention, in particular, the European Court was a sensitive issue, as it entailed Suriname could be placed under some kind of European supervision.

It was no coincidence that Pos raised the issue. The year before, he had visited Paris to discuss the topic of the integration of the overseas territories in the project of European integration, where one key point was that this integration could potentially have negative consequences for those territories. Returning to Suriname, Pos had drafted a report warning of the implications such actions might have, as they could potentially keep Suriname in a set up dependent on European decisions.[142]

These doubts of Pos were perfectly valid. As we have seen, federalist European ideas were highly prominent in the establishment of the Convention, while the perceived character of the ECHR was – from François' point of view – to be found in a distinct European mentality. With or without a facultative Court, the Convention *was* envisioned to be an instrument of European integration, even though the governments had circumvented the more radical provisions in that direction. As such, the Convention had to overcome a firm distrust of European cooperation, which was not uncommon in the overseas territories where it was perceived as a possible 'Empire 2.0'.

140 NL-HaNA, Buitenlandse Zaken/Code-Archief 45–54, 2.05.117, inv. nr. 918, 'Memo from Mr Pos to Regeringsraad, 4 March 1954'.

141 Ibid.

142 Nationaal Archief, Den Haag, Ministerie van Koloniën en opvolgers: Dossierarchief, number access 2.10.54, inventarisnummer 3440, 'Memo 9 December 1953 from directie Suriname to M'.

This was far from a baseless concern. In fact, it was a distinct and very real possibility. Within the Council of Europe, from 1952 onwards, work had progressed on the 'plan Strasbourg', the aim of which was to 'alleviate European economic problems by closer cooperation with the (former) overseas territories'.[143] As such, a proposal was made to increase investment in those areas under guidance of the Council of Europe, in which the Netherlands participated as well. Noting the necessity of 'developing the industrialization of the dependent overseas territories, when it comes to the production of resources', the more profitable industry would have to be kept in Europe.[144] European integration in this regard echoed the old colonial economic structure in which the colonies provided the resources which were transformed into goods in Europe itself. After all, the key to the plan was not to develop the overseas territories for their own sake, but to shape their industries to the benefit of European economic reconstruction.

Pos was wary that, by accepting the Convention, the territories would be drawn into precisely those renewed ties. In preparing a reassuring response to Pos's concerns, the Dutch made an inventory of other European approaches on involving the overseas territories and noted some discrepancies. Whereas France was very willing to include its overseas territories in any form of European integration (clinging to the notion of 'EurAfrique', an idealized European-African tandem for quite some time), Belgium was more reluctant to go this way.[145] Congo, the largest Belgian colony, had little interest in participating in European events. The Dutch ambassador in Leopoldville[146] even noted fear in Congo of the plans for European integration and stated that 'the Colonial had no interest whatsoever in these plans'.[147]

143 NL-HaNA, Buitenlandse Zaken/Code-Archief 45–54, 2.05.117, inv. nr. 20513 'Relations Economiques avec Les Pays D'Outre-Mer 27 August 1952'.

144 Ibid.

145 For details see Peo Hansen and Stefan Johnson, *Eurafrica: The Untold History of European Integration and Colonialism* (London: Bloomsbury, 2014). In France, see Brown, *The Seventh Member State: Algeria, France and the European Community*.

146 Present day Kinshasa.

147 NL-HaNA, Buitenlandse Zaken/Code-Archief 45–54, 2.05.117, inv. nr. 16582, '16 October 1953, Memo from Leopoldville to The Hague'.

The question of Pos thus forced the Dutch government to reflect upon the relation between human rights and Europe: it was clear Suriname did not want to join European integration, so would an extension of the Convention even be feasible? The answer remained ambiguous. In a reassuring note, it was stated that European integration as such was primarily a continental Dutch affair. Any fears Suriname might have had were without foundation: the European project was not meant to form some form of 'closed' group which would threaten the autonomy of the overseas territories, but rather to enhance and safeguard the liberty of the continental state. As such, there could be no objection from Suriname to Dutch participation in this project.[148]

At the same time, the government noted, the protection of human rights was not an exclusively European issue, even though it acknowledged that certain European states also understood the treaty to be a tool to strengthen their ties with the former colonies.[149] However, the ways in which the Convention could achieve European integration were closely connected to the issue of individual complaint: only via this tool could the European Commission and Court truly be reached. Since it was precisely this provision which had not been accepted, both in the Netherlands and abroad, the integrational consequences of the Convention were presented as being very minimal.[150] Suriname, therefore, did not have to worry: the Netherlands took its position into account and reassured Suriname that by not accepting the right of individual petition, the integrational consequences would be minimal.

This explicit reassurance made Suriname accept the Convention: with the expected limited impact and no possibility of a European Court ruling on 'internal matters', the Convention would not hurt its autonomous place in the Kingdom. Ultimately, it was decided the applicability should be the same for the Netherlands and its western dependencies: the Convention was accepted in 1954 as being directly applicable, which would allow local judges to test domestic legislation against the provisions of the Convention, yet without the right of individual complaint.

[148] A rather remarkable notion, since this was not exactly what Suriname had signaled.

[149] NL-HaNA, Buitenlandse Zaken/Code-Archief 45–54, 2.05.117, inv. nr. 16582, 'Memo 13 May 1954'.

[150] Ibid.

This stance was in conformity with the other European powers, who remained hesitant to grant international protection to the inhabitants of their overseas dominions, while granting such protection to their European citizens. Such was a testimony to the distinct 'European' character of the Convention. More than the idea of protecting human rights of all, it was this geographical and cultural location which would be most important in determining the scope of its legal protection. If the Convention indeed had to be seen as the 'conscience of Europe', – as Teitgen himself claimed it was – this was a selective conscience.[151]

As things stood in 1954, the Convention thus started off in a curtailed manner. It enshrined the rights of the European person, and was carefully kept out of the Dutch Kingdom. Moreover, its ambitious beginnings, as pushed by the European federalists, had been carefully dismantled by the governments, who were keen to keep the Convention at bay. Socio-economic rights remained a national concern instead of a human rights issue, and when it came to the Convention's legal value, it was presented as entailing 'nothing new' to the Dutch standards, whereas the right of individual petition was also kept at bay. Yet plenty of issues remained open: this cautious interpretation would be put to the test after 1954, when a new range of actors turned to the Convention to see what its value would be.

[151] As put forward by Teitgen: 'A conscience must exist somewhere which will sound the alarm to the minds of a nation …' cited in Bates, *The Evolution of the European Convention on Human Rights*, p. 44.

CHAPTER 2

1954–1962

The Open Beginning of the Convention

AFTER IT WAS DRAFTED AND RATIFIED, the history of the Convention entered a new stage. In 1954, the Convention had become a part of the law of the land in the Kingdom of the Netherlands, with the exception of Dutch New Guinea. In these early years, the question that was very much open, therefore, was what the impact of European human rights would be on that legal order. It would turn out that the governmental statement that European human rights were completely non-threatening concepts was not meekly accepted. The new situation broadened the range of actors involved, as the early members of the European movement, who we can see returning in key positions, were joined by international and constitutional lawyers. As the first test cases reached the courts, both in the national context as well as at the European level, legal practice started to define the value of the Convention. As such, these initial years form a key episode in the trajectory of the Convention: in 1954–1962, this early period of its existence, the foundation for the Convention's meaning in later decades was laid.[1]

For in 1962, many of the initiatives which had set out to test or enhance the legal value of the Convention reached their end. On the national level, the Hoge Raad quashed a judgement of a lower Court which would have given the Convention a much more prominent position. From that moment on, the battle for the domestic legal value with European human rights was settled – at least for a moment. On the European level, in 1962, an initiative from the Dutch judge to make the European Court

[1] Although to provide a full overview of the initiatives of van Asbeck at the European Court, sources from 1964 are also included.

receive more cases was ultimately dismissed, and after the case of *De Becker* v. *Belgium*, a long period of inactivity for the Court followed. From a broader perspective, 1962 was also the year in which the last vestige of Dutch empire in the 'east', Papua New Guinea, was 'lost'. It was a key moment in the status of the Netherlands, as until 1962, the country had continued to cling to an idea of being a great, imperial nation. Only after 1962, a new sense of morality came to dominate (foreign) politics, resulting in a reappreciation of human rights. Where the interpretation of the legal value of the Convention seemed to close in 1962, a new potential for engagement opened up afterwards as well.

The foundational character of this period is occasionally misunderstood. The notion that these were very *quiet* years for both the European Court and for the Convention in the domestic legal order has been presented as something of a truism. The early years of the Convention's existence usually seen as the years in which the 'Beauty' was still fast asleep.[2] This goes both for the European as for the domestic level. When it comes to the domestic level, the well known stories of a domestic judge who did not possess a physical copy of the Convention, or the notion of a judge who believed that only bad cases could be won by appealing to European human rights, all serve to illustrate the overarching theme: the Convention did not matter until much later. Yet even though it may be true, only few cases reached the Court, and knowledge of its existence was confined to a tiny group of experts, this is a point to problematize rather than to take at face value. After all, the Convention had been the focal point of activism in the years leading up to its ratification. So why was this period of active engagement followed by one of relative silence?

On a closer look, however, the Convention was far from 'asleep' in the domestic legal context. The Convention did not enter the domestic legal framework in a state of inertia, and even though the actors engaging with the Convention shifted from the more activist European movement into the more specialized field of international lawyers, this did not mean that the Convention as such was no topic of attention. To glance over this early period as merely a warm up to a later breakthrough would miss some crucial insights. For instead of being asleep, the Convention

[2] Cf. Bates, *The Evolution of the European Convention.*

entered the legal order in a highly contentious line of cases, which dealt with pressing political issues. Responding to ambitious lower courts, the Hoge Raad ultimately stepped in and 'smothered' the interpretation of the Convention. However, this was no predetermined outcome. Rather, it was a legal choice, which cast its shadow over the national legal value of the Convention for years to come.

Second, when it comes to the peace and quiet on the European level, it should be noted this was part of a distinct legal strategy.[3] Following the experiences of the Dutch member of the Commission, Leo Beaufort and the national interaction with the European institutions, it can be shown that the restraint exercised by this institution was part of a conscious effort to let states accept the right of individual petition in order to further the European integration via the human rights system. Yet this strategy of restraint was not necessarily shared by all actors within the European institutions. For whereas such a strategy may have been the case for the Commission, the personal experience of van Asbeck, the Dutch judge in the European Court, tells a different story. There, due to mounting frustration at the Court's inaction, active campaigns were set up, amongst others by van Asbeck, to make the Court relevant. Their failures were due to the opposition of states, but it shows how the Court was by no means passive in the face of its persistent irrelevance.

Three themes dominated the Dutch engagement with regard to the Convention in these early days after drafting which helps understand the claim these early years were, in fact a very vital period. The first was the institutional future of the Convention and the strategy of key individuals to let states accept the facultative options. Although the Netherlands had accepted the jurisdiction of the – as yet non-existent – European Court of Human Rights, the right of individuals to file a petition directly at the Commission had not been accepted on grounds of sovereignty and fear of abuse. This would be the first major issue in the early years of

[3] There has been debate on this notion, with Jan Eckel posing questions as to whether or not this was truly an example of 'legal diplomacy', as put forward by Mikael Rask Madsen. This chapter supports the reading of Madsen, based on archival materials. Mikael Rask Madsen, 'The Challenging Authority of the European Court of Human Rights: From Cold War Legal Diplomacy to the Brighton Declaration and Backlash' *Law and Contemporary Problems* Vol. 79 Nr. 1 (2016), pp. 141–178.

the Convention: both at the European and domestic level, a campaign would be set up to accept the individual complaint procedure. The role of key individuals such as Leo Beaufort and Polys Modinos needs to be highlighted in this regard, as well as the Dutch struggles over the acceptance of the optional clauses of the Convention and the role played by Empire and Communists therein.

The second was the domestic legal engagement with the Convention. It tracks the first 'test cases' which came before domestic courts and which would define how the legal value of the Convention would be perceived in the following years. In a string of divisive cases, courts came to grapple with a sensitive balancing act of weighing religious freedom as enshrined in the Convention against a constitutional ban on Catholic processions in some parts of the country.

The third was the European Court of Human Rights. After it was installed in 1959, the possibility emerged for states to find themselves in a courtroom for violating 'human rights': this was in itself a revolutionary moment, whereby its supporters envisioned the Court as an institution that would bring about a European public order based on human rights, potentially even taking up the role of a European Supreme Court of Justice. The existence of the Court confronted the member states with important questions: which judges would be installed, and how would the case law of this new institution turn out? Yet as the judges found themselves subsequently sidelined, they did not simply accept the situation. Instead, following the Dutch judge in the Court, van Asbeck, we can see how they launched ambitious reform programmes for the Court, which would provide it with a much more powerful role. Ultimately, these initiatives failed. However, they are illustrative of the many facets of the early years of the Convention. If European human rights were off to a slow start, it was not just because of legal caution, but also because of diverging political views on what to achieve with those rights.

2.1 THE FEARS OF DREES: KEEPING EUROPE OUT

Although the Convention may have been ratified, its potential for reform was slim at first glance. Its most revolutionary innovation, the route of individuals into Europe, remained closed. As the Netherlands had not accepted the right of individual petition, the application of European human rights remained an affair for the national judiciary. As things stood, it was not likely that the Dutch government would accept such a right. Although there had been some internal struggles (the Ministry of Foreign Affairs was very much in favour of accepting, mainly on reputational grounds),[4] the government as a whole was sceptical of the possibility of individuals to move towards a supranational institution. It held the right of individual petition to be a 'slogan' of which the consequences were not directly clear.[5]

A majority in Parliament was strongly in favour, however, precisely because of the euro-friendly dimension which acceptance entailed: it had accepted the ratification of the Convention without the right, but under the direction of the euro-friendly group, Parliament would continue to push the government to embrace it.[6] Yet it was up against some stiff opposition, for accepting the right of individual petition would require Drees himself to turn. The Prime Minister vehemently opposed the option of individuals filing complaints against the sovereign Dutch state. Never overtly fond of European integration as such, which he perceived as a suspicious Catholic project, the social democrat Drees feared the right of individual petition could result in a number of problems.[7]

As a general nuisance, the right was regarded as supporting a troublesome international institution, namely the Court. Moreover, a bureaucratic system would have to be set up, and this would be costly as well: who was going to pay for all the expenses just to give these people a platform to complain? The Court of Justice in Luxembourg, so Drees had heard, employed over eighty people: having comparative numbers at European Court of Human Rights would mean additional costs for the Dutch state.[8]

[4] The Ministry felt there was a matter of prestige on the line as well: European integration was perceived to be a good thing, and 'slacking' in that regard was not beneficial to the reputation of a nation willing to serve the progress of international law.

[5] NL-HaNA, Buitenlandse Zaken/Code-Archief 45–54, 2.05.117, inv. nr. 24887, 'notes council of ministers 19 December 1955'.

[6] Klerk and Van Poelgeest, 'Ratificatie a contre coeur', pp. 240–243.

[7] Hans Daalder and Jelte Gaemers, *Premier en elder statesman; Willem Drees 1886–1988, de jaren 1948–1988* (Amsterdam: Balans 2014), pp. 232–259.

[8] Klerk and Van Poelgeest, 'Ratificatie a contre coeur', p. 244.

Primarily, however, Drees feared the usage of the right and its potential implications for domestic public order. One could, for instance, *abuse* the right of individual petition: abuse would take the form of 'querulants', that is, individuals simply looking for trouble and being heard in Europe. More specifically, Drees feared the usage of the Convention by communists. Although the Communist Party was less substantive in the Netherlands than in other European countries, (and the drafters of the Convention had envisioned their human rights mostly as a safeguard *against* communism), the individual complaint procedure made the issue contentious. Drees was highly concerned – and this feeling was shared by some other Ministers – that communists would be able to claim the route of human rights in order to propagate their ideas all the way up to a European forum. Providing freedom of speech, or freedom of assembly, to communists was one thing; offering them a platform to contest any measures taken to prevent them from exercising those rights (Dutch communists were banned from public service, for example) was another thing altogether.[9]

Other concerns were of a more domestic nature. Drees had some severe doubts as regards the situation in which Catholics would use their right of petition to complain about the ban on processions in certain areas of the Netherlands.[10] As a constitutional rule, Catholic processions were only allowed in the Netherlands in certain areas that had been appointed in 1848. In practice, these were 'below the rivers', in the southern part of the Netherlands, meaning that Catholics in more northern parts of the Netherlands were faced with clear obstructions to exercising their religion. No one disputed the fact that this was an obstruction to their right of religious freedom. This peculiar Dutch constitutional set up was, in fact, a particularly sensitive topic which had led to heated debates in Parliament and demonstrations from 1848 onwards. Moreover, since the rule was enshrined in the Constitution, no ordinary majority would be able to change this situation. Drees felt little impetus to grant Catholics an additional route (least of all if it was a *European*

[9] Ibid.

[10] Nationaal Archief, Den Haag, Ministerie van Buitenlandse Zaken: Code-archief 1955–1964, nummer toegang 2.05.118, inventarisnummer 7601, 'notes ministerraad 25 November 1957'.

route) to challenge this provision: for him, such sensitive matters had to be dealt with in the domestic sphere.

Finally, another element played a role in Drees' negative opinion: the colonial legacy. Already, there had been concern in the Ministry of Justice about claims of Moluccans, a distinct group of Indonesians who had fought in the Dutch colonial army in Indonesia, had been brought to the Netherlands and invoked human rights to further their claims.[11] In the eyes of the Dutch government, offering an additional forum for claims in the form of the Convention was undesirable.[12] Moreover, the Minister of Overseas Territories noted that since the Convention applied in the overseas areas, the issue of individual complaints could also arise from those areas. Should the Netherlands accept such a right, maybe Suriname or the Antilles would decide to join. According to Drees, individuals filing complaints from the Antilles and Suriname would be most undesirable: he warned of the troubles which could arise should a person from the Antilles file a complaint about the freedom of association. In addition, Drees took notice of a more institutional venue which the Convention put forward in this regard: the Convention prescribed that local remedies had to be exhausted before the European venue could be tried, and this could be problematic for Dutch citizens who demanded immediate legal relief.[13]

A particular situation in Indonesia was on his mind here, namely a trial which had just started against a former Dutch military intelligence officer, Leon Jungschläger. Jungschläger stood accused of state-undermining activities in Indonesia in light of tensions over the Dutch position in New Guinea. The Netherlands had been quick to

[11] They relied here on the Charter of the briefly lived Dutch-Indonesian Union in order to protest against housing conditions in the Netherlands and the transport of Indonesian troops to Ambon. See further on this particular line of cases, Van Leeuwen, Karin: Rights for Others, Firing Back?: Decolonization and Human Rights in Dutch Constitutional History, *VerfBlog*, January 27, 2022, https://verfassungsblog.de/rights-for-others-firing-back/ (last accessed August 23, 2022.).

[12] It was an issue which had been raised by civil servant Eijssen in 1952: NL-HaNA, Justitie/Wetgeving/Internationale Organisaties, 2.09.84 inv. nr. 171, 'memo 11 December 1952'.

[13] NL-HaNa Buitenlandse Zaken/Code-Archief 55-64, 2.05.118, inv. nr. 7601, 'Ministerraad 19 December 1955'.

respond and push back on the Indonesian claims, but Drees took these proceedings as an offence and a warning. He warned that, if cases comparable to that of Jungschläger emerged, the Netherlands might have to wait until the entire legal procedure had ended in order to establish whether or not the individuals' rights had been violated. Should Indonesia have been a part of the Convention, it would have been more difficult for the Netherlands to act swiftly. In other words, according to Drees, the Convention would restrict the capacity of the Dutch government to act if overseas territories became part of it.[14] Even though his reasoning was not legally sound (the exhaustion of legal remedies was of concern for individual plaintiffs in order for their complaint to be admissible), it was illustrative of the strong reservations that Drees, supported by, for instance, the Minster of Overseas Territories, held in this regard.

2.1.1 ACTIVISM BY RESTRAINT. THE MISSION OF THE EUROPEAN COMMISSION ON HUMAN RIGHTS. Acceptance was not solely a domestic affair. In order to accept the right of individual petition, the above concerns first had to be addressed. Crucially, alleviating these fears and getting the Netherlands – alongside other states – to accept the right of individual petition was one of the key motivations in the early days of the European Commission. This body proved vital in reassuring the states of the non-threatening character of the Convention. In the institutional set up of the European protection of human rights, the European Commission of Human Rights was foreseen as fulfilling a key role in the functioning of the Convention. Acting as a 'gatekeeper', it decided whether or not cases were admissible, whether cases would be sent to the Court or to the Committee of Ministers, and it deliberated if a breach of the Convention had been found. Although not a 'judicial' body in the strict sense (it did not pass judgement on the merits of cases), its role was essential in the functioning of the system of European human rights protection.

This gatekeeping role mattered even more as the Commission had the ambition of convincing the European states to accept the right of individual complaint, thereby 'completing' that novel part of the

[14] Ibid. The legal merits of Drees' concerns were not necessarily watertight, but it shows his firm reluctance to any form of individual recourse to a supranational instance.

Convention: in order to achieve this goal, the Commission adopted a policy of restraint. After this step, it was reasoned, the way would be open for the acceptance of the Court, fulfilling a supranational oversight over national affairs long thought impossible.

2.1.2 DEFINING THE 'INDEPENDENT' COMMISSION: THE ROLE OF BEAUFORT. The choice of members of the Commission in 1954 was thus an important moment in these early moments of European human rights protection: these were the people who would decide on the complaints and thereby define the nature of the project. In the absence of clearly defined criteria for the nature of membership of the Commission (except for the notion they had to sit in an 'independent' capacity),[15] its composition was left to the discretion of the Member States, who were rather cautious of this new international body. 'Independence' was a flexible criterion, and the leniency granted to certain states led them to nominate civil servants with close ties to their own administration.[16] Italy, for example, put forward its undersecretary of Foreign Affairs, Mr Dominedo.[17] For the Netherlands, having such a potentially politicized Commission was highly undesirable, and this was stated as a matter of principle: the Commission was supposed to be an independent body so it could judge 'without bias'.[18]

The other European states were less concerned, as none of them felt this was worth diplomatic trouble, and the installation of the Commission was not perceived to be a matter of great political concern.[19] Moreover, even though the Dutch position might have been principled at the outset, this did not mean its own candidate was free from any ties with the

[15] Article 23. The requirements for holding office as a European judge further included the moral aspect: 'The candidates shall be of high moral character and must either possess the qualifications required for appointment to high judicial office or be jurists of recognized competence'. art 39(3) ECHR.

[16] Madsen, 'The Protracted Institutionalization', p. 47.

[17] Bates, *The Evolution of the European Convention*, p. 175.

[18] NL-HaNA, Buitenlandse Zaken/Code-Archief 45–54, 2.05.117, inv. nr. 20484, 'memo 14 May 1954'.

[19] Nationaal Archief, Den Haag, Ministerie van Buitenlandse Zaken: Permanente Vertegenwoordiging in de Raad van Europa te Straatsburg, 1945–1954, nummer toegang 2.05.59.02, inventarisnummer 1489, 'Memo 10 June 1954'.

government. The proposed Dutch member of the Commission was, in fact, Père Beaufort. His professional credentials were impeccable: as a professor in international law, with a firm interest in human rights, his expertise on the matter was beyond doubt. He was also very much aware of the political saliencies when it came to human rights in the Netherlands. Not only was he firmly involved in the service of Foreign Affairs, he was also a member of the Dutch Senate for the Catholic party. Being known to the government as a modest, rather conservative figure, Beaufort was a logical choice for this new body.

The Dutch fear of a 'politicized' Commission was therefore mainly aimed at the possibility of states using the Commission as a vessel through which they could conduct (aggressive) foreign policy. Above all, the 'naming and shaming' potential of the Commission was not to be hijacked by foreign states. Therefore, an independent Commission did not mean an apolitical Commission, but rather a 'respectable' Commission, which in turn entailed a Commission keenly aware of the sensitive nature of its own work. Most countries shared this conception, resulting in a rather homogenous body composed of elderly white males, who were mostly well connected in governmental circles.[20]

Beaufort offers a textbook example of this dynamic. Being an international lawyer, the prime cadre in which his intellectual notions on the relation between nations and international treaties had formed was that of the League of Nations, which had little to nothing to say about the position of the individual in international law. Faced with the (legally, at least) revolutionary new instrument of European human rights, the Commission members would think twice about accepting too many claims.[21] The Convention was a document to be handled with care, as state sovereignty was not something to be easily curtailed. However, Beaufort had also forcefully pleaded for strong European integration and a furthering of the individual rights protection via international institutions. In his new position, he was capable of *proving* the added value of individual human rights protection on

[20] Madsen, 'The Protracted Institutionalization', pp. 47–48.

[21] See also the memoirs of Commission member Max Sorensen: because this was such a new and invasive instrument, the 'ground position' was one of restraint: Max Sørensen, 'Les experiences personelles de la Convention. L'experience d'un membre de la Commission', *Revue des droits de l'Homme* (1975), pp. 329–342.

the European level. Yet in order to bring about such change, the states first had to accept the mechanism of individual complaints.

From the inception of the Commission, persuading states to accept the right of individual complaint was high on its agenda. It was a concern that only the 'smaller' European states, such as Belgium and Ireland, had accepted this right, whereas the larger European countries had so far abstained. In particular, it hurt that the UK and France, being instrumental for the idea of meaningful European integration via the Council of Europe, had not taken this step.[22] If European integration and international human rights protection were to be viable, the major European powers would also have to be persuaded to accept the right of individual petition.

A similar line of thinking was shared by actors in the Council of Europe more broadly. In his speech installing the Commission, the French General Secretary, Léon Marchal, had proclaimed the acceptance of the right of individual complaint as one of the steps necessary for the future of the European project. As he set out, 'I take it upon myself today to express the hope that your Commission, by the confidence she is able to inspire, will bring those governments who still hesitate to recognize its right to take up individual petitions'.[23]

To build the confidence of states was therefore one of the key characteristics of the system. In the first report on its activities, the Commission responded positively to Marchal's message, stating that it 'will spare no effort to fulfil its mission'.[24] Such mission statements were seen as remarkable in the national context. Many states were wary of the potentially disruptive consequences such a right would have, and the Netherlands was no exception. 'It is doubtful whether picking a side in this political matter is in fact suitable for the Commission', the Dutch permanent representative stated.[25]

[22] France would not ratify the Convention with an eye on Algeria and the impact human rights oversight could have on its internal wars of decolonization: Bonino, *la France face á le Convention*, pp. 316–330.

[23] NL-HaNA, Buitenlandse Zaken/Code-Archief 45–54, 2.05.117, inv. nr. 20484, 12 July 1954, ibid, p. 8.

[24] NL-HaNA, Buitenlandse Zaken/Code-Archief 45–54, 2.05.117, inv. nr. 20484, 'report first activities, 17 July 1954, p. 26'.

[25] NL-HaNA, Buitenlandse Zaken/Code-Archief 45–54, 2.05.117, inv. nr. 20484, 'Memo from Strasbourg to the Hague, 30 July'.

Beaufort himself had already given observers a taste of his vision on the Commission when he participated in his capacity as senator in the debate on ratification in the Dutch Senate, on 27 July 1954. At that moment, he was already a member of the Commission and could provide some insights into the inner workings of the institution.[26] Even though his own Catholic party had been sceptical, Beaufort strongly supported the right of individual complaint. With an eye on his involvement in the European movement, that was not surprising. In his speech, he actively sought to reassure the government and colleagues and left no doubt as to the Commission being a prudent, reflective body. Granted, the Italian pick might be somewhat contentious, yet the other members of the Commission were all fine jurists or professors; surely no political judgements could be expected of such a distinguished group of people?[27]

Moreover, Beaufort assured the Dutch politicians, the Commission would act strictly and swiftly in order to prevent the feared 'abuse' of the Convention from happening.[28] Here, Beaufort alluded to a restrictive policy of the Commission: the state should not worry too much about intrusive consequences of the individual complaints. If anything, the Commission would make sure the so-called 'querulants' (or communists) would not be able to abuse the Convention: Article 17 thereof explicitly prohibited the abuse of rights.[29]

Although Beaufort did not persuade the government to accept the right of individual complaint in 1954, it was a taste of what was to come: not only would the Commission be very restrictive in the admissibility procedure for individual complaints, it would also *use* that restrictive policy to remove any doubts states might have. Beaufort himself would keep pushing for the acceptance of the right of individual complaint, switching effortlessly between his European and domestic roles. In his public appearances too, he would continue to reassure his audience that the Commission had always declared 'baseless' complaints inadmissible

[26] Albeit a member in consultative fashion, as the Netherlands had not yet ratified the Convention.

[27] 'Goedkeuring Verdrag van Rome' *Kamerstukken I* 1954/55 3043, 611–626.

[28] Ibid, 614–616.

[29] Here Beaufort held a very generous meaning of article 17, which relates to interpreting the rights in the Convention to destroy those very same rights.

before stating the Convention was of little use without 'finalizing' its promise.[30] The restrictive practice of the Commission on the European level hence became an active selling point back home, forming an example of how Beaufort was not isolated to his domestic or European context, but actively combined the two.

2.1.3 GETTING THE STATES ON BOARD: THE ROLE OF POLYS MODINOS. However, as the person transferring national peculiarities towards Europe, Beaufort was only one part of the story. One of the promises the government had made to the Parliament when ratifying the Convention was that it would monitor the practice of the Commission in treating those individual complaints. This brought the government into contact with one of the most ardent supporters of European unity via the route of human rights, Polys Modinos.

Modinos was one of the key players in the early years of the Convention, involved from the very beginning in various institutions. A Greek born in Alexandria, educated in France and diplomat for Cyprus at – inter alia – the Holy See, Modinos served as head of the human rights department of the Council of Europe and secretary of the Commission before he became the adjunct Secretary General of the entire organization.[31] In his role as head of the human rights department, he was the communicator between the Commission and the states and served a key role in establishing the image of the Commission.

His ideas on the role and function of European human rights were very much in line with those of some of the drafters. In a speech for the French Section of the International Commission of Jurists (ICJ) on 29 September 1957, Modinos laid down his beliefs on what the Convention entailed. The audience might have been on the conservative side of the spectrum (in its early years, the ICJ was actively sponsored by

[30] See for example the widely reported meeting with Beaufort and the 'Genootschap voor den Rechtstaat', the Dutch section of the International Commission of Jurists, on 5 March 1956. A search on the digital newspaper database shows that nearly all the major newspapers devoted a page to his message.

[31] Michel Erpelding, 'Juristes internationalistes, juristes mixtes, Euro-Lawyers : l'apport de l'expérience semi-coloniale à l'émergence d'un droit supranational', Clio@Themis [online journal], Vol. 22 (2022).

the CIA to promote a form of 'legal activism' against the Soviets),[32] but Modinos himself also echoed an old conservative take:

> In addition to its very important legal character, our Convention must be regarded, in itself, as a political instrument of great value. At a time when Europe is being built, when the foundations of European unification are being laid [...] we must not lose sight of the fact that this association of European nations, an association of six, seven or 15, an association of character supranational, confederal, federal or other, will necessarily have to define and guarantee its political base.[33]

Modinos hence presented the Convention accurately as both a legal and a political document. At the moment of European unification, Modinos stated, the Convention contained solely what was common to its Member States. Yet, echoing words of Paul-Henri Spaak, the Convention also entailed a very distinct civilizing mission in the eyes of Modinos: 'we Europeans have a message to defend and transmit to the world. Large communities are creating large mass civilizations [...] but there is something special and unique about our European message, which is that in wanting to create more well-being for the masses, we always want save the individual'.[34]

This characterization, reminiscent of the speeches at the Congress at The Hague, placed the Convention directly in a very old tradition of European exceptionalism. The noble idea of human rights was not just to be defended, but was also dependent on European civilization. Any 'decline' thereof would mean the end of an apparent unique message. This was the dual political programme of Convention at display: forward-looking as a means to achieve European unity, but with a traditional view to protect the nation states, their institutional set up and the European civilization against decadent elements.

[32] Howard Tolley, *The International Commission of Jurists: Global Advocates for Human Rights* (Philadelphia: Pennsylvania University Press 1994); See also Mikael Rask Madsen, *La Genese de l'Europe des droits de l'Homme*, p. 302.

[33] NL-HaNA, Justitie/Wetgeving/Internationale Organisaties, 2.09.84, inv. nr. 171, 'speech Modinos for the general assembly of the French Section of the International Commission of Jurists'.

[34] Ibid.

In 1962, Modinos again claimed the Convention was best seen as forming the foundation of 'the European Community of Human Rights' (a clear nod to the other European project), whereas in 1965 he stated that the Convention was to be a 'Constitution for a united Europe'.[35] Yet such a status had to be created first. In his work as secretary and head of the department, Modinos placed special emphasis on the non-threatening character of the Commission, while actively pushing for the right of individual complaint to be accepted.[36]

At the request of the Dutch government, which was pressured by Parliament into monitoring the practice of Commission, Modinos had provided a report of its initial activities employed in 1956. The report was distinctively more than simply a summary of facts or outcomes of decisions. Rather, it was written with an active message in mind, namely to show how 'maturely' the young Commission had acted. The first sentence of the Report addressed the concerns of the governments head on: 'while the European Convention on Human Rights was in course of preparation, certain fears were expressed that recognition of the right of individual recourse to an international tribunal might lead to abuse'.[37] The central message of the report was to allay these fears, and 'being concerned to avoid disturbing governments needlessly', as Modinos put it, the Commission again and again demonstrated its very restrictive practice.[38]

The Permanent Representation of the Netherlands noted this emphasis on the restrictive practice of the Commission. Speaking of the report, it was stated that after the initial surge in applications (although there were not as many as one might have expected), the European

[35] Cited in Bates, *The Evolution of the European Convention*, p. 370.

[36] NL-HaNA, Buitenlandse Zaken/Code-Archief 55–64, 2.05.118, inv. nr. 24889, Report 'Procedure and Jurisprudence of the European Commission of Human Rights in Respect of Individual Applications'. In this report, Modinos set out his beliefs on what the Commission should do.

[37] NL-HaNA, Buitenlandse Zaken/Code-Archief 55–64, 2.05.118, inv. nr. 24889, Report 'Procedure and Jurisprudence of the European Commission of Human Rights in Respect of Individual Applications'.

[38] NL-HaNA, Buitenlandse Zaken/Code-Archief 55–64, 2.05.118, inv. nr. 24889, Report 'Procedure and Jurisprudence of the European Commission of Human Rights in Respect of Individual Applications', p. 7.

Commission had acted decisively by accepting only one of the eighty complaints received.[39] Moreover, it was noted with approval, even when procedural elements (such as the exhaustion of domestic remedies before a complaint was admissible) failed, the Commission 'placed a lot of restrain upon itself, thereby creating a precedent for her future activities'.[40]

On the precise reason for which the Commission exercised such restraint, the Permanent Representative expressed that he presumed it was done on purpose:

> Apparently, the Commission has acted accordingly in a conscious matter, as to remove concerns on the introduction of the individual complaint and possibly remove opposition against this provision. Also, Mr Modinos emphasized in the attached piece[41] in a distinct way the self-restraint of the Commission and the silent way in which it fulfils its duties. This is in line with the general opinion here: also the SG of the C.O.E. expressed himself in optimistic terms to me, frankly relieved and pleasantly surprised, because he had been somewhat anxious about the consequences of this introduction.[42]

However, it was also held that this initial practice did not yet offer enough reassurance for the Dutch government to change its mind regarding the right of individual petition. Too many uncertainties remained, and, as the representative noted, 'it cannot be denied that, no matter how great the independence or how unimpeachable the integrity of its members, the choice of its members has an impact on the functioning of the Commission'.[43] Changes in the Commission's set up could therefore have detrimental effects on its practice. Moreover, the Consultative Assembly of the Council of Europe, frustrated by the lack of follow-up, had already put forward a proposal to expand possibilities for individuals

[39] NL-HaNA, Buitenlandse Zaken/Code-Archief 55–64, 2.05.118, inv. nr. 24889, 'Memo 2 February 1956'.

[40] Ibid.

[41] Meant is the report on the functioning of the Commission.

[42] NL-HaNA, Buitenlandse Zaken/Code-Archief 55–64, 2.05.118, inv. nr. 24889, 'Memo 2 February 1956', the introduction of the right of individual complaint, that is.

[43] Ibid.

to complain against states which did not accept the right of individual complaint.[44] The government thus first had to wait and see before it could make any decision on the issue.

2.1.4 FINAL REASSURANCES: ESTABLISHING THE NON-THREATENING CHARACTER OF THE CONVENTION. When it came to individuals moving towards the European institutions, Dutch hesitation regarding the right of individual complaint was thus primarily shaped by the concerns of Drees. A restrictive policy could convince the Dutch governments that 'querulants' would indeed not find a stage to voice their complaints. Two more concerns remained: the concern about supranational oversight of the overseas territories and the potential for communists to use a European route in order to criticize the Dutch state. However, these concerns were also laid to rest when it turned out the impact of the Convention in colonial settings might be less then feared, whereas the Commission moved decidedly to note how the communists' aim to set up a dictatorship of the people would not be protected by European human rights.

As for the first element, the relation between human rights and Empire was put to the test when, in 1956, it became clear that the British move to expand the Convention throughout its overseas territories could stir up trouble. Decolonization and its relation with human rights entered the Council of Europe as Greece filed an interstate complaint under the Convention against the United Kingdom over the latter's treatment of insurgents in Cyprus. The importance of the complaint was twofold: it showed how the Convention could have the potential for disruption, but also provided a certain reassurance to the states. The disruption in this case was limited to political tensions between member states of the Council of Europe, and did not have any effect beyond those two countries.

The Greek complaint was the result of a colonialism, and was directed against the British administration of Cyprus, which ruled the island at the time. A fierce battle for independence had broken out on the island, resulting in the British deploying numerous counter-insurgency

[44] Meant is the proposal of the Assembly to go via other routes, Recommendation 83, 1955.

measures.[45] To make matters more complicated, the Cypriots expressed a desire to unify with Greece, enthusiastically supported by proponents of the nationalist movement back in Athens. As the UK had expanded the ECHR to most of its colonies (albeit excluding the right of individual petition), a venue had been opened for Greek intervention via the European legal route. Using the interstate complaint procedure, which enabled states to ask the Commission to look into human rights violations committed by other states, Greece shone a spotlight on the situation in Cyprus. The complaint was just as much a human rights claim as it was a political statement, which made the rest of the Council of Europe rather nervous.[46]

London too was most unpleasantly surprised by this turn of events. In expanding the ECHR to apply in the colonies, it had not anticipated any true consequences. Now an interstate claim had turned the Convention into a tool which had returned to 'bite' them.[47] Moreover, there was at least some merit to the complaint: the British response to initial peaceful protests had been harsh, and it was not unthinkable that a violation had indeed taken place.[48] Yet the other signatory states to the Convention also looked upon the complaint with concern. Until then, states had believed that interstate complaints would be extremely rare, as this was a quite drastic diplomatic step to take. However, just two years after the creation of the Commission, the first complaint had already been filed, opening up a political conflict made possible by the European human rights system.

The Dutch spoke here of a 'crisis' which had rocked the Council of Europe. Since the grievances were deemed trustworthy, in The Hague it was expected that the complaint of Greece would be declared admissible.[49] The next step would be an investigation by the Commission,

45 Simpson, *Human Rights and the End of Empire*, pp. 924–988.

46 Indeed, it is reminiscent of more classical 'diplomatic protection' claims, just as later interstate claims under the ECHR, which would always focus on persons perceived to be part of a state's 'own' population. This would only change in the Greek case of 1968, when for the first time it were indeed human rights as autonomous subjects which would form the main argument to file an interstate complaint.

47 Simpson, *Human Rights and the End of Empire*, p. 932.

48 Ibid, pp. 932–934.

49 This would not be a decision on merits, but simply the opening of procedures; still: it was sensitive enough to spark this kind of language.

which would first aim at reaching a reasonable settlement: if such a settlement turned out to be unachievable, the case would be put before the European Court of Human Rights. There was but one problem: said Court did not exist yet at the time, which would place the topic on the table of the Committee of Ministers.

To confront the Ministers with a dispute between two of their own member states was most undesirable, as being forced to take a side in what was essentially perceived as a conflict between two NATO-members would only lead to the erosion of Western unity. As a Dutch diplomat noted '[...] It shows, what kind of crisis emerges now, not only for the Treaty for the protection of Human Rights but also for the authority, if not the existence, of the Council of Europe itself'.[50] This reaction was based on the strong desire for political unity within Western Europe, where discord was most unwelcome. The only positive side to the situation was that the high stakes made British concessions more likely – at least in the view of the Dutch permanent representation. These were some strong words, but they show the level of the concern of the Dutch government about the potential for disruption the Convention could have.[51]

Yet one key element of the case was how the Dutch did *not* take the case as a warning in relation to their own empire, or even as something to consider in the domestic discussion regarding the right of individual complaint. The disruption, or crisis, which European human rights had caused, was purely based on the threat to *internal* European cohesion. The more fundamental – and for the Netherlands directly relevant – issue in the conflict between Greece and the UK, namely the colonial status of Cyprus and its claim for independence, was not addressed by the complaint. Indeed, as the Dutch permanent representative expressively

[50] NL-HaNA, Buitenlandse Zaken/Code-Archief 55–64, 2.05.118, inv. nr. 24890, 'Memo 31 May 1956'.

[51] Indeed, the government of Luxembourg sent out the request to the rest of the 'Benelux' if it was not possible to remove this case out of the political sphere and pass it onto the Court in order to prevent the ministers of dealing with a case which would affect Western unity. The answer was short (no), but hope was expressed it would not lead to that and a settlement would be reached. NL-HaNA, Buitenlandse Zaken/Code-Archief 55–64, 2.05.118, inv. nr. 24890, 'Memo 6 July 1956'.

stated, the colonial character of the conflict *could* not be addressed via European human rights.[52]

For the Dutch, the concern about the Greek complaint was rather the threat it posed to western unity in the context of the Cold War, not the idea that Convention could provide for decolonization or scrutiny within the Dutch empire itself. In fact, as we have seen before, the Convention was perfectly compatible with empire. The Greeks made a subtle note here: this was about *European* human rights. Although the UK found itself faced with a complaint on what amounted to colonial violence, the Greek government made a careful distinction. Not *all* colonial struggles were the same. 'The case of the Cypriots differs from that of other peoples of the world still fighting for their freedom in that the Cypriots are Europeans nourished on Western civilization and have a level of culture at least as high as that of other peoples in Mediterranean Europe', the Greek complaint noted.[53] A key element of the complaint, the flogging of prisoners, was also detached from wider colonial violence. As the Greeks argued, 'though the UK may still think fit to inflict this punishment on its coloured subjects, in no circumstances can this practice be tolerated in countries of Greco-Latin culture, where it was long ago abolished as degrading'.[54] As such, the Greek government actively supported the civilizational element: the problem wasn't colonial violence as such, but rather that it was now unleashed upon those who could claim to be European.

Ultimately the case fizzled out. The application was declared admissible, after which the Commission dispatched an investigation to the island to research the possible human rights violations. However, history caught up with the case, as the independence of Cyprus was negotiated in parallel, and as part of this broader process, the Commission eventually decided to terminate the procedure.[55] Yet the focus on the distinctive European element of the violence inflicted also helps to explain why

[52] NL-HaNA, Buitenlandse Zaken/Code-Archief 55–64, 2.05.118, inv. nr 24890, 'Memo 31 May 1956'. The Convention, after all, lacked (and still does) a right to national self-determination.

[53] Quoted in Simpson, *Human Rights and the End of Empire*, p. 930.

[54] As put forward in the Greek application to the commission. See also the legal argument in paragraphs 192/193, *Greece* v. *UK*. (no. 176/56).

[55] Simpson, *Human Rights and the end of Empire*, p. 1052.

no immediate concern was voiced with regard to the Dutch own colonial context. The complaint was rather perceived as a conflict between two states in the European family instead of a test case for human rights in decolonization as such.

In addition, the concerns on the domestic level with regard to the Commission would most decisively be settled when the Commission decided on the admissibility of a complaint of the German Communist Party in the summer of 1957. Dissolved by the German Constitutional Court and forbidden from continuing its activities, members of the party had turned to the European Commission for aid. By prohibiting the party, the applicants stated, their rights of freedom of expression, thought and assembly had been violated. Prima facie, this was simply an admissibly test, the likes of which the Commission had seen quite a few by then. However, the case was about much more than that. Only a year previously, the Hungarian uprising had confronted Western Europe with harsh communist interference. This was a case which was highly anticipated as it went to the core of what the Convention meant. Were European human rights also available for those considered to be its main enemy?

The case was closely followed in Europe, maybe with particular interest in the Netherlands, where it came to serve as litmus test on whether or not the Commission could be trusted in letting the states deal with sensitive topics. For the case came at a pivotal moment in the Dutch domestic debate on the right of individual petition. Under constant pressure from Parliament, the Ministries of Justice and Foreign Affairs had worked on a number of memos in order to convince the government to accept the provision. With a new Minister of Justice, convinced Europeanist Ivo Samkalden, the tide was turning in favour of such an initiative. What was remarkable, however, was the close coordination of these ministries with Beaufort, who acted as contact person between the two Ministers. After the Minister of Justice was convinced to support the proposal, he contacted Beaufort in order to coordinate the enterprise with Foreign Affairs.[56] Such involvement in politics by an independent member of the Commission was apparently not frowned upon. Introduced by the

[56] Klerk and Van Poelgeest, 'Ratificatie a contre coeur', p. 243.

two Ministers, a proposal to accept the right of individual complaint was scheduled for October 1957, three months after the decision of the Commission on the German case.

With the two ministries most involved in the matter in favour, the eyes of the highest civil servants turned to the Prime Minister. It was well known Drees had been wary of the possibilities of communist propaganda being supported via the Commission. With the other fears (the costs and the 'baseless complaints') more or less debunked via the restrictive admission policy of the Commission, this case would show whether communists indeed could take the European route.

One of the civil servants, Pieter Eijssen, advisor to the Ministry of Justice, paid particular attention to the case. Moreover, he was in contact with Modinos. In conversation, Eijssen had explicitly mentioned that Dutch acceptance would be very much dependent upon what decision the Commission would take with regard to the German communists.[57] As the decision of the Commission neared, it seemed almost inconceivable that Beaufort was not aware of the attention the case was attracting in the Netherlands: as he was himself involved in domestic politics and the initiatives, pressure on him to take this domestic context into account will have been very real.

When, on 20 July 1957, the Commission decided on the admissibility of the complaint, it therefore knew it was dealing with a very sensitive case. The Commission's reasoning was very clear. Taking into account the fact that the aim of the Communist Party was to 'establish a socialist-communist system by means of a proletarian revolution and the dictatorship of the proletariat', it declared these objectives to be incompatible with the Convention, 'even if it could be proved that the Party's present activity is directed towards the seizure of power solely through the constitutional means afforded to it in the Basic Law of the Federal Republic of Germany'.[58] A dictatorship, it was duly noted, was not allowed under the Convention, and the application was declared inadmissible.

[57] NL-HaNA, Justitie/Wetgeving/Internationale Organisaties, 2.09.84, inv. nr. 171, 'Memo 17 August 1957'.

[58] *Communist Party of Germany* v. *Federal Republic of Germany*, European Commission on Human Rights, App. No. 250/57.

The result was, legally speaking, not very surprising: the Commission was basically following its earlier precedent by being extremely adverse to entertaining complaints.[59] More important, however, was the fact that, instead of the Communist Party voicing its grievances on a European platform, the *Commission* was gifted a major opportunity to showcase its non-threatening character. The case was hailed as a major sign of reassurance for the Western European governments: the Convention was here to protect democracy, meaning in practice the existing nation states, whereas enemies of the status quo would not be granted a podium.

Moving back to the Netherlands, Beaufort wasted no time in publicizing the result, and he used his connections in Europe to help steer the domestic decision-making process. Swiftly after the decision, Modinos reached out to the Ministry of Justice in the Netherlands: 'Professor Beaufort was kind enough to inform me about your Excellency's interest in the work of the European Commission of Human Rights', Modinos noted, before sending an overview of the most recent activities of the Commission, emphasizing in particular the recent decision on the admissibility of the German Communist Party.[60]

This explicit European reassurance added to the domestic pressure on the government to accept the right of individual complaint. This pressure had come from multiple angles. First, there was the euro-friendly side of the national Parliament, which let little opportunity go to waste to press for action on this issue. Second, there were diverging views within the government itself.[61] The Ministry of Foreign Affairs continuously put pressure on Drees to accept the right, and Foreign Affairs also took the communist case as a welcome gift: for their pro-European civil servants, this was the ideal argument they could use to negate any concerns voiced

[59] With the benefit of hindsight, one might also state the decision was completely justified as well. Democracy was still fragile, especially in early post-war Germany.

[60] NL-HaNA, Justitie/Wetgeving/Internationale Organisaties, 2.09.84, inv. nr. 171, 'Letter Modinos to Ministry of Justice, 29 July 1957'; 'M. le Professeur L. J. C. Beaufort a bien voulu me faire part de l'intérêt que votre Excellence témoigne aux travaux de la Commission européenne des Droits de l'homme'.

[61] The role of Suriname and the Antilles was minimal in this discussion: it was clear there was no desire to expand this right to those areas, but that left the European part of the Netherlands free to do so.

by Drees.[62] The case offered the clearest example of how the Commission would take into account the concerns of states and was sold accordingly. 'Now, no reason exists to not accept the right of individual complaint', civil servant Eijssen proclaimed.[63] He was right: fears of abuse, empire and communism had been effectively dealt with by the Commission. Even Drees grudgingly agreed in the end and condoned the right of petition. After receiving word from Suriname and the Antilles, they had neither any interest in joining the individual complaint procedure nor any objection to the Netherlands accepting it, there were no longer any hurdles. On 24 May 1960, a new legal venue was opened up: any person could now complain to a European body and claim the state had violated his or her human rights.

2.2 DOMESTIC ENGAGEMENT: DEFINING THE MEANING FOR YEARS TO COME

Pressure to accept the right of individual complaint therefore came from key actors within Parliament and from Europe itself. Yet, this section seeks to show how broader engagement with the Convention was still fairly limited. This was not surprising: human rights engagement in general was very minimal. In fact, 'human rights activism' did not even exist yet. Human rights could serve as moral standards, as happened in the engagement with colonial struggles in Algeria, where the Universal Declaration was used as a moral yardstick to protest against French violence.[64] However, a distinct focus on human rights as such, or on human rights as legally enforceable claims to further justice, let alone distinctive 'human rights groups', were lacking in the domestic framework.

[62] The facultative acceptance was seen as troublesome: Foreign Affairs received a lot of pressure from the European level to 'complete' the commitment to the Convention. Also, as neighboring states (such as Belgium) accepted the right, there was feeling the Netherlands could not 'remain behind'. Klerk and Van Poelgeest, 'Ratifcatie a contre coeur', pp. 240–246.

[63] Klerk and Van Poelgeest, 'Ratificatie a contre coeur', p. 244.

[64] Niek Pas, *Aan de wieg van het nieuwe Nederland: Nederland en de Algerijnse oorlog 1954–1962* (Amsterdam: Wereldbibliotheek, 2008), pp. 171–181.

A story drawn up in 1956 by the famous Dutch cartoonist Marten Toonder was emblematic for engagement with human rights in the Netherlands. In the story, a king had set out to look for the elusive 'rights of man' and found, to his great joy, a 'league for the exaltation of humanity'. Sure that he would find human rights there, the king was told the rights of man were a marvellous product of Western civilization, which should be exported to primitive tribes in Borneo. After enquiring if one should not first possess something in order to be able to export it, the king was thrown out by the offended league, and forced to continue his search. In the end, he did not find the paper version upon which the rights of man had been written; it turned out to have been burned. Even though the king worked his way around this hurdle by noting that human rights existed independently of the paper on which they were written, the conclusion, 'rights of man are still the right of the strongest' was a bleak one. The story nicely sums up the situation at the time in which human rights were still rarely seen in the public, political and legal debate, however.[65]

2.2.1 THE CONVENTION AND THE INTERPRETATIVE COMMUNITY. If something comparable to present-day human rights groups was present, it was to be found in a legally orientated and distinctly conservative 'gentlemen's club'. Affiliated to the International Commission of Jurists (ICJ), the commission of lawyers protecting individual rights was the elitist 'Genootschap voor den Rechtstaat'. Although the 'Genootschap' had proclaimed itself a proponent of the right of individual complaint, in practice the group was more a debating group on constitutional affairs rather than a 'human rights' society.[66] It was a closed, elitist club with a numerus clausus focusing above all on the protection of the 'rechtstaat', a concept which was – from the perspective of the members of the Genootschap at least – quite easily translated into 'law and order'. This stance was not at all exceptional: all over Europe, early 'human rights engagement' took place in these distinct groups of

[65] Marten Toonder, *De Rechten van de Mens* (Amsterdam: De Telegraaf 1956).

[66] Beaufort was invited to speech there on the Convention for example: he knew the chair of the Genootschap, the jurist N. J. C. M. Kappeyne van de Copello quite well.

eminent, (male) and relatively conservative jurists and lawyers.[67] Human rights were not yet a broadly shared language for action; instead they were common amongst only a very limited group of legal academics.

Even within that realm, the concept of human rights was a remarkable outlier in, for instance, the basic legal education at universities. Curricula were primarily focused on private law, which took up the majority of compulsory courses, with jurisprudence, constitutional law and criminal law as exceptions.[68] In fact, human rights was not a separate academic field at all. If studied, human rights formed part of a distinct sub-question in international law, namely that of the position of the individual as a subject of international law. When charted, the trajectory of (legal) human rights was painted as one of growing international protection of – a very distinct version of – individuals.[69] Topics covered ranged from the diplomatic protection of one's own nationals (citizens) vis-à-vis other states, to the religious freedom clauses for Christian subjects of the Turkish Sultan (much advocated by European states),[70] ending with the present-day safeguards of individual liberties 'under the protection of the society of states'.[71]

As for the question of individuals in international law, this was still a matter of academic dispute. In 1954, J. P. A. François,[72] author of the leading handbook on international law in the Netherlands, noted that it was a matter of interpretation, but had clear preferences for a more state-orientated approach. François dismissed the claims of Lauterpacht, who saw the individual as bearer of fundamental

[67] This was by no means a unique situation: all over Europe the groups which were engaged in this early form of human rights engagement were part of these conservative jurist groups. See for more detail the analysis of the British, French and Scandinavian groups in Mikael Rask Madsen, *La Genese de l'Europe des droits de l'homme.*

[68] Nationaal Archief, Den Haag, Collectie 451 van Asbeck, nummer toegang 2.21.183.03, inventarisnummer 118, 'notes study of international law'. An outline of the study programme can be found in *Nederlands Tijdschrift voor Internationaal Recht* Vol. 10 Nr. 4 (1963), p. 440.

[69] This as opposed to the more philosophical traditions, ranging back to the various 'Grand Declarations'.

[70] See also Moyn, *Christian Human Rights*, p. 153.

[71] NL-HaNa, van Asbeck, 2.21.183.03, inv. nr. 59, 'study materials sixth ecumenical congress for lawyers'.

[72] Indeed, the same as who had advised on the ratification of the ECHR.

rights and instead opted for a firm intergovernmental reading of international law. For François, Lauterpacht's ambition was 'a mere theoretical construction and unreal'.[73] Afterwards, he turned to the situation of distinct treaties protecting 'human rights' which had led to the 'human rights problem' as he labelled it.[74] Speaking specifically of the European Convention, François was sceptical of the institutional set up, which might allow 'propaganda before an international forum against a State'.[75]

However, these traditional notions of international law had come under some pressure. After the Second World War, a way of thinking had entered Dutch academia which actively pushed for the limitation of national sovereignty in order to advance, or protect, the position of the individual. The problem of 'the individual in international law' featured prominently in many of the works of leading Dutch scholars of international law. Beaufort himself was a prominent part of this movement, advocating an international rule of law based on the human person. In Leiden, Prof. van Asbeck was the main voice calling for an international law based on the individual, and this went hand in hand with his religious inspiration. For van Asbeck, individual rights were to shape the 'common ethos' of international affairs. Inspired by the Swiss jurist Max Huber, whom he considered an example in many ways, van Asbeck approached international law from a distinct personalistic, ecumenical perspective, and as an ethos of international law, in his opinion, human rights were in therefore very much Christian in nature as well, and indeed formed part of a common European legacy.[76]

In his teaching, van Asbeck placed emphasis on this new form of international control, thereby not only supporting this specific 'Huberian' interpretation of international law, but also laying the seeds for a new generation which would take this message and build upon it. As such, he inspired his students to follow up upon this subject-oriented

[73] J. P. A. François, *Grondlijnen van het Volkenrecht* (Zwolle: Tjeenk Willink 1954), p. 228.

[74] Ibid.

[75] Francois, *Grondlijnen van het Volkenrecht*, p. 230. 'Human rights' were consequently written between quotation marks in this work.

[76] This harks back to Huber, who stated that law should never depart too far from its social foundations, meaning in this case the common European Christian tradition.

interpretation of international law.[77] Many of his former protégées, such as Hein Schermers, Jos Kapteijn and Menno van Emde Boas, would indeed later turn up in positions of power, some in the Council of Europe and even in the European Commission on human rights.[78]

Van Asbeck's counterpart in Groningen took a more activist approach. A veritable giant in the world of international law, Bert Röling had been a judge at the Tokyo trial before returning to the Netherlands to specialize in the laws of war and conflict. His interest in human rights and individual justice had grown out of his experiences in the East, which had led him to discard the idea of unlimited state sovereignty, and he closely followed the initiatives in this field at the UN and in Europe. However, the unifying force of human rights played a major role in his thinking as well: for Röling, individual human rights were the 'beginning of a new era, in which the supranational community of humanity starts to play a role'.[79] The European experience would be the first step onto a global field.

Driven by these ambitions, but also well aware of the doubts in the domestic sphere concerning the acceptance of the right of individual compliant, Röling advocated this right in a rather influential article, which was subsequently picked up in the Dutch political debate in order to continue pushing for more European integration.[80] For Röling, acceptance was both a logical step in the furthering of both the position of the subject in international law, as well as safeguard of 'true democracy' based on individual liberties and human personality, which would be the basis for future cooperation.[81] Praise for this stance did not only come from domestic Parliamentarians: Modinos also expressed his gratitude for 'the support which you gave in your article

[77] NL-HaNa, van Asbeck, 2.21.183.03, inv. nr. 36, 'letters of students'.

[78] Most notably H. G. Schermers and Van Emde Boas, who were later involved in the European institutions themselves.

[79] Nationaal Archief, Den Haag, Collectie 544 B.V.A. Röling, 1915–1985, nummer toegang 2.21.273, inventarisnummer, Röling, inv. nr. 112, 'Lecture on the United Nations'.

[80] B. V. A. Röling, 'Het individuele klachtrecht in de Europese Conventie voor de mensenrechten' *Nederlands Juristenblad* Nr. 13 (1956), pp. 293–315. The article was discussed extensively in, for example, Vaststelling Hoofdstuk III (Buitenlandse Zaken) *Kamerstukken I* 1955–1956, 4100, 416–417.

[81] Röling, 'het individuele klachtrecht', p. 315.

to the continuous effort [...] to urge the acceptance of the optional terms of article 25 para 1'.[82]

The turn to these distinct academic circles related to a broader change in actors who engaged with the Convention. As we have seen, early domestic engagement with the Convention had been primarily a matter of concern to members of the European Movement. However, as time went on, that particular group increasingly turned its attention away from the Council of Europe and human rights, and instead, the promise of European integration was taken over by the EEC. The European Parliament and Commission offered more promising and trustworthy sources of European idealism, in particular after the Council of Europe proved hampered by its intergovernmental nature.

This move to the 'other' Europe was also reflected in legal research, where doing research into 'Europe' swiftly became synonymous with 'the EEC'. Illustrative here are the various 'Europe-institutes' set up in the mid-1950s in Amsterdam and Leiden. In these institutes, Universities conducted research on European law, but work was much more focused on the works of the European Communities. Although not necessarily at odds with research into European human rights, (in fact, Evert Alkema, later a leading scholar on the Convention would do his research in one of these institutions), the Europe-institutes would mainly pay attention to the benefits which economic integration might bring about for European unity. The Dutch 'association for European Law' attested to the focus on economy by associating itself with the journal on 'social-economic legislation'. European integration, which the early proponents of human rights had hoped the Convention would help to achieve, increasingly became the realm of this primarily economical-oriented discipline. The distinct 'Euro-lawyer', with a focus on the internal market, would overshadow the 'human rights route' in the years to come.

The focus of the EEC on the market had – aside from the more active institutions in that organization – another key advantage over the study of human rights in the Council of Europe. Although both routes clearly moved in the direction of limiting the nation state, the EEC was considered

[82] NL-HaNA, Röling, 2.21.273, inv. nr 81, 'Letter Council of Europe to B. V. A. Röling, 20 April 1956'.

to be distinctively 'modern'. The study of the market itself had undergone a renovation, and (economic) scientific planning was at the core of many initiatives in Western Europe. A bright future could be achieved by scientific means: economics itself came to be seen as a distinct scientific field where experts could predict the best outcome. Europe, in the form of the EEC, offered precisely such a venue, also for lawyers to thrive in. The new field of European Law breathed the technocratic, supranational spirit of coordinated economic progress. The supposedly apolitical and scientific economic cooperation of Europe was fit perfectly with a period in which the 'political' was distrusted and specialization and expertise were the buzzwords. In the time in which buildings of Le Corbusier dotted the landscape, it was efficiency, not aesthetics, which was to be lauded. In contrast to the top-down expertise of the 'Economic Europe', the state-oriented, and rather romantic focus of the Convention promised little in terms of specialization. This added value of the technical route thereby attracted the attention of lawyers with a keen interest in economy, a topic that was far more modern and 'scientific' than 'human rights', the latter above all harking back to older conceptions of what it meant to be European. In this context, it mattered that the European Convention had always been more about restoration than about revolution. In contrast, the Economic Europe promised a break with the past: its supranational structure was a radical departure from the central position of the nation state.[83]

Ultimately, it would thus be a small group of international lawyers who took up the task of interpreting the merits of the Convention. With the first cases emerging before Dutch courts, the question turned from the political aspect of the Convention to the legal: what would be its value?

2.2.2 THE CONVENTION IN DOMESTIC COURTS: A CONTESTED BEGINNING. European human rights were quickly tested in the domestic courts. There was no fixed jurisprudence, and no stable precedent; rather the future and character of the Convention was very much open. From the late 1950s onwards, cases involving the Convention started to reach the Hoge Raad. The vast majority of cases, and the most contentious ones in particular, dealt with religious freedom. One strand

[83] Klaus Patel, *Project Europe*, pp. 122–132.

of cases reflected a direct response to one of the most fundamental shifts in state power as it occurred in Western Europe: the emergence of the social welfare state. The welfare state, as it was being set up in the Netherlands, was a massive project. For the first time in history, the state was establishing a social security net for its most vulnerable citizens. Although the prime benefactors of the welfare state would be the national working class (meaning, in practice, white males), the implications in the field of health care and safety were unprecedented. This, in turn, led to a tremendous increase in the regulatory regime of the state, and under the banner of social security followed a vast expansion of coercive state power. Solidarity among citizens was not something which appeared out of thin air: in order to provide for all citizens, all citizens had to participate.

In establishing social welfare, the state stepped into previously untouched areas of individual behaviour. Most of all, the state touched upon areas which had been the domain of the churches for centuries. Most notable in this aspect was the social security of vulnerable citizens. With the introduction of the General Old Age Pensions Act, the question emerged of how much the state could ask of its traditionally religiously exempted citizens. Could the new social state be allowed to force individuals to pay a premium, even if the individual in question was a preacher who, according to the rules of the reformed church, was to be supported by their own flock?[84] In other words, how far could the state reach into the individual lives of strongly religious people in the name of national solidarity? As human rights landed in the Netherlands, the first cases dealt with Article 9 of the Convention, relating to freedom of religion and – occasionally – Article 1 of the first protocol, dealing with the right to property.

There were no claims the other way: human rights would not be invoked to *support* the welfare state.[85] As we have seen, European human rights were never intrinsically bound up with the social welfare state to begin with. Rather, from early on they were invoked in a number of

[84] This was the question at the heart of a stream of cases which ended up before the HR 13-04-1960, ECLI:NL:HR:1960:123, *NJ* 1960/436.

[85] On this absence, see Moyn, *Not Enough: Human Rights in an Unequal World.*

cases in order to curtail the state.[86] At first sight, the attempted use of the Convention as a 'shield' vis-à-vis an intrusive welfare state might not come as a surprise. Its drafters specifically had in mind an all-too-intrusive 'socialist' government when it was set up, leading to the absence of social rights in the Convention. Yet although the welfare state might be a new deal in Europe, it turned out that, unlike in the United States, national judges were rather reluctant to strike down its provisions.[87]

The Hoge Raad proved wary of using this new document to exempt individuals from the mandatory social scheme. Despite acknowledging the direct applicability of Article 9 of the Convention, it swiftly moved to defuse any potential explosive claims. Faced with the question of prioritizing individual freedom of religion or shared social welfare, the Court took the side of the government. What is more, the Court stated that the contested provisions of the social welfare state did not even touch upon Article 9 of the Convention. No conflict therefore existed, no exceptions had to be tested, and the government could proceed with its policy.[88]

In doing this, the Hoge Raad refused to engage in detail with the articles of Convention in the domestic context, thereby establishing a practice which would shape the domestic engagement with the Convention for a decade to come. What is more, the prominence of the religious character of these early claims matters for a number of reasons. Not merely because of the results of the cases, but also because it tells us a lot about the people using the Convention and its role in these early years: contemporary key elements of European human rights law, such as free speech, privacy, or the right to a fair trial, were almost never seen in the domestic setting in these early years. Nor were practices that discriminated against women put forward as human rights violations. The mandatory resignation of women from employment after marriage had crossed the minds of lawmakers when the Convention was being drafted, leading one to question whether this would be in conformity with the

[86] For a detailed review of all the cases, see Damiaan Meuwissen, *De Europese Conventie en het Nederlandse Recht* (Leiden: Sijthoff, 1968), pp. 365–405.

[87] One reason for that difference is the traditionally much more hesitant role of the Dutch courts: the prerogative of Parliament to see if measures violated fundamental rights was, and remains, a strong constitutional tradition.

[88] Cf. HR 13 April 1960 NJ 1960, 436; Meeuwissen *De Europese Conventie*, pp. 373–377.

new European human rights document. Yet in practice, no legal claims based on the Convention entered the legal setting, nor were human rights arguments used in the parliamentary debate on this practice.[89]

As the cases around pensions showed, the role of the Convention as a tool to fend off the welfare state was minimal. Yet there was also another way in which the Convention started to be used. This was, in fact, the most contentious stream of cases of the late 1950s in the Netherlands: the decisions on the constitutional ban on Catholic processions. This had been one of the fears of Prime Minister Drees all along: a European rule trumping the sensitive topic of processions. This Catholic custom was a regular sight in the traditionally Catholic southern parts of the Netherlands, yet had been a source of consternation between Catholics and Protestants ever since the constitution of 1848 had proclaimed that processions were only permitted in that areas where it was legal *at that time.* In effect, the Dutch constitution had thus frozen the practice in place. Much to the dismay of Catholic citizens, subsequent parliamentary initiatives and legal routes to open up the provision amounted to nothing. Although the practice was not as stringent as the law stated (Catholics were rarely persecuted or jailed, and usually the authorities only acted when a Protestant community filed a complaint), the freedom of Catholic citizens remained very much hampered.[90]

In the 1950s, driven by the new potential of the Convention, cases that questioned the state of affairs began to emerge, and in the Netherlands, the tiny medieval city of Geertruidenberg would become the centre of this activity. Despite being in the southern part of the Netherlands, its inhabitants were primarily Protestant. When, in 1957, Catholic inhabitants marched in procession through the city, thereby provoking the Protestant population, they did so with the explicit aim of testing the constitutional rule in court, and this time, the plaintiffs thought they had a chance. National law was no longer the only option to claim rights: one of the main legal strategies of the Catholic plaintiffs

[89] Although the European Convention did not play a role in the debate, the United Nations initiative on equal treatment and payment for women was important: see *Kamerstukken II*, 1955–1956, 2732, 2 May 1956.

[90] P. J. Margry, *Teedere quasties: Religieuze rituelen in conflict: confrontaties tussen katholieken en protestanten rond de processiecultuur in 19e-eeuws Nederland* (Hilversum 2000), pp. 418–420.

was to test the precedence of Article 9 of the Convention over the Dutch constitution.[91]

What followed was a back-and-forth of cases which spanned five years of legal debate. In the first phase, somewhat to the dismay of annotator Röling, the international question was avoided. The case went to the Hoge Raad but focused narrowly on the interpretation and proof of whether the procession would have been allowed in 1848. A lower judge ruled that this would indeed be the case, and it was confirmed by a higher judge, before the case ended up before the Hoge Raad in 1959, which disagreed with the earlier rulings and sent it back to a lower court.[92]

It was there, at the court in Arnhem, where the question of the compatibility between the Constitution and the Convention would finally be addressed. In a judgement as short as it was explosive, the Court held that Article 9 of the Convention had indeed been violated. The grounds of exception, that is whether the constitutional provision was necessary in a democratic society on the grounds of public order, were swiftly dealt with. This question, the Court stated, had to be answered in 'light of present day conditions': the constitutional provision, forcing the interpretation to look into the situation of 1848, did not offer sufficient guidance in this aspect. As a result, the ban on processions, which had been constitutionally entrenched for over 100 years, was declared invalid.[93]

At first sight, this interpretation was perfectly reasonable, at least legally speaking. The Convention was of a higher order than the constitution, a test was carried out, and a domestic rule was found in violation of a higher norm. However, the case soon became a much larger test than just an interpretation of the ban of processions: it went straight to the question of the position and role of the Convention in the domestic legal order. Basically, the domestic court used the Convention in order to force a radical break in Dutch legal doctrine. Traditionally, the Dutch

[91] Although it should be noted this was not the only route the plaintiffs took: European human rights were but one of the options. The other one was a claim on a recently signed 'Friendship treaty' with the United States, which also included an article on religious freedom.

[92] HR 15-05-1959, ECLI:NL:HR:1959:15 *NJ* 1959/560.

[93] Hof Arnhem 08-03-1961, ECLI:NL:GHARN:1961:40 *NJ* 1961/424.

courts had been wary of setting aside constitutional provisions, which were regarded as an area in which the legislature should act.[94] Also, viewing the interpretation of the Convention in light of 'present day conditions' (reminiscent of the much later European case law invoking the same terminology) gave an autonomous meaning to the article and opened the door for a versatile judicial use of this international legal document. This was new: until then, the Dutch legal tradition had mostly been on the more restrictive side of review against international law. But most of all, the judgement sparked a keen interest in the role of the Convention, and the large academic and public debate made the case into something more than a simple legal discussion.

2.2.3 CURTAILING THE CONVENTION: TOWARDS THE HEARING OF THE HOGE RAAD. 'Ban on processions silently lifted by Treaty of Rome', the liberal newspaper *Het Vaderland* noted on 13 April 1961.[95] In a 'remarkable judgement', the self-assured position of the government upon ratification of the Convention had turned out to be premature, the paper noted, and the consequences were enormous: 'this judgment leaves no single doubt as whether in the present day situation, with an appeal upon the Treaty, anywhere in the Netherlands, at any time, a procession is permitted'.[96] It is telling that the legal aspect of the case was remarkably prominent in the press coverage, and also in light of the constitutional reforms of 1953, which had opened up the Dutch legal order to the prevalence of international law, this was a major showcase to highlight the implications of that reform. Indeed, the lifting of the ban on processions was one thing, but the fact that it happened through an appeal to an international treaty was another. 'Treaty prevails over law', the liberal newspaper *NRC* noted with approval.[97]

Not only the newspapers accorded importance to the legal element of the case, but the academic community was also triggered by the case.

[94] Meuwissen, *De Europese Conventie en het Nederlandse Recht*, pp. 424–425.

[95] Nationaal Archief, Den Haag, Nederlandse Permanente Vertegenwoordiging bij de Raad van Europa te Straatsburg, nummer toegang 2.05.278, inventarisnummer 1004 'newspaper clippings permanent representation'.

[96] NL-HaNa, P. V. Raad van Europa Straatsburg, 2.05.278, inv. nr. 1004, ibid.

[97] 'Processieverbod en de Europese Bescherming van Mensenrechten', *NRC* 17 April 1961.

Their debate dealt mainly with the interpretation of the Convention, and one voice in particular stood out: that of lawyer D. J. Veegens.[98] In his vision, the Convention offered plenty of room for a progressive jurisprudence, although this was dependent on 'the personal convictions of those in the Commission and the Court and the results of the process of European integration'. At the same time, such a development was also desirable. For Veegens, the Convention was meant to be used as 'an instrument to expand the common understanding of and shared respect for the fundamental rights of man'.[99]

Veegens' reading mattered, as he would put this specific interpretation to the test as the lawyer for the Catholic priests before the Hoge Raad. According to Veegens, the Convention could not be interpreted as allowing states to derogate from fundamental rights provisions merely on the grounds of national legal tradition. Instead, the treaty offered a certain, not overtly low, minimum of fundamental rights, which indeed had to be interpreted in light of present-day circumstances.[100]

The further the case progressed, the more it seemed as if the Convention would upset the carefully guarded equilibrium of Dutch domestic law: the advice given by the 'Procureur Generaal' to the Hoge Raad leant towards the interpretation proposed by Veegens and went in the direction of a firm European protection of fundamental rights. Clearly, the procession was covered by Article 9 of the Convention on Freedom of Religion. The question therefore turned to the grounds of exceptions: would the argument of 'necessity to protect public order' suffice in order to curtail the freedom of the Catholic citizens?[101] This was not the case according to the Procureur Generaal: in his interpretation, the Convention entailed a strong protection, as the words 'necessary' had to be interpreted very strictly. The chance of disturbing the public order

98 D. J. Veegens, 'Het Europees Verdrag tot bescherming van de rechten van de mens en het nationale recht' *Mededelingen van de Nederlandse Vereniging voor Internationaal Recht* Nr. 43 (1960), pp. 42–82, 46.

99 Ibid.

100 Ibid, p. 59.

101 Article 9(2) Convention: 'Freedom to manifest one's religion or beliefs shall be subject only to such limitations as are prescribed by law and are necessary in a democratic society in the interests of public safety, for the protection of public order, health or morals, or for the protection of the rights and freedoms of others'.

to a degree of seriousness required would be inconceivable 'in present day Netherlands', it was concluded.[102] Therefore, the consequence would have to be that the Constitutional provision had to be set aside in favour of European human rights. What the Procureur General proposed had wide-ranging implications, not only in practice. Here, two manners of interpretations stood in opposition to one another: an autonomous interpretation of the Convention in light of present-day circumstances versus a more cautious interpretation of the Convention in the light of a classical domestic history of 1848. Which choice would prevail would set the standard for subsequent developments of the ECHR in the Dutch context.

The Hoge Raad would prove reluctant to go with the advice it was given. Instead of using the Convention in the way the applicants would have hoped, as a tool for reform, the Hoge Raad 'smothered' it.[103] It proved extremely hesitant to attach great worth to the Convention in interpreting it. In the words of annotator Röling, the Hoge Raad 'greatly restricted the possibilities for judicial review'. For one, it decided that the 'content' of the grounds of exception in Article 9(2) of the Convention were 'in principle' not suitable for judicial review and should remain the domain of the national legislature.[104] Moreover, the domestic tradition was what mattered in assessing the value of the public order exception. The question the Hoge Raad decided to answer was whether the rule of 1848 would be unreasonable 'per se' in 1962: not if an interpretation was needed on grounds of a present-day state of affairs.[105] In doing so, it not only 'domesticized' the ECHR (by interpreting it in light of domestic constitutional law), it also showed that it would not lightly use the Convention to set aside domestic provisions.

The judgement was far from inevitable. As the advice of the Procureur Generaal showed, the other route, (using the Convention

[102] HR 19-01-1962, ECLI:NL:HR:1962:22, *NJ* 1962, 107.

[103] Taken from P. van Dijk, 'De houding van de Hoge Raad jegens de verdragen inzake de rechten van de mens', in B. Baardman (ed.), *De plaats van de Hoge Raad in het huidige staatsbestel. De veranderingen in de rol van de Hoge Raad als rechtsvormer* (Zwolle: W. E. J. Tjeenk Willink, 1988), pp. 173–209.

[104] Although this requirement was softened somewhat in later case law.

[105] Joke de Wit, *Artikel 94 Grondwet Toegepast: Een onderzoek naar de betekenis, de bedoeling en de toepassing van de woorden 'vinden geen toepassing' in artikel 94 Grondwet* (Rotterdam, Doctoral Thesis, 2012), pp. 90–95.

as a tool for reform) was just as feasible, legally speaking. This judicial restraint was arguably the result of various circumstances, as traditionally the Dutch Hoge Raad had been quite restrictive in setting aside domestic rules. In that sense, the judgement might not have been a surprise.[106] Another reason for the restraint was the high stakes involved: the case dealt with one of the most contentious issues in Dutch society since the prohibition was put in place in 1848, and such sensitive topics were not likely to be easily put aside by law. It did not help, for that matter, that the bench was composed of a majority of Protestants.[107] Combined with the traditional restraint of the Hoge Raad, this made the outcome perhaps less surprising. All in all, the expectations of the Dutch government upon ratifying had turned out to be true: the highest court would 'not find easily a tool in this treaty to block Dutch legislation'.[108]

2.2.4 THE FALLOUT: DOMESTIC RESTRAINT, EUROPEAN CONCERN. The judgement was immediately celebrated in the reformed Protestant community in the Netherlands. Should the Hoge Raad have agreed with the priests, 'Rome would have won', the paper of the Reformed Party noted with joy.[109] The government was also relieved: the status quo had been preserved, a hot topic was laid again to rest, and the wide deference the judiciary left to the state would seem to entail that the Convention would not radically alter the domestic legal order.

But where, then, did the judgement leave the status of the Convention in the Netherlands? Broadly speaking, there was a legal and a political consequence. Speaking of the legal implications, the Hoge Raad 'tamed' European human rights, which were interpreted to be subject to a limited

106 As some administrative and constitutional lawyers indeed stated. *Ars Aequi* Vol. 11 Nr. 5 (1962) 'annotation Prins', pp. 135–144.

107 There were, in fact two protestant judges (Smits and de Jong), one Catholic (Petit) and two Liberals: Wiarda and Hulsmann. As for the liberal judges, they too fitted in the culture of judicial restraint.

108 See Chapter 1 on the concerns with regard to the ratification of the Convention.

109 *De Banier: Partijblad van de SGP*, 15 February 1962. Would the decision of the Hoge Raad have been otherwise, the paper noted, 'emigration or resistance until the end' were the options.

judicial review, on the one hand, and presented as merely a restatement of domestic fundamental rights traditions on the other.

In fact, even the majority of the academic reception was positive about the judgement: as it fitted neatly in the tradition of judicial restraint, the decision was deemed wise and was applauded for 'placing the choice back in the hands of the legislator'.[110] However, this was also because the judgement had attracted the attention of constitutional lawyers rather than the 'usual suspects' in international law. This more nationally oriented group of lawyers differed in their reading from the international lawyers, by placing more emphasis on the traditional Dutch reference of fundamental rights protection to Parliament. Indeed, support for the Convention as a tool for reform was found only amongst a limited group of mostly international lawyers. Röling for instance, was critical of the judgement, which he believed 'firmly limited the possibility of judicial review'.[111]

Strong disappointment was also voiced back in Europe: a communique of the Council of Europe was explicitly devoted to the line of cases.[112] In the text, the judgement in Arnhem was lauded: 'the judges in Arnhem are men of wisdom'.[113] The story was supposed to end here, the communique noted, if not the Hoge Raad had decided otherwise. However, there was still hope: the plaintiffs could take their case to the European Commission of Human Rights, and, as the communique noted, such a step could yield a different outcome: 'because for the lawyer, the arguments can work in either direction'.[114] Röling indeed hoped such a step would be taken: this would lead to a European clarification of whether or not the ban on processions was in conformity with the Convention.[115]

However, this step was never taken. The reasons for this lack of follow-up are not clear, and in the absence of any source, all explanations are a guess.[116] A lack of knowledge or practice does not seem truly

[110] *Ars Aequi* Vol. 11 Nr. 5 'annotation Prins', pp. 135–144.

[111] *NJ* 1962/107 'Overtreding Processieverbod' annotation Röling.

[112] Quoted in the speech of Ivo Samkalden, Kamerstukken I, handelingen 12 November 1963.

[113] 'Les juges d'Arnhem sont gens de sagesse'.

[114] Ivo Samkalden, Kamerstukken I, handelingen 12 November 1963, 'car pour le jurist, les arguments ne manquent ni dans un sens, ni dans l'autre'.

[115] *NJ* 1962/107 'Overtreding Processieverbod' annotation Röling.

[116] There seems to be no archive available to provide information on why this step was not taken.

convincing: the priests were helped by a lawyer (Veegens) who knew the workings of the Convention. Moreover, the other line of cases (which used the Convention as a tool against the welfare state) *did* take the European route. The elderly pension act was brought before the Commission in 1963, where it was swiftly decided this did not entail a violation of the Convention. The final result, therefore, was that almost the entirety of Dutch complaints before the Commission stemmed from this religiously inspired stream of cases, aimed at excluding individuals from the welfare state project, cases which were distinctly not covered by the Convention.[117]

The legal implications of the case were lasting: instead of engaging a broad part of academia and practitioners from the start, constitutional lawyers could maintain that the Convention offered nothing new for the Netherlands. Legal engagement with European human rights would therefore remain the field of international lawyers, tucked away in a niche far away from mainstream legal debates. Offered the opportunity, the Hoge Raad shied away from the consequences of using European human rights as a tool to open up the constitution. It may have mattered here that these early cases dealt with highly politically salient topics, namely the welfare state and the position of Catholics in the Netherlands. Interference in those areas via human rights would sit uneasily with the traditional defence of the Dutch judiciary. However, in co-opting the Convention into this restrictive reading, the Hoge Raad set a precedent of restraint which would last well into the 1970s.

In the short term, the cases also had a more political implication. In particular, it had consequences for the acceptance of the other fundamental rights document of the Council of Europe: the European Social Charter. Set out as the pendant to the Convention, but focusing on the social aspect of human rights, the instigators saw it as the 'second step' in European human rights protection. However, in particular, the legal counsel of the Ministry of Internal Affairs had been unpleasantly surprised by the procession cases. To the Ministry, it was clear the potential

[117] For extensive study of these developments, Menno van Emde Boas, 'The Impact of the European Convention of Human Rights and Fundamental Freedoms on the Legal Order of the Netherlands' *Nederlands Tijdschrift voor Internationaal Recht* Vol. 13 Nr. 4 & Vol 14. Nr 1. (1966–1967), pp. 337–330.

implications of human rights treaties, which Foreign Affairs was so keen to sign, had been underestimated. In a letter to the Minister, the legal counsel strongly opposed the signing of the European Social Charter. Writing some months before the Hoge Raad had given its judgement, the counsel warned of the danger of underestimating the unforeseen implications, explaining that

> the entire matter of human rights – and in particular as far as the social fundamental rights are concerned – has so many constitutional implications that one should take that well into consideration in advance. One cannot simply wave those concerns away in the belief that an international covenant cannot differ from the constitution; later it will turn out that one will be confronted with all kinds of constitutional troubles [...] examples of such are the freedom of procession [...] relating to the treaty of Rome.[118]

This concern over the Social Charter was remarkable, as the treaty had not been taken very seriously before. After all, this project of socio-economic rights deserving European protection as distinct human rights was hamstrung from the start.[119] Proposed by the Assembly in early 1954, the Committee of Ministers accepted a call for such a charter not much later that year. Yet it soon became clear the hurdles to any substantial treaty were too high. The main reason for this was the fact that the states (the Netherlands included) were opposed to any legally binding rules on social rights. Indeed, most governments did not see socio-economic rights as being 'human rights' in the first place, which fundamentally limited their willingness to engage in any strong treaty.[120] The Netherlands were no exception here: it did not believe social rights were on equal footing with classical liberal rights and was not in favour of a strong supervision mechanism.[121]

118 Nationaal Archief, Den Haag, Ministerie van Binnenlandse Zaken: Bureau Juridisch Adviseur, nummer toegang 2.04.63, inv. nr. 28, 'Memo to minister, 5 October 1961'.

119 For an extensive treatment see David Harris and John Darcy, *The European Social Charter* (New York: Transnational Publishers, 2001).

120 Hilde Reiding, *The Netherlands and the Development of International Human Rights Instruments* (Antwerp, 2007), p. 156.

121 Hilde Reiding, 'The Netherlands Gradually Changing Views on International Economic and Social Rights Protection' *Human Rights Quarterly* Vol. 34 Nr. 1 (2012), pp. 113–140, 120–123.

This position of the states resulted in a flexible text: the provisions were to be guidelines for further implementation, and any firm supervision was lacking, with only a duty to report on progress as burden for the states. The provisions would not be self-executing, and individuals would not be able to claim these rights before national judges. A supervisory mechanism comparable to the Convention was disregarded: no court would rule on social rights. Instead, the reports were scrutinized by a commission of experts and non-binding recommendations could be proposed by the Committee of Ministers.[122] As a result, the document was regarded to be of limited importance, or at least this was the position of the Dutch government, which attached very little weight to the Charter. With its minimal legal impact, it was labelled a 'propaganda treaty', which gave the impression it had been signed solely in order to express values.[123]

Those were rather specific values, to be sure. Regarding what could considered to be 'social' rights, a distinct approach was taken. Also because of close cooperation with the ILO and employer and labour organizations, the Charter was more focused on the 'working' citizen than on the citizen as such (as a consequence, the Charter was focused on the working 'man' rather than women).[124] Work, the protection of working conditions, and inclusion of health care provisions as means to reintegrate into the working life, all revolved around the issue of labour. Work was, in fact, so central to the Charter that when it was signed in Turin in 1961, this was done in the context of an international exhibition on 'man and his work', celebrating technological progress and new energy sources.[125] On the occasion of signing, it was even left to the states' discretion to

122 Article 29 of the European Social Charter.

123 NL-HaNA, Justitie/Wetgeving/Internationale Organisaties, 2.09.84, inv. nr. 266, 'memo November 1962'.

124 Women were of limited importance in the Charter, which labelled the family 'the fundamental unit of society' – although there was a provision on maternity leave and on some social benefits for wife and child. Most protective was article 8(4) of part 2 of the Charter which asked the signatory parties 'to prohibit the employment of women workers in underground mining, and, as appropriate, on all other work which is unsuitable for them by reason of its dangerous, unhealthy, or arduous nature'. In the revised version of 1966, this was changed into 'pregnant women, women who have recently given birth or who are nursing their infants'.

125 NL-HaNA, Kabinet Minister-President, 2.03.01, inv. nr. 3000 'signing in Turin 1961'.

choose which articles they would declare themselves bound to: a minimum of five articles was deemed enough. Necessary as this might have been to reach European consensus on the topic, the result was rather meek. The social Europe and European human rights would remain separate stories: contrary to its proclaimed status as the other side of the coin of European human rights, the Charter would never reach a similar status as the Convention. Limited by its legal status, Europe therefore offered little extra in this regard: the national venue offered a much more promising legal venue to improve one's position.

The fact that even such a 'toothless' treaty was met with concern in the Dutch political deliberations was therefore mainly a result of caution due to the experiences from the recent past with what had been deemed another harmless document, namely the Convention. That case had proven that even non-threatening human rights treaties could potentially come back to bite the signatory state. This feeling was enhanced when, upon closer examination, the Ministers found the Charter to pose some problems in light of domestic law. In particular, the provisions on the right of civil servants to strike were met with concern (in the Netherlands this was prohibited for the personnel of the railways, for example), but provisions on social benefits also raised questions.[126] The result of these concerns was a compromise: the Netherlands would sign the Charter, yet negotiate further on ratification, which ultimately would be signed as late as 1980. Hesitation about signing up to new international treaties was therefore one of the outcomes of these early days of the Convention in the Dutch context.

Ultimately, the great deference shown by domestic Courts to the legislature and refusal to engage with the provisions of the Convention in their own way would focus the attention on the European system. If no solace could be expected from domestic courts, could the European Court offer guidance in that respect?

[126] Nationaal Archief, Den Haag, Ministerie van Binnenlandse Zaken: Bureau Juridisch Adviseur, nummer toegang 2.04.63, inventarisnummer 28, 'Memorandum of legal advisor to Minister', 5 October 1961; Nationaal Archief, Den Haag, Ministerraad, nummer toegang 2.02.05.02, inventarisnummer 1057, 'notes Ministerraad, 6 Oktober 1962'. The Ministries of Justice and Internal affairs were most adamantly opposed to signing the Charter.

2.3 EUROPEAN INTEGRATION FRUSTRATED: VAN ASBECK IN THE EUROPEAN COURT

Guidance from the European Court was indeed one of the hopes when, in 1959, the European project was being celebrated in Strasbourg. The tenth anniversary of the Council of Europe was filled with the laudatory speeches one might expect of such an event. Gifts were exchanged, and a movie festival was held for the occasion, with every nation submitting its finest cinematographic productions.[127] Despite struggles in the organization of the Council of Europe, where the Consultative Assembly consistently clashed with the Committee of Ministers, the ideal of European Unity had not yet disappeared from the institution. A new page was written when, under the watchful eye of chairmen of national parliaments, fifteen eminent men were solemnly sworn in as judges of a new institute: the European Court of Human Rights. The 'crown jewel' of the Council of Europe had become a reality in 1959.

Subsequently, however, the Court found itself with hardly any work at hand. In most accounts, this has been explained by the hesitation of states and a conscious legal strategy of restraint to build trust in the system.[128] However, there is also something missing in this story: surely, the Court had its own agenda and sensibility to the need to build legitimacy, but one should also not overstate its influence. When zooming in to the micro level, it is apparent that 'legal diplomacy' was but *one* of the initiatives the Court employed. Its relatively marginal position was not lost to the experienced bench. In fact, the Court was fundamentally unhappy with its minimal role and actively sought to expand this. This story, of how the Court grew frustrated with its marginalization, adds a more political layer of the Court's relationship with the domestic context. By focusing on the experience of the Dutch judge van Asbeck, one can see the more nuanced historical reality behind this 'protracted institutionalization'. This account not only expands upon

[127] The Dutch submission 'en de zee was niet meer' was a curious mix of nostalgia and hope as it showed the emergence of new land where once there was sea, but also the loss of tradition.

[128] Madsen, 'The Protracted Institutionalization of the Strasbourg Court: From Legal Diplomacy to Integrationist Jurisprudence', pp. 43–61.

the more socio-legal narrative but also has implications for our understanding of the further development of the Court. Ultimately, it was the Member States which remained firmly in the driving seat of the Court's set up and future.

2.3.1 DIVERGING EXPECTATIONS OF STATE AND JUDGE. There were high hopes for the European Court of Human Rights: still in the late 1950s the Consultative Assembly had pushed for the Court to become a general court which could rule over all the treaties of the Council of Europe.[129] This would have resulted in a sort of 'European Court of Justice', much in line with the federalist thinking which was still quite prominent in the Council of Europe. Reality proved more resilient. The Assembly's expectations for the Convention paired with a European supreme court, like many of its federalist ideals, proved a bridge too far for the States, who routinely blocked such proposals. Apart from broader concerns on European integration, which was perceived to be better off in the specialized European Communities than the general Council of Europe, it was the nature of the Convention in the first place which made the Dutch government wary of promoting such a European supreme court.

In fact, it was precisely the nature of human rights as legally binding concepts which made the Dutch government reluctant to expand the Court. Fears of an intrusive European Court were much larger with regard to the European Court of Human Rights than they were regarding the Court of the European Communities. 'Human rights touch on everything, and go in that regard, way beyond the Europe of Coal and Steel', as a memo summarized the difference between the two Courts.[130] The specialized nature of the European communities acted as a reassurance: yes, that other European Court would be powerful, but also confined to the detailed realm of economics. What bothersome intrusion in domestic legal contexts could be expected from a Court in that segment of life?

The Court was not immediately active: a number of signatories had to be reached first, and this had been foreseen for 1959. This brought up

[129] Bates, *The Evolution of the European Convention*, p. 183.

[130] NL-HaNa NR Buitenlandse Zaken/Code-Archief 55–64, 2.05.118, inv. nr. 7610 'memo 6 sept 1962'.

the question of the election of judges: who would be eligible and which persons were preferential? The year before, the governments had deliberated on this topic, mostly bringing up the question of incompatibilities. The Convention set out that judges merely had to possess 'a high moral character', but did not explicitly mention any other requirements.[131] Fernand Dehousse, the chair of the Consultative Assembly, summarized the position of the judges: 'the function of judge is not a full day job, for which they will not be paid a salary but merely a compensation. Moreover, the function is therefore compatible with another function, including a political one'.[132] This remarkable openness (it was common for international courts to include a section on incompatibilities) was the result of the drafting process of the Convention: to keep the text as lenient as possible, the requirements were not too strict. However, much like with the instalment of the Commission, the Dutch government was not overly thrilled about the presence of politicians in the European Court. Despite the formal compatibility with other functions, the judges should be independent, which precluded appointing any politicians or civil servants.[133]

This strong Dutch focus on the independence of the judges led the government to select its candidates from within a distinct sphere, with a preference for lawyers of some stature, with time on their hands and with experience of international law and comparative constitutional law. Moreover, the search for proper candidates would need to take place in 'circles of judges, lawyers, professors and retired civil servants'.[134] The candidate list was a perfect example of such individuals, and three candidates were put forward in order of preference:

131 Article 21 of the Convention (nowadays amended as to include incompatibilities).

132 NL-HaNA, PV Raad van Europa Straatsburg, 2.05.278, inv. nr. 994, 'Memo from Perm. Rep to the Hague, 8 October 1958'.

133 It would seem this point of view was shared by other states: the first bench was a composed of mainly professors and judges with close connections to national elites: Mikael Rask Madsen, 'The Legitimatization Strategies of International Justices: The Case of the European Court of Human Rights' in Michal Bobek (ed.), *Selecting Europe's Judges: A Critical Review of the Appointment Procedures to the European Courts* (Oxford: Oxford University Press, 2015), pp. 259–278.

134 NL-HaNA, PV Raad van Europa Straatsburg, 2.05.278, inv. nr. 994, 'Memo from Foreign affairs to Perm Rep. 15 November 1958'.

van Asbeck, Beaufort and international lawyer Jan Verzijl.[135] Of those three, Beaufort had in fact already communicated he would not be willing to be both judge and Commission member at the same time, which subsequently led to the election of the first candidate on the list (van Asbeck) to the Court.

The choice of van Asbeck was a choice for someone with deep connections in the corps diplomatique. After his involvement in Indonesia, he had settled in Leiden to teach international law, but remained in close touch with the government. The new function offered to him was highly welcome, as he felt his work in the university had started to confine him. In the late 1950s, the academic life in Leiden was changing. van Asbeck was part of a generation which had a distinct view of the university as a place offering a slightly elitist group of people the room to breathe. Studying as a way of life. The university, however, was starting to attract more and more students and demanded more and more in the terms of education. 'I cannot express how much the focus on teaching at the University oppresses me', van Asbeck wrote to a colleague. 'I feel the notion and treatment of the University as primarily a place of education is a deadly danger for the University and for the spiritual life and substance of the West. Russia treats the University as a school, and we know the consequences [...] The infection, also the American infection, has also implications for us...'[136]

When he retired in 1959, wary of the university he left behind, van Asbeck looked forward to his new job in Strasbourg. Already in his teaching, he had expressed his hope for a further protection of the individual in the 'society of states'. Since in his eyes the individual was ultimately the subject of international law, it was only logical that international law should strive for the protection of the individual.[137] As van Asbeck saw – and taught – it, one of the most promising attempts to create that protection was the European Convention, and the opportunity to play a part in this new endeavour was highly exciting. The European character of

[135] Verzijl was another rather classical international jurist, noting how international law was distinctive 'European' in nature.

[136] NL-HaNa, van Asbeck, 2.21.183.03, inv. nr. 117, 'Letter to A. W. van Der Pot'.

[137] NL-HaNa, van Asbeck, 2.21.183.03, inv. nr. 61, 'college 20 May 1959'.

the Court appealed to him: he had been pushing for a strong stance on European integration, and to be able to be an active role in this was not an opportunity to be wasted. The Court therefore offered to play into two desirable elements: the protection of the individual, and European integration at large.

2.3.2 THE FIRST CASES BEFORE THE COURT: DEFERENCE TAKES HOLD. The beginning of the Court's activity was characterized by major political stakes from the start. It so happened the first case to appear before the Court was – just like the first case before the Commission had been – a highly salient one. That case, of Lawless, the suspected IRA-fighter who was detained without trial under emergency-powers law, was aided by the later Nobel-Prize winner Sean MacBride, with the case ultimately ending up before the European Court of Human Rights, has been extensively studied.[138] This was not just the first case before an international court on human rights, it was also a politically loaded one. Behind the screens, the Irish government expressed major concerns, and the case invoked the close interest of other states. Already in 1958, when the complaint arrived at the European Commission, it was noted that this was an important moment. 'This is undoubtedly disappointing for the Irish government, which has gone through a lot to shelve the complaint'. Since this has not happened, it will become much more difficult for the Irish government to take repressive measures against the 'Irish Republican Army', the Dutch Ambassador in Dublin noted.[139]

Irish concern only grew further when the Commission began to draw up its report in 1959. With the Court now in place, the possibility existed that the Commission would send the case there, and the ambassador in Dublin noted increased consternation.

[138] Brian Doolan, *Lawless* v *Ireland: The First Case Before the European Court of Human Rights: An International Miscarriage of Justice?* (Aldershot: Ashgate 2001); William Schabas, 'Ireland, the European Convention of Human Rights and the personal contribution of Sean MacBride' in John Morison, Kieran McEvoy and Gordon Anthony (eds.), *Judges, Transition and Human Rights* (Oxford: Oxford University Press 2007), pp. 252–274.

[139] NL-HaNA, PV Raad van Europa Straatsburg, 2.05.278, inv. nr. 998, 'Memo from Dublin to The Hague, 7 September 1958'.

> The Irish Government is still far from feeling secure over the ending of this case. Should this fall to her disadvantage, the top civil servant[140] does not exclude the possibility such an ending would bring other Governments to greater reservations as far as this international justice is concerned.[141]

The Irish warning was not without merit. Its line of defence, the state of emergency, was not uncommon in Europe in those days when violence was still lingering. The United Kingdom had invoked the same defence in the Cyprus case, while France, although it had not ratified the Convention at the time, had also declared a state of emergency the previous year over the crisis in Algeria. Should European human rights indeed prove to be an obstruction to these exercises of power, the position of the supervision mechanisms might indeed have become precarious.

It was all the more remarkable, therefore, that the Commission indeed sent the case to the Court. It did not have to do this. In fact, its confidential report to the Committee of Ministers had found no human rights violations, yet as the case 'raised legal issues of fundamental importance in the application of the Convention', the Commission found it desirable that the Court would have the last say in the matter.[142]

The Court would, after careful deliberation, side with the state.[143] The state of emergency proved sufficient to provide for a derogation on the duties under the Convention. It was a taste of things to come: in the early cases before the Court, it would be careful to offer the states a wide room of manoeuvre. As such, it laid the foundations for a very cautious engagement with human rights on the European level. The Court would, much like the Commission, not easily find a violation. Still, this moment was celebrated in Strasbourg. Hopes flared high after *Lawless*, decided only two years after the Court was operational. As 'radio

140 The ambassador had a conversation with the procureur-general of the Irish government.

141 NL-HaNA, PV Raad van Europa Straatsburg, 2.05.278, inv. nr. 998, 'Memo from Dublin to the Hague, 16 December 1959'.

142 *Lawless* v. *Ireland* (no. 3), 1 July 1961, Series A no. 3.

143 van Asbeck himself was not on the bench for this case: the judges were chosen by chance.

Strasbourg' of the Council of Europe happily announced, these were 'historical hours [...] Democracy possesses a new instrument ...!'[144]

2.3.3 THE COURT'S FAILED INITIATIVES AND THEIR LESSONS. These high hopes were swiftly dashed, and the stream of cases before the Court would rapidly dry out. After the Lawless Case, there followed the case of *De Becker* in 1962. After that, there was a six year hiatus until the Belgium Linguistics case of 1968.[145] This lack of cases was not how van Asbeck had imagined the Court to function, nor indeed how he perceived his role in furthering the protection of the individual in the international legal framework. This calm before the Court has been presented as an act of legal diplomacy as well; however, this did not imply that the Court remained passive in this state of affairs. 'Authority building' was distinctively *not* understood in the Court as being idle. Far from it, the Court was actively trying to expand its role. The actions of van Asbeck show how he played an active role in trying to expand the importance of the Court via institutional reforms. He was one of the most senior members of the Court and had been highly influential in drawing up the rules of procedure before in 1959.[146] Later proposals for reform also carry his fingerprints, and an insight into his experiences in these early years therefore shows a much more nuanced view on the workings from within the European Court.

For in this period, the Court desperately tried to get involved and put forward a number of ideas in order to receive more cases. The first battle for reform was an expansion of the power of the Court via advisory opinions. An idea had been put forward which would allow it to provide advice on application of the Convention, should a national Court find itself in situations where it had to apply the Convention, a procedure comparable to the preliminary ruling procedure of the European Communities. This was an idea which nowadays is reflected in Protocol 16, which entered into force in 2018. The idea did not come only from

144 'Des heures historiques... La Démocratie possède un nouvel instrument'. NL-HaNA, PV Raad van Europa Straatsburg, 2.05.278, inv. nr. 998, 'transcript radio 4 July 1961'.

145 Bates, *The Evolution of the European Convention*, pp. 528–529.

146 H. Petzold, 'The Dutch judges of Strasbourg 'in R. Lawson and E. Myjer (eds.), *50 jaar EVRM*, pp. 585–595.

the Court, but had been around for quite a while: already in 1960 the Consultative Assembly had put forward this proposal to governments, which were subsequently urged to reflect on the issue.[147] These were initiatives to get the system going.

Yet it soon became clear there would be little support from the states. In a damning memo, the legal counsel of the Ministry of Foreign Affairs denied the added value of such a proposal. It expressed major reservations regarding the expansion of powers of the Court and asked explicitly why *this* Convention would have to be altered in such an intrusive matter.[148] The initiative went directly against what the states had in mind when the Convention was drafted, the Ministry noted: the limited powers of the Court had been a conscious choice of the states in the first place. If anything, the Court was supposed to have a very minimal role. Laying out the ideal situation, the memo concluded how 'one can only rejoice if the judges in this Court have very little on their hands'.[149] It was not up to the Netherlands to change that situation.

The opposition of states did not immediately persuade the Court to stop its attempts. Two years later, in 1962, the proposal was still on the table. In fact, the Court had brought up even more proposals to expand its competences. Van Asbeck, who was one of the judges pushing for a more active Court, was not content with merely making proposals. He also sought to influence the domestic sphere by meeting with the expert on the Convention in the civil service of the Netherlands: Hein Schermers. They knew each other well, as van Asbeck had been the PhD supervisor of Schermers. In August 1962, the two sat down for a meeting and van Asbeck explained the proposals the Court had put forward to expand its powers. Apart from the possibility of advisory opinions to national judges, the Court also proposed it should become possible for governments to ask similar advice on laws which entailed a human rights element. This would guarantee that national laws would be in conformity with the Convention from the outset.[150] The argumentation

[147] Recommendation 232 (1960) of the Consultative Assembly.

[148] NL-HaNA, PV Raad van Europa Straatsburg, 2.05.278, inv. nr. 995, 'memo JURA, 16 March 1960'. Emphasis in original memo.

[149] Ibid.

[150] Ibid.

van Asbeck put forward with regard to the advice to national courts was twofold. First, it would help in creating a larger uniformity in the application of the Convention. Second, it would prevent judgements which were not in line with the common European standard. These proposals would have placed the Court firmly at the centre of attention and granted it a major role in the development of European human rights law.

Schermers did not agree with his Doktorvater. Since the recommendation of the Assembly, the Netherlands had been strongly opposed to any such measures. Even a conveyance of a commission of experts on the question was deemed unwise: alongside Norway and Sweden, the Netherlands actively tried to prevent such a meeting from ever taking place.[151] Any expansion of the powers of the Court was neither necessary, nor desirable.[152] Reflecting upon the ideas brought forward by van Asbeck, Schermers shot down these two provisions *precisely* because of the argumentation van Asbeck provided.

Expanding the power of the Court could, as Schermers held, result in conflicts. The Court itself was deemed a problematic institution for the state, as flexibility needed to remain a key feature of the Convention. 'The Court only rules on the basis of the law, whereas the Commission has much more flexibility, also to reach a friendly settlement. This conciliatory function is absent at the Court'.[153] As far as the advice on legislation went, that element was also seen as undesirable. What if the Commission later had to check if something was in conformity with the Convention? And what if domestic opponents of the law in question would ask if advice had been requested? This would result in an overtly bureaucratic and unworkable situation, Schermers noted.[154]

The Netherlands would continue to shoot down all proposals the Court put forward. Its powers were, and should remain, limited. Ideally,

[151] NL-HaNA, Buitenlandse Zaken/Code-Archief 55–64, 2.05.118 inv. nr. 7610, 'memo 7 June 1960'.

[152] Ibid. Although ultimately unsuccessful, these states did manage to firmly strip the proposal of any meaningful content; see article 1, second protocol.

[153] NL-HaNA, Buitenlandse Zaken/Code-Archief 55–64, 2.05.118 inv. nr. 7610, 'memo 6 September 1962'.

[154] Ibid.

the matters would be dealt with by the Commission, where the possibility of friendly settlements provided both more leniency and less political problems. The issue of advisory opinions was ultimately dealt with in the second protocol and was stripped of all the contents the Court had put forward. Even after the Court had compromised and – grudgingly – removed its wish for national courts to ask them for advice, governments would not overturn their original intent. Advice could only be given at the request of the Committee of Ministers (which would have to agree by a two-thirds majority) and could not deal with 'any question relating to the content or scope of the rights or freedoms defined in Section I of the Convention [...] or with any other question which the Commission, the Court or the Committee of Ministers might have to consider in consequence of any such proceedings as could be instituted in accordance with the Convention'.[155] This stripped the provision of any meaningful content and basically left the Court in limbo. Its preferred option, a preliminary ruling procedure comparable to that which existed at the European Court of Justice, had been trashed and would remain unfeasible.

This only added to the disappointment of van Asbeck, but still was not the end of the initiatives of the Court. Van Asbeck swiftly put forward a second attempt at institutional reform. In an internal note drawn up for his colleagues in 1964 to expand on for further proposals, he expressed his dismay with the situation. Speaking of the idle situation the Court found itself in, he noted: 'this state of affairs is an insult to a Court such as ours, on which it was originally intended to confer a role of primordial importance and on which thousands of men have based their hopes of a better human society in Europe'.[156] The situation was dire, van Asbeck wrote. The Court faced numerous institutional problems which went beyond anything that could be solved by simple amendments. The choice to insert the Commission before the Court resulted in the inaction the Court found itself in, as it was dependent on others to bring forth cases. And who would refer a case to the Court? Not the

[155] Article 1 second protocol ECHR.

[156] NL-HaNa, van Asbeck, 2.21.183.03, inv. nr.111, 'memo institutional reform 25 May 1964'.

states, as they were not at all eager to land in front of an international court. Conversely, the Commission had not brought a case before the Court in years.

Van Asbeck therefore proposed a mandatory system: governments and the Commission should decide, as a rule of practice, that a case involving a state which has recognized its compulsory jurisdiction, should be submitted to the Court.[157] As for the advisory opinions, van Asbeck expressed his disappointment. These changes were cosmetic and would not have any practical effect, although that did not mean that nothing should be done. 'The only thing for us to do at the present moment and in the immediate future is to follow the discussions closely and keep our eyes open for any opportunity offered of extending the Court's sphere of advisory activity', van Asbeck urged his colleagues.[158] His conclusion was bleak. Unless the mandatory system of sending cases to the Court was put into place, 'our court's inertia must inevitably continue for quite some years to come'.[159]

Yet van Asbeck's fear did not address the notion that for his own state, this inertia was precisely how the Court should function. Also, this second proposal of van Asbeck did not crystallize into anything substantial due to the persistent resistance of the states. What these failed efforts show are a clash of conceptions of the Convention. For van Asbeck and some of his colleagues, the Court was called in existence to fulfil a promise of providing protection to the individual. It was unacceptable that the Court would be left dangling as a rare trinket in the European legal order: that was not the original promise. The government saw matters somewhat differently. To them, the Court was an ultimum remedium, of which it was better if it did not do anything in the first place. In that context, it was not surprising the proposals of the Court were not taken up and subsequently forgotten.

As the Convention emerged from these early years, it would seem it had little to add to the existing legal frameworks. The Dutch

157 Ibid.

158 Ibid.

159 van Asbeck would send the same request to Foreign Affairs a year later, urging the Ministry to promote the sending of cases to the Court. See the portrait of van Asbeck by H. G. Schermers in Lawson and Myjer, *50 jaar EVRM*, pp. 535–539.

government was highly cautious in its stance on the Convention, the domestic courts had 'smothered' its legal value, and engagement was predominantly confined to a small group of international lawyers. On the European level, restraint prevailed and initiatives in the opposite direction had been rejected. This resulted in an image of the Convention as a document with little legal value, an image, even though this was a contested characterization, which was pervasive as the Convention went into the 1960s.

CHAPTER 3

1962–1968

From European Rights to Human Rights

IN 1962, AFTER ITS CONTESTED BEGINNING, the status of the Convention seemed relatively settled. It was not a pretty sight. On the domestic level, the Hoge Raad had successfully smothered any ambitious interpretation it might have, whereas on the European level the initiatives to activate the Court had failed. It would seem the Convention was destined to occupy a very minimal position in legal practice, and at first sight these were the 'years of crisis' for the Court and Convention. A persistent lack of legal activity made that 'the clouds of doubt' were floating over the system of the Convention.[1] When Henri Rolin, Vice President of the Court, gave a speech in 1965 titled 'Has the European Court of Human Rights a future?', it was by no means clear if this was a rhetorical question.[2]

However, from the grassroots, a new engagement with human rights in general, and with the Convention more specifically began to emerge.[3] As such, the early 1960s formed a crucial period of transition in which

[1] Bates, *The Evolution of the European Convention*, p. 184. On the 1970s as defining moment in the history and 'breakthrough' of human rights in general, see most prominently Jan Eckel and Samuel Moyn (eds.), *The Breakthrough: Human Rights in the 1970s*. For a similar moment in the Convention, Mikael Rask Madsen, 'The Challenging Authority of the European Court of Human Rights: From Cold War Legal Diplomacy to the Brighton Declaration and Backlash', *Law and Contemporary Problems* Vol. 79 Nr. 1 (2016), pp. 141–178.

[2] Quoted in Bates, *The Evolution of the European Convention*, p. 184.

[3] In contrast to commonplace explanations, which usually turn to the 1970s or 1980s to frame the breakthrough of the ECHR, this chapter seeks to nuance these claims, by showing how these shifts were the result of a 'bottom up' movement which started to use human rights as new claims. Only later did this tie in with institutional legal developments at the Council of Europe, such as the growing leniency of the Commission to refer

the meaning of the Convention began to shift from a treaty focused primarily on European integration to a document focused on human rights *as such*. In this period, a distinct break with the status which had been so carefully cemented in the preceding decade can be observed. As this shift took place beyond the courtrooms, be they national or European, it has remained relatively out of sight of the legal narrative. Yet if one broadens the scope beyond the legal discussions, certain distinctively new elements can be discerned which shed new light on the development of the Convention.

For in these six years some fundamental developments took place which began to alter the conservative, minimalistic status quo which had characterized the Convention up to 1962. To be clear, the shift from 'European' document to 'human rights document' was never clear-cut or binary. Legacies of the European ideal cast a long shadow over the developments in the 1960s, and often, the two points of view intertwined. Still, a subtle shift can be discerned in how human rights could function. First, two broad societal developments in the Netherlands, namely 'depillarization' and the emergence of a new public memory regime, allowed for a new engagement with human rights to emerge. Second, decolonization proved vitally important. In 1962, the Netherlands lost control of the last vestige of the Dutch Empire in the 'East', New Guinea. This opened up a new direction in Dutch foreign policy focused more on 'right' instead of 'might'. However, all of this took place in a world where, legally, the Convention was still very much kept at bay. Aside from certain individual academics, human rights were not prominent sight in the courtrooms. Both on the domestic and on the European level, the Convention seemed to offer individuals little protection. In particular, on the European level, the institutions were still deeply politicized, resulting in a great deal of state-friendliness. The defining change in this disposition emerged when the Dutch joined an interstate complaint against Greece in 1967. The case stood out as a direct consequence of these earlier shifts in society and foreign policy, and as such, heralded the beginning of a new understanding of the Convention.

to the Court later on in the sixties or a presumed shift from 'legal politics' to 'technical law', see Bates, *The Evolution of the European Convention*, pp. 261–262.

3.1 A NEW SOCIETY: NEW HUMAN RIGHTS?

First of all, human rights did not escape the broader societal developments in which they functioned. The Convention had been born from a distinct environment, drafted to suit imperial societies in the context of the emerging Cold War. It was a document which smelt of the classical world of international law, a place of chesterfields and cigars, a place which had remained its natural habitat in the 1950s.[4] However, in the early sixties, human rights were starting to be used in a different way. Two important shifts led to a new frame of reference in the understanding of human rights in general, and of the European Convention in particular.

First of all, in the 1960s, a new kind of political engagement emerged. In particular, so-called 'depillarization' left its mark on Dutch society and opened up space for individual engagement, transcending former divisions based on religious convictions. These old divisions had shaped Dutch society so as to separate communities, as each of them, Protestant, Catholic, liberal or socialist, had their own distinct 'pillar' which provided for church, party, newspaper, and school, but those were rapidly disappearing in the early 1960s. In particular, the structuring of society along religious lines became loosened. This 'decolonization of the citizen', as one journalist dubbed the trend, was above all presented as a break with the past and a 'modernization' and individualization of society.[5] New political parties, such as Democraten'66 or the Politieke Partij Radicalen, sought to dismantle the classical, closed political system and promised democratic renewal. Institutional religion seemed on the back foot, as churches emptied swiftly.[6]

Yet it would be an overstatement to claim that in the course of several years the Netherlands turned from a conservative, religious country into an individualistic secular nation. The historian Peter van Dam has argued in this regard how 'depillarization' should best be seen as a

4 Such as the 'genootschap voor den Rechtstaat', described in Chapter 2.

5 Henk Hofland, cited in Peter van Dam, *Staat van Verzuiling: over een Nederlandse mythe* (Amsterdam: Wereldbibliotheek, 2011), p. 77.

6 James Kennedy, *Nieuw Babylon in Aanbouw: Nederland in de Jaren zestig* (Amsterdam: Boom 2017), pp. 106–110, 197–205.

shift from 'heavy' to 'light' communities. What took place in the 1960s was a fundamental shift in the way people organized themselves. 'Heavy' communities can be characterized as being focused on a strong integration with the in-group and by their exclusionary character. This was the essence of the pillar structure. In the 1960s, however, people turned to 'lighter' communities which, in contrast, are much more open: instead of a predetermined notion of who could belong, these lighter communities revolve around communal ideas or interests. A strong focus on individual freedom of choice was pervasive, and these groups were open to all who felt attracted to their ideas.[7]

This analysis is of particular importance when it comes to human rights. The new political movements of the 1960s, being 'light' communities, focused on specific issues or revolved around shared values, and anyone who was interested could join. The human rights movement was precisely one of those movements; indeed, it was among the more successful ones, although there were various other routes to be taken. Environmental protection was another particularly successful 'light' community.[8] Humanitarian groups that promoted campaigns for development aid also experienced a breakthrough, while the broader 'solidarity' movement, which turned to suffering elsewhere in the world, also started to emerge in this decade as well.[9]

One side effect of this new political engagement in light communities was an increase in the use of an emotional discourse. This is not to say that emotions had been absent from debates on the Convention until then, however, they were used in a different manner. In fact, the link between emotion and human rights was explicitly pejorative. Human rights were seen as 'serious business': yet this presupposed seriousness was exclusionary in character. An emotional appeal based on

[7] Peter van Dam, *Staat van Verzuiling*, pp. 19–20.

[8] Half of the global sales of the Club of Rome's report *Limits to Growth*, went over a cashier in the Netherlands, totalling one million (!) copies sold in the Netherlands; James Kennedy, *Nieuw Babylon in Aanbouw*, p. 86.

[9] For a concise overview, see Jan Eckel, 'The Rebirth of Politics from the Spirit of Morality: Explaining the Human Rights Revolution of the 1970's' in Jan Eckel and Samuel Moyn (eds.), *The Breakthrough: Human Rights in the 1970s* (Philadelphia: University of Pennsylvania Press 2015), pp. 226–261.

human rights was suspect. As we have seen in the reasoning behind the decision not to extend the Convention to the overseas territories in the 1950s, such a move was deemed undesirable because of the 'emotional way' in which people would use the legal possibility of human rights.[10] In essence, this was classic patriarchal way of thinking, which applied to a variety of issues. In a gendered way, it drew on the archetypical 'hysterical' women, and it would take the feminist movement to establish the idea that women's rights were, in fact, human rights.[11] In a colonial setting, it referred to the 'lightly inflammable' inhabitants of the colonies whose societies were 'not yet mature enough' to deal with human rights.[12]

What took place in the late 1960s was a change in the appreciation of emotion and in particular, a remarkable rise in emotional *engagement*.[13] This was a broad shift. Via the new medium of television, moving images entered the households of every individual. Television in particular allowed for a direct confrontation with the suffering of others far away. The famine in Biafra of 1967 carved the images of children with bloated bellies in the public conscience and formed the beginning of a broader international humanitarian movement.[14] The Vietnam War became a focal point of solidarity movements and protests precisely because of the abundance of shocking images of the conflict available to the public. Witnessing suffering simply became more widespread. Yet a witness is

10 See Chapter 2 and further in this piece. Yet also think of the fears of Drees for 'querulants': people (troublemakers) simply looking for a platform to frame grievances.

11 Of all the early cases in the Netherlands appealing to the Convention, *none* related to rights of women, almost all to freedom of religion.

12 The patriarchal aspect here is the view of colonial residents as children rather than full-grown persons: not yet ready to take on the responsibilities of a functioning human rights system.

13 Emotional engagement was not new as such, obviously. Solidarity with persecuted Christians had a long history; the Algerian war evoked pleas of compassion in the 1950s. What was new was the more universal character (suffering *as such* became a concern, rather than the group to which the person belonged to) and the *scale* of the engagement: although the mass movements would truly bloom in the 1970s, its roots lay in the 1960s.

14 Lasse Heerten, 'The Dystopia of Postcolonial Catastrophe: Self-Determination, the Biafran War of Secession, and the 1970s Human Rights Moment' in Eckel and Moyn (eds.), *The Breakthrough: Human Rights in the 1970s*, pp. 15–33.

never just a passive bystander. It is no coincidence that one of the earliest slogans and strategies of Amnesty International was the emotionally loaded 'mobilization of shame'.[15] Shame cut both ways here: this was an appeal to shame governments for their actions, but also an appeal to the shame of the audience: Amnesty appealed to a vicarious shame on the treatment of fellow human beings.

The exclusionary consequences of emotions in human rights might seem paradoxical, but this also underlines the importance of the shift which took place. In many ways, an appeal based on human rights was put forward as an inherently emotional claim: a claim upon empathy, a 'shocked conscience', or indeed on sympathy for a fellow human being.[16] The emergence of a regime which allowed for expressions of such empathy to be broadly shared and 'taken seriously' was therefore more than just a cultural revolution propelled by the flower power of young hippies. Rather, it fulfilled a requirement for these human rights claims to thrive.[17]

3.1.1 A CHANGE OF MEMORY AND MORAL REFERENCE. Second, and closely related to the suffering of others, was the central place the Holocaust began to acquire in Dutch public memory.[18] This

[15] Although it would take until the 70's before this human rights NGO truly became a player of considerable size, see Bastiaan Bouwman, 'Outraged, yet moderate and impartial: The rise of Amnesty International in the Netherlands in the 1960's and 1970's' *BMGN- Low Countries Historical Review* Vol. 132 Nr. 4 (2017), pp. 53–74.

[16] I follow the analysis of Rorty in this regard: Richard Rorty, 'Human Rights, Rationality and Sentimentality' in S. Shute and S. Hurley (eds.), *On Human Rights: The Oxford Amnesty Lectures 1993* (Oxford: Oxford University Press, 1994), pp. 111–134. Martha Nussbaum and others, most prominently Lynn Hunt, follow this line of reasoning. The extensive scholarship on 'law and emotions' is not directly relevant here, as they draw upon the same basic idea that a claim upon human rights is inherently connected to emotional connections. However, see for a concise and clear notion Emily Kidd White, 'Till Human Voices Wake Us: The Role of Emotions in the Adjudication of Dignity Claims' *Journal of Law, Religion and State* Vol. 3 (2014), pp. 201–239.

[17] The link which was forged in this way with 'solidarity' can also help explain why human rights as a public discourse in the Netherlands have always more or less been reserved to *foreign* realms: solidarity in the national sphere had already been 'bureaucratized' by the welfare state.

[18] Samuel Moyn has argued that the rise in Holocaust memory contributed to the breakthrough later in the 1970s: I tend to agree, yet also would like to frame the changing

mattered greatly, as the shared memory served as leading national moral benchmark. The Second World War had been ever present in the public memory of the Netherlands, yet this remembrance had taken the form of a story of *national* suffering. The occupation had been a tragedy which had befallen the small and innocent nation of the Netherlands, and as such, was a narrative aimed at restoring the nation state. The heroic resistance was celebrated, and suffering was presented as a shared, not an individual experience. References to specific Jewish suffering were met with silence or not acknowledged at all. As one survivor remembered her arrival back in the Netherlands, the initial response had been 'quite a lot of you came back. Just be happy you weren't here – how we suffered from hunger!'[19] However, the narrative began to shift in the mid-1960s. The national element of collective suffering passed to the background as a shift was made from innocence to guilt, and from a collective burden to individual – in particular, Jewish – suffering.

When the Eichmann trial was held in 1962, this was more than just a prosecution. It was also a showcase of cruelty and documentation of the crimes perpetrated, broadly picked up by leading national figures.[20] Much in line with what Hannah Arendt would argue, Eichmann was not presented in the Dutch context as the 'monster', a stereotype created by the Nazi-chiefs. Rather, he was seen as a terribly ordinary man, capable of doing horrible things embedded in a bureaucratic system. For the Dutch, this image also entailed a confrontation with their own actions in the war. Three years later, in 1965, the monumental work of historian Jacques Presser, 'Ondergang' was published, which explicitly placed the fate of the Jewish population at the centre of attention. As much an *in memoriam* as a *j'accuse*, the work was instrumental in breaking the pervasive silence on the topic.[21] Presser confronted the Dutch with their silent complicity. Noting the assistance to the Nazi's of the railroad workers, the

memory culture in terms of national suffering to individual suffering. Samuel Moyn, *Human Rights and the Uses of History* (New York: Verso, 2014), pp. 87–99.

[19] Quoted in Tony Judt, *Postwar*, p. 806.

[20] Leading public intellectuals such as Mulisch and Herzberg were defining in this regard for the Netherlands. See further Van Vree, *In de schaduw van Auschwitz*.

[21] Van Vree, *In de Schaduw van Auschwitz*, p. 104.

police, or the civil servants, the question as to whether this was indeed an innocent nation emerged.

The importance of this shift in remembrance culture lies in its relation to the central point of moral orientation: the memory of the war. When this turned to the suffering of the other, here the Jewish population, the focus on the nation came to be replaced by a focus on the individual, and the evil which could befall it at the hands of the state. Although it would take until the late 1980s for the specific site of Auschwitz as universal moral topic and the concept of human rights to become intrinsically linked, it was in the 1960s that the shift towards connecting the war, individual suffering, and guilt took place. More importantly, it also opened up the possibility of a new moral use of the Second World War. State-sanctioned violence, which incurred individual suffering, now was increasingly met with a strong moral counterpart: that of the lessons of the war.[22]

Clearly there were limits to this consciousness when it came to political reality. These were also the years during which a first, but limited reckoning with Dutch colonial violence in Indonesia took place. In the so-called 'excess nota' of 1969, it was noted how the 'excesses' that Dutch soldiers had committed in Indonesia were just that, namely singular and isolated outbursts of violence. Human rights language was shunned, however. The notion of 'excesses' was in fact inserted to replace the label of 'war crimes', which had been present in the draft of the nota. As such, the nota helped *preserve* a broader sense of innocence. Colonial violence was the work of 'bad apples', not part of systemic violence.[23]

Still, these broad developments provided new frames of understanding and ways to see the world, and this also had an impact on human rights and the Convention more particularly. By placing the individual in the foreground, a new approach to the Convention could be adopted, focused much more than before on the individual needs it protected, rather than its promise of European integration.

[22] Ibid, p. 105.

[23] See Maurice Swirc, *De Indische Doofpot: Waarom Nederlandse Oorlogsmisdaden in Indonesië nooit zijn vervolgd* (Amsterdam: Arbeiderspers, 2022).

3.2 THE END OF EMPIRE AND THE EXPANSION OF HUMAN RIGHTS

A crucial element in the conservative outlook on the Convention was, as we have seen in Chapters 1 and 2, its relation to the concept of Empire. Indeed, the persistent 'crises of Empire' in which the European states found themselves in the late 1950s and 1960s had formed a crucial element in why states did not participate fully in the system of the Convention.[24] Only with the burden of the colonial territory (and related colonial violence) removed, were the states able to participate more freely with regard to the Convention, or so the story goes.[25] However, the Dutch case offers a perfect case study to show that the situation was less black and white. For the Netherlands, the end of empire propelled a new interest in moral values such as human rights, but at the same time, imperial distrust in the extension of human rights remained present in positions adopted in the Council of Europe.

Decolonization may seem a peculiar notion in this timeframe, as Indonesia had no longer been part of the Netherlands for some fifteen years. However, in the early 1960s, also the final remnant of the Dutch Empire in the eastern hemisphere, Western New Guinea, became independent from Dutch rule.[26] The implications were substantial. As one influential author has described it, after the 'loss' of New Guinea, the Netherlands found in human rights engagement a new niche in foreign politics, fitting with its new status of a 'small nation'.[27] Also within the rest

[24] Martin Thomas, Bob Moore and Larry Butler, *Crises of Empire: Decolonization and Europe's Imperial States* (London: Bloomsbury 2015).

[25] The case of France is most obvious in this regards: embroiled in a colonial war in Algeria (legally a part of France), there was very limited impetus to join the Convention. As for the United Kingdom, the colonial context had already offered troubles (as we have seen in Chapter 2); Madsen, *La Genese de l'Europe des droits de l'Homme*, pp. 300–308.

[26] I follow here the notion of Floribert Baudet and Peter Malcontent among others that only after the end of empire an active engagement with human rights was possible. Baudet and Malcontent, 'The Dutchman's Burden? Nederland en de internationale rechtsorde in de twintigste eeuw' in B. de Graaff, D. Hellema and B. van der Zwan (eds.), *De Nederlandse Buitenlandse Politiek in de twintigste eeuw* (Amsterdam: Boom, 2003), pp. 69–104.

[27] Alfred E. Pijpers, 'Dekolonisatie, compensatiedrang en de normalisering van de Nederlandse buitenlandse politiek' in N. C. F. van Sas (eds.), *De Kracht van Nederland. Internationale positie en Buitenlands beleid* (Haarlem: Becht, 1991), pp. 204–218.

of the Kingdom, things began to shift. When, in 1964, the right of individual complaint was extended to Suriname, the Netherlands made it possible for individuals far removed from the 'civilized' continent to complain to an international institution over violations of human rights.

3.2.1 DECOLONIZATION: NEW GUINEA AND THE TURN FROM MIGHT TO RIGHT. In order to understand the impact of decolonization on engagement with these specific European human rights, some background information is needed on the situation in Western New Guinea. Decolonization in general took on many forms, from all out colonial wars to relatively calm transfers of sovereignty, but the common denominator was the profound transformation of the European states from global empires into European nation states.[28] The Dutch case was no exception here. Although the largest Dutch colonial territory, Indonesia, had achieved independence relatively soon after the Second World War, West New Guinea had remained tied to the imperial Dutch construction. Relatively low on resources, industry, or tactical position, the Dutch nonetheless held on to this last vestige of the former eastern empire with conviction. Despite mounting pressure from Indonesia, the United States and recently independent states to provide independence of the Papuans, the Dutch held firm. New Guinea had become a symbol, signifying the Dutch grander ambitions in the world as imperial power.[29] After Indonesian independence, it was New Guinea which still allowed the Dutch to see, feel, and present themselves as a global power, its attention in foreign policy focused overseas rather than towards the European continent.

The legitimization of Dutch presence in New Guinea was the development of the population. As the argument of the Dutch government rang, the administration was there to safeguard the right to national self-determination of the Papuans. Before that right could be invoked, however, a certain level of development first had to be reached, which the Dutch were willing to help in achieving, for example, by making New

[28] Even though that distinction was obviously not immediate or clean cut: the European project can be very well seen as desire to *maintain* an imperial foothold cf. Peo Hansen and Stefan Jonsson, *Eurafrica*.

[29] Arend Lijphart, *The Trauma of Decolonization, the Dutch and West New Guinea* (New Haven: Yale University Press, 1966), p. 285.

Guinea a key focus area in the newly established development aid programme and by providing cultural sponsorships and education.[30]

The imperial leftover had implications for political and legal positions, which were in line with those of other imperial states. For one, it led to a focus on political partnerships with fellow European powers. In the Suez crisis, the Dutch had supported France and the United Kingdom over the invasion of Egypt and was equally surprised by the critique of the United States on this kind of 'imperial' policy.[31] The legal consequences were most directly seen with regard to initiatives taken at the level of the UN. With an eye on its partners and own position, the Netherlands was reluctant to take an active position on human rights related issues, for example, on the human rights covenants being drafted.[32] In particular, the right to national self-determination, indeed the very right the Dutch used to legitimize its presence in New Guinea, proved to be the main source of contention.

For national self-determination had become the leading legal claim of the decolonization movement during the late 1950s.[33] Newly independent states would aim to get national self-determination accepted as more than just a principle, which was its legal status at the time. Rather, they campaigned to enshrine it as the 'mother' of all other human rights. This meant a turn from principle to law, from promise to fact. According to these states, the human rights covenants at the UN would have to open with an acceptance of this right: in doing so, national self-determination had moved into the realm of human rights.[34] This

[30] See Vincent Kuitenbrouwer, 'Beyond the Trauma of Decolonization: Dutch Cultural Diplomacy during the West New Guinea Question, 1950–1962' *The Journal of Imperial and Commonwealth History* Vol. 44 Nr. 2 (2016), pp. 306–327.

[31] Baudet and Malcontent, 'The Dutchman's Burden?', pp. 69–104.

[32] Castermans-Holleman, *Het Nederlandse mensenrechtenbeleid in de Verenigde Naties.*

[33] Ronald Burke, *Decolonization and international human rights* (Philadelphia, University of Pennsylvania Press, 2010), pp. 35–59. For nuance on the different means self-determination could serve, that is, independence of federalist futures, see Gary Wilder, *Freedom Time: Negritude, Decolonization and the Future of the World* (Durham: Duke, 2015).

[34] The notion of Samuel Moyn that the struggle for national self-determination was not a human rights struggle holds if one sees human rights as individual rights, lifted above the structure of the state. The fact that national self-determination seeks to establish that state sits uneasy with this definition. However, the use of national self-determination in the human rights discourse, and the campaign to see it accepted *as* a human right were very real nonetheless, cf. Moyn, *The last Utopia*, pp. 116–119.

placed the Dutch in a precarious position. The Netherlands had always presented national self-determination as a principle – an important principle, perhaps, yet not a matter of international law as such. Faced with the campaign of the newly independent states, a choice had to be made. Would the Netherlands support the right of self-determination, thereby risking to antagonize its European partners but being consistent in its reasons for being in New Guinea? Or would it side with the imperial policy of keeping national self-determination a principle rather than a right, but undermining its own position in doing so?

It was Beaufort who first addressed this tension. In his capacity as a representative at the United Nations and an expert on human rights, he found it increasingly difficult to defend the Dutch (and indeed, the European) position that self-determination was not a 'right' but a principle to be granted in due time, and he experienced a 'strong sense of discomfort' in pursuing this course.[35] In his vision, continuing on this path would hurt the position of the Netherlands in the international context, where colonialism was receiving ever more criticism. Instead, the Netherlands should behave much more flexibly, and even consider accepting national self-determination as a right. Although he gathered some support for his vision, the direct implications remained minimal. In its foreign policy, the Netherlands continued to side with fellow Western partners over questions of decolonization, for example, by actively supporting Portugal, a country which evaded critique on colonialism by flat out denying that it possessed any colonies to begin with.

The lukewarm position of the Dutch changed in 1960, when Resolution 1514 was put to a vote in the General Assembly. This resolution, condemning colonialism and affirming the independence of colonial areas, enshrined the right of national self-determination as an essential component of the decolonization process. The vote put the Dutch position to the test. France and the UK would vote against the resolution, while the United States (pressured by the UK) would abstain.[36] A traditional Dutch

[35] NL-HaNA, Buitenlandse Zaken/Code-Archief 55–64, 2.05.118 inv. nr. 25719, 'report meeting on national self-determination, 19 May 1958'.

[36] Nationaal Archief, Den Haag, Nederlandse Permanente Vertegenwoordiging bij de Verenigde Naties te New York, Number Access 2.05.273, inventory number 2062, 'Code message from New York to The Hague, 12 December 1960'.

answer to this situation would have been to side with the Western European partners – the position of the 'big three' had been a lodestar for foreign policy choices ever since the end of the Second World War. However, New Guinea, and with it the embrace of national self-determination, had come to occupy such a central position in Dutch policy that any concession to this right was deemed a danger for the Netherlands' tactical position.[37] Abandoning its European partners, it voted in favour of Resolution 1514: 'because we agree with the principles it contains, which are also the principles by which we are guided in our administration of the only non-self-governing territory under our administration'.[38] Choosing to support its own empire led the Dutch not just to break with its partners, but also – and slightly paradoxically – to tie itself to the anticolonial movement and the campaigns for national self-determination as a human right.

In the meantime, the situation in New Guinea escalated quickly. Indonesia had been frustrated that the area had remained outside the transfer of sovereignty and had been claiming the area for years. Military intrusions had become commonplace and only escalated further in 1961 and 1962. The dispatchment of a Dutch warship led to an increase in the tensions, and shots were fired at Indonesian marines. It took intense pressure from the United States on the Dutch and Indonesians to reach a compromise in 1962. The Netherlands would relinquish sovereignty, and let the area pass over to the Indonesian administration, and the Papuans would then be asked in a referendum whether or not they wanted to remain with Indonesia or not.[39]

The farewell of New Guinea meant the end of the final vestige of an idealized empire. Clearly, it did not mean the end of overseas possessions. Suriname and the Antilles remained in the Kingdom, but were formally self-governing territories with a modest, but ultimately a level of

[37] NL-HaNA, PV Verenigde Naties, 2.05.273, inv. nr. 2062, 'Code message from the Hague to New York, 13 December 1960'.

[38] NL-HaNA, Buitenlandse Zaken/Code-Archief 55–64, 2.05.118, inv. nr. 25577, 'Report on GA session, 14 December 1960'.

[39] P. J. Drooglever, *Een Daad van Vrije Keuze: De Papoea's van Westelijk Nieuw Guinea en de grenzen van het Zelfbeschikkingsrecht* (Amsterdam: Boom, 2005). The referendum (or plebiscite) has remained contentious, as it took place under close Indonesian military supervision.

self-rule. The implications, however, were clear. If New Guinea allowed the Netherlands to think of itself as a moderate imperial power, now the country had definitively found itself in the ranks of smaller European states.[40] More important was the notion that this entailed, namely that the Netherlands had a new mission in foreign policy. No longer tied to its imperial legacy, the Netherlands doubled down on its previous policy concerning self-determination and human rights. The loss of New Guinea was one thing, but any additional loss of credibility was to be avoided. 'We have a moral responsibility', Luns wrote to the Dutch representative at the UN with regard to the political constellation after 1962. According to Luns, it should be clear the Dutch had been sincere in their support for the right of national self-determination and, by extension, in their support of human rights. This urge to maintain at least the moral high ground was reflected in a new policy at the UN concerning Portugal. Unlike in previous years, the Dutch now withheld their support of the Portuguese state, a NATO member, stating as a reason the incompatibility with Resolution 1514.[41]

Additionally, the loss of New Guinea opened up space for more active participation in the drafting of the human rights covenants. With the conflict over the inclusion of national self-determination out of the way, it became much easier to accept international human rights. Even the legal opinion on the covenants changed. Whereas there had previously been a strong opinion that a collective right such as national self-determination could not be accepted as a type of 'human right', Schermers, advising on the topic, now urged the government to embrace it, indeed as the start of the Declarations. As he noted: 'a political right of an individual without the connected right of collectivity is useless'.[42] With the end of empire, the road seemed free for an alternative moral programme, that of human rights: it was a turn from might to right.[43]

[40] To the horror of some, the 'same rank as Denmark!'; H. Baudet, Nederland en de rang van Denemarken. *BMGN – Low Countries Historical Review*, Vol. 90 Nr. 3 (1975), pp. 430–443.

[41] NL-HaNA, PV Verenigde Naties, 2.05.273, inv. nr. 2053, 'Instructions to the Dutch delegation, 1962'.

[42] NL-HaNA, Buitenlandse Zaken/Code-Archief 55–64, 2.05.118, inv. nr. 25719, 'Memo to DIO, 15th November 1962'.

[43] This is not the place to repeat the entire debate on the supposed character of a 'Guiding Nation' of the Netherlands, yet for a concise overview see Baudet and Malcontent,

3.2.2 EUROPEAN HUMAN RIGHTS IN THE SHADOW OF COLONIALISM. It is important, however, not to overstate the direct implications of decolonization with regard to human rights. In particular with an eye on the Convention, a more differentiated image emerges. On the one hand, the Netherlands distinctively took up a more active position in the UN, and Dutch politics began to embrace the Convention as benchmark of democratic values in other venues. For instance, when it came to association of the EEC, the requests of Spain and Portugal to that end, the Convention emerged as the benchmark against which to evaluate those requests, in particular in Dutch debates.[44]

Yet the Council of Europe was a different forum. Apart from the fact that the Convention did not contain the right to self-determination (unsurprisingly, the minority protection regime which was based on this right had not functioned too well in the interwar period), any legal links between New Guinea and the Convention had been avoided by the Dutch administration. However, decolonization and its effects did echo in the Council of Europe. There too, decolonization played a role in the orientation towards a new future, and the connection of newly independent states with the European Convention attracted attention in particular. In this forum, the Dutch approach was still one of caution and imperial thinking.

The best example of such continuity in colonial thinking can be seen in 1962, when the Consultative Assembly proposed opening up the Convention for non-member states of the Council of Europe, specifically to address the consequences of decolonization.[45] Since the Convention only applied to members of the Council of Europe – membership of which was reserved for European states – the independence of overseas territories resulted in them losing membership of the Council of Europe. By gaining independence, the (potential) protection of individuals by the Convention was therefore lost. Such had been the case in Cyprus, which

'The Dutchman's Burden?' in B. de Graaff, D. Hellema and B. van der Zwan (eds.), *De Nederlandse Buitenlandse Politiek in de twintigste eeuw*, pp. 69–104.

[44] Ronald Janse, 'The Evolution of the Political Criteria for Accession to the European Community, 1957–1973' *European Law Journal* Vol. 24 Nr. 1 (2018), pp. 57–76.

[45] NL-HaNA, Justitie/Wetgeving/Internationale Organisaties, 2.09.84, inv. nr. 173, 'Council of Europe Doc. 1418, 27th April 1962'.

only joined the Council of Europe two years after its independence, but applied more broadly now that ever more former dependencies were becoming independent states. In order to solve this issue, the Assembly requested that the Convention should be open for non-European states to join as well. This was the most extreme attempt since the plans of the 1950s to include Parliaments from overseas territories, and to turn the Convention into something more than a regional human rights instrument. Should the proposal have been taken up, it would have created a genuinely international forum for protection of individuals. However, the initiative failed, and a majority of states firmly rejected it.

In this European forum, the classical 'imperial' distrust of the new states remained an important factor. Although the benefits of this proposal were clear, as it expanded the protection for human rights, a welcome development in the absence of international rules (the Covenants of the United Nations were signed only in 1966), the downsides weighed heavier. The advice of Dutch Foreign Affairs warned of the possible consequences of extending the human rights protection, above all of the heightened instability of the supervisory mechanism it expected that this extension would result in. The inclusion of former colonies could lead to a situation where 'the Commission and the Court would be confronted in greater quantity with disputes relating to internal political struggles in the "new" states' – an undesirable situation. Moreover, it could lead to 'emotional reactions' from the unsuccessful party, which might include a government, 'Foreign Affairs reasoned'.[46]

What stood out even more was the fear that, should newly independent countries be admitted, the composition of the Commission and Court would change fundamentally. Under the rules of the Council, each state had one member in both Commission and Court. This was deemed problematic to the Dutch in light of potential extensions, as in their opinion, the experts from the new states might not be up to the standards of the functions. As the advice went:

> the members of Commission and Court have to fulfil high demands. Only when they have substantial judicial authority or rich experience will they

[46] NL-HaNA, PV Raad van Europa Straatsburg, 2.05.278, inv. nr. 1005, 'memo 13 September 1962, from the Hague to Perm Rep'.

> be able to build the necessary trust. To what extent the potential joining non-European countries could send sufficiently qualified lawyers for the work in these institutions I cannot say for sure, but doubt seems to be [...] justified.[47]

This was a reasoning reminiscent of the earlier debates on why the Convention was not extended to Suriname and the Antilles. The new states would not be 'ready' to join the international supervision mechanism on human rights. The fear that these areas would be less 'reluctant' to use the Convention or, again, more 'emotional' in fact reflected the perception that they were regarded as a mirror image of the nations of Europe, supposedly civilized and stoic.

3.2.3 EXPANDING EUROPE: THE NEW DISPOSITION OF SURINAME. Bearing in mind the resilience of imperial language in the Council of Europe, it makes it all the more remarkable that two years later, the right of individual complaint was extended to Suriname. In the 1950s, this move had been deemed unwelcome by both sides. At that time, Suriname did not want to be involved in any kind of European integration, wary of the Plan Strasbourg and fearful of the consequences that might entail for its own economy and position, whereas the Netherlands feared an unrestrained and excessive use of human rights in the Surinamese context. In 1964 this had changed. By introducing the right of individual complaint in the Surinamese legal order, the Netherlands was the first country of the Council of Europe which took the remarkable step of extending the international human rights complaint mechanism towards 'non-Europeans'.[48]

The symbolism of the move was unmistakable. For one, the 'European' protection of human rights was extended to places previously excluded from its scope, pulling these areas closer into the orbit of the European project. On the other hand, it also meant the protection of the individual had moved beyond the realm of what had previously been an exclusive, civilized group of states, leading to the question: who was worthy

[47] Ibid, 'Memo 13 September 1962'.

[48] A similar declaration had once been made by Denmark with regard to Greenland, although that was a different matter than the imperial colonial areas.

of human rights protection? From 1949 onwards the Convention had protected only the 'civilized citizens', so opening up its institutions to all persons in Suriname also entailed a subtle turn from the 'European' aspect to the 'human rights' element of the Convention.

What had changed in the discussions on the status of the Convention was Suriname's openness to European integration, as the decision to accept the right of individual petition ultimately rested in the hands of the government in Paramaribo, not in The Hague. As an autonomous part of the Kingdom of the Netherlands, Suriname could decide on a range of topics by itself, including the choice of whether or not it desired this European supervision.

The position of Suriname on the issue had consistently been dismissive. The personal convictions of Pos, the Surinamese representative in The Hague, stood out in this regard. He had expressed his opinion on the issue a number of times since the question had first come up and always advised negatively.[49] In 1957, Pos again put forward his – slightly elitist – position. 'Suriname is a country with a young democracy: it is therefore understandable that persons and groups in Suriname will have a less clear understanding of the necessary limitation of the fundamental rights and freedoms than exists in older democracies, and will be more easily inclined to see a displeasing measure as an infringement of their human rights'.[50] Still as late as 1963, Pos had let the Dutch government know there would be no reason to expect any active engagement from Suriname with regard to the Convention.[51] However, in the same year,

[49] Partly because of a journey to Paris in 1953, in which he met with several prominent French thinkers, who had warned him for the consequences of joining, Pos was wary of such a move. The fear was that Germany and Italy would produce goods cheaper and put the overseas territories out of competition. Now, was the European integration within the framework of the Council of Europe something different from the European Communities, or the European Coal and Steel Community, yet the reluctance of being involved in an all too encompassing European integration was a constant factor in the advices of Pos. NL Ha-Na, Ministerie van Koloniën, 2.10.54. inv. nr. 3340, 'Memo from direction Suriname to Minister, 9 December 1953'.

[50] The results would be, according to Pos, an influx of complaints. NL Ha-Na, Gouverneur Suriname/Kabinet, 2.10.26, inv. nr. 918, Letter of Pos to PM, 28 November 1957. It is noteworthy how Pos, himself from Suriname, used the same argumentation as the Dutch elite.

[51] NL-HaNA, Kabinet Minister-President, 2.03.01, inv. nr. 812, 'Meeting Council of Ministers for the Kingdom, 26 April 1963'.

Pos undertook a career switch and moved to Cuba to serve as ambassador, making space for Suriname to adopt a new position on the issue of European human rights protection.

With Pos elsewhere, political opinions had started to change in Suriname. Two developments in particular led to a new approach to European cooperation: the wish of Suriname to act in a more autonomous way in international affairs, and the re-evaluation of the European project. To a large extent, the two trends intertwined. When Suriname ultimately signed an association agreement with the EEC in 1964, this was celebrated as a recognition of the autonomy of the country as well.[52] What was important for Surinamese politics was the establishment of Suriname as a relatively independent actor within the Kingdom in the realm of foreign politics. By constantly voicing this desire for 'emancipation' and by taking concrete action, such as applying for associate membership of UNESCO, Suriname pressured the Netherlands for more leeway. This caused quite some discomfort in The Hague: the Statute of the Kingdom did not allow for such an 'Alleingang' and in general Surinamese initiatives in this regard were deemed problematic.[53]

In particular, 'Europe' had ceased to be a threatening concept in Paramaribo. The association with Europe and, more specifically, its accompanying European Development Fund were seen as desirable to tap into. Development, or the desire for development, had taken up a central place in Surinamese politics. Again, this tied in with the first desire, as a more developed country would have a better chance of pursuing its own independent path. It had stung that the Dutch government poured more money from the European Development Fund into New Guinea than into Suriname, and being included in the European development programme would be another way of acquiring more funds. Association with Europe had, in the minds of the Surinamese politicians, become a tool for further independence, rather than posing a threat of continued imperialism.[54]

[52] Klinkers and Oostindie, *Knellende Koninkrijksbanden*, p. 68.

[53] Ibid, pp. 63–70. See also Nationaal Archief, Den Haag, Kabinet van de Vice-Minister-President en Kabinet voor Surinaamse en Nederlands-Antilliaanse Zaken, nummer toegang 2.10.41, inventarisnummer 72, 'notes meeting 14th June 1963'.

[54] NL-HaNA, Kabinet Vice-MP/KabSNA, 2.10.41, inv. nr. 72, 'notes meeting 28th December 1959'.

The acceptance of the right of individual complaint should be seen in light of these developments. Over the years, the reasoning behind not accepting such a right was the notion that Suriname was *not* a European nation. To be controlled in any way by a mechanism of European supervision was unacceptable. With the change of heart on how European integration should be assessed, joining the Convention seemed less of a threat as well. Moreover, this was a decision coming from Suriname itself, not from The Hague, which helped in making that decision.[55]

At the same time, one should not overestimate the practical results of the decision to extend the right of individual petition. The fears of an overly zealous and emotional population flooding the Commission with cases were highly exaggerated – in fact, to the contrary, almost no attention was given to the topic. The largest legal journal in Suriname devoted not a single page to the Convention or the petition mechanism in the year after it was announced.[56] This lack of attention to the Convention was combined with a limited accessibility of information. A letter sent to the Hague provides an illustration of the situation. The local government had encountered a problem: a Surinamese lawyer had asked for a paper copy of the Convention, as the only available copy in the entirety of Paramaribo was to be found in the library of the Ministry of Justice. With none available, the Hague kindly had to be asked to provide a paper copy to distribute.[57] Such silence later led Alkema, the leading scholar on the Convention in the Netherlands, to note that no complaint had ever been filed from Suriname with the European institutions.

This was actually an exaggeration: *one* complaint had been filed. The complaint, *Cabell-Bouman against the Netherlands*, dealt with an individual

[55] See for a comparison also L. Moor and B. Simpson, 'Ghosts of Colonialism in the European Convention on Human Rights', who focus on the British example. The British Colonial Office was 'adamantly hostile' to extend the individual petition to its dependencies. The UK only accepted the jurisdiction of the Court and right of individual petition for its own island in 1966, before extending those – in rather erratic fashions to overseas territories in later years. In 1967 it extended it to a first group of dependencies, including Gibraltar and the Isle of Man (all of these were quite small, however, and none of which had the same numbers of inhabitants as Suriname).

[56] The 'SJB', or the Surinaams Juristen Blad'.

[57] NL Ha-Na, Gouverneur Suriname/Kabinet, 2.10.26, inv. nr. 918, 'Letter of 17 March 1964 to the Hague'.

who had been removed from his office as a notary in Paramaribo. Unable to appeal the decision, and after discussion with professors in Utrecht and Leiden, he petitioned first the Governor, before turning to the European Commission, alleging a violation of the Convention (without referring to specific articles). Since his complaint was filed well over the six-month time limit, however, it was deemed inadmissible.[58]

Yet such cases were absolute outliers. At the same time, this extension to Suriname, important as it was, should not be seen as a full embrace of human rights in the entire Kingdom. Despite the novelty and symbolism of the move of Suriname, the situation was different in the Antilles. Here, the local government, despite its cooperation in the association agreement with the economic Europe, was still adamantly opposed to the possibility of investigation by European human rights institutions, and it would take roughly ten more years before the step was finally taken to also include these areas in the European human rights framework. Part of the explanation lies in the difference between Suriname and the Dutch Antilles when it came to an independent foreign policy. The small islands were much less prone to articulate a strong opinion about these matters (it would be 'suicide' it was noted), and as a result, more wary of signing up to international covenants by themselves. Moreover, the financial and other potential unforeseen consequences were seen with distrust by the local government, which had limited funds to spare for international commitments on human rights issues.[59]

3.3 ENGAGING WITH THE CONVENTION

Despite its expansion overseas, in the continental Dutch context the position of the Convention remained ambivalent. There existed a small but active group of academics in the realm of international law who pushed for an appreciation of the Convention, mostly found in Leiden and Amsterdam. These places were the 'hotspots' of the movement,

[58] Historisch Documentatiecentrum voor het Nederlands Protestantisme (1800-heden) VU, W. F. De Gaay Fortman, Collectienummer 338, inv. nr. 201, 'application no 3646/68, *Cabell Bouman* v. *Netherlands*'.

[59] NL Ha-Na, Ministerie van Koloniën, 2.10.54. inv. nr. 10181, 'Letter of Willemstad to the Hague, 30th March 1953'.

not only because of the presence of a 'Europe institute' in those cities, which pushed for there to be more attention to legal developments in Europe (although primarily focused on the European Communities), but also because of the legacy of van Asbeck. He might have retired from academia, but as a judge at the ECtHR, van Asbeck kept close ties with some of his pupils. He remained in touch with H. G. Schermers at the Ministry of Foreign Affairs when the Court set out its proposals for a more dynamic Convention, yet also after the failure of these initiatives, van Asbeck remained connected to the Leiden circle, actively pushing for them to pay more attention to the Court.

As such, the late 1960s stand out in particular as the time of the beginning, if scattered, study of the topic of human rights. For one, this had to do with the increase of attention to the topic in international law more generally. In 1966, international law had become a mandatory course in Groningen and Rotterdam and then at both universities in Amsterdam a year later. The growing importance of European law, at the time still a variety of international law, was put forward as one of the reasons for the move, alongside the more general notion of the existence of the Convention.[60] One major advance in bringing 'human rights' into the academic discipline was the step the University of Amsterdam took in 1967 when it instituted a special chair in 'human rights'. The lectorate was given to Theo van Boven, who had recently finished his dissertation on human rights and had swiftly established himself as one of the leading experts in this field. Combined with a number of detailed works and dissertations appearing on the topic, very small steps were taken towards establishing human rights as distinct scientific topics.[61] In a move which would slowly take it out of the confines of international law, the study of human rights as a set of autonomous topics of law paved the way for

[60] L. Erades, 'De Proeve 1966 en de artikelen 60-67 van de Grondwet', *NJB* nr. 26 (1966), pp. 603–610, 609.

[61] Apart from the work of Alkema in Leiden, 1968 also saw the emergence of a lengthy dissertation on 'The European Convention and Dutch Law' by D. H. M. Meuwissen, which was one of the first books on the topic. D. H. M. Meuwissen, *De Europese Conventie en het Nederlandse Recht* (Amsterdam, 1968). Also, beyond the legal realm, they gained interest, however. In political sciences, a young Peter Baehr swiftly found his niche in 'human rights', following the earlier interest of his mentor Tammes.

inclusion in a wide variety of legal settings.[62] Although van Boven mostly focused on the UN and the role of human rights in the truly international setting, his position at the University of Amsterdam was a first step in the broader 'scientification' of human rights as a topic of study.

Out of these academic groups emerged a network of individuals who stayed in close contact with each other. The network included Schermers, who, after serving at the Ministry of Foreign Affairs on the issue of fundamental rights, became a professor at the University of Amsterdam in 1963 and established himself as a leading academic on European legal integration. Then there was Prof. H. F. van Panhuys, who had taken over the chair in international law in Leiden from his former promoter van Asbeck, and Evert Alkema, a young academic who was brought into the Europe Institute in Leiden in 1966. There, as a novice in the area, Alkema had to deal with the 'leftovers' his colleagues did not have time for or interest in, meaning human rights.[63] By studying these leftovers, Alkema took a specific interest in the Convention and would establish himself as the first legal expert *specifically* working on the Convention, whereas another former student of van Asbeck, Menno van Emde Boas, was also based in Leiden before joining the Council of Europe at the directorate on human rights. In Utrecht, the young professor Jos Kapteyn, a former PhD candidate under van Asbeck, also developed a keen interest in the law of the European communities and did some research on the Convention on the side. It was a small, but dedicated group. A modest network was thus being set up of academics publishing on case law of the Commission and urging colleagues to see the Convention's potential. It was this new input in academia which sought to solve one of the more structural issues concerning the use of European human rights in the Netherlands: the lack of practical information about the Convention.

[62] Compare the slogan of Cassin in 1970: 'we need to establish human rights as a science', quoted in Henette Vauchez, 'the ECHR and the Birth of (European) Human Rights Law as an Academic Discipline' in Antoine Vauchez and Bruno de Witte (eds.), *Lawyering Europe: European Law as a Transnational Social Field* (Oxford: Oxford University Press, 2013), pp. 117–137.

[63] See also the analysis of Van Rossum, 'The roots of Dutch strategic human rights litigation', pp. 387–399, 392.

Their publications were supported by the activist lawyer J. H (Jacq) Smeets, who supported the plaintiffs in some of the very first complaints against the Netherlands.[64] Smeets in these years was almost synonymous with the legal engagement with the Convention. For years, he had been more or less the sole lawyer invoking the Convention, with the result it had even begun to be dubbed the 'Smeets Treaty'. Smeets himself was accused of not having enough 'respect' for the Convention, as he referred to it so often.[65] Although he was a pioneer in the field, it did not help the Convention's reputation that Smeets was also the lawyer for more activist members of society, such as Trotskyist arms smugglers into Algeria, Portuguese deserters who did not want to fight in Angola, or the so-called 'provo's', a youthful Amsterdam anarchist counter-culture group.[66] As such, he was regarded with slight suspicion by the rest of the Bar, who accused him of 'building castles in the sky' by invoking the treaty.[67] The somewhat fringe character of these cases also reflected on the Convention: if the only lawyer consistently using European human rights was one also defending weapon smugglers, it was best to stay clear of such a tool if one wished to retain a 'respectable' reputation.

All in all, it was a very small group indeed. This was also one of the main barriers to wider usage of the Convention, as it entailed that knowledge on its system was scarce. In 1961, when the yearly meeting of international lawyers focused on the Convention as its theme and expanded upon the potential of the document for the Dutch legal order, this discussion remained confined to the realm of the – more academic – international lawyers. For the ordinary lawyer, the Convention offered little of added value. When later that year, a complaint was uttered by a lawyer about the limited availability of the text of the Convention, it illustrated the broader problem. The Convention had only been published in the official 'Tractatenblad' of 1951 'which had been long sold out'. Although at the request of Parliamentarians a small booklet had been

[64] Smeets supported the American C. W. Wallace when he filed a complaint, in 1963. *C.W. Wallace v Netherlands*, 1983/63. See also HR-13-09-1963, ECLI:NL:HR:1963:16, *NJ* 1964/389.

[65] Wera de Lange, 'Jacq Smeets, Advocaat', *De Waarheid* (02-05-1984).

[66] 'Jacq Smeets', *De Waarheid*.

[67] Leiden, 19 September 2019, Interview Alkema.

printed, this 'did not contain the original texts' and was, according to the lawyer, a rather sloppy effort which contained pagination mistakes.[68]

The improvement of basic availability of the Convention, or indeed simply raising awareness of the – potential – role of the Convention, would be the focus point of this group of academics. Nearly all mentions of the ECHR in the largest legal journal of the Netherlands, the Nederlands Juristenblad, reflected the belief that the Convention had the 'potential' to become a highly important text.[69] However, with the number of cases reaching the Commission, European Court, or even national judges remaining very limited, this was a message which increasingly lost credibility. Still, the same spirit of letting the Convention live up to its potential animated Schermers, and he published a small book containing the text of the Convention with one commentary per article.[70] The book contained the Dutch, French, and English texts as well as the European social charter. Relatively limited in terms of analysis, the book was truly meant as a 'first meeting' for Dutch lawyers with the Convention. The introduction written by van Asbeck was illustrative of the aim of the booklet. As he emphasized the possibilities the Convention offered and pushed for an interpretation and use of the document, he hoped to elevate the text above its status as part of a cabinet of legal curiosities: this was a 'cri de coeur' for relevance.

However, these activist notions were up against some tough opposition. For one, the 'activist' interpretations of the great potential of the Convention were not shared by other key players. Other scholars such as Beaufort and Riphagen put forward a much more classical image. Both had been involved in drafting the Convention and wrote their analyses accordingly. Beaufort in particular was an insider to the system, and even though he had pushed for the acceptance of the right of individual petition, he very much subscribed to the way the Convention had been set up. To Beaufort, it needed to be and remain a diplomatically cautious system with a lot of room for states. Still in 1965, when the right of individual

[68] J. H. Van Wjk, 'Een uitgave van het verdrag van Rome noodzakelijk' *NJB* Nr. 14, (1961), p. 310.

[69] Based on a survey of references to or articles devoted to the ECHR in the NJB.

[70] H. G. Schermers, *Het Europese Verdrag tot Bescherming van de Rechten van de Mens en de Fundamentele Vrijheden* (Zwolle: Tjeenk Willink, 1964).

petition had already been granted for five years, Beaufort had strongly defended the diplomatic and reluctant stance of the Commission against allegations from a colleague parliamentarian that the entire process of human rights protection was being 'hidden and inaccessible' by noting this cautious step-by-step approach was *precisely* where the strength of the system lay.[71]

3.3.1 A DOCUMENT OF LITTLE LEGAL VALUE. When it came to the domestic usage of the Convention, claims of its great potential were difficult to maintain in a consistently dismissive legal order. The Hoge Raad continued to follow a restrictive approach in its application of the Convention. Even after the Procession saga, there were attempts to use the Convention in strategic ways. It seemed for a while the Convention offered broadcasters a reasonable chance to circumvent national rules concerning television broadcasting in the Netherlands, for instance. This was a highly regulated affair by the government, and timeslots were distributed among the 'pillars' in society: the Catholics had their own slots and programmes, and the same for the Protestants. What mattered greatly in this context was that the Convention, as far as the freedom of expression went, seemed to offer a broader protection of fundamental rights than the national Constitution.[72]

But also despite the potential of the case to open the Dutch legal order for review against the Convention, the Hoge Raad kept the door firmly shut. It did not even get to making a review based on substance: 'since weekly radio programmes were not information which everyone had the right to receive or impart within the meaning of article 10', they ruled that there was no violation of Article 10 whatsoever.[73] Again, the decision

[71] Nationaal Archief, Den Haag, Ministerie van Buitenlandse Zaken: Code-archief 1965–1974, nummer toegang 2.05.313, inventarisnummer 4279, '"Enerzijds Anderzijds", *Nieuw Europa*, March 1965'.

[72] Both in wording (opinions and ideas in the Convention versus 'thoughts and feelings' in the Constitution) and in substance (the Convention also accepted the notion of *receiving* information and ideas, whereas the Constitution remained silent on this topic). Article 10 ECHR, article 7 Grondwet.

[73] Ibid. This was arguably less straightforward then the Court stated. When Televizier took the case to the Commission of Human Rights, and the complaint was declared admissible, this was an indication of the difficulty of the case. See also Th. J. Vondraek, 'The

in a high-profile case in which the Convention was invoked was underwhelming for those who championed its potential. In that sense, the case confirmed the belief that despite the pleas of the small group of scholars, the Convention indeed did not have much value in the domestic legal system.

It was not surprising, therefore, when in 1968, on the invocation of Article 6 of the Convention, an Advocate General at the Hoge Raad would note that 'the article apparently is aimed at legal systems in which, unlike in the Netherlands, the rights of the suspect are not properly guaranteed'.[74] With the Hoge Raad as reluctant as it was, the appeal of the academics seemed destined to fall flat. All this led one commentator to note with regret that the Convention was reminiscent of 'das Mädchen mit dem die Kindern nicht verkehren durften'. It might be known in certain circles, but popular? Very much to the contrary.[75]

Illustrative of the limited status of human rights more generally was the Dutch experience when the 'International Human Rights Year' was proclaimed in 1968.[76] The formalities and festivities were taken up by the Ministry of Culture with close ties to the academic world, with the 'coordination committee' of the year in the hands of the Europe Institute in Amsterdam. Schermers himself had taken up the secretariat, and was joined in the organization by colleagues such as van Boven. Yet although active, these early academics were also still a minority in their line of thought. When a proposal was sent to the Ministry for a series of lectures on how the Netherlands dealt with its obligations regarding equal pay for men and women, the civil servant in place dismissed the plans as 'left-wing forced propaganda'.[77] Another proposal, to organize a conference on conflicts between the Dutch legal order and international human rights law, was shut down, as it was deemed impossible by the

Netherlands-The Televizier Case: Two Conflicting Concepts of Freedom' *The American Journal of Comparative Law* Vol. 15 Nr. 3 (1966), pp. 537–546.

74 Quoted in Kuitenbrouwer, *NRC*, 10 February 1975.

75 J. H. Smeets, 'de proeve van een nieuwe Grondwet en de grondrechten' *NJB* Nr. 18, (1967), pp. 478–479.

76 Although the year was an initiative of UNESCO, the Council of Europe swiftly joined in order to promote the Convention.

77 NL-HaNA, CRM, 2.27.19, inv. nr 1985, 'Notes 3 January 1968'.

relevant committee to find enough incompatibilities between Dutch law and international human rights standards to spend an entire day on.[78]

The limited engagement with the Convention ran throughout society. Despite the tiny groups of academics and the odd individual lawyer, it is important to note that the limited scale of attention for human rights in the early 1960s was also the case in (civil) society at large, which did not use the term too often, or too successfully. One of the best examples in this regard is the fate of the Dutch section of Amnesty International. With the later success of NGOs like Amnesty or Human Rights Watch, it is easy to forget in hindsight the troubles Amnesty had in its infant years: for instance, the Dutch national section struggled enormously with its organizational set-up and had trouble attracting broad resonance.[79]

Although Amnesty was one of the first groups in the Netherlands to focus *exclusively* on human rights,[80] it remained a tiny group composed of high-profile individuals but without any proper impact. After struggling for two years with administrative overload, little revenue, and lack of attention from the public, the organization got dissolved in 1964. Clearly, organizational matters had made things worse, but the fate of the early years of Amnesty also serves as an illustration of the limited appeal that the language of human rights had in civil society in the early 1960s. It would take another four years until Amnesty was re-established in the Netherlands in 1968, but this time as a completely different organization focusing on shared membership and inclusive action. This 'second' Amnesty would turn out to become one of the most successful NGOs of all time in the Netherlands, precisely because it differed so significantly from its previous iteration, with a new character which only emerged after the distinct failure of the predecessor organisation.

78 Nationaal Archief, Den Haag, Ministerie van Cultuur, Recreatie en Maatschappelijk Werk, nummer toegang 2.27.19, inventarisnummer 1985, 'Notes meeting 8 March 1968'.

79 Bastiaan Bouwman, 'Outraged, yet moderate and impartial: The rise of Amnesty International in the Netherlands in the 1960's and 1970's' *BMGN-Low Countries Historical Review* Vol. 132 Nr. 4 (2017), pp. 53–74.

80 The Dutch section of that other major international organization of the time, the International Commission of Jurists (the Genootschap voor de Rechtstaat) was, although concerned with the rule of law, not focused on human rights as such.

3.3.2 DIPLOMATS, NOT JUDGES: THE EUROPEAN SPHERE IN PRACTICE. The minor significance of human rights was also reflected in the actual use of the European legal route to claim these rights. Despite the extension of the Convention, the number of (successful) complaints was very small. Although the microcosm in Strasbourg congratulated itself on being a moral example to the world (as the Convention was taken as a source of inspiration for the Nigerian constitution in 1960, and the Latin American system of human rights protection also looked to the European example, which was celebrated as a big success), in practice the Convention formed a moral example in which only *two* cases had been judged before its flagship institution, the European Court of Human Rights.[81]

As we have seen, this was due in part to a conscious effort of the Commission to set up a non-threatening system. However, two additional observations should be made here. First, some very practical reasons were of direct relevance to the practice of filing complaints: the Commission's secretariat was small and in the process of being set up, resulting in some troubles when dealing with complaints that arrived in languages other than English or French. Since not all plaintiffs (or their lawyers) were bilingual, the interaction of individuals with the European system was constrained.[82] Second, the political character of the Commission was also not necessarily the result of a desire for authority or legitimacy: it also flowed from a different understanding of how the Convention was supposed to function.

One example of an experience of one Dutch plaintiff in the early 1960s can shed some light on the first aspect. After sending his complaint to the secretariat, the plaintiff received his files back, with the remark that the application had to be worded in either English or French. In practice, this would mean that either a translation bureau had to be hired, or the person who filed a complaint would have to know one of

[81] Something someone like Vasak noted with no small amount of pride: Karel Vasak, 'The European Convention of Human Rights beyond the Frontiers of Europe' *The International and Comparative Law Quarterly* Vol. 12 Nr. 4 (1963), pp. 1206–1231.

[82] All the more since both the UK and France had not accepted the right of individual complaint at that time, resulting in the situation where the preferred languages of the Secretariat were not spoken by any potential plaintiffs.

these languages and do the work him/herself.[83] The plaintiff, being a persistent person,[84] created some commotion about this response and contacted the Ministry of Foreign Affairs, writing to see if there was a solution 'in order for also the poorest and most insignificant fellow human being to be able to receive his human rights'.[85]

Although this might have been a somewhat poetic petition, the problem was very real. Legally speaking, the situation was flexible. On the one hand, there was no hard requirement to provide an entire document in French or English and it was possible to present a complaint in another language, should the individual desire to do so. However, as Schermers noted in his analysis of the situation, 'a translation of some kind will have to be necessary, which the plaintiff has to provide for'.[86] Now even though there was some financial aid available from the secretariat for necessary translations, this remained a barrier to the practical accessibility for individuals. Conversations with Beaufort and McNulty, the head of the secretariat, provided some further information. Both were of the opinion it should be possible to file complaints in Dutch in order to provide the best possible access; however, there was one problem, namely that 'the DG for human rights does not entail any Dutch speaking civil servants – although there is a vacancy'.[87]

Since the secretariat received many letters, and it was not sure whether they contained complaints or requests for information, any letters received in a language which was unknown to the employees were

[83] NL-HaNA, Buitenlandse Zaken/Code-Archief 55–64, 2.05.118, inv. nr. 25057, 'letter to Ministry of Foreign Affairs, 31 October 1961'.

[84] The plaintiff, Alexander Mertens, was quite well known in legal circles at the time: he was the subject of a famous judgement of the Hoge Raad in which it was ruled that 'electricity' could be seen as a 'good' after he was convicted of theft in a groundbreaking case on the meaning of 'any good', a case which is still considered an absolute classic in Dutch criminal law. After that case, he had acquired a criminal record, of which the information had been spread by the Dutch state after the Second World War. This policy of sharing publicly his criminal record was the subject of his complaint to Strasbourg.

[85] NL-HaNA, Buitenlandse Zaken/Code-Archief 55–64, 2.05.118, inv. nr. 25057, 'letter to Ministry of Foreign Affairs, 31 October 1961'.

[86] Ibid.

[87] NL-HaNA, Buitenlandse Zaken/Code-Archief 55–64, 2.05.118, inv. nr. 25057, 'Memo 19 March 1962'.

promptly returned to their senders.[88] This situation would continue provoking confusion for some time: it would take until 1971 (when, to be clear, the aforementioned vacancy had been filled for quite some time) for a procedure to be completed fully in Dutch by a plaintiff.[89]

As for the second point, the political character of the Commission, this was already a hot topic at the time. With its restrictive policy, the Commission invited criticism from the more activist members of the Council of Europe. The progressive Dutch Catholic senator, Willem Siegmann, had expressed his concern about the Commission in the Consultative Assembly, accusing it of being more a 'guarantee for the rights of states rather than for the rights of the individual human being'.[90] For Siegmann, it was clear that for most of the members of the Commission, being 'diplomats, no judges', the route of the political Committee of Ministers was more appealing than taking a case to the Court. To make matters worse, since the entire process played out behind closed doors, it was impossible to properly check the procedure. The result? 'A ghost Court, vegetating, inactive and without work'.[91]

Siegmann's critique struck a nerve with his fellow Catholic senator, Père Beaufort, who defended the course pursued by the Commission. Beaufort did not dispute the critique that the Commission was 'political', but he did set out the reasons behind this. The task of the Commission was conciliatory in nature: this required a gentle touch without the openness usually required in Court cases. In fact, *precisely* in order to better protect the individual, it was most useful to take a closed and diplomatic approach aimed at states in order to stop possible violations in an inconspicuous way. This was also the reason Beaufort trusted that the number of successful complaints, even though it could probably go up somewhat, would never reach a 'high number'.[92]

[88] Ibid. It is unclear how many applications were sent back in this way.

[89] NL-HaNA, PV Raad van Europa Straatsburg, 2.05.278, inv. nr. 917, 'Memo from Perm. Repr. to the Hague, 25th August 1971'.

[90] NL-HaNA, Buza/Code-archief 1965–1974, 2.05.313, inv. nr.4279, 'Enerzijds Anderzijds', *Nieuw Europa*, (March 1965).

[91] Ibid.

[92] Beaufort added on a personal note: 'Fortunately!'

Beaufort's answer to the critique of Siegmann is illuminating in understanding the practice of the Commission. Whereas Siegmann pushed for a much more active interpretation of the Convention by calling for the curtailing of the political route of the Committee of Ministers in favour of the Court, Beaufort was wary of bothering states with expansive legal procedures. But his motivation for pursuing this restrictive course was not only to 'build authority' or establish the legitimacy of the Commission: it was a deeply felt belief that such a course was also the *better* way to deal with the system. To Beaufort, it was clear the system was a distinctive compromise, which was there to be safeguarded.

Over the years, this reluctance and cautionary approach had also been the position of the Dutch government. When Beaufort passed away, on 9 June 1965, opening a vacancy for a new member of the Commission, the choice for a replacement was made for continuity. Much like Beaufort, an individual was chosen who was just as much a politician as a lawyer. The Protestant W. F. De Gaay Fortman combined jobs as professor of civil law, rector of the Free University, and member of the Senate for the 'Anti Revolutionary Party'.[93] Choosing De Gaay Fortman was above all a move for continuity: the Commission was again filled by an individual well connected both to the political leadership in the domestic context as to the legal profession. A moderate, both in politics as well as in his legal opinions, De Gaay Fortman was not expected to revolutionize the human rights policy of the Commission.[94]

3.3.3 AN IDLE COURT SHAPED UNDER BELGIAN PRESSURZE.

As a result of the restrictive policy of the Commission, the years from 1962 to 1965 had been idle for the Court. No cases had been referred by the Commission (much to the frustration of the judges and van Asbeck) and the initiatives deployed had not resulted in any tangible reforms. It was the tragedy of van Asbeck, who was deeply engaged in these attempts and had hoped to see the Court become a true supreme

[93] See also A. Buyse, 'Portret van W. F. De Gaay Fortman' in Asbeck' in Lawson and Myjer (eds.), *50 Jaar EVRM*, pp. 495–501.

[94] De Gaay Fortman fits, again, neatly in the 'legal diplomacy' framework of Madsen. Mikael Rask Madsen, 'the protracted institutionalization'.

European Court, that he never experienced a single case on the bench. Even so, in 1965, one of the most high-profile and sensitive cases the Commission had to deal with was referred to the Court: the Belgian Linguistic case.[95]

The case formed an important moment in the trajectory of the Convention. It dealt with a highly political salient topic: the Belgian language regime, which formed (and forms) a core issue of Belgian national identity and is central in the sensitive relations between the different language groups in the country. The Belgian government believed this was an internal domestic issue, and as the case progressed, fears about the future of the Conventional system turned out to be very real. It would become a test case for the acceptance of both the Convention as well as the Court.[96] The *Belgian Linguistic Case* was only the third case which came before the Court, but it evoked furious reactions in Belgium. More than once during this time, Belgium threatened to retreat from the Convention, or refrain from extending the period in which it accepted the jurisdiction of the Court.

As the case inched towards its hearing at the Court, it started to make an impact on Dutch policy with regard to Strasbourg. Above all, the case's influence was felt in the election of a new judge for the European Court. After van Asbeck resigned from the bench in May 1966 for health reasons, the question was, who would take up the blue robes in his place? It was a matter of replacement, as the new judge would take over his position and fulfil van Asbeck's term. In light of the Linguistic case, the Belgian government had asked the Netherlands to make haste in sending its selection. In October of that year, the Court would convene to begin with the case. With an eye to the close relation between Belgium and the Netherlands and the simple fact that the Dutch judge would speak Dutch (a language which, according to the Belgian government, had to be protected in the Linguistic case), a swift replacement of the Dutch

95 After learning of the referral of this case by the Commission van Asbeck seems to have been relieved and urged some restraint in the terminology of further proposals by the Court to increase the number of cases before it. See H. G. Schermers 'Portret van F. M. Baron van Asbeck' in R. A. Lawson and E. Myjer (eds.), *50 Jaar EVRM*, pp. 535–538, 538.

96 For a close read, see Bates, *The Evolution of the European Convention*, pp. 225–239.

judge would be highly appreciated.[97] After all, as the Belgian Permanent Representative noted, 'it seems necessary to have a Dutch judge in the Court [...] even more so because Professor Cassin, the President of the Court, has the French nationality'.[98]

In choosing the next Dutch judge, the question emerged whether a diplomat or a judge should sit on the bench. The more political option was proposed by the Ministry of Foreign Affairs, influenced in its stance by the Belgium pressure, whereas the more 'legal' option was the choice put forward by the Ministry of Justice. In making its first selection and spurred on by the Belgium demand for a swift choice, the Ministry of Foreign Affairs proposed a former Minister of Justice, Ynso Scholten.[99] Although a lawyer by profession, he had no specific expertise on the Convention and lacked firm academic standing. However, he was closely connected to the political realm and had already expressed his interest in the position.

The Ministry of Justice put out an alternative option, however. Scholten was switched in favour of a member of the Dutch 'Hoge Raad', Gerard Wiarda.[100] Wiarda, according to the Minister of Justice, Ivo Samkalden, was a man of impeccable legal qualities, with some international experience and wide knowledge on questions of administrative law.[101] Any objections to the 'double hat' Wiarda might have, being part of both the Hoge Raad as well as the European Court, were unnecessary, as for example, the French Judge Cassin was also a member of the French Conseil d'Etat.[102]

A quick comparison between Wiarda and Scholten made clear that, as a matter of legal expertise, Wiarda was by far the more experienced candidate. He had been a judge and enjoyed a significant prestige as a professional and sharp legal mind. Scholten, on the other hand, had the

[97] NL-HaNA, Buza/Code-archief 1965–1974, 2.05.313, inv. nr. 22910, 'Memo from Secretary General Foreign Affairs, 21 June 1966'.

[98] NL-HaNA, Buza/Code-archief 1965–1974, 2.05.313, inv. nr. 22910, 'Memo from Belgian Perm. Rep. to Belgian Ministry of Foreign Affairs, 12 May 1966'.

[99] Ibid, 'Memo JURA, 1 June 1966'.

[100] Id NL-HaNA, Buza/Code-archief 1965–1974, 2.05.313, inv. nr. 22910, 'Memo of Ministry of Justice to Foreign Affairs, 22 July 1966'.

[101] See also G. J. W. Steenhoff and R. J. Q. Klomp, *G.J. Wiarda: Schets van Leven en Werk* (Utrecht: G. J. Wiarda Instituut, 1998).

[102] Ibid.

political experience, a trait which at this stage was almost equally important in Strasbourg.

In the choice between the two, the Belgian case emerged as a decisive factor. Speaking in favour of Scholten, the Ministry of Foreign Affairs made the link explicit by noting that this was 'Without a doubt, the most important case the Court has had before it and it would seem therefore, also with regard to Belgium, desirable to present a candidate who holds authority also outside the field of legal expertise'.[103] Moreover, if the Belgian government will be on the losing side, this will be not taken lightly. 'Only the prestige of the judges will protect the governments of the states of which the judges decided contra the Belgian government from the ire of the Belgium government and prevent the latter from rejecting the Convention altogether'.[104]

But to Minister Luns, it was precisely the political aspect of Scholten which made the matter more contentious for him: 'It would not seem practical should the Netherlands expose itself more than necessary in the Belgian Language case'.[105] In this context, the professional expertise of Wiarda was more desirable than the purely political preference for Scholten. The choice of the judge hence was a deeply political affair, and if the judge was perceived as having a close connection to the national administration, this could well backfire. Wiarda then became first choice, also based on the desire to minimize political exposure. His legal credentials, and therefore 'neutral' expertise, could help minimize critique should a decision be taken which went against political preference.

Although the election of judges is always an inherently political process, the choice between Scholten and Wiarda was also about something more than just simple preferences. The political character of Scholten ultimately worked against him: when faced with political pressure, it was precisely the judge's legal qualities which were valued and perceived to hold the least downsides in the potentially explosive context of the

[103] NL-HaNA, Buza/Code-archief 1965–1974, 2.05.313, inv. nr. 22910, 'Memo Justice to Minister, 29 July 1966'.

[104] NL-HaNA, Buza/Code-archief 1965–1974, 2.05.313, inv. nr. 22910, 'Memo from JURA to SG, 30 August 1966'.

[105] Ibid.

Belgian sensitivities. The choice of Wiarda ultimately prioritized legal expertise over political expediency, and entailed the choice of a judge over a diplomat. The implications of this would be felt years later, when Wiarda started to bring back the legal insights gained at the European level into the domestic context.

3.4 TURNING HUMAN RIGHTS INTO SHARED CONCERNS: THE IMPACT OF THE GREEK CASE

Amidst the turmoil of the Belgian Linguistic Case, the system of European human rights protection was rattled by another key moment in the transformation the Convention went through in the late 1960s.[106] In 1967, when a military coup d'état overthrew the government in Athens, Greece became a focal point for transnational human rights activism.[107] As it tied into the structural shifts in society, solidarity with Greece became a cause which brought together people from various political backgrounds in support of a new creed: 'human rights'. Moreover, it would lead to a shift in governmental position: from a document which was shunned, the Dutch government would file an interstate complaint against Greece for violating the Convention, heralding a new beginning of governmental engagement with European human rights.

[106] Ed Bates has argued the case can be seen as a shift in the course of the Convention. In his view, the result of the complaints was a disillusion in the capability of the Council of Europe to prevent a country in slipping into dictatorship. The 'collective pact against totalitarianism', which was the 'original promise' of the Convention had proved to be insufficient. Consequently, this led to the gradual abandonment of this idea in favour of a different course focused on the protection of the individual. However, the idea of the Council of Europe being able to prevent the return of totalitarianism had always been doubted, well before the Greek case took place. The Greek case was no watershed in this regard. Rather, the two ideas went hand in hand: the protection of individuals required a democratic government. Moreover, the reactions to the Greek departure of the Council were not at all overtly negative: especially in the Scandinavian countries, this was greeted as a success rather than a failure. The exclusion of a dictatorship from an international organization was a sign the Convention had in fact functioned properly. Bates, *The Evolution of the European Convention on Human Rights*, pp. 270–271.

[107] Barbara Keys, 'Anti-Torture Politics: Amnesty International, the Greek Junta, and the Origins of the Human Rights "Boom" in the United States' in Akira Iriye, Petra Goedde and William Hitchcock (eds.), *The Human Rights Revolution: An International History* (Oxford: Oxford University Press, 2012), pp. 201–214, 205.

Instigated by domestic pressure, for the first time the Dutch government used the Convention to criticize a fellow European state. With the case progressing to a final climax, where Greece dramatically left the Council of Europe altogether, its consequences were substantial. It brought human rights into the picture, closing down certain options with regard to the Convention but also opening up windows of opportunity at the domestic level at the same time. By invoking human rights in a foreign policy setting, the Netherlands not only tied itself to these standards but also propagated interest in the Convention back home. In itself, this was a clear break with the past. Traditionally, the Ministry of Foreign Affairs had been highly reluctant to criticize other states for their political actions, least of all in relation to the notion of human rights.[108] Confronted with the situation in Greece, however, the government not just expressed concern, but it took direct steps to confront the dictatorial regime in Athens.[109]

3.4.1 TOWARDS A COMPLAINT: THE EXTERNALIZATION OF INTERNAL POLITICS. There was a remarkable component about the interstate complaint procedure against Greece: for the first time, a European state found itself confronted with an interstate complaint under the Convention over how it was treating its own citizens. Previous interstate complaints had always related to more or less competing claims of citizenship and territory: Greece had challenged the UK over the situation in Cyprus, while Austria and Italy had their own troubles in South Tirol. Yet this time, a complaint had been filed by three Scandinavian countries (Denmark, Norway and Sweden) and by the Netherlands, dealing with a situation at completely the other side of Europe. As such, this was already peculiar. Greece was a NATO member and was considered a partner in the Cold War. Even though the Détente

[108] For a still very complete overview, see M. Kuitenbrouwer and M. Leenders (eds.), *Geschiedenis van de mensenrechten: bouwstenen voor een interdisciplinaire benadering* (Hilversum: Verloren, 1996).

[109] In turn, it heralded a new beginning for human rights engagement, flowing from the 'Boomerang effect' of invoking human rights in international settings. M. E. Keck and K. Sikkink, *Activists beyond Borders: Advocacy Networks in International Politics* (New York: Cornell University Press, 1998), p. 13.

had opened up space for a less rigid view of the West-East division, criticizing an ally remained a delicate matter.[110]

Indeed, the first response of the Dutch government was to do nothing. In particular, the Minister of Foreign Affairs, Joseph Luns wasn't keen on fracturing western unity.[111] However, by 1967 circumstances had changed. 'Solidarity' became a buzzword and seeped into politics as well. For one, people were genuinely shocked at the news of the coup in Greece, but they also were spurred into action. Greece was one of the first focus point for a broader 'solidarity movement' which had sprouted up all over Europe. In the new era of public engagement, the responses to the coup saw a blooming of committees, marches, and demonstrations, mostly supported by student associations, declaring the junta as 'fascists' who placed their political opponents in concentration camps.[112]

As protests over the coup arose in the Netherlands, one particular committee stood out in this regard, namely the 'Comité Vrij Griekenland'. In principle, a solidarity committee was nothing new. The so-called 'country committees' which aimed to keep attention focused on the situation in specific foreign states, had existed before.[113] What was new, however, was the composition of this specific group. For one, it possessed political weight, with politicians from the left and right joining in. It also involved academics with a special interest in the topic of human rights.[114] Peter Baehr, a political scientist who would later become one of the leading voices on human rights in the Netherlands, participated, as well as the

[110] Kim Christiaens, 'Communists are no Beasts: European Solidarity Campaigns on Behalf of Democracy and Human Rights in Greece and East-West Détente in the 1960s and Early 1970s' *Contemporary European History* Vol. 26 Nr. 4 (2017), pp. 621–646.

[111] N. Aukes, *Nederland en het Griekse Kolonelsregime* (Leiden: Instituut voor Internationale Studiën, 1984), p. 12.

[112] Collectie Comite Vrij Griekenland, International Institute for Social History, ARCH00314, nr. 1. 'cartoons'.

[113] As for instance the 'Algeria Committee', protesting the violence committed by the French state.

[114] At least Baehr and Kooijmans had consciously experienced the War: Baehr even had to go into hiding. Later on they would note how this formed their later involvement in themes relating to justice (something similar can be said of Van der Stoel). See the lecture Baehr delivered as head of Amnesty on the 4th of May (IISG Archives), Nico Schrijver, 'A Portrait of Judge P. H. Kooijmans' *Leiden Journal of International Law* Vol. 27 Nr. 4 (2014), pp. 839–858.

later diplomat and judge Pieter Kooijmans, and the young professor in International law, Jos Kapteyn. The engaged lawyer J. H. Smeets acted as secretary and a contact person to more radical protest groups. From the lawyers in the group came: to file an interstate complaint under the Convention.[115]

The lobby of the Comité was swiftly translated into parliamentary action, helped by the parliamentarians involved. The left wing in Parliament proved most susceptible to the pressure, with the Labour party in particular being open to input. This party had, under the leadership of Joop den Uyl, shifted distinctively to a more 'activist' left direction and used its position in opposition to voice this activism.[116] It was Labour parliamentarian Max van der Stoel in particular who kept the pressure on the government. After filing a motion asking that the government, should the Greek situation not improve, would file an interstate complaint, the parliamentary majority threw their support behind this action and continued to do so in subsequent motions. In light of such constant parliamentary pressure, Luns was forced to reconsider his original position.

What had changed the situation was that, in the meantime, the Scandinavian countries (Denmark, Norway and Sweden) had filed a formal complaint. This ensured the Netherlands was not alone in filing a complaint, and made Luns opt for joining in the procedure, despite protests from the Ministers of Economic Affairs and Agriculture, who feared it would hurt trade incomes. It is important to note the discrepancies between the mood in Parliament, shaped by concern for Greece, and the disposition of the government. The decision to file the complaint was not based on altruism, but on pressure from Parliament. As was explained to the Permanent Representation in Strasbourg, the action was pursuing two aims. First, by turning the issue over to the Commission on Human Rights, the government would have its hands free in relation to additional claims of parliament. In addition, the lengthy period of investigation would provide the Greek government ample opportunity

[115] See also Aukes, *Nederland en het Griekse Kolonelsregime*, p. 32.

[116] Although the parliamentary pressure was supported by the Catholics and liberals as well.

to prepare for a return to parliamentary democracy: the step would safeguard some peace and quiet.[117]

Individual parliamentarians would find different ways to express themselves. Dutch involvement was substantial in the Consultative Assembly of the Council of Europe, for example. In a parallel track alongside the investigation of the Commission, the Assembly was conducting investigations of its own into the situation in Greece. Compared to the government's rather reluctant way of acting, the parliamentary mission was the different side of the coin. Here, the Dutch showed a more activist side, delivering the two rapporteurs who led the investigations of the Assembly. In particular to Max van der Stoel, this role formed a first step in what would become a life of human rights advocacy.[118] His report was scathing: with no freedom of expression, demonstration or possibility to visit the political prisoners on the islands where they were held, Greece was a dictatorship with little hope of improvement.[119]

3.4.2 INTO THE PROCEDURE. Having taken the first step of filing the complaint, the Dutch turned to their Scandinavian counterparts to coordinate their procedures and focus on the admissibility of the case at the Commission. From the start, the two parties entered the case with different expectations. For the Dutch, the preferred outcome would be a friendly settlement by the Commission and a diplomatic solution to let Greece return to a democratic way, while the Scandinavian strategy was focused on addressing the individual human rights violations in detail.[120]

One factor here was the report of Amnesty International on torture. This resonated deeply with the Scandinavians, who built their complaint primarily around that issue. However, precisely there, the Dutch approach differed. The Netherlands did not join the additional Scandinavian complaint stating a violation of Article 3 (the prohibition

[117] NL-HaNA, PV Raad van Europa Straatsburg, 2.05.278, inv. nr. 971, 'letter from Foreign Affairs to Strasbourg, 27 September 1967'.

[118] Anet Bleich, *De Stille Diplomaat: Max van der Stoel, 1924–2011* (Amsterdam: Balans, 2018), p. 116.

[119] NL-HaNA, PV Raad van Europa Straatsburg, 2.05.278, inv. nr. 350, 'Report on meeting Assembly, 14 May 1968'.

[120] Evensen himself thought from the start a friendly settlement was almost impossible.

of torture), arguing that such a clause would be very hard to prove, and further deteriorate relations with Athens.[121] By delegating the investigation of the complaint to the Commission, the Dutch government felt it had done enough to satisfy parliamentary pressure and it could await its verdict with relative flexibility.

The two visions clashed already in the first coordinating meeting in Copenhagen.[122] As the Dutch representatives explained their vision of how a friendly settlement should always remain possible, the Scandinavians revealed their doubts and scepticism on the feasibility of that option. For them, the aim was to compile as much evidence as possible in order to prove torture took place. After all, no derogation under Article 3 was possible in a time of emergency, which the Greek government surely would invoke.

The Greek strategy was more political, however: Greece argued it was not bound to the Convention, being a 'revolutionary government', which had saved the country from a communist takeover. Thus, it argued, it was in a different legal situation than a regular government and should enjoy more leniency for action. What they put forward was, in essence, a political argument, leaving the states with a choice between the colonels or the communists.[123]

Such an argument was less surprising than it may seem. After all, one key element of the Convention had been to protect European civilization against communist threats. During the drafting process of the Convention, the Greek civil war had been raging and no one had claimed human rights for communists then.[124]

Still, this argument forced the Dutch government to reflect upon the meaning of the Convention. Was it indeed still the document as set out in the 1950s? Or did the Convention apply to *all* individuals, even communists? In this reflection, the Dutch made a clear choice. The purpose

121 NL-HaNA, PV Raad van Europa Straatsburg, 2.05.278, inv. nr. 974 'Memo 31 May 1968'.

122 Ibid, inv. nr. 971, 'Notes of first coordination meeting in Stockholm 7 December 1967, 15th December 1967'.

123 NL-HaNA, PV Raad van Europa Straatsburg, 2.05.278, inv. nr. 972, 'Memo to Evensen, 10th January 1968'.

124 See i.a. the Traveaux Preparatoires of the Convention, the verbatim records of the Congress of Europe, and Marco Duranti, *The Conservative Human Rights Revolution*, pp. 107–108.

of this Convention was the protection of 'the rights of man'.[125] Which particular type of government violated those rights, or any political preference of those invoking these rights were of no concern: 'neither of these circumstances can possibly be invoked to deprive the individual of protection of his rights under the Convention'.[126] What emerged here was an embrace of the idea of the Convention as being all about the rights of the individual as such. It would prove to be the beginning of a period in which the 'European' character would increasingly give way to the 'individual' enshrined in the Convention.

3.4.3 CLAIMING THE MORAL VICTORY. As the complaint proceeded, the question emerged whether or not a friendly settlement could be reached between Greece and the Dutch and Scandinavians. Yet negotiations proved difficult: the aim of the complaining states was a return to the demands of the Convention. This would require, among other things, a release of political prisoners, a reinstatement of a free press, and the possibility of free elections.

Yet the Greek response left much to desire. On the political prisoners, the Greeks remained silent for instance, but at the heart of the matter stood the issue of torture. Greece denied any responsibility for cases thereof which had taken place before the friendly settlement. Should accounts of torture arise after the settlement had been reached, Greece would accept an investigation of the matter. Such an investigation should be placed in the hands of the International Red Cross, but any member of the investigation committee had to be accepted by the Greek government.

The proposals were unacceptable to the four governments. Not only did it entail nothing trustworthy on the factual improvement of human rights, but it also left the Greeks too much leeway in their possible implementation. Lacking credibility, 'the tone in which they were stated, the attitude of the Greek government and the reinforcement of

[125] NL-HaNA, PV Raad van Europa Straatsburg, 2.05.278, inv. nr. 972, 'Memo to Evensen, 10th January 1968'. Underlining in the original.

[126] Ibid. Something remarkable happened here: indeed, the Convention had set out to protect the individual, yet also had been about European Unity and *which* individuals were worthy of that protection was indeed very much depended on who had counted as Europeans (compare the non-extension to New Guinea).

the dictatorship' made further discussion on the matter completely futile, the Dutch agent noted.[127]

Even pressure from other allied states, such as Germany and France, who urged for more flexibility with regard to the Greek situation would not alter the thinking of the Dutch government. For even though it had launched the procedure out of an ambition to keep its own hands free and aim for a friendly settlement, in the meantime the Dutch had committed itself to the Convention as safeguard for individual human rights. In the end, the Franco–German diplomatic pressure could not deal with the more fundamental underlying problem, namely the Greek regime's complete unwillingness to commit to human rights standards. The procedure had simply progressed too far to backtrack on the earlier demands without losing all credibility.[128]

Faced with insurmountable opposition, a legal judgement of the Commission at hand and a motion of the Assembly which called upon the governments to suspend Greece from the Council of Europe, the Junta did not await formal suspension. Late in 1969, Greece unilaterally proclaimed its retreat from the Council of Europe and denounced the Convention. This was celebrated as a success: the Danish representative spoke of the joyful notion that one could exclude a dictatorial regime from an international organization on a question of human rights.[129] Max van der Stoel, the main voice for action in the Netherlands and driving force behind the parliamentary pressure (both domestic and European), spoke of a 'moral victory'.[130]

3.4.4 THE BOOMERANG RETURNS: THE IMPLICATIONS OF THE GREEK CASE. Yet maybe more important than the direct consequences of the Greek case (with Greece leaving the Council, the legal effects were rather minimal), were the implications it entailed for future actions. On the one side, this removed a number of policy

[127] NL-HaNA, PV Raad van Europa Straatsburg, 2.05.278, inv. nr. 986, 'Memo 12th September 1969'.

[128] Ibid, 'Memo 26th September 1969'.

[129] NL-HaNA, PV Raad van Europa Straatsburg, 2.05.278, inv. nr. 986, 'Letter from embassy in Copenhagen to the Hague, 17th December 1969'.

[130] Bleich, *De stille diplomaat*, p. 118.

options with regard to the Convention. On the other hand, it opened up a window of opportunity for a new engagement with human rights, based on solidarity and individual suffering. The programme of the Convention shifted, with the emergence of the idea that it could also hold a promise of expanding the programme of human rights.

As for the first notion, the longer the procedure went on, the more the Dutch government tied itself to the rights entailed in the Convention. When starting the procedure, the idea behind this had been to get rid of extensive scrutiny of domestic pressure groups and Parliament. And although the actual Dutch participation in the case was never as intense as that of its Scandinavian counterparts, ultimately the government was forced to opt for individual rights rather than political leniency. Even political pressure from its closest allies could not alter that remarkable notion. Yet this also had consequences for the way in which the government approached the *Belgian Linguistic* case and Belgian initiatives with regard to the Convention flowing from that case. After the appointment of Wiarda had somewhat settled the Belgian urge for a Dutch-speaking judge in Strasbourg, the distrust in the Court had not faded. It was felt that the conviction of Belgium would deeply hurt Belgian interests, and so to prevent such a situation, it went on the offensive.

For one, the Belgian government proposed a 'reinterpretation' of the Convention to the Ministers and possible amendments of certain articles. This was desirable, according to the Belgians, since over the years, 'troubles' had risen in the application of the Convention.[131] Although such a proposal was not remarkable per se, the Dutch suspected a more cynical goal. The procedure over the Belgian linguistic policy was still open, and this proposal was arguably meant to force the Court in a certain direction.[132] Moreover, there were strong indications as to how seriously the Belgians took the case. As the Permanent Representative noted, a modest proposal for reinterpretation of the Convention by the Council of Ministers might not be the only course of action which could

131 NL-HaNA, PV Raad van Europa Straatsburg, 2.05.278, inv. nr. 934, 'Memo Brussels to The Hague, 5th September 1967'.

132 NL-HaNA, PV Raad van Europa Straatsburg, 2.05.278, inv. nr. 934, 'Memo from Strasbourg to The Hague, 7th July 1967'.

be expected. In private, his Belgian colleague 'spoke of the need to pressure the judges of the Court'.[133]

Would the Netherlands support such a course of action? Here, the Greek case, and in particular the attention under which it had placed the Convention, emerged as a decisive factor *not* to meddle in the system as it stood. 'With an eye on the Greek question, which has resulted in a large amount of public attention for the Convention in our Country [...] this moment to address the interpretation of certain articles of the Convention would not be opportune', Foreign Affairs noted.[134] This approach gained extra weight with an eye on the European reputation at stake: 'every derogation of the system of laws under the Convention would strongly devaluate the growing European prestige in this field [...] the importance of the Belgian conduct is thereby extra important'.[135]

What mattered here was how the domestic political engagement and governmental steps into using the Convention had an impact on subsequent action in the Council of Europe. For years, the field of European human rights had remained isolated from any substantial form of (public) attention. Yet Greece had altered that situation. Faced with a sudden scrutiny of its approach to the Convention, the Dutch proved hesitant to take or support steps which could damage the system. When later on, the German and French attempts failed to sway the Dutch, this was an illustration of the same notion: one could no longer freely commit to human rights claims without being scrutinized at home. In a perfect example of 'talk the talk, walk the walk', the Dutch government found that its political room for manoeuvre with regard to the Convention had been significantly limited.

However, and this was the other side of the coin, the case also showed the new ways of engagement which were possible regarding the Convention. Put simply, the case generated an enormous amount of attention for human rights. And what was more, activism, it had turned out, could produce results. It had been a committee of professors and politicians which

133 Ibid.

134 Ibid.

135 Ibid. The result of such attention was to stand on the break on any Belgian initiatives: the original proposal was, also after pressure from the Dutch side, reframed to a very modest proposal to call for a study by the committee of experts.

had set in motion a movement which ultimately led to the interstate complaint. Again, the story of Amnesty offers a fine example here: although it had been founded for the second time after the complaint had already been filed, it then swiftly grew in size, not least by actively focusing on the Greek situation.[136] Combining the renewed focus on wartime memory (one flyer stated 'we have been liberated from the Germans in Germany, but not from the Nazi's within ourselves')[137] the main aim of Amnesty was to pay attention to political prisoners. The Greek prison islands were the ideal screens on which to project this new engagement.

Added to this renewed engagement was distinct choice of language of such action. 'Human rights' were a slogan which resonated both in progressive leftist circles as well as liberal or even conservative circles. As the 'Comité Vrij Griekenland' had shown, it was possible for people of entirely different political backgrounds to come together under one banner: that of human rights. Even the victims of the Greek junta ('communists!') became a source of concern, as *even* communists were entitled to human rights. If some on the left had previously suspected human rights as a means of harbouring and safeguarding bourgeois interests, when it came to suffering, this was a cause all could join.

In academia too, the case served as an illustration of a new interest in the Convention. Before the Greek case, most of the articles on the Convention had been in specialized journals, read by few other than the already interested group of international lawyers. However, with the blossoming of interest in the story, the main legal journal (the NJB) opened up pages for a discussion of the Convention and published a couple of articles on the matter in order to explain the details of the case.[138]

Above all, it was this activist notion of human rights as a programme which would remain after the Greek case had ended. It was the preamble of the Convention which was taken up by those individuals engaged. Smeets, for example, took his experience in the Comité Vrij

136 NL-HaNA, PV Raad van Europa Straatsburg, 2.05.278, inv. nr. 988, 'exerpt *NRC* 13-04-1970'.

137 Ibid.

138 See P. J. G. Kapteyn and O. C. De Vries, 'Griekenland en de Mensenrechten' *NJB* Nr. 28 (2 September 1967), pp. 753–762; E. Alkema 'Griekenland en de Mensenrechten II' *NJB* Nr. 19 (11 May 1968), pp. 468–471.

Griekenland with him into his daily life as a lawyer, for example. To him, the Greek case made clear how the Convention was not something to be kept safe, but also entailed a programme of progressive expansion of human rights for the individual.[139] The experience with Greek victims of torture, intersecting with wartime memory, made this particularly acute. 'The Convention is no empty slogan', he would remark later, looking back on the period.[140]

The next decade would see the turn towards the individual in the European Convention fulfilled. Where this process remained rather convoluted in the 1960s, for example, with the prevalence of imperial distrust in members from the former colonies, in the 1970s, on the waves of this new kind of activism, the Convention would come to be seen as a tool for individual justice. This new wave of engagement was not only confined to the action groups: the group of engaged academics actively took part in this turn, and with the election of 'the most progressive cabinet of all time' in 1973, Max van der Stoel was installed as Minister of Foreign Affairs. In governmental circles as well, this activist approach now took space, leading towards a surge of new initiatives with regard to the Convention, sometimes to the surprise of the other members. Yet the most striking aspect was how these initiatives were no longer employed in the name of 'Europe' but were used to protect 'the individual'. In that regard, the Greek case formed a fundamental shift in that direction.

139 J. H. Smeets, *NJB* Nr. 27 (1971), pp. 784–785.
140 'Jacq Smeets' *De Waarheid* (2-05-1984).

CHAPTER 4

1968–1979

European Human Rights in the Age of Activism

AFTER THE GREEK CASE, the idea that the European Convention could foster change began to settle in the Netherlands, and in its wake, a new phase in the engagement with (European) human rights was taking shape. Above all, it was the link with 'action' which became prevalent. No longer confined to the more conservative right-wing groups, human rights served as a rallying cry in the broader solidarity movement and were turned into a shared language to address human suffering. This was a global phenomenon. Amnesty International attracted more people to the cause of human rights than ever before and won the Nobel Prize in 1977. In the Helsinki Agreements, human rights became a shared concern in both East and West, with 'Helsinki human rights watches' emerging on both sides of the Iron Curtain. Under the presidency of Jimmy Carter, human rights started to function as a moral lingua franca in international foreign policy, demonstrations in solidarity with Chile appealed to human rights, while Portugal and Spain joined the Council of Europe after their transitions to democracy.[1] In the Dutch context, the crown on a decade of bottom-up human rights activism was when the government formally installed human rights as foreign policy aims in 1979.[2]

Also, the European Court seemed to jump the human rights bandwagon. In a legal revolution, the European Court set out that

[1] On the EC and human rights, see Sara Lorenzi, Umberto Tulli and Illaria Zamburlini (eds.), *The Human Rights Breakthrough of the 1970s: The European Community and International Relations* (London: Bloomsbury, 2022).

[2] Jan Eckel and Samuel Moyn, *The Breakthrough: Human Rights in the 1970s.*

the Convention had to be interpreted in light of present-day conditions and was therefore best characterized as a 'living instrument'.[3] Connected to the findings that the Convention entailed autonomous concepts which were not dependent on the meaning given to those concepts on the national level, this was the Court's '*Van Gend and Loos*' moment, laying the basis for an era of progressive human rights jurisprudence.[4]

Yet such a coming-of-age story cannot be seen in isolation from the fundamental changes which occurred on the national level. Instead of a Court-driven approach, the grassroots and the European sphere mutually reinforced one another. Crucially, in the 1970s, the Convention was picked up by an expanding group of actors. Not only action groups, but also a new set of academics began to harbour a renewed interest in the potential of human rights that went beyond the early interest of relatively isolated individual scholars. The 'human rights scholars' of the 1970s were closely related to the action groups using human rights, and the emergence of human rights as academic discipline was hence deeply connected to the broader wave of activism and solidarity, often involving the same people.

The relevance of this movement lies in the fact that it lay the foundation for the 'rights revolution' which occurred later. This revolution, as coined by Charles Epp, entails 'a fundamental transformation in the behaviour of a country's highest courts away from dealing primarily with business disputes and property rights claims brought by corporations and wealthy individuals, towards protecting and expanding the individual rights of ordinary citizens'.[5] Such revolutions do not occur out of thin air: crucially, for such a judicial rights revolution to take place, a firm legal support structure has to be in place.

3 *Tyrer* v. *the United Kingdom*, 25 April 1978, Series A no. 26.

4 Albeit without the explicit claim of the EEC to an autonomous legal order, which was – as we shall see soundly rejected by the states.

5 Charles Epp, *The Rights Evolution: Lawyers, Activists, and Supreme Courts in Comparative Perspective* (Chicago: University of Chicago Press, 1998), pp. 2–3. By its focus on the *courts*, Epp's work needs to be distinguished from the more general notion of Ignatieff that after the 1940s, and in particular after the civil rights movements of the 1960s, a 'rights revolution' permeated society. Ignatieff focuses more on rights 'talk', Epp rather on rights adjudication. Michael Ignatieff, *The Rights Revolution* (Toronto: Anansi, 2000).

What can be observed in the early 1970s is the establishment of such a 'legal support structure'. European human rights expanded from the grassroots into the respectable circles of academia and legal practice, thereby normalizing appeals made on those grounds. Even though the domestic courts remained reluctant to deal with European human rights, pressure grew due to growing numbers of appeals, as well as new interpretations being brought forward. From little-known instruments, European human rights turned into tools with which one could pursue change at the domestic level.

But, these new groups did not just foster a growing engagement with the Convention. They also put forward a new *meaning* of European human rights. Well aware of their limited potential in positive law, academics and activists appealed not merely to the law, but also to the 'spirit' of the Convention. Understanding this shift in meaning provides more clarity as to the definitive *legal* breakthrough of the Convention itself, roughly a decade later. Long before the European Court declared the Convention to be a 'living instrument', these claims could already be heard in the realm of activists and early scholars on human rights who, by making these claims, brokered an interpretative revolution which fundamentally changed the way the Convention was perceived. Finally, the human rights revolution of the 1970s should not be understood as a primarily European affair.[6] Rather, it had implications throughout the entire Kingdom of the Netherlands.[7] As European human rights became connected to issues of migration and (potential) independence, they acquired a new place in the Kingdom for all areas involved.

[6] E. A. Alkema, *Studies over Europese Grondrechten* (Deventer: Kluwer, 1978), p. 11; H. K. Fernandes Mendes, *Onafhankelijkheid en Parlementair Stelsel in Suriname: Hoofdlijnen van een nieuw en democratisch staatsbestel* (Zwolle: Tjeenk Willink, 1989), p. 74; Klinkers and Oostindie, *Knellende Koninkrijksbanden*, pp. 130–131.

[7] An element which is often forgotten. The exception, Brad Simpson, *Human Rights and the End of Empire*, focuses on the UK and ends his story before the 1970s, however. Also, Ed Bates devotes some pages to the British considerations with regard to the colonial aspect, but very limited. Madsen draws on this secondary literature to show how colonial considerations mattered in the initial phase of the Convention, but remains very much focused on the institutional European developments.

4.1 BUILDING A SUPPORT STRUCTURE: THE INTELLECTUAL REVOLUTION

First, the interpretative revolution of European human rights as it was brought forward in the 1970s merits attention. New actors from the grass-roots turned to human rights in order to use the Convention as a tool for domestic change. In doing so, two elements which had defined and shaped Dutch engagement with the Convention were altered, namely a lack of widely shared knowledge and a firm belief in the redundancy of European human rights.

For the Convention as it emerged from the late sixties, lived a quiet life. One reason for this lack of activity lay in the fact that lawyers and plaintiffs simply did not know of the system, how it worked, and whether or not to apply it.[8] As we have seen, engagement with the Convention was a niche that was occupied by a few international lawyers. When it came to legal education in the Netherlands, human rights rarely figured in the existing curricula. In 1975, the Asser Institute in The Hague made an inventory of where and how human rights featured in education. Its conclusion was that human rights were either absent, at best scattered, but mostly barely present at all. Although there was the lectorate of Theo van Boven in Amsterdam devoted to (international) human rights, even the 'Europe institutes' throughout the Netherlands considered the Convention a mere side activity. Simultaneously, there were no journals or handbooks devoted to the topic, leaving human rights to be a matter one could occasionally stumble upon, but most likely miss out on altogether. The result was a Convention which was little known, and as such, little loved.[9]

This had clear consequences for legal practice, as it deterred lawyers from using the Convention in the first place. As one commentator had held, 'with such chicanery, only bad cases can be defended'.[10] An example can be found in the experiences dealing with one particular element

[8] Cf. Myjer, 'Over hoe het EVRM verzeild raakte in de Nederlandse Strafrechtspleging' in *40 jaar EVRM*, pp. 271–296.

[9] Asser Instituut, Verslag Colloquim, p. 6. 'onbekend maakt onbemind'.

[10] I. Samkalden, 'de Universele Verklaring van de Rechten van de Mens en haar doorwerking' *Internationale Spectator* (1964), 672–673, cited in E. Myjer 'Over hoe het EVRM verzeild raakte in de Nederlandse strafrechtspleging' *40 jaar EVRM*, pp. 271–296, 275.

of the Dutch legal order, which could potentially be in violation of the Convention. The so-called Crown's appeal', amounted to an appeal procedure with the government itself, (in this case, an Administrative Litigation division of the Council of State) and had been perceived as potentially constituting a lack of fair trial.[11] However, when advised to bring an appeal based on Article 6 ECHR to the Council of State, stating that – as this was the government controlling the government – the Council could not be seen as an independent tribunal in the sense of the Convention. The response of the lawyer was incredulous: 'But sir, I have to plead there again one day!'[12] As a lawyer appearing before the same court, it was 'not done' to accuse the Council of State of violating human rights. Put bluntly, it would be an insult.

Such was and remained the position throughout the 1970s for those aiming to use the Convention in the domestic courts: any legal claims on the Convention would face some stiff opposition. Some individual cases started to come through which began to break with the famous dismissive position of the domestic courts, but these remained isolated incidents. Even the decision of a local judge who – for the first time – declared a formal law to be non-binding due to conflict with the Convention, (a decision hailed by commentator and later judge at the European Court Egbert Myjer as a 'Dutch swallow' which could herald a spring of human rights protection), proved a mirage.[13] With the Hoge Raad consistently dismissive on the Convention, one commentator noted in 1977 that the ECHR still resembled a 'freedom flag to cover up for political power', rather than a proper human rights document.[14]

Also, the European Court itself was a distant institution. Cases against the Netherlands were few, with even less making an impact. When they did, their direct *legal* implications were relatively minimal. The realm of

[11] The same procedure which would later in *Benthem* v. *Netherlands* be declared in violation of article 6 ECHR.

[12] Interview E. A. Alkema, Van Rossum, 'The Roots of Dutch Strategic Human Rights Litigation', p. 395.

[13] Myjer, 'tekenen van een Hollandse lente' *NJCM Bulletin* Vol. 5 Nr. 1 (1980), pp. 21–30; Myjer, 'overzicht' *NJCM Bulletin* Vol. 5 Nr. 3 (1980), pp. 148–153.

[14] For an overview of dismissed claims on the Convention, see Peter Baauw, 'het europees verdrag en het nederlandse straf(proces)recht' in *Rechten van de Mens in Mundiaal Perspectief* (Nijmegen: Ars Aequi Libri, 1978), pp. 99–139.

the two cases in which the Netherlands was found to have violated the Convention were relatively niche legal topics, such as military discipline and the rights of mentally ill patients. Clearly important, these did not touch on the broader legal framework, and with small changes in the procedure, the rights of the individual were deemed to be safeguarded enough.[15]

Therefore, the knowledge which *did* exist on the Convention was relatively clear: people who wrote on the Convention had to note again and again how it would be of little to no use in the domestic legal system. Moreover, when it came to the European developments, the key Dutch interpreters were still the 'insiders' to the very reluctant system, with Riphagen and Beaufort defending the cautious course of the Commission and Court as part of its *raison d'etre*, presenting European human rights as a careful compromise reserved only for the worst of situations.

From precisely this kind of reasoning, the human rights activism of the 1970s broke away. In their attempts to use and expand knowledge of the system, a flurry of activist lawyers, scholars and others heralded a new meaning of the Convention as a veritable tool for individual human rights protection, with firm consequences as to how European human rights would be perceived in the following years. They were quite aware of the limited value of the Convention in the law: however, that was something to be changed, rather than to be taken at face value.

4.1.1 NEW ACTORS OCCUPY THE FIELD: FROM ACTION TOWARDS ACADEMIA. The interpretative change was engineered following the waves of activism which emerged in the late 1960s and continued into the 1970s. This intersection between human rights and the broader solidarity movement would be vital for the development of rights talk in general as 'rights' took on a new meaning. Actions of solidarity were organized with regard to Chile, for instance, or in protesting against the apartheid regime in South Africa, which attracted

[15] See the analysis in NJ 1980, 114: EHRM, 24-10-1979: Winterwerp and the annotation of Alkema.

huge numbers of people.[16] From these solidarity groups, human rights engagement became a topic for the masses themselves.[17]

These broad solidarity movements turned to human rights suffering abroad. Amnesty International (what's in a name?) was statutorily obliged to devote its attention to human rights violations abroad. Yet from the same seed of activism, a different engagement with rights claims sprouted which took up the language of 'the law' in pushing for justice. 'Rights' became a source of action, not just on the streets in solidarity with far flung places but also inwards in the national context.

These were organizations of a different kind: in those usually small-scale, legally orientated action groups, a new engagement with the Convention emerged which provided the soil on which the later breakthrough in legal practice could grow. These groups emerged alongside a broader 'legal aid' movement, which altered the legal landscape.[18] When in 1970 the student-run legal journal *Ars Aequi* fiercely criticized the Bar and the legal profession for being undemocratic, inaccessible and systematically geared towards the wealthy few, this was a starting point of a new engagement with the conservative legal world. Expensive lawyers, high entry fees and a lack of choice among lawyers led to a structural disadvantage of the less well off in the courtroom, the writers argued. As a solution to these systemic biases, the authors called for the rise of the 'social' lawyer, aiding the individual citizen in its cases against the more powerful government. In itself a sign of the times, the document stood at the beginning of the emergence of a distinct new movement, namely widespread social legal aid.

Social legal aid exploded and took on many forms: 'collectives' of lawyers offered their services to those in need, while the emergence of mostly student-run 'wetswinkels' (legal aid boutiques) ensured free legal

[16] Duco Hellema, *Nederland en de jaren zeventig* (Amsterdam: Boom, 2012), p. 69.

[17] One could also point to the turn to 'non material values', as proposed by Ronald Inglehart. This has been taken up by Peter Malcontent, *Op kruistocht in de Derde Wereld* (Hilversum: Verloren, 1998).

[18] Tetty Havinga and Leny de Groot-van Leeuwen 'Onder de microscoop en door de verrekijker: 25 jaar rechtssociologie in Nijmegen' in Paul Minderhoud (ed.), *De Januskop van het Recht* (Nijmegen: Wolf, 2007), pp. 1–11.

advice to visitors.[19] As multifaceted as the social aid lawyers were, what united them was the desire to alter the way the law functioned and to democratize the legal profession by ensuring more and more people could claim their rights in practice. Indeed, this was among the most lasting legacies of the movement: the opening of justice to previously disenfranchised groups and claims. Aided by social lawyers, people who previously had little incentive or little means to claim their rights, now could – and would – turn up in court. Conscripted soldiers, prisoners and the mentally ill, for example, all saw their concerns transformed into legal claims.

These activists applied the human rights framework to national issues, and in doing so, played a vital role not just in the discovery of the Convention as a legal tool, but also in its 'domestication'. Crucially, these groups were not the mass movements of the 1970s, but rather small-scale initiatives, mostly the realm of legal experts.[20] This was by no means a specifically Dutch phenomenon. Inspiration was drawn most prominently from the United States and the civil rights movement, sometimes very directly. Leading Dutch academics such as Peter Baehr, Toon Peeters, Kees Schuyt, or Cees Flinterman encountered the American protests first-hand when they were doing research in the US and brought these ideas back to the Netherlands.[21] The effects were tangible, as Peeters, for instance, served as a leading figure in one of these new organizations bringing forth a new vision on the law: the Coornhert Liga, based mostly around Utrecht University.[22]

[19] Mies Westerveld et al., (ed.), *35 jaar sociale advocatuur* (Den Haag: SDU Uitgevers, 2010). Rubiah Balsem et al., (eds.), *De Amsterdamse Rechtswinkels in beeld: 40 jaar sociale rechtshulp in beeld: 1970–2010* (Amsterdam, 2010).

[20] As such, these organizations have flown under the radar of most of the historical studies on human rights of this period, which have focused on successful mass-movements or major human rights NGOs, or Foreign Affairs, thereby also confirming the story of human rights being of relevance *elsewhere*.

[21] Baehr and Flinterman would, as professors with close connections to practice and governmental positions, leave a lasting mark in the human rights field of the Netherlands, Schuyt made a name as leading figure in socio-legal research, with Toon Peeters being influential in the realm of criminal law.

[22] Hans Smits, *Strafrechthervormers en Hemelbestormers: opkomst en ondergang van de Coornhert-Liga* (Amsterdam: Amsterdam University Press, 2009), p. 36.

Named after an early modern humanist, the Liga sought the 'humanization of the penal law system' in order to ensure the 'optimal guarantee of individual fundamental rights and freedoms'.[23] Via notions of 'humanization', it did not take long before 'human rights' came up as a tool to be used in this context. 'The respect for the rights of man should be taken as leading ethical consideration in the treatment of the individual', the Liga held.[24] This meant that certain entitlements for detainees, such as privacy, humane work with pay and recreation, weren't just privileges, but 'human rights'. Even though these claims were *known* to be unlikely to succeed, the motivation was precisely to test the existing status quo against a new understanding of these rights.

Another example of such legal activism was the founding of the 'Dutch lawyers committee for human rights', the Nederlands Juristen Comite voor Mensenrechten (NJCM).[25] The NJCM was an example of an organization which merged solidarity, idealism, action and – highly importantly – academia. Starting out as a platform for lawyers and jurists to campaign for South Africa, it swiftly turned into a self-standing expert group. In close connection to academics at Leiden University, to which its founders were linked, it was a new kind of organization 'which would set out to work, with as much idealism as expertise, on the transnational effectuation of human rights'.[26]

The NJCM established itself as the leading domestic legal group engaging with human rights when it took over the mantle of Dutch section of the International Commission of Jurists (ICJ) in 1975. The ICJ, one of the largest transnational organizations for the protection of fundamental rights, had itself embarked on a transformation as well. Since its establishment as a CIA-sponsored conservative NGO to help win the Cold War, new chairmen such as Sean McBride and Neil MacDermot had moved into a more progressive direction. Via contacts at the University of Leiden, it was suggested that the NJCM took over membership of the ICJ from the

23 Hans Smits, *Strafrechtshervormers*, p. 27.

24 Archief Coornhert Liga, International Institute for Social History, ARCH03001, inv. nr. 1, 'board meeting 18 June 1973'.

25 Wiebe Hommes, 'het NJCM: Een schets van de geschiedenis' *NTM* Vol. 42 Nr. 4 (2017), pp. 577–583.

26 NJCM Archief, Ingekomen post 1975 'korte inleiding notulen' 20 August 1974.

existing Dutch section, the Genootschap voor den Rechtstaat' – whose ageing board was quite happy to shift over to the 'new generation'.[27]

It was a clear symbolic shift: legal human rights engagement moved from chesterfields and cigars into leather jackets and jeans. More substantively, however, it entailed an important change in how human rights were approached. From a group focused on the constitution and deeply conservative (one of the members of the Genootschap published a defence of Apartheid not long after the membership had shifted), human rights were now upheld by a group of engaged academics who saw it as their aim of making their promise a legal reality.[28]

A final step in the transformation of human rights engagement in the Netherlands was how human rights research *as such* found a centre of its own, marking a definitive breakthrough of 'human rights scholarship'. When in 1981 the Studie-en Informatiecentrum Mensenrechten (SIM) was founded in Utrecht, a centre exclusively devoted to human rights research, education and documentation, research into human rights had found a dedicated platform. Again, the link to activism was strong. The SIM grew out of the same activist human rights world of the early 1970s. Its founder, Hans Thoolen, had also founded the NJCM some years before, whereas other leading voices such as Pieter van Dijk, Egbert Myjer, Jenny Goldschmidt and Evert Alkema were involved in at least one of the two institutions. Therefore, although the SIM was a formal research centre, as opposed to the more 'action-orientated' NJCM, it was also a continuation of the same ambition: to make human rights relevant.

4.1.2 BRINGING FORTH A NEW MEANING OF THE CONVENTION. The crucial contribution of these groups was that they employed initiatives to further a new interpretation of the Convention. In their activist zeal to alter the situation in the domestic legal context, they set out to *change* the legal order using human rights. As activism was taken up in academic scholarship, a new interpretation of the Convention was embraced, which put forward human rights as progressive values whose potential was far greater than their actual legal value had been hitherto.

[27] Hommes, 'het NJCM: Een schets van de geschiedenis' *NTM*, p. 578.

[28] NJCM Archief, Correspondentie met ICJ, letter 14 June 1976.

This new interpretation of European human rights didn't remain confined to the ivory tower of academia in which it was first conceived. Rather, it branched out to wider legal education, media and – crucially – into the Dutch Bar.

First, the idea of the Convention as a tool of individual rights which should be expanded – and had the legal potential to do so – became increasingly enshrined as the *correct* legal interpretation. A first step in enshrining this new activist interpretation was the emergence of the first domestic academic journal on human rights. This was done via the so-called 'NJCM-Bulletin' in 1976. Initially set up as a stencil for members of the action group, the publication soon started to function as the outlet for the 'research' side of the NJCM and grew into a veritable academic journal of its own. Working groups of the NJCM which specialized in distinct areas of law could publish in the journal, just as other academics working on human rights. As the Bulletin grew in size and professionalized, it heralded a new development in the legal engagement with human rights in the Netherlands.[29] With the introduction of the Bulletin, the NJCM took on a Janus-face with regard to human rights. Not only did its members think, teach or demonstrate about the trajectory of human rights law, they could also publish those views, thereby shaping and steering the trajectory. Soon, the Bulletin came to function as the leading journal exclusively devoted to human rights in the Netherlands, thereby becoming a prime vehicle for broader academic discovery and interpretation of the early cases of the Convention.

For the bulletin, regularly checked domestic developments against ECHR standards and provided a fixed segment for an analysis of European jurisprudence. When the case of *Klass* v. *Germany* was dealt with by the European Court, it was immediately taken up in the Bulletin as an example of how the Dutch surveillance laws were also potentially in conflict with the new Strasbourg minimum.[30] As such, the journal tied directly into one of the aims the NJCM had formulated: to research

[29] Incidental studies had appeared in the *NJB*, *Bestuursrecht* and other journals, but none of these was explicitly devoted to human rights.

[30] See, for example, the 'jaarverslag' 79–80, in which all these elements were brought up *NJCM Bulletin* Vol. 5 Nr. 5 (1980), pp. 326–332.

whether the 'full potential of the Convention' in the national context was being reached. Clearly, multiple articles concluded that was not the case. As publications poured in on situations in which European human rights could play a role, this was a distinctively new way of engaging with human rights.[31] Via these kinds of publications, the Bulletin played a vital role in translating European case law into the Dutch legal context.

A second moment, and illustrative of the connection between the academic and human rights worlds, was when in 1977 a post-academic course on human rights was organized jointly by the NJCM and Pieter van Dijk of the Europe Institute in Utrecht. Although such a course was in itself not earth-shattering, it stood at the beginning of a more durable development. The course led to the publication of a book series on human rights, leading the way in a new way of disseminating knowledge, educating students with regard to human rights. It filled a niche: human rights had always been scattered around different disciplines. With the emergence of a specialized series, it was relatively easy for the new human rights scholar-activists to monopolize the field.[32]

Finally cementing this dynamic interpretation in the scholarly realm was the publication of the first Dutch handbook on the ECHR in 1979. This was a crucial moment in which this new 'activist' interpretation took hold as 'the correct' interpretation of the Convention. In itself, the publication of a handbook was already a major step in the mainstreaming of the Convention. Previously, monographs had been published, yet always from a Dutch constitutional point of view.[33] The handbook, on the other hand, was the first true structural study of the European case law, its development, and relation to national systems.[34]

[31] Demonstrations, police practices, alcohol tests – in all these issues it turned out the Convention could play a role. See for example the 'jaarverslag' 79–80, in which all these elements were brought up *NJCM Bulletin* Vol. 5 Nr. 5 (1980), pp. 326–332.

[32] What mattered as well was how Wiarda, as both president of the Hoge Raad and member of the European Court was more than willing to explain the details of the Convention 'back' in the national context. In doing so, he lend his personal authority to the Treaty.

[33] The studies of Alkema and Meeuwissen were essential in establishing first contact with the Convention, but did not offer a purely 'European' perspective, let alone a systematic overview of its case law.

[34] A translation of Robertsons had been present, but achieved little attention aside from the small group of experts.

'De europese conventie in theorie en praktijk', authored by Prof. Pieter van Dijk (later judge at the European Court of Human Rights) and Fried van Hoof with assistance of Leo Zwaak, was a work which merged insights in the latest case law and theory on the Convention.[35] Importantly, it was *successful* in doing so. The entire first edition of 1,500 books sold out. Picked up by the relevant audiences, it became well known and used in practice. Fragments and analyses of the book emerged in motions of Parliament and were copied into pleadings before domestic courts.[36] In a testament to the work's status, even the legal division of the Ministry of Foreign Affairs referenced the book when deciding on the meaning of a provision.[37]

From the beginning it was clear the book's authors saw the Convention as something destined to play a greater role than it had done so far. In doing so, they took a strong normative position in describing the Convention, which had, 'the potential to become a common legal order for the signatory states, to which the national law was subservient'.[38] Much like what had taken place in the EEC, the Convention could, and ideally should, develop a form of primacy. The fact that the Convention dealt with human rights, 'fundamental, one might say constitutional rights and freedoms', was enough reason on its own for such a statement, the authors held.[39]

The normative attitude towards the Convention could be found throughout the book. Where there was room for disagreement or where matters were not yet settled – of which there were many, be it case law or institutional questions – the advice was consistently to expand the European system in favour of individual rights

[35] It went on to have a remarkable afterlife. After two reprints in Dutch, it was translated into English, becoming one of the more prominent international handbooks on the ECHR (Theory and Practice of the European Convention).

[36] van Dijk and van Hoof, *De Europese Conventie in Theorie en Praktijk* 'Voorwoord tweede druk' (Utrecht, 1982).

[37] Nationaal Archief, Den Haag, Ministerie van Buitenlandse Zaken: Code-archief [periode 1975–1984], nummer toegang 2.05.330, inventarisnummer 22105', memo Van der Wal, 22 maart 1982'.

[38] Pieter van Dijk and Fried van Hoof, *De Europese Conventie in Theorie en Praktijk* (Nijmegen: Ars Aequi, 1979), p. 11.

[39] van Dijk and van Hoof, *De Europese Conventie*, p. 11.

protection.[40] Instead of seeing the Convention as a compromise which should take the position of the state deeply serious, van Dijk and van Hoof pushed for a dynamic, individually oriented system. The contrast with the interpretation endorsed by Beaufort roughly ten years earlier was almost absolute.

The book also contained a domestic agenda. According to van Dijk and van Hoof, the reason for the famous domestic reluctance in using the Convention was a knowledge gap, which prevented the relevant actors from engaging with the Convention. Lawyers, judges and plaintiffs were simply not yet fully aware of the opportunities the Convention offered, which subsequently led to inaction. An increase of legal knowledge and expertise was therefore required in order to help individuals and judges to progress. Such steps had to come bottom up. Should national judges be confronted with an active and well-equipped bar, this situation might change. The handbook itself was a first step into this direction and actively served as a call to action for domestic lawyers.[41]

As such, the book enshrined 'une certaine idée' of the Convention. The demarcation between 'activist', in the sense of aiming to expand the system of the Convention, and 'academic', in the sense of a statement of fact, was not easily drawn. The book was therefore more than a 'neutral' handbook: it was also written from a firm moral conviction in the value of human rights, on how their legal protection should be expanded, and it offered an active encouragement for the system.

Faced with the actual legal value of the Convention, the academic turnabout seemed to remain wishful thinking. But some small steps seemed to indicate things might be changing. It was Gerard Wiarda himself, the Dutch judge in Strasbourg, who broke open the discussion.[42] In an influential

[40] From the potential of the Court to give advisory opinions to the plea to refer as many cases as possible to the Court, a vision emerged of a system which should be dynamic and progressive in nature; pp. 144, 422.

[41] Ibid, pp. 404–409.

[42] Gerard Wiarda, 'de betekenis van art. 6 lid 1 van het Europese verdrag tot bescherming van de rechten van de mens voor de Nederlandse administratieve rechtsgangen' in P. Abas and N. J. P. Giltay Veth (eds.), *Non sine causa* (opstellen aangeboden aan Prof. Mr G. J. Scholten) (Zwolle: Tjeenk Willink, 1979), pp. 459–474.

article of 1979, he held that Article 6 (1) could have dire consequences for the so-called 'appeal on the Crown' – which the lawyer of the COC had been afraid to invoke out of fear of insulting the judges and requirements of the Convention. By attaching his own personal stature as undisputed authority on administrative law, former president of the Hoge Raad, and judge at the European Court to such a critical reading of Dutch law, Wiarda was sending a clear signal.[43] If a person with the stature of Wiarda, not known to make rash legal judgements, thought Dutch law could be in violation of the minimum standard of Europe, things were probably serious.[44]

But discussion did not equal change: even though Wiarda played a role in drawing attention to the standards as they were being defined in Europe, the general attitude of the Dutch judiciary with regard to the Convention continued upon the tradition as established in the previous decades: hesitant and dismissive.

4.1.3 DISSEMINATION: ACADEMIA, MEDIA, BAR. What did emerge, however was an academic institutionalization of knowledge. From there, knowledge of the Convention was disseminated over other fields. The SIM, for instance, played an important role in 'unlocking' European case law. Part of what set SIM apart was its focus on compiling and rendering accessible case law on human rights. In doing so, it responded directly to the complaints that human rights law was inaccessible and distant. By compiling datasets and creating Strasbourg Case law digests providing an article-basis overview, SIM also served a key role in bringing the ECHR from the distant European publications (only accessible in French and English) into the domestic legal system.

Such compilations might seem trivial, yet they addressed a key problem of the Convention: the limited accessibility of case law and judgements in a pre-internet age. These digests made the material accessible to domestic

[43] For an overview of the discussion, see E. Hirsch Balllin, '*Tot welke wijzigingen in het Nederlandse Recht dienen de beginselen van behoorlijke rechtspraak, neergelegd in het Europees Verdrag tot Bescherming van de Rechten van de Mens en de Fundamentele Vrijheden, alsmede in het Internationaal Verdrag, aanleiding te geven?' Preadviezen NJV, Handelingen NJV* (Deventer: Kluwer, 1983), pp. 4–6.

[44] Such was also the idea of Alkema, who emphasized the importance of Wiarda's engagement with the topic as one of the reasons for the 'breakthrough' of the Convention.

lawyers and offered a clear, systematic overview of case law. The initiative would be gradually expanded over the years to include national case law as well, emerging as a key resource for both academics and lawyers.[45]

Another area in which the new interpretation of the late 1970s made an impact was in the realm of legal education.[46] In Utrecht, for example, human rights started to figure prominently as the penal law department shifted to a more critical point of view. Via the work of often young pioneers such as Peter Baauw and Frank Kuitenbrouwer, Strasbourg was brought into the limelight. Both of those scholars had been interested in the idea of European human rights protection and undertook trips towards Strasbourg to get in touch with the institution and integrate the Convention in their lectures on penal law.[47] All of this found its way back into the classroom, with a distinct mission: 'we need to bring up a generation of people who think in terms of human rights', Mark Biesheuvel of the NJCM noted in 1976.[48]

This message was also pursued in other venues. After his time in Utrecht, Kuitenbrouwer would leave academia and join the liberal newspaper NRC. With his background in law, he was one of the very few journalists who had a keen eye for the distinct legal side of human rights and for the Convention in particular. Brought up in the tradition of human rights-friendly interpretations of the law and in very close contact with the world of human rights scholars, Kuitenbrouwer was one of the first voices in the national media, if not the first, to provide continuous attention to the legal implications the Convention might have.

In writing about the Convention, Kuitenbrouwer remained committed to how he had taught the Convention, namely as a project to be developed and expressed these notions consistently in his coverage. In doing so, he helped to bring about awareness of the Convention by choosing

[45] Erin Jackson, Brianne McGonigle Leyh, *A History of SIM: The Netherlands Institute of Human Rights since 1981* (Utrecht, 2016), pp. 83–92.

[46] That is not to say it was only due to these scholars human rights education became part of the academic programme. However, by including it in their own lectures, they ensured it became an increasingly common sight in the legal education.

[47] C. Kelk, *De historie van het Willem Pompe instituut* in W. M. J. Bekkers and e.a. (eds.), *Rechten in Utrecht* (Deventer: Kluwer, 2002), pp. 45–77, 67.

[48] 'Eigenlijk moeten we een generatie kweken die meer in termen van mensenrechten denkt' *Mare Universitair Weekblad* (24 August 1978).

to address topics which otherwise would have remained unnoticed. New academic publications on the Convention or court cases in which European human rights were invoked were not usual topics for media coverage. Kuitenbrouwer specialized in these however and showed in his reports how the Convention could matter in Dutch society, thereby fuelling the legal human rights revolution which started to take place.

For in his writing, Kuitenbrouwer was critical of the attitude held by most lawyers and judges at the time that the Convention was not relevant for the Dutch context. 'Human rights', Kuitenbrouwer noted, 'are too often seen in the Netherlands as something which predominantly matters as support for those weakest shoulders in the family of nations'. Instead, they were a central problem area which deserved far more attention, also in the Netherlands itself.[49]

Finally, Kuitenbrouwer's colleague at Utrecht, Peter Baauw, would play a major role in bringing human rights into another audience: that of legal practice. This was a crucial spillover. Baauw would combine penal law and human rights throughout his career as practising lawyer. As such, he also did not shy away from using the Convention, offering advice to plaintiffs on how to take the Strasbourg route, making a name for himself as one of the very few to do so along the way.[50]

His bridge function between academia and practice became most tangible when – confronted with the increase in human rights claims – the Dutch Bar Association held its annual conference in 1981 on the topic of human rights.[51] In earlier talks, the Bar Association had contacted the NJCM on how more attention could be given to human rights in legal practice, after criticism had emerged on the absence of human rights in the education and training of lawyers that the Bar offered.

As the Bar invited two experts in order to educate the audience, these were precisely those with a clear idea and programme for the Convention in mind: Baauw and Alkema. As a result, what the Bar learnt was the

[49] Frank Kuitenbrouwer, 'Nederland en de rechten van de mens', *NRC* (10 Februari 1975).

[50] Archive NJCM, Diverse Post, 26 februari 1982, 'Brief aan NJCM'.

[51] Peter Baauw, 'Advocaat en mensenrechten: strafrechtspleging en straatsburg' *Advocatenblad* Vol. 61 Nr. 15 (1981), pp. 322–347; Evert Alkema, 'Advocaat en mensenrechten: vuistregels en vooruitzichten' *Advocatenblad* Vol. 61 Nr. 15 (1981), pp. 298–322.

'new' interpretation of the Convention. Providing their analysis of the state of Dutch lawyers and the Convention, both academics called for a more active role of the bar. If the lawyers did not dare to take the step to Strasbourg or to make appeal based on the human rights enshrined, no further clarification could be expected. Therefore, it was in the hands of the lawyers to breathe life into the Convention and by doing so, to make their own lives easier along the way.[52]

Alkema and Baauw urged their audience there were good reasons to invoke the Convention. From pretrial detention times to the rights of the suspect, all were topics where Strasbourg could be of assistance.[53] In order to help with those promising cases, the entire day was set up to get the Dutch lawyers acquainted with the Convention. Getting the basics right was a priority. In order to achieve a good command of the system, a checklist was provided, as well as a 'route map' on filing a complaint in Strasbourg, and the form with which to file a complaint.[54] Again, these steps could be seen as trivial in themselves. However, they provided the Dutch Bar with very practical tools and information on the merits and potential of the Convention. In a situation where the Convention had been very far removed from daily legal practice, it was these little things which could already make a difference.

What connected this wide range of initiatives is the shared zeal to *make* European human rights relevant. Be it the journal, the human rights groups, or the legal aid, all sprang from the same source: the activism of the 1970s and a desire to alter the status quo. As these turned to European human rights law, they altered its meaning. From something that was conservative and shunned, human rights turned into a tool to be invoked to break open the system.

4.1.4 INTERLOCKING ACTION AND ACADEMIA: THE CASE OF ENGEL. Nowhere is the impact of the interaction between the new academic approach and the legal aid movement better illustrated than in the case of *Engel and others* v. *the Netherlands.* For as the case progressed

[52] Ibid.

[53] Baauw, 'strafrechtspleging en Straatsburg'; Alkema, 'vuistregels en vooruitzichten'.

[54] To be found as appendix in *Advocatenblad*, Vol. 61 Nr. 15 (1981), p. 348.

from the grassroots, it was the firm help of academia that meant the case would ultimately end up in Strasbourg and lead to the first conviction of the Netherlands by the European Court. A closer examination of the case sheds light on precisely how these new engagements with human rights took place in practice.

The case was brought forward by the 'judicial committee' of the Union for military servicemen, the VVDM. As such, that was a striking example of how pervasive the legal aid movement was. After all, the fact that the VVDM *had* a judicial committee, which urged its members to 'know their rights' and voice their grievances in those terms as well, was a direct consequence of legal aid in practice. As the VVDM became the prime forum for conscripted soldiers to voice complaints, most requests on legal aid related to military discipline. This was done in a highly efficient manner, but to be judged by one's own officer seemed a far cry from having an independent judge. Moreover, punishment could be harsh. To the judicial committee it seemed this was very much a form of criminal punishment instead of the administrative punishment it was legally. As such, the legal standards should be the same as well.

The solution to this problematic military discipline was to be found in the Convention. Despite the relatively minor status the document enjoyed at the time, the judicial committee of the VVDM was convinced of its potential, as the military discipline would be 'in violation of the spirit of the Treaty of Rome' (as the Convention, being signed in Rome, was better known at the time), which 'holds supremacy over the national law.[55] To be judged by one's own officer did not seem to fit the bill of the need for an 'independent judge'. Here, the judicial committee saw an opportunity to test the discipline against Articles 5 and 6 of the Convention: Were the soldiers being deprived of their liberty in a fair trial?[56]

[55] The Convention went by many names in its history, but was commonly referred to as the 'Treaty of Rome' or the 'Rome treaty' due to its place of signature, which should not be confused with the *other* Treaty of Rome relating to the EEC. Emphasis added on 'the spirit' of the Convention as legally speaking, the soldiers had little to go with: tying into the new attention for human rights, however *was* promising. Archief VVDM, IISH, ARCH01547 inv. nr. 598, 'memo 8 January 1970'.

[56] The legal problem was if military discipline could be equated with penal law or not: if it did, the Convention would apply. If not, other routes would have to be pursued. The aim of the VVDM was to get a judgement on precisely this point.

The VVDM did not expect much success at the domestic level. However, that was seen as a distinct advantage: since all domestic remedies had to be exhausted (which the committee foresaw wouldn't take much time), a principled case could be sent into Strasbourg.[57] Precisely on that ambition, it would receive help. After all, the road to Strasbourg was not often taken and was rarely successful. When cases surrounding disciplinary sanctions started to emerge in the national news, the VVDM were contacted by the young academic from Leiden, Evert Alkema.[58] He approached the board with a proposal: 'if you are serious about those human rights, you have to go to Strasbourg, and I would be willing to help'.[59]

His motivation to lend a hand to potential plaintiffs was a deeply personal matter. To Alkema, the Convention, as 'the most tangible legacy of the Nuremberg trials' needed to needed to be 'activated'. As such, he would scout promising cases in the domestic system and aim to get them to Strasbourg, in order to 'prime the pump' of the system: *Engel* was one of these cases.[60] As such, he was a key figure in the early discovery of the Convention in the Netherlands.

Throughout the procedure, his help to the VVDM would be of vital importance.[61] As he helped in ironing out the legal niceties of the case, he was particularly crucial in getting the case declared admissible. He stood in close contact with Anthony McNulty, the secretary of the Commission, with whom Alkema tested the waters to see whether or not the Commission would act on such a case. Receiving a positive answer from Strasbourg, Alkema ensured a reinforcing tandem, of active individual plaintiffs at the domestic level and an eager and responsive secretariat on the European field.[62]

What eased the matter forward was that on the domestic level, the complaint coincided with the drafting of a new law on military discipline.

57 Archief VVDM, IISH, ARCH01547 inv. nr. 598, notes 'legal committee, 28 July 1969'.

58 Van Rossum, 'The Roots of Dutch Strategic Human Rights Litigation', p. 392.

59 Leiden, 19 September 2019, interview E. A. Alkema.

60 Alkema remained involved in a number of cases after Engel, for instance, the case of *X&Y* v. *Netherlands*; Leiden, 19 September 2019, Interview E. A. Alkema.

61 Van Rossem, The Roots of Dutch Strategic Human Rights Litigation', p. 393.

62 L. Lavrysen, 'Strasbourg was something new' *Tijdschift voor Rechtsgeschiedenis*, pp. 543–544.

This conjunction had some implications for the expected resistance from the government. The law was drafted under the shadow of the procedure, but things had come to somewhat of a standstill in Parliament, a judgement would have the potential to shape the legal requirements. This entailed that things were already moving, and that strong resistance of the government was not to be expected – an important element in putting forward a successful complaint.

4.2 THE REAPPRAISAL OF THE EUROPEAN COURT

Reaching Strasbourg, *Engel* kicked off a remarkable activity and became intertwined with a second development. For on the European level, the Dutch government started to see the Convention, and in particular the Court, in a new light, namely as a distinct solution to political problems which began to emerge in the Committee of Ministers. This shift in how the Court was perceived cannot be seen in isolation from the grassroots developments. For with the emergence of individual complaints, political contestation followed. In turn, this helped influence one of the most substantial shifts in the system of the Convention: a reappraisal of the European Court of Human Rights. The famous 'waking up' of the Court in this period cannot be seen in isolation from this political conflict.

The institutional set up of the Conventional system had created the possibilities for such conflicts to emerge. The European Commission on Human Rights could sent cases either to the Court or to the political body of the Committee of Ministers: keenly sensitive to the concerns of the states of an intrusive Court, it consistently opted for the latter option. Getting to the Court therefore entailed 'going through the eye of the needle' that was the Commission.[63] The involvement of the ministers traditionally had been rather limited: its treatment of cases moved along without notable conflict, rubber-stamping the reports of the Commission.

Yet in the 1970s, an influx of cases reached the Commission and were subsequently sent to the Committee of Ministers. The rising number

[63] Armin von Bogdandy and Ingo Venzke, *In Whose Name? A Public Law Theory of International Adjudication* (Oxford: Oxford University Press, 2014), pp. 63–71.

of applications flowed from the European-wide growth of use of the Convention on a domestic level, and although the numbers of rejections remained high (around 95 per cent of applications was dismissed), the Ministers increasingly were confronted with questions on issues of law. Certain 'hard cases' started to appear before the Committee of Ministers, itself a political rather than a judicial body, meaning that contentious decisions on law were pulled into the political sphere, and thereby opening up room for diplomatic conflicts.

Confronted with these developments, the Dutch government did something remarkable: it set out to change the system. The proposed answer to problems in the Committee was as simple as it was radical: the Ministers would need to get the Court involved. In two simultaneous developments, the Netherlands started initiatives within the Committee of Ministers to reinvigorate the system of the Convention. The Court, rather than being a problem, now emerged as a solution, to which these hard cases should be referred.

4.2.1 A NEW DISPOSITION IN EUROPE. The first sign that matters had changed for the Dutch government were found in its response to the case of *Engel.* Faced with the complaint of the soldiers, the Dutch government opted for a remarkable move. Influenced by the new Minister of Justice, Dries van Agt, who, inspired by both personal idealism as well as pragmatic considerations, supported a more active engagement with the Convention, the government proposed asking a question to the Court, under Article 1 of the Second Protocol of the Convention.[64]

This protocol had been the result of the campaign for the Court to increase its own activity and, as such had also swiftly been disarmed by the governments.[65] The barriers were high: a two-third majority in

[64] 'The Court may, at the request of the Committee of Ministers, give advisory opinions on legal questions concerning the interpretation of the Convention and the Protocols thereto'. Van Agt was aided by the transfer of Joseph Luns to NATO in 1971. Luns had been opposed to an excessive position of the Court and preferred bilateral diplomatic agreements. With his influence gone, room was opened for a more active policy with regard to the Court.

[65] As described in Chapter 2.

the Committee of Ministers needed to agree with the question, and a prohibition to go into the 'content or scope of the rights or freedoms defined in section 1 of the Convention [...] or with any other question which the Commission, the Court or the Committee of Ministers might have to consider in consequence of any such proceedings as could be instituted in accordance with the Convention' made the advices of the Court extremely difficult to come by.[66]

To Riphagen, the legal advisor at the Ministry of Foreign Affairs, the initiative was doomed to fail. Having been involved in the drafting of the protocol, he was of the opinion there was no realistic chance the questions would ever be admissible.[67] To Van Agt, however, the limited potential under the protocol was something to change rather to accept. As was set out, 'there is a risk, in the very small possibilities of the protocol. It seems as if a somewhat narrow interpretation of article 1 would take away the meaning of the whole procedure by which the opinion of the Court can be asked. This certainly would make no sense'.[68] As such, the Netherlands proposed the Committee of Ministers to ask the Court for clarification. Did the military disciplinary detention fall under Article 5 of the Convention? And what was the meaning of 'criminal charge' in Article 6 exactly?

Yet the response from the other states was cold. The Italian representative noted the obvious: the questions on the content of paragraph 5 of the Convention were inadmissible under Article 1, paragraph 2, while to the other member states, the argument that the protocol would 'take away the meaning of the whole procedure' wasn't convincing. After all, it was meant to be just that.[69]

As such, the Dutch initiative was destined to fail. Yet the episode was a first indicator of an emerging trend: breaking with the traditional restraint in the Committee, the Netherlands *did* try to get things moving within the set-up of the Convention. The problem was, however, that this attempt was done via the second protocol, which formed a formidable

[66] ECHR, 2nd protocol, article 1(2).

[67] NL-HaNA, Buza/Code-archief 1965–1974, 2.05.313, inv. nr. 4281, 'Memo 6 September 1971'.

[68] Ibid, 'Note from Strasbourg to the Hague, 18 February 1972'.

[69] Ibid, 'Memo from Strasbourg to the Hague, 28th December'.

barrier because of its very strong wording. This second attempt would be broader in its ambition and aim at a more substantive change in the procedure of the Convention.

4.2.2 POLITICAL CONFLICT IN THE COMMITTEE. For *Engel* was but one of the cases which started to emerge before the Commission. Inspired by the new interest in human rights, the number of complaints started to rise.[70] One of these was the case of *Scheichelbauer* v. *Austria* of 1969.[71] At the centre of the case stood the question of whether recordings made in collaboration with the police, without the knowledge of the person, could be used in Court.[72] The Commission had found no violation but was divided. Seven members thought the practice admissible, while four, including the Dutch member, found that it entailed a violation of the Convention. In line with the usual referral policy, the report was sent to the Committee of Ministers. There, the standard policy was to follow the majority of the Commission and proceed to terminate the case. It seemed business as usual.[73]

However, the Ministry of Foreign Affairs was concerned. This had to do with the fact that the voting record of the Dutch member, De Gaay Fortman could not easily be ignored. The practice of using recordings was under scrutiny in the Dutch domestic legal debate as well, which made this a topic of particular importance. 'Since the Dutch member of the Commission had a different opinion and this is a very sensitive issue, consultation with the Ministry of Justice seems necessary'.[74]

From that consultation, it emerged that the Ministry of Justice in fact did consider this to be a very principled point, and considered this practice to be a blatant violation of rights.[75] Such strong statements did not miss their effect: in the next meeting of the Committee, the Dutch minister noted it would not simply go along with the findings of the

[70] Bates, *The Evolution of the European Convention*, p. 240.

[71] *Scheichelbauer* v. *Austria* No. 2645/65.

[72] Ibid.

[73] NL-HaNA, Buza/Code-archief 1965–1974, 2.05.313, inv. nr. 22889, 'Memo 25th May 1971'.

[74] Ibid, 'Memo 1st June 1971'.

[75] Ibid, 'Memo 23 June 1971'.

Commission. Instead, he proposed a paragraph for inclusion in the final resolution which would state that in principle, 'the recording of a private conversation unbeknown to the participants or one of them constitutes an interference with privacy', thereby affirming the notion that this right was protected under the Convention.[76]

To the Dutch this may be a matter of principle, other states were less convinced.[77] Austria unsurprisingly voiced the clearest critique. 'To adopt this position, is to endorse the minority in the Commission', the Austrian representative declared.[78] Germany sided with Austria, the Directorate of Human Rights supported the Netherlands. A rift had emerged in the Committee of Ministers on the basis of an individual human rights complaint.

In particular, the Austrian resistance was firm, and when the Austrian ambassador in the Netherlands left a statement that any alteration of the conclusions of the Commission was deemed 'highly undesirable' for the Austrian government, the Dutch understood they might need to compromise in order not to risk an open diplomatic conflict.[79] Finding compromise in a resolution which both let Austria off the hook by finding no violation and assuring the Netherlands that this was only the matter because of the very specific case, further conflict was ultimately avoided.[80]

But to Van Agt, the discontent rising from this case was reason to seek to alter how the system itself worked. It had not been the first time the Committee of Ministers had used its political character to the perceived detriment of the proper procedure for human rights protection, but 'in the case of Scheichelbauer [...] the downsides connected to the treatment of an individual complaint by the Committee of Ministers ... have clearly surfaced', Van Agt noted.[81] 'The risk clearly exists that political considerations influence how complaints are dealt with and even that a certain judgement of the legal question at hand will be seen as an

[76] Ibid, 'Memo from Perm. Rep. to The Hague, 5th July 1971'.

[77] Ibid, Memo 23 June 1971'.

[78] Ibid.

[79] Ibid, 'Memo 16th August 1971'.

[80] Ibid, 'Memo 23th August 1971', emphasis added.

[81] Ibid, 'Memo 5th October 1971'.

unfriendly act by the other state'.[82] The reason for this conundrum lay in the institution itself: the Committee was a 'non-independent institution with a non-legal signature' and as such 'not fit to answer questions on law with authority'.[83]

The solution here was to change the forum which should decide those matters: from the Committee this should go to the European Court. It formed the beginning of a campaign to change the referral policy of the Commission, investigating whether there was not some merit in prescribing a 'main rule' to refer to the Court, should the procedure concern a complaint against a state which had accepted the jurisdiction of the Court.[84]

This campaign to change the referral policy of the Court benefitted from domestic circumstances. In particular, after the installation of the government of Joop den Uyl in 1973, labelled 'the most progressive government' the Netherlands had ever seen, support for human rights thinking soared. Those ministers dealing with the Convention were strong supporters of an independent legal system. Max van der Stoel, already familiar with the promise of the Convention after his work on the Greek case became Minister of Foreign Affairs. De Gaay Fortman moved from the Commission back into the national context to become minister of Internal Affairs and was in charge of the relationship with the overseas territories.[85] Moreover, Laurens Jan Brinkhorst, a young professor of European Law from Groningen and avid 'Europeanist', became secretary of European affairs. Coming from Groningen, Brinkhorst remained in quite close contact with his former colleague, Evert Alkema, who in private had already presented Brinkhorst with some ideas to strengthen the Convention – in particular through a change in the referral policy of the Commission.[86]

Despite this support from the Dutch context, most other states supported the political freedom the system offered. In particular, the United

[82] Ibid.

[83] Ibid.

[84] The jurisdiction of the Court. NL-HaNA, Buza/Code-archief 1965–1974, 2.05.313, inv. nr. 22889, 'Memo 29th November 1971'.

[85] He was replaced by C. H. F. Polak, a former minister of justice and senator, keeping with the tradition of electing member of the Commission with close ties to the government.

[86] NL-HaNA, Buza/Code-archief 1965–1974, 2.05.313, inv. nr 4283, 'Memo 29th October 1973'.

Kingdom, Belgium and Austria embraced the possibility of political influence and were wary of a purely legal approach to the matter. This came as no surprise: all these states had been confronted with sensitive cases, after which they had resorted to political pressure. Belgium had experienced the *Belgian Linguistic* case and was actively delaying the treatment of another case.[87] The United Kingdom had already diminished the period of acceptance of the right of individual complaint from three to two years to express its discontent with the system.[88] West Germany expressed firm support for the system and its mix of politics and law, because the 'vagueness of the concept of human rights' set it apart from other fields of law. Precisely the uniqueness and sensitivity of human rights law made the carefully balanced legal system of the Convention, between politics, all the more valuable. From the Commission itself, little change could be expected, according to the representative, as it had expressed its preference to 'take the political route in sensitive cases against the member states, rather than to involve the Court'.[89]

Without the clear support of the other member states, the Dutch decided it would be counterproductive to needlessly 'irritate the tempers in the Commission'.[90] Rather, an indirect and unofficial policy should be pursued to influence the 'climate' around the Commission and wait for openings to arise.

4.2.3 DEADLOCKS AND SOLUTIONS. The wait proved to be short. The year after *Scheichelbauer*, another Austrian case, *Huber* v. *Austria*, provoked discord in the Committee. In it, the Ministers were confronted with an unexpected situation when the report of the Commission noted a violation of the Convention while in a very comparable case (*Neumeister* v. *Austria*), the Court itself had held there was no violation.[91] What should

[87] The *Les Fourrons* case, again on language policy, was kept off the agenda of the Committee by Belgium as a way to delay a judgement.

[88] NL-HaNA, Buza/Code-archief 1965–1974, 2.05.313, inv. nr 4283, 'Memo from Strasbourg to the Hague, 4th December 1972'.

[89] Ibid.

[90] NL-HaNA, PV Raad van Europa Straatsburg, 2.05.278, inv. nr. 917, 'Legal Advice 27th April 1972'.

[91] *Huber* v. *Austria*, app. No. 6821/74; *Neumeister* v. *Austria*, 27 June 1968, Series A no. 8.

the ministers do when the report of the Commission was in apparent contradiction with a judgement of the Court?

The legal issue at hand in both cases (who flowed from the same proceeding) was one of extreme delay in a criminal procedure.[92] Neumeister and Huber were both caught up in the same lengthy criminal case on account of fraud, ranging to some twelve years in the case of Huber. The practical reason for such a tremendous delay was that the Austrian authorities were largely dependent on authorities in third countries which proved hard to reach and cooperate with. Yet in the face of such extreme delays, the question surfaced if this was all within reasonable time as held in Article 6 (1) ECHR. The Court had held that this was indeed the case. Depending on the complexity of the case and the dependency on foreign authorities, these delays were unfortunate, but not enough to establish a violation of the Convention.

Conversely, some years later in the case of *Huber*, the Commission *did* find a violation of Article 6(1).[93] Twelve years, the Commission held, was a very long time to be part of a criminal procedure. It was now up to the Committee of Ministers to delve into a tricky legal issue. In principle, the Court was the prime interpreter of the Convention, yet now the Commission endorsed a different view.

To Austria, the case was deeply unwelcome: it went as far as to label findings of the Commission 'legally unfounded'.[94] But it also noted something which caught the attention of Dutch diplomats. 'The Committee is primarily a political organ, competent to rule on purely legal questions [...] only in exceptional cases', the Austrians held.[95] What was before it now was precisely this sort of legal twist, which was explicitly not something for the Committee. In the eyes of the Austrians, the Ministers were now 'overtaxed by a request to decide on a purely legal question'. Such notions were music to the ears of the Dutch, who saw in these statements

92 The case against Huber and Neumeister flows from the same proceedings.

93 Although the Commission tried to explicitly note the differences between Huber and Neumeister, the fact the two were faced with the same proceedings made that quite tricky.

94 NL-HaNA, PV Raad van Europa Straatsburg, 2.05.278, inv. nr. 942, 'Memo 1 October 1974'.

95 Ibid.

support for their own campaign to turn over legal questions to the Court rather than to the Ministers. Legal questions should belong with the proper legal institutions, now the Austrians also seemed to think.

The case proved difficult to decide: in particular, the 'smaller' countries endorsed a more legalistic approach, with the Scandinavian states, the Netherlands and Ireland accepting the Commission's report, whilst Italy and Germany, for instance, urged for a non-approval of the report.[96] This latter position was cherished by the larger states, led by the UK, traditionally the most opposed to any form of supranational legal authorities. According to the UK, it was desirable to keep this flexibility for cases such as these in 'grey areas' to deal with the opinion of the Commission.[97] Austria indicated it could accept the report, albeit only if the Committee of Ministers did not impose 'unacceptable obligations as to indemnifications' on Austria.[98] It was a middle ground: formally accepting the report, yet without any consequences.

The positions could not be squared, however: on the one hand, there stood the states who sought to overrule the Commission, on the other hand, the more legalistic ones sticking to the report. It had turned into a fundamental debate on what the role of the Committee of Ministers should be: not afraid to intervene in legal proceedings or reluctant of its own power to overrule the legal experts? With none of the governments willing to give ground, the rubberstamp-machine of the Committee of Ministers had ground into a deadlock in deciding on the case of an individual – thereby extending the already lengthy procedure Mr Huber found himself in. To acquiesce in the deadlock proved to be the only way forward: the solution was found in simply doing nothing, meaning a non-finalization of the procedure. The Netherlands was harshly critical of this development: 'this way of not-ending the procedure was in violation of the spirit of the Convention'.[99]

Yet precisely at this point, the campaign to involve the Court kicked in again. Throughout the saga, the Dutch had continued to express their preference for the judicial solution and tied this into their envisioned

96 Ibid, 'Notes committee of Ministers 30 October 1974'.

97 NL-HaNA, PV Raad van Europa Straatsburg, 2.05.278, inv. nr. 942, 'Report 15 April 1975'.

98 Ibid.

99 Ibid, 'Notes committee of ministers 15 April 1975'.

larger role for the Court. In response, the Dutch attempted to create a different 'mood' around the referral policy in these years. This was taken up in a couple of ways.

First, the Netherlands got the Court involved on its own instigation in the case of *Engel*. The Netherlands had made it clear to the Commission it saw no problems in a referral to the Court and applauded it when it took that step.[100] Moreover, the government offered further support by actively joining the Commission in referring the case to the Court.[101] In pushing its 'own' signature case to the Court and making clear to the Commission this was a desirable course of action the Netherlands actively gave the Court a say in the matters. It was not alone in this strategy: another state which turned to the Court for solace was the United Kingdom, albeit with a very different goal in mind. When the United Kingdom referred the case of *Golder* to the Court for example, it did so with the explicit motivation to curtail an interpretation of the Commission it deemed to go too far.[102] Here, the Court in fact benefitted from its conservative reputation. As states were confronted with a more active Commission, the past experience with the more reluctant Court was a reason for reassurance and cause for action. In comparison to the more active Commission, the Court was no longer the most threatening party.

A second way to achieve change was by seeking to influence the ecosphere around the Commission. Brinkhorst would not cease to convey concerns on the 'politicization' of human rights – that the Court was increasingly being sidelined in favour of the Committee of Ministers – when he met leading figures within the Council of Europe, and pushed for an enlarged role of the Court.[103]

100 NL-HaNA, Buza/Code-archief 1965–1974, 2.05.313, inv. nr. 4284, 'From the Hague to PV 21 October 1974'.

101 Under the system of the Convention, both the Commission and the Member State could bring a case to the Court. Earlier, the United Kingdom had done so in *Golder* but with a completely different motivation. Whereas *Golder* was meant as a warning to the Commission (and expecting the Court to be more restrictive in its approach), *Engel* was meant as *encouragement* of the Commission to involve the Court and further develop the system.

102 Bates, *the Evolution of the Convention*, pp. 294–297.

103 NL-HaNA, Buza/Code-archief 1965–1974, 2.05.313, inv. nr. 4284, 'Memo from Brinkhorst to DRW 17th July 1974'.

And indeed, the Commission did refer more cases to the Court, the latter became more involved in the second half of the 1970s. Even though the majority of cases were still transferred to the Committee of Ministers, certain hard cases in which the Commission failed to find a comfortable majority were now sent to the Court, for example.[104]

Now clearly, the reasons for this new activity of the Court are diverse and range from the dynamics released by France and Switzerland's accession to the system, to the growth of cases more generally. Moreover, although no direct causal link can be discerned, these 'soft' attempts to create a different mood around the referral policy were all too real. As we have seen, the members of the Commission were closely connected to the governmental elites of the states they represented. Sensitive to the political climate surrounding its actions, the Commission had actively refrained from involving the Court, following a longstanding distrust in the institution from more sceptical member states. But in the period of 1970–1974, the Court was increasingly seen as a solution and not as a problem: with states such as the Netherlands pushing for its involvement, the diplomatically keen Commission was bound to pick up on this new dynamic.

4.2.4 REJECTING THE IDEA OF THE ECHR AS 'NEW LEGAL ORDER'. But even if this was an atypical period of 'Strasbourg friendliness', the support for the system was not unconditional. Getting the Court involved was one element, but when it came to more foundational shifts in the structure of the Convention, the states remained famously hesitant. When again an initiative to create a preliminary ruling mechanism for the European Convention was deployed in 1979, its fate was telling of how the states believed the system should work.[105] The general aim of the initiative, proposed by a committee of experts, was simple: to ensure more uniformity in the interpretation of the Convention and to more

[104] For example, the sex education case, *Kjeldsen, Busk Madsen and Pedersen* v. *Denmark*, 7 December 1976, Series A no. 23, where the Commission could not agree on a violation of article 2 of the first protocol and sent it to the Court to be decided there.

[105] Nowadays, this possibility is – with some differences – enshrined in protocol 16 of the Convention.

fully integrate the Convention into the judicial system of the Contracting states.[106]

The Court itself supported such a step. It advocated an 'optional protocol, which would grant to national courts the right – but not the obligation – to request preliminary rulings and provide that the Court would give advisory opinions – but not judgements – on the issues thus raised'.[107] Moreover, the committee saw similarities between the Convention and the law of the European Community. The Convention, it was held, established in the field of civil liberties a 'new legal order designed to substitute for the particular systems of individual states a common European system'.[108] The preliminary ruling procedure would greatly aid and accelerate the penetration of the Convention into domestic law, just as Article 177 of the Rome Treaty had accelerated the penetration of Community law in Member States law.[109]

This was a rather bold reading of the Convention, and precisely on the point of 'substituting' national rights, the states intervened. Uniform interpretation might have been necessary for community law, that made it precisely undesirable for Convention law, which consisted of a vital mix between diplomacy and law after all, the aim of the Convention was to provide an international guarantee of certain rights, which might be restricted in a different manner in different countries, according to national conceptions. The Convention, it was held, was not designed to replace national rules, but requires that they contain nothing against it.[110]

This sensitivity to domestic preferences was a disposition also seen at the European institutions themselves. President of the Court, Balladore Pallieri, noted in 1975, for example, how it was not the job of the Court to protect human rights, but rather to protect the Convention as such.[111]

[106] NL-HaNA, Buza/Code 1975–1984, 2.05.330, inv. nr. 21796, 'Report on Preliminary Rulings, p. 6'.

[107] Ibid, Report on Preliminary Rulings, p. 7 'opinion of the Court'.

[108] Ibid, Report on Preliminary Rulings, p. 11.

[109] Ibid, Report on Preliminary Rulings, p. 17.

[110] NL-HaNA, Buza/Code 1975–1984, 2.05.330, inv. nr. 21796, 'Final Report on Preliminary Rulings, pp. 6–10'.

[111] Cited in P. J. Baauw, 'Het Europees verdrag en het Nederlandse straf(proces)recht', *Rechten van de mens in mundiaal en Europees perspectief* (Nijmegen, 1978), pp. 99–139, 128.

Doing so required an awareness of the many compromises which had shaped it from its foundation in order to keep the states on board.

4.3 HUMAN RIGHTS BEYOND EUROPE: A DIFFERENT DISPOSITION

These tendencies of the government to voice support in the Council of Europe give rise to an image of a cautious, but otherwise firm supportive Dutch state when it came to European human rights protection. But a more nuanced image emerges if the broader setting of the Kingdom is taken into account. For what was desirable for the Netherlands was not always perceived as desirable in the Dutch relation with its overseas territories. In this context, a first example of how the Dutch government thought of European human rights as a threat pertains to issues of migration into the Metropole. As such, the Netherlands worked actively to keep the fourth protocol of the Convention pertaining to migration at bay in order to prevent an influx of fellow citizens. Second, European human rights emerged in unexpected ways in the discussion surrounding the independence of Suriname. Where for Suriname independence ultimately entailed the definitive end of European human rights protection, for the Antilles, independence emerged as a key motivation to *become* fully part of the system.

4.3.1 THE FOURTH PROTOCOL: KEEPING EUROPEAN HUMAN RIGHTS AT BAY. The clearest example of the Netherlands' ambiguous approach to the Convention is the way the Dutch government struggled with the ratification of the fourth protocol of the Convention. Here, European human rights were perceived as posing a tangible threat to the political freedom to regulate migration into the metropole. As a consequence, Dutch civil servants stepped in to keep human rights out of the discussion.

The protocol provided in Article 2 the right of every citizen to freedom of movement within the territory of a state and the freedom to choose residence for everyone lawfully within the territory of a state.[112] Should this be

[112] 4th protocol ECHR, article 2 (1).

accepted, it might have an effect on existing, or potential, barriers to free movement within the Kingdom of the Netherlands. Put simply, all citizens of the Antilles, Suriname and the Netherlands shared the same nationality: the Dutch one. Yet not all citizens were free to move or choose residence freely within the Kingdom: here the protocol could possibly have a significant impact by allowing such free residence to emerge.

All three parts of the Kingdom were confronted with this potential impact. For Suriname and the Antilles, such a right to free movement and residence seemed to go directly against existing legal hurdles which had been erected to control immigration into those areas. These rules were put in place in colonial times to prevent the entrance of 'agitators' but after the Second World War, they were embraced by the governments of Suriname and the Antilles in order to protect the social fabric of the states. Since their societies were comparatively small in comparison to the Netherlands, an influx of Europeans would have intrusive and unsettling effects on the socio-economic set up of the countries.[113]

A potential solution would be to not expand the protocol to Suriname and the Antilles, thereby safeguarding the existing barriers. However, the exclusion of these areas was not a decision which could be made by the Netherlands alone: Suriname and the Antilles had the final word over whether they would like the protocol to apply in those territories. Discussion between the three governments was therefore necessary, as in principle, it was deemed desirable to apply the same standards of human rights protection throughout the Kingdom. After all, the image of unequal human rights standards for former colonial subjects did not fly well on the international level.[114]

For the Netherlands itself, there was a different potential conflict with the protocol. The right to free movement of all citizens was starting to have visible consequences, and from the late 1960s onwards, the Netherlands was turning from an emigration country into one of immigration. A major influx of migrants came from Suriname and the Antilles. This migration was perfectly legal, as no rules existed on migration from

113 Oostindie and Klinkers, *Knellende Koninkrijksbanden*, pp. 228.

114 NL-HaNA, Justitie/Wetgeving/Internationale Organisaties, 2.09.84, inv. nr 195, 'Notes to the SG from W. Breukelaar, 15 February 1971'.

those parts of the Kingdom into the Netherlands. Yet with growing numbers of migrants, voices were emerging in favour of installing a more stringent migration policy.

Civil servants from different ministries were most active in this regard. From the 1950s there had already been concerns about the asymmetric rules on migration within the Kingdom, yet migration levels from the Antilles and Suriname into the Netherlands had steadily risen in the 1960s, from a negligible number of several hundred in 1960 to almost ten thousand in 1971.[115] The volume of migration and perceived otherness of these people concerned the civil servants.[116]

This influx of what were perceived to be culturally distinct fellow Dutchmen required a change in migration policy, or so they held.[117] A lack of screening of who came into the country supposedly resulted in the 'import of a socially troublesome group, rather than potential working forces'.[118] Therefore, higher control of migrants was needed, alongside possibly creative solutions (it was proposed to let migrants take the boat instead of the plane to allow the idea of settling in the Netherlands to mature during the time at sea) in order to make integration into Dutch society run more smoothly.[119]

Yet such a shift in integration policy would require legal changes. In this light, the potential impact of international treaties on such limits deserved further scrutiny. Here the fourth protocol emerged as a matter of discussion, as it could pose a threat to the potential to control migration from the overseas territories into the Netherlands.[120] Legal experts

115 Oostindie and Klinkers, *Knellende Koninkrijksbanden*, p. 231.

116 This only increased when, in the years right before Surinamese independence, the number skyrocketed to 35,000 in 1975; Oostindie and Klinkers, *Knellende Koninkrijksbanden*, p. 231.

117 NL-HaNA, Justitie/Wetgeving/Internationale Organisaties, 2.09.84, inv. nr. 195, 'advice working group CRW, 2 September 1971'.

118 Ibid.

119 Ibid.

120 NL-HaNA, Justitie/Wetgeving/Internationale Organisaties, 2.09.84, inv. nr. 195, '8 July 1971, memo to W. Breukelaar, legal advisor min. Justice'. The central role of civil servants is more important than it seems: as Saskia Bonjour has argued, only later in the 1970s would politics shape the migration policy, before then there was a lot of leeway for civil servants. Saskia Bonjour, *Grens en gezin. Beleidsvorming inzake gezinsmigratie in Nederland, 1955–2004* (Amsterdam, Aksant, 2014), pp. 116–117.

were divided, but some had spotted a very clear reason to be concerned about migration in the context of the European Convention. Recently, the European Commission had declared a relatively comparable case, admissible, namely that of the 'East African Asians'.

In this case, the issue was about citizens seeking to migrate from the former British colonies in East Africa into the United Kingdom. More specifically, the Commission heard the complaints of Commonwealth citizens of Asian origin who were being discriminated against (mostly in Kenya) and subsequently sought to move to the United Kingdom.[121] Confronted with an influx of migrants, the UK had made a distinction in its admission policy of UK citizens and installed a law which imposed controls on migrants, which could only be avoided for those people who themselves – or whose parents or grandparents – were born in the United Kingdom.[122] In doing so, it created subdivisions amongst its commonwealth citizens, providing a minor status to those who were not born in the United Kingdom. Subsequently, when East African Asians, who were commonwealth citizens but were not born in Europe, were barred from entering the UK, some had filed a complaint under the Convention.

When the Commission declared the complaint admissible, reactions from London were very critical. UK diplomats were furious with the Commission, and held the Commission failed to respect the 'democratic rights of states'.[123] For the British Foreign Office, the complaint had come as a surprise. Clearly, the Convention was expressly *not* meant as a document which would have an impact on the relation between a geographical European state and its former colonial components.[124]

[121] Ian Sanjay Patel, *we're here because you were there: Immigration and the End of Empire* (London: Verso, 2021), pp. 209–243.

[122] Richard Plender, 'European Commission of Human Rights: Decision on Admissibility of Applications by East African Asians against United Kingdom' *International Legal Materials* Vol. 10 Nr. 1 (1971), pp. 6–55.

[123] NL-HaNA, Buza/Code-archief 1965–1974, 2.05.313, inv. nr 4283, 'Memo from Strasbourg to the Hague, 4th December 1972'. The sensitivity of the topic was illustrated by the fact that the Council of Ministers kept the critical report of the Commission a secret until 1981: see Bates, *The Evolution of the Convention*, p. 234.

[124] Britain and the Netherlands were unique in that they had expanded the Convention. The other colonial empires had not taken that step. For France, see Pauline Bonino, *La France face à la Convention européene des droits de l'Homme (1949–1981)*. For Belgium, see in short Johan VanDe Lotte, *Handboek EVRM: algemene beginselen* (Antwerp: Intersentia,

The admissibility decision of the Commission was thus also a reason for alarm in the Netherlands, where it was feared it'd have an impact on its own migration policy. Telling of the still very close relations between Commission and Member States, the Ministry of Foreign Affairs sought contact with the Dutch member of the Commission, De Gaay Fortman, expressing that the Netherlands were eager to be kept up to date with the English pleadings before the Commission, in particular to remain aware of the developing legal details of the case and to be able to study its potential implications for its own policies.[125]

As the complaint progressed, it became clear how different the two situations were. This had to do with the nature of the post-imperial structure of the relation between the two European states and their former colonial areas. In the British Commonwealth, there existed a significant variation in terms of citizenship status. Citizens of the former colonial areas might be part of the Commonwealth, but they enjoyed less status and rights than those of 'full' citizens of the United Kingdom, which gave rise to the validity of the complaint of the East African Asians. However, in the Dutch setting, such a distinction in citizenship did not exist, and a comparable complaint was thus not considered possible.

Still, the issue raised serious concerns in the Dutch Ministry of Justice. In light of a potential involvement of the European institutions in the context of migration, it was better to be safe than sorry and not to ratify the protocol.[126] The Netherlands did not share these considerations with Suriname and the Antilles, who would substantiate their position on the protocol, unaware of the Dutch hesitation. The Surinamese government had doubts of its own, as it was unsure about whether its own policy on migration was in conformity with the Protocol. Since it attached greater value to safeguarding its immigration policy over joining the European protocol, it made the choice to maintain the barriers and not

2004), p. 556. An extensive study on the status of the Convention in relation to Belgium and its colonial context is still missing.

125 NL-HaNA, Kabinet Vice-MP/KabSNA, 2.10.41, inv. nr. 79, 'Letter to de Gaay Fortman, 16 October 1972'.

126 NL-HaNA, Kabinet Vice-MP/KabSNA, 2.10.41, inv. nr. 77', notes meeting 27 June 1972'.

to participate in the protocol, thereby leaving it up to the Netherlands and Antilles to continue the conversation.[127]

As a result, the challenge was to come to an agreement between the Netherlands and the Antilles on how to follow up on the protocol. The Ministry of Justice decided in that context to delay the ratification of the protocol, in particular as it could 'throw up a barrier' against migration rules for the Netherlands, effectively halting the process for years to come.[128] What emerged here was how the legacy of the imperial past continued to influence engagement with European human rights within the Kingdom. Although human rights were ever more embraced by the Dutch government in light of its foreign policy, the consequences of human rights with regard to the internal relations within the Kingdom were deemed sufficiently disruptive not to accept them. In the Kingdom, the relative absence of the Convention can therefore be explained not solely by a lack of significance, but precisely because certain provisions thereof were in fact deemed to be too significant, so much that they would pose a threat to migration policy.

4.3.2 TOWARDS REFORM AND INDEPENDENCE: HOW THE CONVENTION GOT LOST IN THE KINGDOM. The second way in which human rights were part of debate in the Kingdom lies in the lead up to the independence of Suriname.[129] The final result of this independence, the loss of European human rights protection, might have come as no surprise. It was rather self-evident within the system of the Convention. The Council of Europe had debated decolonization and a possible extension of the human rights system to newly independent 'non-European' states and firmly rejected such ideas.[130] Yet in this

[127] NL-HaNA, Justitie/Wetgeving/Internationale Organisaties, 2.09.84, inv. nr. 195, 'Memo from Antilles to the Hague, 28 January 1972'; 'Memo from Suriname to the Hague, 27 March 1972'.

[128] NL-HaNA, Justitie/Wetgeving/Internationale Organisaties, 2.09.84, inv. nr. 195, 'Memo to Minister of Justice, 27 July 1972'.

[129] H. G. Hoogers and G. Karapetian, 'Hoe grondrechten in het Koninkrijk zoek raakten: een beschouwing over de binding van koninkrijksorganen aan grondrechten' *Tijdschrift voor Constitutioneel Recht* Vol. 8 Nr. 1 (2017), pp. 4–36.

[130] See Chapter 3.

overarching context, the Convention emerged in the discussions leading up to Surinamese independence in unexpected ways.

The discussions on independence and the position of the different countries in the Kingdom were held in the so-called 'Koninkrijkscommissie', a gathering of experts and politicians which had set out to prepare a new legal framework for the Kingdom of the Netherlands. The old legal framework, 'the Statuut', put down the legal connection between the Netherlands, Suriname and the Antilles, was perceived to be too restrictive, particularly in light of demands for further autonomy and ultimately, independence. In order to open up the Statuut and to accommodate a new future relation between the three areas, the Commission was installed to 'make a choice among constitutional and international legal alternatives' which could consist of the new basis for a cooperative relation. Swiftly, its scope broadened to reflect on the economic, social and cultural development of the countries, providing the potential for a more fundamental revision of any future relation.[131]

Human rights were one of the many topics discussed. In discussions on development aid, military cooperation, nationality regulation, and border divisions, fundamental rights seemed to be of a less pressing nature. Yet they were proper topic of discussion, with one (sub)commission entirely devoted to their position. Their inclusion was the result of work from the delegations from Suriname and the Antilles, who pushed most actively for attention to international human rights protection. In the earliest discussion papers, they flagged the topic as being highly important. Their motivations for engaging with human rights protection differed, however.

Most outspoken in this regard were the Antilles, whose position was rather clear from the beginning: in a personal note from the governor to the prime minister of the Netherlands, the line of thinking was set out. For one, the Antilles did *not* seek independence. Such a move would leave the islands vulnerable and without proper perspective.[132] Therefore, some changes would be needed to the legal set up of the

[131] Oostindie and Klinkers, *Knellende Koninkrijksbanden*, pp. 88–98.
[132] NL-HaNA, Kabinet Vice-MP/KabSNA, 2.10.41, inv. nr. 76, 'Letter Governor to PM, 13 August 1971'.

Statuut, primarily to remove some of the discontent which could have arisen in the Netherlands, and some of those changes were in the field of fundamental rights.

How did this perceived discontent of the Netherlands come to be? In 1969, a violent riot had occurred on the streets of Willemstad, in Curaçao. Dutch marines were ultimately deployed to restore order, but the outburst of violence had shocked many. In particular, it was the Dutch engagement in order-keeping which emerged as a source of legal concern. In the Statuut of the Kingdom, which regulated the legal bonds of the Kingdom, protection for fundamental rights, legal certainty and sound government were seen as an affair of the entire Kingdom.[133] Should one of those issues be neglected, one of the three countries (in practice, the Netherlands) could be required to step in and ensure protection.

What the islands feared was the Dutch discomfort with this requirement. After the riots, the Antilles had experienced Dutch interference in internal affairs, but also had perceived how The Hague was not particularly pleased with the fact it had to step in to restore order. What the Antillean government wanted to avoid was that the requirement on the Netherlands to protect fundamental rights might motivate The Hague to render the Antilles independent, simply to get rid of this burden of protection. Therefore, the Antilles proposed an internationalization of the issue. 'We need to discharge the Kingdom of this burden [...] the supervision will have to be submitted to arbitration or legal judgement', the Antilles held.[134] It was again a sign of the discovery of the Court as a solution for political sensitivities, only this time for issues internal to the Kingdom.

Such a notion signalled a major shift away from previous political preferences. Throughout all negotiations on, for example, the right of individual petition at the ECHR, the Antilles had refused any international legal oversight over its internal affairs.[135] Those investigations would be potentially costly and constitute an unwanted interference in

[133] Nowadays, article 43 of the statue.

[134] NL-HaNA, Kabinet Vice-MP/KabSNA, 2.10.41, inv. nr. 76, 'Letter Governor 13 August 1971'.

[135] See the earlier discussions in Chapters 2 and 3.

domestic affairs. Yet in light of possible independence, it now embraced those options of legal control, precisely to prevent its own sovereignty from emerging in full.

In coordination with the Dutch government, a solution could be found in the European framework to address these concerns. The Dutch section noted it would be then desirable for the Antilles to accept the right of individual petition under the Convention. The term of the past declaration of acceptance of the right in the Netherlands (which was renewed every five years) ended in 1974. It was therefore strongly encouraged that the Antilles should join in the new declaration of renewal and accept the possibility of individuals to complain at the European Commission.[136] Such a notion had always been strongly contested in the Antilles, but in the changed political set up this offered an ideal route forward. The system of the Convention now came to function as the 'international legal supervision' on fundamental rights in the Antilles. The motivation to remain part of the Kingdom, with human rights protection as an international, not merely a Dutch affair, ultimately – after some Dutch encouragement – led to the acceptance of the right of individual petition in 1974. This did not mean that the Kingdom was discharged of any responsibility, but rather it ensured the decision of whether there were human rights violations taking place could be 'outsourced' to an international body. What should happen if such a violation was found remained an open question.

The step did not raise a lot of attention: it was more or less neglected by newspapers and academic commentaries.[137] However, this was a sign of the different engagement with the Convention in the Antilles: the acceptance of the right of individual complaint, or attention for the Convention at large, was not carried forward by a grassroots movement, but rather by a more political desire to maintain a constitutional link to the Kingdom. Lacking popular attention or desire, it was a monumental step nonetheless. For the first time, the full legal venues that European human rights had to offer were now open to *all* within the Kingdom.

[136] NL-HaNA, Kabinet Vice-MP/KabSNA, 2.10.41, inv. nr. 85, 'Notes Dutch Delegation on Fundamental Rights, 16th April 1973'.

[137] Based on a survey of leading newspapers in the Antilles (Amigoe).

4.3.3 SURINAME AND EUROPEAN HUMAN RIGHTS IN THE QUEST FOR INDEPENDENCE. In Suriname, the situation was different. The firm aversion of the Antilles towards independence was not shared in Paramaribo. Although independence was an option which was perceived to be still very far removed and undesirable at first sight, it was a possibility which was being debated in politics as well as academia.[138] With regard to the new set up of future cooperation, Suriname initially held this would ideally take the form of a Commonwealth. This would mean all countries would be independent states bound together, preferably with a shared head of state: the Queen or King of the House of Orange.[139] As far as international fundamental rights were concerned, an original proposition was put forward: 'since fundamental rights are of paramount importance for the preservation of sound governance [...] a Commonwealth Court could be installed to keep oversight on these issues'.[140]

Such a 'Commonwealth Court of Human Rights' was a novelty. It would consists of three judges from each area, and would be able to provide binding judgements on whether or not one of the states had violated its human rights obligations.[141] This would ensure that even after the possible loss of the protection of the Statuut (and international arrangements), a supranational oversight would be kept in place. As the Surinamese delegation held, such oversight did not constitute an undesirable interference in internal affairs, since the UN had also held human rights to be a matter of international concern.

The role human rights played in the Commission caught the Dutch members somewhat by surprise. Contrary to what the Antilles believed, the Dutch had not expected human rights protection to function very prominently.[142] However, pushed by the initiatives of the other two

[138] In particular, the Surinamese lawyer, Clemens Biswamitre, had a special attention for the nexus between independence and fundamental rights, arguing it would entail a loss of the Convention rights, but how that could be mitigated by putting the rights of the ECHR in the domestic constitution.

[139] NL-HaNA, Kabinet Vice-MP/KabSNA, 2.10.41, inv. nr. 81, 'Report Surinamese Delegation 1 August 1972'.

[140] Ibid.

[141] Ibid.

[142] In the earliest reports, very little attention was given to the topic. See NL-HaNA, Kabinet Vice-MP/KabSNA, 2.10.41, inv. nr. 77, 'Notes Meeting Dutch Section Int. Law,

parties, they had to reflect on the possibilities of rights protection in the Kingdom, and grapple with the option of a shared human rights court.

The point was discussed when the sections of the three parties gathered in Paramaribo, in August 1972. How were they to square sovereignty and fundamental rights in a commonwealth set up? Although consensus existed on the need for international protection, the details on how this should be done and what form it should take still caused quite some confusion. From the Dutch side, labour Parliamentarian Van Lier noted the Netherlands had some experience with the matter, since 'in Europe, we have the European Convention of Human Rights, and a Court with the possibility of individual complaint', in apparent ignorance of the fact the Convention applied to Suriname and the Antilles as well.[143]

It was via the Dutch engagement with these questions that the ECHR entered the discussion. The legal experts were responsible for its inclusion: the leading legal mind in the Dutch delegation on the human rights court and other venues for the protection of fundamental rights was Willem Riphagen. For the first tripartite meeting of the section 'international law' of the Commission, Riphagen was commissioned to produce an initial proposal of what such a Commonwealth Court could look like, while simultaneously presenting some ideas on the possibilities of fundamental rights protection.

His aim was to take the rights embodied in the ECHR as a template. As the chair of the commission summarized: 'the creation of such a court would require all three the countries to ratify the European Convention on Human Rights'.[144] There was an additional benefit of using the Convention as a template: it refrained from being overly ambitious. As it neatly tied into a classical conception of human rights, its focus on civil and political rights excluded the potential Court from taking socio-economic rights into account. This exclusion of socio-economic rights was a conscious choice from the Dutch delegation and hinged

3 July 1972', which provides some details on the manner, but in a reactive way to claims of the other parties.

143 NL-HaNA, Kabinet Vice-MP/KabSNA, 2.10.41, inv. nr. 81 'Notes Meeting 28/31 August 1972'.

144 NL-HaNA, Kabinet Vice-MP/KabSNA, 2.10.41, inv. nr. 77 'Notes Meeting Dutch Section Int. Law, 3 July 1972'.

on the perceived justiciability thereof. These rights were 'of a different nature' when compared to classical liberal human rights, and best not to be fully judicialized. To the Dutch section, their inclusion in a document which could be judged upon by a court would be 'undesirable, even while accepting how worthy these rights were of attention for Suriname and the Antilles'.[145] Suriname and the Antilles went along with the proposal, and as a consequence, the demands 'to take the economic, social and cultural development' into account, were not included in the field of law and remained confined to more political flexible notions on development aid, for example.

As for the notion of the Commonwealth Court of Human Rights, the Dutch section on international law found itself in a tricky position. In light of the desire of Suriname for a continuation of rights protection in a new set up, the Dutch section had argued in sincerity for a proposition for such a court.[146] Yet when the format was laid out by the experts which made up the section to the entirety of the Dutch delegation, problems emerged. At the core of the discussion was the fact that such a Court was a desire from the other parties to safeguard fundamental rights. However, with the Antilles now covered by the Convention, it had become a particular Surinamese affair.

To the Dutch delegation, such a Court was of little to no priority since any loss of fundamental rights protection in case of independence would occur elsewhere. 'The "European" Dutchmen already possess a very good access to the European Court', it was held.[147] Conversely, an additional court would only create confusion and overlap: the Netherlands merely had a derivative interest in supporting the creation of such a Court. Put briefly: fundamental rights protection after independence was not a Dutch problem, so why bother at all? Alternatives were not keenly eyed. One member noted how the creation of the Court was perfectly fine with him, as long as it did not hold any jurisdiction over autochthonous Dutchmen.[148]

145 NL-HaNA, Kabinet Vice-MP/KabSNA, 2.10.41, inv. nr. 85, 'Notes Dutch Delegation on Fundamental Rights, 16th April 1973'.

146 NL-HaNA, Kabinet Vice-MP/KabSNA, 2.10.41, inv. nr. 85, 'Notes 18 April 1973'.

147 NL-HaNA, Kabinet Vice-MP/KabSNA, 2.10.41, inv. nr 79, 'Notes Meeting 5 July 1973'.

148 Ibid. The chairman shared this opinion, making any further progress in this direction unfeasible.

Moreover, was it not more desirable for Suriname to join the UN treaties on human rights or the Inter-American Court of Human Rights?[149]

Therefore, the delegation determined that fundamental rights protection in the form of a Court was undesirable if it included the Netherlands in any set up. If a Court would indeed be something which needed to emerge, then it was something for the Antilles and Suriname to take up.[150] The international law section raised concerns on this finding but was ultimately overruled. As the Netherlands removed its support from the initiative, its memos changed in character. To prevent an all too blunt rejection, caution was urged. Far better than an outright dismissal would be to show how such a Court would not have the value the other sides might attach to it, thereby altering their opinion.[151]

In practice, this meant a different set of arguments became more articulated. Instead of a flat political refusal, the Dutch unwillingness to join in a new supranational Court was hidden behind legal tactics. Such 'objective formulations' would, according to a member, further 'mask the fact there was a catch here'.[152] Although Riphagen had already mentioned this in the case of independence, a strong legal connection to the Netherlands could serve as impediment for Suriname to join the UN, indeed this was now actively brought forward as a warning to the Surinamese delegation.[153] In subsequent legal analyses, Suriname was warned *not* to maintain a close legal connection to the Netherlands by means of the courts if it wanted to be seen as an autonomous player in the world. The Dutch delegation was well aware that its position would not be welcomed in Suriname: the new strategy was described as a 'cold shower' for the Surinamese emphasis on international protection of

[149] Ibid.

[150] NL-HaNA, Kabinet Vice-MP/KabSNA, 2.10.41, inv. nr. 85, 'Preliminary Report Dutch Section, 20 September 1973'.

[151] NL-HaNA, Kabinet Vice-MP/KabSNA, 2.10.41, inv. nr. 79, 'Notes Meeting Dutch Section, 5 July 1973'.

[152] NL-HaNA, Kabinet Vice-MP/KabSNA, 2.10.41, inv. nr. 79, 'Notes Meeting Dutch Section, Input Member van Lier 26 October 1973'.

[153] NL-HaNA, Kabinet Vice-MP/KabSNA, 2.10.41, inv. nr. 79, 'Notes Meeting Dutch Section, 26 October 1973'; NL-HaNA, Kabinet Vice-MP/KabSNA, 2.10.41, inv. nr. 85, 'Preliminary Report, 20 September 1973'.

fundamental rights.[154] That the Dutch refusal to cooperate was disguised as a friendly offer of help did not alter that basic fact.

However, as it was deliberating, political developments caught up with the Commission. With the election of the new government of Den Uyl in the Netherlands, the pressure from the Netherlands to aim for full independence of Suriname grew and the Commission lost its momentum. Suriname itself had stopped participating in the Commission after May 1973. Yet the breakthrough came from Suriname itself: after an election, a new government stepped up with a very clear idea. Suriname needed to become independent, ideally before 1976.[155] This created an entire new dynamic. The new government was much more inclined to break with existing bonds than previous ones, and the issue of the Court, and indeed the international protection of fundamental rights, was regarded as burdensome rather than desirable. Such a shift surprised the Dutch delegation but made things easier at the same time. With the two governments now in agreement, the commonwealth Human Rights Court was out of the picture.

Moreover, the new push for action meant the Commission was back on track to prepare the cadres in which independence should take place. However, the position of the new Surinamese government had caused some consternation in the ranks of its own delegation. Members of the Surinamese opposition, who for the past years had pressed for international fundamental rights protection, saw the issue completely disappear from the meetings. In this context, the Convention came to serve as the most prominent example of things which would be lost when independence was achieved. Surinamese politician Jnan Adhin flagged the issue and warned of the emergence of a 'vacuum of human rights protection'. 'If Strasbourg disappears [...] no international forum for appeal would exist anymore in the case of a human rights violation'. Was this not something which should be considered?[156]

The Dutch session was not inclined to take any side in what it perceived to be an internal Surinamese dispute and responded in line with

154 Ibid.

155 Oostindie and Klinkers, *Knellende Koninkrijksbanden*, pp. 120–126.

156 NL-HaNA, Kabinet Vice-MP/KabSNA, 2.10.41, inv. nr. 83, 'Notes Trilateral Meeting Int. Law, 14 August 1974'.

its previously determined position: this was entirely a matter for Suriname to take up. The Dutch now explicitly put Suriname in the realm of the South American system. As one of its members told the Surinamese delegation, 'it is up to you, as a South American country, to refine, alongside with your South American sister states, the machinery of the treaty of Bogota or whatever it is called, on human rights and to make this into a treaty which is worth mentioning'.[157] Gone were any remnants of considering Suriname as part of the European human rights framework.

Adhin, in particular, was dismayed. He raised the issue again in the finalizing plenary session, urging the Commission to at least make sure no vacuum would emerge on fundamental rights. He expressed his distrust in the future of the South American human rights system, a continent of which the countries 'did not have a reputation of great concern for fundamental rights'. International protection was necessary however: was it not possible to see if membership of the Council of Europe could be continued in any way in Suriname?

But his notion of continuing ties to Europe was precisely what triggered the new nationalistic government of Suriname and its members in the Commission. In a firm critique, Adhin's fellow delegate Komproe noted:

> it is hard to maintain we need to cling onto the ECHR for our protection of human rights. Let's find that protection at the UN, in our own region! Moreover, I would like to comfort Mr Adhin, that until this day, no single Surinamese has used this possibility.[158] It is expensive, it is complicated, it is a mere academic affair.[159]

In a way, Komproe was right to note the limited practical importance the Convention had possessed in Suriname and echoed earlier concerns when Suriname indeed had declined to join the system out of fear of being integrated too closely in a new European system. Yet the point of Adhin was more fundamental: 'the mere existence of such an institute has merit' he held. The 'paper reality' the Surinamese government

[157] NL-HaNA, Kabinet Vice-MP/KabSNA, 2.10.41, inv. nr. 83, 'Member Van Santen, 14 August 1974'.

[158] Of complaining at the ECHR.

[159] NL-HaNA, Kabinet Vice-MP/KabSNA, 2.10.41, inv. nr. 80, 'Notes Meeting Plenary Commission, 3 October 1974'.

set out, stating that the Constitution and preamble would be enough, was even more naïve than his 'academic' position.[160] Yet Adhin's pleas were akin to hoping to board a ship which had already sailed. In the discussions, the new Surinamese government had accepted the Dutch preference for the UN and South American systems and did not seem to be keen to remain tied to any form of legal connection with Europe. Independence – and a swift one, at that – was what mattered.

The final conclusion was therefore perhaps unsurprising. Suriname would aim to protect human rights via its own constitution and, as a replacement for years of European orientation, would seek to join the UN and initiatives in its own region. Adhin and other members of the opposition filed a minority statement in the report of the Commission calling for the need to prevent the loss of international rights protection, but the position was never again a topic of debate.[161]

Thus, human rights disappeared from any agreement or template for independence. The new constitution of the freshly independent state was hastily written (in The Hague with support of Dutch legal experts) and was more inspired by the Dutch constitution than by the ECHR. It was therefore all the more surprising when roughly a year later, the government of Suriname filed a demand at the Council of Europe to formally *rejoin* the Convention. As its letter to the secretariat set out:

> I have the honour to inform you that, by a verbal note of 16 December 1976, the Minister of Foreign Affairs of Suriname informed the SG of the Council of Europe that the Republic of Suriname wished to be bound by the European Convention on Human Rights, which had been made applicable to the territory of Suriname, before it became independent, by the Kingdom of the Netherlands.[162]

Why was there this turn around in the Surinamese disposition? It had to do with the aim of the negotiations. These had been aimed primarily

[160] NL-HaNA, Kabinet Vice-MP/KabSNA, 2.10.41, inv. nr. 80, 'Notes Meeting Plenary Commission, 4 October 1974'.

[161] NL-HaNA, Kabinet Vice-MP/KabSNA, 2.10.41, inv. nr. 80, 'Rapport van de Koninkrijkscommissie's Gravenhage, October 1974', p. 49.

[162] NL-HaNA, Buza/Code 1975–1984, 2.05.330, inv. nr. 22128, 'Memo 19 January 1977 from Council of Europe'.

at achieving swift independence: only after that aim had been achieved could proper consideration – also internally within Suriname – on future human rights protection take place. Yet the Surinamese request, for clear legal reasons, could not be granted, as only members of the Council of Europe could join the Convention. Suriname, as a non-European state, was not eligible for such membership.

Legally speaking, this is and was, a correct assessment. The Convention remained tied to the European project, and initiatives to include former colonial areas had consistently been rejected. For Suriname, this refusal meant the definitive end of maintaining European human rights protection. Yet it was no self-evident rule of history this should have happened. The Netherlands clearly pushed for a solution with as few strings attached as possible, and alternatives which would have kept certain ties in place were denied by both Surinamese and Dutch politicians. The resulting final outcome left little room for human rights, but was by no means a predetermined one.

CHAPTER 5

1979–1989

The Defining Decade: How the Convention Became 'Mainstream'

In 1983, a remarkable situation occurred in the district Courthouse in Groningen. During a session focused on simple offenses committed by students, a judge was driven to despair. One after another, the students appealed to their European human rights, safeguarded in the 'Treaty of Rome' until finally – the appeals went on forever – the judge cried out in anguish: 'you are not in Rome, you are on the Grote Markt in Groningen!'[1]

It was a sign of a fundamental shift in the status of the Convention. For whereas the 1970s stood out for the emergence of an activist interpretation of the Convention, the defining element which came to characterize human rights, and the Convention more specifically, in the 1980s was how remarkably 'mainstream' they had become. This 'mainstreaming' relates to how human rights, from NGOs to governmental policy, became the embodiment of claims for justice and, moreover, grew in scope: as ever more areas previously seen as exclusive competences of the government or simply not important enough to constitute a connection to human rights were being drawn into the orbit of human rights language.[2] As the Ministry of Foreign Affairs took its first steps towards streamlining Dutch support for human rights, the concepts were presented by an internal commission as a kind of 'sourdough', the flavour of which would permeate the entire department.[3]

[1] F. Kuitenbrouwer, 'Het universele geweten in Nederland', *NRC* 10 December 1983.

[2] See in this vein Ignatieff, *The Rights Revolution*, pp. 1–6.

[3] NL-HaNA, Buza/Code 1975–1984, 2.05.330, inv. nr. 6233; Adviescommissie Mensenrechten, *In dienst voor de mensenrechten.*

The most important element in this development was how mainstreaming also took place in the courtroom. After all, the Convention had long been kept at bay by the domestic judiciary. These norms were after all 'serious business', not to be used lightly. But over the course of a decade, human rights evolved from fringe anomalies into commonly accepted legal arguments, which – importantly – started to win cases, both on the domestic as on the European level.[4] Looking back at the 1980s, former president of the European Court Ryssdall saw a trend by which the Convention and its Court 'moved from the obscurity of a peripheral international tribunal of interest only to the initiated few' into a far more widely accepted institution as a proper constitutional court of Europe.[5] As such, the courts fulfilled the 'rights revolution', building on the legal infrastructure set up in the previous decade.[6]

Yet – much like sourdough – its taste wasn't for everyone. For although the new zeal of the courts was welcomed by activists and scholars, the government grew increasingly wary of human rights and their new implications. The expansion of human rights was far from uncontroversial. This opened a fracture in support for the Convention and planted the seeds for present-day public debates on the limits that European human rights place on governmental freedom.

For this mainstreaming of the Convention was not 'uncontroversial'.[7] In fact, it was so controversial that partly because of this pushback,

[4] Mikael Rask Madsen, 'The Challenging Authority of the European Court of Human Rights: From Cold War Legal Diplomacy to the Brighton Declaration and Backlash' *Law and Contemporary Problems* Vol. 79 Nr. 1 (2016), pp. 141–178, 154.

[5] Quoted in Bates, *The Evolution of the European Convention* p. 400. Also, Madsen turns to this quote to characterize the period; Madsen, 'The Challenging Authority', p. 167.

[6] Epp, *The Rights Revolution*; see in this light also Pieter van Dijk, 'Domestic Status of Human Rights Treaties and the Attitude of the Judiciary, the Dutch Case' in Mannfred Nowak, Dorothea Steurer, Hannes Tretter (eds.), *Progress in the Spirit of Human Rights: Festschrift Für Felix Ermacora* (Kehl, 1988), pp. 631–649.

[7] Madsen notes how the position of the European Court was strengthened by deciding on a list of more or less uncontroversial issues: that is surely true in relation to the position of the Court itself, as it dealt with much less highly political interstate complaints, yet this is not to say everything was smooth sailing. Rather, the impact of its findings on fair trial and family law proved quite controversial indeed, if only on a domestic level. Madsen, 'The Challenging Authority of the European Court of Human Rights', p. 154.

human rights lost some of their radical feathers.[8] With the mainstreaming of human rights, they were on the one hand inserted into areas where they were had been kept from, such as migration. But they also turned from protest language into legalized tools of action and policy considerations. This in turn entailed their domestication: human rights law as enshrined in the Convention could succeed in cutting the rough edges off, but could not fundamentally challenge the system.[9] With some of the more ambitious options abandoned along the way, a key outcome of the decade was how in the Netherlands the minimum standard as enshrined in the international legal order was embraced as the default option, turning the Strasbourg minimum into the domestic maximum.

5.1 'THE UNIVERSAL STANCE OF EVERYONE TOWARDS EVERYTHING': HUMAN RIGHTS IN THE 1980S

This mainstreaming of human rights was not lost to contemporaries. In his 1990 novel *Immortality*, Czech writer Milan Kundera made an observation on a development he had seen emerging from the midst of the 1970s: the rise in prominence of human rights talk. For Kundera, himself having fled a communist dictatorship, it was striking how commonplace these lofty terms had become. With slight exaggeration, Kundera noted how, over the course of a decade, 'parking on the sidewalk' had become a human right, explaining:

> because people in the West are not threatened by concentration camps and are free to say and write what they want, the more the fight for human rights gains in popularity, the more it loses any concrete content, becoming a kind of universal stance of everyone toward everything, a kind of energy that turns all human desires into rights...[10]

[8] Jessica Whyte, *The Morals of the Market: Human Rights and the Rise of Neoliberalism* (New York: Verso, 2019); Samuel Moyn, *Not Enough: Human Rights in an Unequal World* (Cambridge: Harvard University Press, 2018).

[9] As we shall see in, for example, migration.

[10] Milan Kundera, 'The Gesture of Protest against a Violation of Human Rights', *Immortality* (London: Faber & Faber, 1990).

Kundera touched upon one of the most striking transformations which had taken place with regard to human rights in the 1980s. From being presented as 'serious business' in the 1950s and 1960s which only were threatened in totalitarian states, they were transformed into commonplace claims, moving beyond small academic circles and engaged individuals into the societal, scholarly and political mainstream. Kundera took the French context as a model for his vision of 'the West', yet he could just as easily have placed this story in the Netherlands.[11]

Kundera had a point. Human rights were increasingly seen in all facets of society. They emerged in newspapers, as a call for action, or in courts as legal claims. Politicians used it to address undesirable situations (although mostly exclusively in a foreign policy setting), while philosophers came to defend and embrace human rights as the new intellectual *vogue*.[12] The presumed apolitical claim of human rights fitted nicely with the turn to depoliticized expertise.[13] Human rights thrived in the managerial style of politics that emerged in the same period, which increasingly left it up to the judge-expert to decide on whichever political question lay underneath the supposedly neutral new regulations.[14] The decade was neatly summarized in the French slogan 'Management, Minitel, Human Rights'.[15]

In legal education, the battle for the meaning of the Convention had already been decided and would steadily be cemented. In the human rights hubs of Leiden and Utrecht most prominently, the Convention was now a commonplace element in the curriculum. With the Dutch member of the Commission, Henry Schermers, treating countless of

[11] A very similar critique indeed emerged not long after in Michel Korzec, *Ik kan alles uitleggen* (Amsterdam: Prometheus, 1994), pp. 43–56.

[12] Luuk van Middelaar, *Politicide; De moord op de politiek in de Franse filosofie* (Groningen: Historische Uitgeverij, 2011), pp. 142–158.

[13] Van Middelaar, *Politicide*, pp. 142–158.

[14] On management language see Wendy Brown, *Undoing the Demos. Neoliberalism's Stealth Revolution* (New York: Zone Books, 2015).

[15] 'Leur credo prêche le management, le Minitel et les droits de l'homme' François Bernard Huyghe and Pierre Barbes, *La Soft-Idéology* (Paris: Laffont, 1987), p. 12. The 'Minitel', an early French variant of the internet, was a hugely popular device in the 1980s, albeit mostly confined to France.

his students in Leiden to the insights and cases he experienced in Strasbourg, the Convention was made ever more common within Dutch legal education.[16]

From the governmental side of things, the formal inclusion of human rights as a Dutch foreign policy objective in 1979 can be seen as a starting point for a more active engagement with human rights. The necessity to take fundamental rights into account led to an increase in attention for the topic and formed the basis of an expanding realm of committees and initiatives when it came to including human rights in governmental action.

One of the initiatives which stood out in this regard was the so-called 'advice committee on human rights', instituted in 1984, under the direction of human rights expert Peter Baehr. This committee, mandated to give non-binding reports on human rights-related issues concerning Dutch policy in Foreign Affairs, was set up with the aim of providing an independent check on how human rights could be best implemented in policy. Baehr himself had high hopes for the committee. In his opening speech, he set the tone, remarking that when Dutch Ministers of Foreign Affairs had sleepless nights, they should ask themselves whether or not they had done enough for human rights.[17] This used to be, or in fact still was, the language of an activist, but now it had become a part of the governmental circles themselves.

The first report of the committee is illustrative of the great expectations which were placed upon human rights in the 1980s. The report dealt with the place of human rights in – among other contexts – the education for civil servants, and found the existing amount of human rights education to not be in conformity with its importance as one of the pillars of foreign policy (in a Freudian slip, the authors of the report initially wrote '*the* main pillar of foreign policy').[18] Perhaps unsurprisingly, the committee

[16] Illustrative is the institution of the Mordenate College, a group for talented students following a special curriculum with more personal attention devoted, amongst other to Schermers own experiences at the commission. See one of its early publications: Henry Schermers (eds.), *The Influence of the European Commission of Human Rights* (The Hague: TMC Asser Instituut, 1992).

[17] 'Interview Peter Baehr', *NRC* (24 March 1988).

[18] Emphasis added.

proposed that there should be a much stronger emphasis on human rights education and awareness throughout the entire governmental system.[19]

The mainstreaming of human rights was explicitly embraced as a policy aim. A central tenet in the report was the idea that the gap between policy makers and citizens had to be narrowed. 'The socialization of human rights', as it was dubbed, formed a key feature in the proposed policy: human rights were too important to be left to policy alone. Instead, society as a whole would have to be involved. To achieve that goal, the committee recommended close cooperation with the same NGOs who had driven the human rights moment in the first place. This led to the recommendation to let Amnesty International or the SIM in Utrecht provide coaching and training sessions to the civil servants.[20]

Without exaggerating the immediate impact of this committee – which received quite some pushback from civil servants – it was a sign that human rights were becoming more commonplace in considerations in the Ministries. In particular the relation between the government and NGOs stands out in this regard. Human rights engagement had experienced its breakthrough on the streets, with marches for Greece and protestors carrying signs of Amnesty international. Yet in the 1980s, human rights became increasingly institutionalized as engagement moved from the streets to the meeting tables.

5.1.1 THE INSTITUTIONALIZATION OF ACTION AND THE TURN TO HUMAN RIGHTS LAW. This intertwinement between government and social movements is closely connected to the professionalization of social movements which occurred in the 1980s. The action groups which had emerged in the 1970s faced a dilemma in the 1980s: should they continue upon the loosely organized path of activism, with a small but active base of volunteers, or become more institutionalized, usually as a mass membership organization? Amnesty took this latter route, turning into a mass organization with fewer active members, but with a strong and

[19] NL-HaNA, Buza/Code 1975–1984, 2.05.330, inv. nr. 6233; Adviescommissie Mensenrechten, *In dienst voor de Mensenrechten: Buitenlandse Zaken en de rechten van de mens* (The Hague, 1984), p. 10.

[20] NL-HaNA, Buza/Code 1975–1984, 2.05.330, inv. nr. 6233; Adviescommissie Mensenrechten, *In dienst voor de mensenrechten*, p. 15.

stable basis of passive contributors combined with a growing professional secretariat.[21] It was a development which can be discerned in a wide variety of social movements as the character of grassroots movements of the 1970s, slowly but surely shifted into professionalized organizations.[22]

A consequence thereof was that it became increasingly common for grassroots movements and NGOs to have close relations with the government. This was poignant in the realm of human rights activism, which – supported by the government's ambition to cooperate with these NGOs – was drawn ever closer into policymaking.[23] To be clear, both the government and the NGOs supported this shift towards increasing intertwinement. The best example of this dynamic is how, after 1979, a wide variety of NGOs were invited by the government to join the so-called 'Breed Mensenrechten Overleg' (BMO), a formalized platform for discussion on how to improve attention for human rights in Dutch foreign policy. The meeting consisted of a colourful mix of NGOs, ranging from larger groups such as Amnesty and Pax Christi, to more loosely organized, single-issue movements. One participant, a textbook activist who had been active trying to propagate human rights since the late 1960s, could not contain his surprise when, after a decade of little to no attention for the issue of human rights, 'suddenly countless societies, committees and other groups had arisen out of nowhere, which all in high tones were dealing with human rights'.[24]

In itself, the existence of such a forum was illustrative of the attention human rights had started to receive, but it was also constitutive of a new role for human rights and human rights organizations. For these NGOs, the forum offered a formalized venue to exert influence on governmental policy, which made participation all the more attractive. For the government, on the other hand, it was a good way to tap into the human rights

[21] Bouwman, 'Outraged but Impartial', *BMGN*, p. 73.

[22] Hans Beerens and Marc Broere, *De Bewogen Beweging: Een halve eeuw mondiale solidariteit* (Amsterdam: KIT Publishers, 2004), pp. 117–118.

[23] See also de Liagre Böhl, 'Consensus en Polarisatie spanningen in de verzorgingsstaat, 1950–1990' in R. Aerts, *Land van kleine gebaren: een politieke geschiedenis van Nederland 1780–1990* (Nijmegen: Boom, 2007), p. 337.

[24] Nationaal Archief, Den Haag, Tweede Kamer der Staten-Generaal, nummer toegang 2.02.28, inventarisnummer 4995, 'Studiecentrum universele rechten van de mens, November 1979'.

expertise of the NGOs, a realm in which these were occasionally better equipped than the government itself.[25] Moreover, the opportunity to 'touch base' before decisions ensured a certain connection to societal groups and ensured that policymakers could evade the most damning critiques.

The implications of the BMO were twofold. First, NGOs were increasingly moulded into becoming 'human rights NGOs'. By integrating a variety of societal groups into a particular forum dedicated to human rights, it bonded them together on that topic. In this manner, those activist groups were guided into using a particular set of speech and action, that is, the language of human rights.[26] Second, it ensured that human rights activism became firmly engrained in the fabric of government and society. As a consequence, it did lose some of their radical feathers: it simply became more difficult to fundamentally criticize decisions if one was present and discussing them throughout the drafting process.

With the professionalization of activism came a renewed focus on human rights as human rights law. For one, the institutionalized conversations with the government nudged activists towards this path. Grand Utopian narratives were simply less effective at the meeting table with policymakers than the precise phrasing of legal obligations. One needed to speak the language of the administration in order to be heard. As the same old school street activist noted with disappointment in the first meeting of the BMO, 'it is highly frustrating how human rights [...] have been drawn completely into the realm of nitty gritty legal work...'[27]

Unfortunately for the activist in question, the nitty-gritty legal work was there to stay. Also in terms of action, law proved a useful tool to change situations. Now this is clearly not to say that no attention for law existed before the 1980s. Much to the contrary, we have seen how law was foundational, with the legal aid movement closely connected to the protests of

[25] More than once, ministries reached out to these action groups to hire experts on the topic. As a result, members of Amnesty and NJCM, for example, ended up in Foreign Affairs or the Ministry of Justice, further strengthening the connection between the legal experts in government and NGOs.

[26] Making it difficult along the way to address issues not easily caught in the human rights discourse, such as poverty.

[27] NL-HaNA, Tweede Kamer, 1945–1999, 2.02.28, inv. nr. 4995, 'Comments on Nota Human Rights'.

the 1970s. However, as NGOs evolved from mass movements into institutionalized players, the way the law was used also became professionalized. Had the earlier engagement been one of getting people to 'know and use their rights', in the 1980s strategic litigation by specialized lawyers was brought to the forefront on a much wider scale. Amnesty, for example, began to hire lawyers, drawing upon a surge of interest in the potential for (public interest) human rights litigation after the Dutch ratification of the UN treaties in 1978.

One movement stood out when it came to pushing for equality via legal venues and is illustrative of the growing commonplace of human rights in the 1980s. The feminist movement, long rather sceptical of using human rights language, would turn to the language of law and, increasingly, human rights and the courts as solutions for undesirable situations. For a long time, the relationship between human rights and women's rights was a complicated history.[28] Yet in the 1980s, the two became increasingly aligned.[29] This coincided with a new zeal of feminist lawyers. In the Netherlands, the Clara Wichmann Institute, specifically focused on the law in order to further emancipation by engaging in strategic litigation. Alongside a specified journal, *Nemesis,* which approached the law from a feminist perspective, the institute fulfilled a role in disseminating knowledge and claims on usages of law for feminist purposes to a much broader group of interested lawyers.[30]

This intertwinement of human rights groups, government and the turn to human rights law ensured human rights became ever more common in policy and regulation. But their mainstreaming was completed by an ever more impactful change, namely the change in status of the Convention in the legal realm.

5.1.2 THE JUDICIARY IN THE REGULATORY STATE. For all these developments may have easily remained marginal, had they not

[28] Celia Donert, 'Women's Rights in Cold War Europe: Disentangling Feminist Histories', *Past and Present* Vol. 218 supplement 8 (2013), pp. 180–202.

[29] Arvonne S. Frazer, 'Becoming Human: The Origins and Development of Women's Human Rights', *Human Rights Quarterly* Vol. 21 Nr. 4 (1999), pp. 853–906.

[30] Margreet de Boer and Marjan Wijers, *Vrouw en Recht: De beweging, de mensen, de issues* (Amsterdam: Amsterdam University Press, 2009).

gone hand in hand with a trend which proved key in reinforcing this new zeal for human rights: the new role of the domestic judiciary. This was part of a structural change within the legal system. What stood out in particular was how, in the 1980s, the judiciary saw an immense growth in its power, due to a change in how the state was organized. As the 1980s came to be known as an age of liberalization and privatization, with the government retreating from the public sector, it was the judiciary which took on a new role. In fact, the retreat of the government emboldened independent judges to step in and become more active in society. Crucially, in the 1980s, the position of the judiciary was enhanced as it became the prime institution for safeguarding the individual liberties of the citizens. This development has been described as a transition from a positive state – a form of governance characterized by direct interventions in the economy and a focus on budget spending – to a 'regulatory' state, characterized by rule-making, outsourcing and subsequent reliance on independent experts – the judiciary most of all – to control these new regulations of the government.[31] With judges growing increasingly comfortable in this active role, appeals on human rights could land in a more fertile ground at the courts in the 1980s then in any earlier period.

The courts themselves grew increasingly accustomed to this role. Confronted with an increase in cases, the traditional restraint of the judiciary was ever less suited to the new circumstances, in which the judge had to act as problem-solver. In particular, the principle of equality came to function as a newly found tool to limit the power of the government, heralding a new division between a protective judiciary against an overtly intrusive government.[32] Moreover, the late 1970s were a period in which the judges started to see the law less as a set of rules and more as a set of values, which allowed for more creative interpretation. Crucially, this was done with an eye for the interest of the individual. In that sense, the

[31] Giandomenico Majone, 'From the Positive to the Regulatory State: Causes and Consequences of Changes in the Mode of Governance' *Journal of Public Policy* Vol. 17 Nr. 2 (1997), pp. 139–167, 156. Further, G. Majone, 'The Rise of the Regulatory State in Europe' *West European Politics* Vol.17 Nr.3 (1994), pp. 77–101.

[32] Rob Schwitters, *Recht en Samenleving in Verandering: een Inleiding in de Rechtssociologie* (Deventer, 2008), pp. 61–63.

judge was almost bound to become more active in protecting the citizen vis-à-vis an increasingly powerful government.[33]

In this new role, international law became the most readily available tool for the courts. In light of the constitutional openness of the Dutch legal system, which grants a strong position to directly applicable international legal provisions, international law offered the standards against which judges could check legislation.[34] They did not need to look far: the new role of the judiciary coincided with a growth of legal possibilities in the field of international and European law. From the late 1970s onwards, the judges could find plenty of those tools in an expanding range of international law to intervene in the legal landscape. Most prominently, the regulations of the EEC grew significantly and presented judges with ever increasing powers to check governmental legislation.[35] With an eye to human rights, the Dutch ratification of the international human rights treaties, the ICCPR and ICESCR, in 1978, meant a strong increase of the possibilities of judicial engagement, and served as an encouragement for human rights claims in themselves.

Clearly, the possibilities for the judiciary with regard to the Convention had been exactly the same since 1954 when the Convention was ratified. But it was the attitude of judges which ultimately determined the way the Convention was interpreted, and precisely that was shifting in the eighties.[36] For within the options available to the judiciary, the Convention began to take up a central place in its role of protecting the citizens. The number of cases which included an appeal on the Convention tell a distinct story: in 1980, thirty-five cases before the Hoge Raad contained a reference to the ECHR. In 1986 it had already grown

[33] Ybo Buruma, 'Wat is een goede rechter? Een mentaliteitsgeschiedenis (1900–2020)' Inaugural lecture (Nijmegen, 2016), pp. 36–40.

[34] Soeharno takes this as one of the reasons for increased judicial control. J. E. Soeharno, 'From Guardian of the *Rechtsstaat* to Ruler in the Rule of Law: An Inquiry into the Increased Role of the Judiciary' in van Hoek, A., Hol, A. M., Jansen, O. J. D. L. M., Rijpkema, P. and Widdershoven, R. J. G. M. (eds.), *Multilevel Governance in Adjudication and Enforcement* (Antwerp: Intersentia, 2006), pp. 157–178.

[35] Alter, *Establishing the Supremacy of European Law*, pp. 1–32.

[36] van Dijk, 'Domestic Status of Human Rights Treaties', pp. 631–649.

into 102, in which 12 violations were found.[37] The next year, in 1987, the NJCM signalled 178 relevant cases in which the Convention played a role as compared to 36 in 1979: roughly five times as many.[38]

Lawyers played an important role here. In Chapter 4, we saw how knowledge of the Convention had become disseminated from a select few academics into the bar more generally. This ensured how, in the 1980s, appeals on the Convention definitively moved beyond the actions of engaged individuals (although those clearly led the charge) into the relative mainstream of legal tools. Conversely, the growing acquaintance with the functioning of European human rights had their impact beyond the own domestic legal order. Very practical, increased knowledge of the Strasbourg option increased the chances of success for the plaintiff there as well. For example, it had been rare for early plaintiffs going to Strasbourg to receive proper legal aid: less than one in ten plaintiffs had help from a lawyer before 1970, and even if plaintiffs were awarded legal advice, lawyers were not fully aware of how the procedure functioned. In 1987 this had grown to over five in ten, which as such led to a more streamlined procedure, with a bigger chance of success in getting an application to be declared admissible.[39]

Therefore, the judiciary increasingly became an answer for political problems. This was a feeling shared by both the government and activists. For when it came to establishing change, the activist zeal of the 1970s in political innovation had ebbed away. As one disillusioned activist lawyer noted in 1988: 'in the 1970s, we had put our hopes in government and Parliament, but in the 1980s, it became clear they were not of that much use anymore…'.[40] But the solution was not to give

[37] Pieter van Dijk, 'Domestic Status of Human Rights Treaties and the Attitude of the Judiciary, the Dutch Case', p. 642.

[38] 'Jurisprudentieoverzicht' *NJCM Bulletin*, Vol.13 Nr. 8, pp. 820–823.

[39] C. A. Groenendijk, 'mensenrechten tussen retoriek en praktijk: gebruik van het klachtrecht in Straatsburg en de bescherming van vreemdelingen' in L. Heyde, J. Leijten and Th. Mertens en B. P. Vermeulen (eds.), *Begrensde Vrijheid: Opstellen over mensenrechten aangebonden aan Prof. Dr D.F. Scheltens bij zijn afscheid als hoogleraar aan de Katholieke Universiteit Nijmegen* (Zwolle: Tjeenk Willink, 1989), pp. 191–203.

[40] A. H. J. van den Biesen, 'Sociale advocatuur en mensenrechten' in Tom van Hoogenboom (ed.), *Sociale Advocatuur en de rechten van de* mens*: Congresverslag Maastricht* (Nijmegen: ars Aequi Libri, 1989), pp. 1–8, 2.

up on social ideals, but rather turn to a different forum: the courts. As such, the activism of the previous decade increasingly shifted from politics to law – where it was now met by a much friendlier counterpart than in previous years.

5.2 THE DOMESTIC LEGAL REVOLUTION

Arguably the most important change in the 1980s with regard to the Convention was its change in usage by the judiciary. As judges grew accustomed to their new roles as the guardians of equality and increasingly put limits on governmental legislation, they looked to the Convention as a tool to do so. In this decade, the Convention became *perceived* to be of great importance by lawyers, judges and plaintiffs. On paper, the possibilities for revision against the Convention had always existed. They were, in fact, extremely strong. Yet only in the 1980s, the domestic judiciary started to embrace the potential of European human rights as checks on governmental policy.

A symbolic moment in the proclamation of the new legal status of human rights was the Dutch constitutional revision of 1983. Long in the making, the revision was the result of a longstanding desire to modernize the somewhat archaic constitution and revolved primarily around fundamental rights.[41] Their importance was reaffirmed by rearranging them and placing them in the opening chapter of the constitution. New rights were added, such as the right of non-discrimination and the right to bodily integrity, but also social rights, such as the duty for the government to provide employment opportunities. As the editorial board of the *NJB* noted, 'for the first time since 1798 the constitution puts emphasis on fundamental rights [...]it makes those into a frame of reference and orientation for the entire legal system'.[42]

The direct legal consequences for fundamental rights may have seemed slim at first sight. The new constitution did not lead to a surge in litigation in itself: the ban on constitutional review made such a role

[41] Tom Barkhuysen e.a., *De Nederlandse Grondwet geëvalueerd: Anker of verdwijnpunt?* (Alphen aan den Rijn: Kluwer, 2009), pp. 44–45.

[42] Redactioneel, 'Een nieuwe Grondwet' *NJB* nr. 7 (1983), p. 201.

impossible. However, it did signal political support for the strong legal protection of fundamental rights. This statement of support was important in light of the reason for which domestic courts had been traditionally reluctant in their application of fundamental rights, namely a desire not to touch upon the prerogative of the legislator. The legislative support and attention for fundamental rights were helpful in diminishing that hesitance.[43]

In this context, it is important to note that the ECHR was but one of the fundamental rights treaties which could be used in the newly found judicial zeal. The UN treaties formed another option. Sometimes, the Convention – not the most ambitious of human rights programmes after all – did not fit with the aims pursued by legal activists. The most important of these limitations was the principle of non-discrimination as enshrined in Article 14 of the Convention, which was (and is) not a self-standing right but needs to be connected to other rights in order to claim discriminatory treatment. It was a legacy of the drafting history when women's claims were dismissed, and a general principle of equal treatment had not been taken up in the final text. Claims based on non-discrimination and equality were the central arguments, however of the feminist legal movement, which, as its legal advice went, was better off with appeals based on other international treaties.[44]

Still, even with this caveat, the Convention came to outshine the other treaties as the most vital tool for fundamental rights protection.[45] But the Convention wasn't brought to life solely in a top-down manner. Spurred on by lower judges, the Hoge Raad started to go (much) further than the European demands prescribed and began to use the Convention on its own account to change the Dutch legal system. Moreover, the Convention was increasingly made to matter in areas previously considered beyond

[43] Janneke Gerards en Carla Sieburgh (eds.), *De invloed van fundamentele rechten op het materiele recht*, p. 533.

[44] Stichting NJCM Boekerij, *Vrouw en Recht* (Leiden: NJCM, 1984), pp. 3–5.

[45] It should therefore be kept in mind that the Convention offered a *specific* protection: not all claims to justice came to be incorporated in European human rights claims. We have already seen the absence of socio-economic rights in this context, but one can also think of migration (see beyond) and equality in this context. The breakthrough of the Convention was therefore a success story, yet one with inherent limitations.

the reach of human rights by a combination of lawyers and academics who saw their claims land in increasingly fertile soil. This was indeed a domestic legal revolution, but established through a constant interaction between the domestic and European level.

5.2.1 CATERING TO EUROPEAN DEMANDS: THE PROCEDURAL REVOLUTION OF ARTICLE 6. The most visible impact of the ECHR in the Dutch legal order in a 'top down' manner can be identified in the change that Article 6 of the Convention brought about by inserting its procedural demands on fair trial a variety of legal areas. The first of those areas was criminal law. The prominence of that field was not surprising: most of the early attention to human rights in the legal system had been in the context of criminal law, where people like Baauw, Myjer and Peeters had actively pushed for incorporating human rights and where there existed an acute awareness of its potential.[46]

This impact of the ECHR on the criminal procedure could be felt from the late 1970s onwards. Its requirements entered the spotlights when a high-profile case of a Dutch war criminal was declared inadmissible because of a violation of the 'reasonable time' requirement of Article 6 ECHR.[47] Although later reversed by the Hoge Raad, it proved the beginning of an ever-increasing relation between criminal law and demands flowing from the Convention.[48] It was telling when, already in 1981, the president of the Hoge Raad would note how human rights treaties, and in particular the ECHR, were increasingly influencing cases relating to criminal law.[49] Also illustrative of the growing engagement of the Dutch legal profession with the Convention was when, in 1983, the 'Nederlandse Juristen Vereniging', the 'umbrella organization' of legal professionals in the Netherlands, spent the day discussing the implications which Article 6 of the Convention could have on the Dutch

[46] See Chapter 4.

[47] See HR 22-05-1979, ECLI:NL:PHR:1979:AC6587, *NJ* 1979, 301 – the Menten case.

[48] Even though this was by no means a smooth or easy way: Myjer had to note how his proclaimed 'Dutch spring' did not truly kick off, with local judges dismissing appeals on article 6. Myjer, 'overzicht rechtspraak' *NJCM Bulletin* Vol. 5 Nr. 3 (1980), pp. 148–153.

[49] P. van Dijk, 'De houding van de Hoge Raad jegens de verdragen inzake de rechten van de mens', pp. 173–209, 202.

legal order. Even though the potential implications sometimes met with incredulous reactions ('if I hear all this, I believe it might be best to cancel the Treaty and continue as we have always done', a member of the audience stated), the meeting made it increasingly clear that the Convention was here to stay.[50]

Meanwhile, the Hoge Raad struggled to define its position vis-à-vis Article 6. The consequences which should be attached to violations of the reasonable time requirement remained vague for quite some time. As the criminal procedure needed to be brought in line with European demands with regard to the reasonable time requirement, confusion ensued on how exactly to do so.[51] The judiciary therefore went along in a somewhat trial-and-error manner. For a while, the Hoge Raad opted for a quite restrictive approach before it would settle for a more nuanced approach, and rather than declaring the case inadmissible outright, it would open the possibility for a limitation of punishment as well, something more in line with the European demands as well.[52]

Later in the 1980s, the procedural requirements would further be refined by seminal cases *Kostovski* v. *Netherlands* and *Brogan and Others* v. *U.K.*[53] The consequence of both cases was how key components of the Dutch criminal code needed to be reviewed. In *Kostovski*, the European Court found that the way in which the Dutch criminal procedure allowed for the usage of anonymous witnesses (inaccessible to the suspect, not present in Court, interrogated by members of the public prosecutor, and in the end conclusive to the ruling) was in violation of Article 6 of the Convention.[54] In *Brogan*, directed against the UK, the time requirements of temporary custody were defined by the European Court, noting that a period of four days and six hours were not in line with the Convention.[55] Much to the surprise of those dealing with

[50] Redactioneel commentaar, *NJCM Bulletin* Vol. 8. Nr. 4 (1983).

[51] See, for example, *Wemhoff* v. *Germany*, 27 June 1968, Series A no. 7.

[52] HR 07-04-1987, ECLI:NL:PHR:1987:AB9733, *NJ* 1987/587. See Evert Alkema, *Over implementatie van internationaal recht: De internationale rechtsorde is de onze nog niet* (Leiden, 2005), p. 10.

[53] *Kostovski* v. *the Netherlands*, 20 November 1989, Series A no. 166, *NJ* 1990, 245; *Brogan and Others* v. *the United Kingdom*, 29 November 1988, Series A no. 145-B.

[54] *Kostovski* v. *the Netherlands*, 20 November 1989, Series A no. 166, *NJ* 1990,245.

[55] *Brogan and Others* v. *the United Kingdom*, 29 November 1988, Series A no. 145-B.

Dutch criminal procedure, which worked on a comparable time frame, it turned out that such timing did not count as 'promptly' in the meaning of the Convention.[56]

These cases had an immediate impact on the Dutch national system. As the president of the Hoge Raad looked back on the occasion, it was even felt as a 'disruption' of the legal machinery.[57] As a result, European demands became firmly integrated in the domestic criminal law system and came to serve as the key document in which the rights of suspects were enshrined.

The changes put forward by European case law on Article 6 did not stop there. The second field where the procedural revolution of Article 6 could be felt was administrative law. Here, the right to a fair trial, in particular the demand to appear before an 'independent and impartial tribunal', caused a small earthquake in the Dutch legal system in 1985 when the case *Benthem* v. *Netherlands* the European Court declared that the 'appeal on the crown' was not up to the standards of the ECHR.[58]

The judgement came a shock.[59] The story of Evert Benthem, a small entrepreneur from Groningen, had gripped the Dutch legal world for quite some time, but when the case was finally decided by the Court in Strasbourg, also newspapers picked up its importance. It was evident something remarkable had happened here. Not solely because of the strong David versus Goliath thematic the judgement provoked and the tragic backstory which accompanied the case (the lengthy procedure had left Benthem bankrupt and divorced before proven right), but also because it was the first time the European Court had delivered such an impactful judgement against the Netherlands. With *Benthem*, a defining

[56] E. Myjer, 'The plain meaning of the word "promptly"', in P. Mahoney e.a. (eds.), *Protecting Human Rights: The European Perspective – Studies in memory of Rolv Ryssdal* (Heidelberg: Carl Heymanns Verlag, 2000), pp. 975–992.

[57] W. E. Haak, 'De taak van de Hoge Raad in Europa en het Koninkrijk' *NJB* Vol. 17 (2004), pp. 881–888.

[58] *Benthem* v. *the Netherlands*, 23 October 1985, Series A no. 97 Wiarda had written an article before, stating how European demands could be construed as not in conformity with Dutch practice, yet to no avail.

[59] For an overview of commentaries, see the annotation of Alkema in *NJ* 1986/102: EHRM 23-10-1985, ECLI:NL:XX:1985:AC9055.

element of the Dutch legal system had been declared to constitute a violation of human rights. As one newspaper noted, the judgement 'hit like a bomb'.[60]

It was followed by swift action to redesign the administrative procedure in order to comply, and after a period of confusion, some three years later a new law ensured the venue to constitute a truly independent tribunal. Yet the case stood for more than just a change in an administrative procedure – this was 'a pearl out of the Crown', it was noted, and with it, the idea of an infallible Dutch legal system was resolutely buried.[61] In essence, it was the definitive end of the myth of Dutch legal innocence.

5.2.2 MOVING BEYOND STRASBOURG: THE DISCOVERY OF ARTICLE 8. A different field of law can shed light on how the Convention wasn't just made relevant in a top down manner through the European Court. For when it came to Article 8, a veritable 'bottom up' movement turned the Convention into a tool for the judiciary to engineer change in the realm of family law. At first sight, this was not the first realm of law one expected human rights law to play an active role. The product of local domestic sensitivities, it was long regarded as a purely domestic state of affairs. Still, it became the prime area in which a new engagement with the Convention was formed. It began with the *Marckx* case, in which the European Court decided a Belgian division between 'legal and natural' children to be discriminatory in nature.[62] The case stood at the basis of a flurry of activity by the Dutch courts, which found in Article 8 a provision to truly alter family law.

For some years after *Marckx*, the Hoge Raad, embarked on an adventurous trip to change Dutch family law. It set out this trajectory in a case concerning divorce. As a rule, this implied the automatic end of parental authority and the need to appoint guardianship over the child, but the Hoge Raad found this to be a violation of Article 8 ECHR, thereby opening the door for a reading of parental authority

[60] 'Het Benthem-arrest sloeg in als een bom', *Het Parool* (16 December 1986).
[61] See the annotation of Alkema, *NJ* 1986, 102.
[62] *Marckx* v. *Belgium*, 13 June 1979, Series A no. 31.

which could also exist beyond marriage.[63] That in itself may not seem surprising, yet in doing so, the Hoge Raad went – on its own account – beyond what the European Court had set out. No precedent for such use of Article 8 existed in the European jurisprudence, which entailed the Hoge Raad was prepared to give precedence to European human rights, even when no significant European developments pointed in that direction.[64]

Now clearly, the European system allowed for such a usage of the Convention. It had been stressed how it served as a minimum standard, but states were free to adopt more far-reaching protections.[65] In the Dutch context, it came as a surprise though, in particular because a year later, the Hoge Raad continued with this active approach. The next year, it was decided a right to visit would be granted to a man who did not have any legal connections to a child after breaking a relation with the mother.[66] Again, one year later, the Hoge Raad found Article 8, read in conjunction with Article 14 ECHR, to entail that also unmarried parents could enjoy parental authority together.[67] These small steps in the end culminated in a judgement in which the Hoge Raad set a completely new standard on family life. In deciding on Article 8 in situations regarding parental visitation rules, the Hoge Raad constructed how family life in the meaning of Article 8 already existed *de jure* if a plaintiff was the biological father of a child.[68]

Such a reading went far beyond any existing European jurisprudence.[69] What took place here was therefore fundamentally new in the domestic legal approach to European human rights. Rather than the traditional hesitant approach, the Hoge Raad took a provision of directly applicable international human rights, interpreted it on its own account

[63] HR 04-05-1984, ECLI:NL:PHR:1984:AG4807.

[64] See also Leo Zwaak 'Netherlands' in Blackburn and Polakiewicz, *Fundamental Rights in Europe, the ECHR and Its Member States, 1950–2000* (Oxford: Oxford University Press, 2001), pp. 595–624.

[65] See also article 53 ECHR.

[66] HR 22-02-1985, ECLI:NL:PHR:1985:AG4966, *NJ* 1986, 3.

[67] HR 21-03-1986, ECLI:NL:PHR:1986:AC9283.

[68] HR 10-05-1985, ECLI:NL:PHR:1985:AG5018, *NJ* 1986, 5; HR 15-07-1985, ECLI:NL:PHR:1985:AC4250, *NJ* 1986, 6 and HR 16 May 1986, ECLI:NL:PHR:1986:AC9342, *NJ* 1986, 627.

[69] European Commission, 15 March 1984 appl. 9558/81 (BRD).

and used it to alter Dutch family law. In doing so, human rights law had suddenly become a key provision in the hands of the judiciary.

Encouraged by the willingness of the Hoge Raad to liberally interpret the Convention, lower judges on occasion went further still. In lower courts, a right of recognition and a right to shared custody for a parent who did not recognize his child, but lived together was being composed on the basis of Article 8.[70] Moreover, this new course generated a flood of new procedures of plaintiffs eager to base their claims on Article 8, which – after all – could very well work in their favour.[71] The practice of the Hoge Raad therefore also resulted in activating new claims on the Convention, which would end up in Strasbourg to be decided.[72]

The way things stood in 1987 can be described as the absolute peak of active judicial engagement with the Convention. As things progressed over the mid-1980s, the judiciary had put itself into a uniquely powerful position. In its new role of not just protecting, but also furthering individual rights protection, it had presented itself with the power to anticipate developments on the European level, and subsequently go beyond the level of protection granted by the European Court or Commission. Such a position tremendously enhanced the potential of judicial review: it meant judges were free to interpret on their own account what international human rights norms entailed and use those interpretations to set aside formal legislation. To those academics who had pushed for the Conventions activation, this was a laudable position indeed: in light of human rights protection, things could not be (and go) 'fair enough'.[73]

5.2.3 MAKING THE CONVENTION MATTER IN MIGRATION LAW. Through a combination of European demands and self-standing domestic legal activism the Convention therefore gained

[70] W. Elzinga, 'Ontwikkelingen in het Nederlandse familierecht in het licht van EVRM en BUPO', in *Sociale Advocatuur en de rechten van de mens: Congresverslag Maastricht*, pp. 91–101; Rb Amsterdam, 17 December 1987; RB Amsterdam, 4 May 1987, *NJ* 1987, p. 842.

[71] M. de Langen, 'De betekenis van artikel 8 EVRM voor het familierecht' *Handelingen Nederlandse Juristen Vereniging, 1990 I* (Zwolle: Tjeenk Willink, 1990), pp. 85–185, 164.

[72] Ibid.

[73] E. Myjer, 'Dutch interpretation of the European Convention: a double system?' in F. Matscher and H. Petzold, (eds.), *Protecting Human Rights: The European Dimension. Studies in Honour of Gérard J. Wiarda* (Köln, Heymanns, 1988), pp. 421–430.

increased relevance in the Dutch legal order when it came to criminal, administrative and family law. Yet in the 1980s, a fourth realm of law became drawn into the orbit of European human rights law, illustrating how domestic (legal) activism and European jurisprudence cannot be seen in isolation.[74] This was the realm of migration law.

Migration is nowadays a key component of the European human rights framework, posing limits on expulsion, providing for family reunification and entailing obligations for countries when confronted with people claiming asylum. Yet this situation is somewhat perplexing from a historical point of view. The ECHR does not offer any rights of asylum, for example.[75] So how did the Convention end up so intimately connected to migration? As in the other areas of law discussed here, migration and asylum only saw the impact of human rights law emerge during the 1980s.[76] For usually, the ECtHR's engagement with these questions is situated as beginning in 1989, when in *Soering v UK* the European Court found the expulsion of a German national to the United States to constitute a violation of Article 3 ECHR.[77] Yet as much as *Soering* can be seen as a beginning, it was also the end of a movement which was set in motion much earlier on a local level by a diverse coalition of academics, judges and activists.

The connection between migration and human rights needed to be explicitly created. For although Article 14 of the Universal Declaration sets out the right to seek asylum as a human right, legally speaking, human rights were notoriously absent from the realm of immigration law as it was beginning to take shape in the 1970s. In fact, immigration law itself was in its infancy, hardly a proper field of law and although

[74] See for a comparable approach, but focused on the Danish case, Thomas Gammeltoft-Hansen and Mikael Rask Madsen, 'Regime Entanglement in the Emergence of Interstitial Legal Fields: Denmark and the Uneasy Marriage of Human Rights and Migration Law', *Nordiques* [Online], Nr. 40 (2021), pp. 1–18.

[75] See Prisca Freile, 'Asylum and immigration under the European Convention of Human Rights: An Exclusive Universality?' in Helmut P. Aust and Esra Demir-Gürsel (eds.), *The European Court of Human Rights: Current Challenges in Historical Perspective* (Cheltenham, 2021), pp. 133–156.

[76] A. H. J. Swart, 'Het recht op gezinsleven in het Europees Verdrag en het vreemdelingenrecht (preadvies)' in: *Handelingen Nederlandse Juristen-Vereniging 1990-I*, pp. 185–262.

[77] Marie-Bénédicte Dembour, *When Humans Become Migrants: Study of the European Court of Human Rights with an Inter-American Counterpoint* (Oxford: Oxford University Press, 2015), pp. 196–197.

the influx of Dutch citizens from the overseas territories had become increasingly prominent, immigration numbers remained quite modest overall.[78] The domestic legal field dealing with migration was therefore very minor, comprising at best a handful of individuals who engaged in the practice.

On the other hand, the Convention was distinctively *not* set up to accommodate migration. Within the European jurisdiction, it provided protection to all residing there. But by no account would it protect those *outside* that scope, or those wishing to enter the realm of human rights. Therefore, on the European level, very little to no jurisprudence existed on the link between the Convention migration.[79] Expulsion, immigration and human rights remained – and, bearing in mind the hesitancy of the Dutch government in ratifying the fourth protocol of the Convention, were *kept* – separate worlds.[80]

As a result, lawyers and campaigners for asylum would focus on domestic law or the Refugee Convention, not on human rights or the ECHR. Asylum was a distinct field, which legally and in terms of discourse was not expressed in human rights terms.[81] What made matters more complicated was how the first lawyers in this area were basically operating in a legal vacuum. There was little scholarship to go by, little to no jurisprudence, and to make matters worse, the governmental document laying out the legal framework, the 'vreemdelingencirculaire', was kept a secret, making it inaccessible to both immigrants as well as any lawyers seeking to establish violations.[82] In this context, wherein immigration was very much seen as a prerogative for the state, expulsions were rarely successfully challenged in court, either domestically or European.[83]

However, change was underway. When in 1988 the slogan 'asylum rights are human rights' was uttered, it was a sign of how the two had

[78] Leo and Jan Lucassen, *5 eeuwen migratie: Een verhaal van winnaars en verliezers* (Amsterdam: Atlas Contact, 2018), pp. 160–178.

[79] Gammeltoft Hansen, Madsen, 'Regime Entanglement', pp. 10–11.

[80] With Dutch ratification of the protocol only taking place in 1982, after the independence of Suriname.

[81] Marcel Reurs and Martijn Stronks, *Pioniers in het vreemdelingenrecht* (Utrecht: SDU Uitgevers, 2011), p. 11.

[82] This situation would remain that way until the 'circulaire' was made public in 1982.

[83] Dembour, *When Humans Become Migrants*, p. 504.

become synonymous.[84] Via the agency of NGOs, migrants themselves and engaged lawyers, the link to human rights talk was made, and this was increasingly reflected in the legal procedure. Lawyers turned to Strasbourg and the Convention to find extra options and time for their clients. In turn, the success they had in those venues spurred on the domestic judges to act in a more 'human rights friendly' manner in expulsion cases.[85]

The first step was made in the realm of human rights activism. Since the early 1980s, Amnesty International and other NGOs started to forge the connection, which may seem remarkable on first sight. The human rights NGOs as they had appeared in the 1970s were, with the small exception of the more legally oriented ones, primarily focused on human rights violations *abroad*. Yet as ever more attention was being devoted to the troublesome human rights situations in foreign countries, this also dragged the question of immigration, and specifically of expulsion, into the domestic human rights discussion.

The formal incorporation of human rights into the foreign policy of the Netherlands in 1979 formed a key moment in this development. This made that NGOs were presented with a 'hook' onto which they could attach their claims. In the mid-1980s it became increasingly evident that the invocation of human rights in situations abroad could have clear connections to domestic policy considerations, and the Ministry of Foreign Affairs began to note a recurring pattern: NGOs increasingly connected Dutch commitments to human rights to the principle of non-refoulement.[86]

In particular, Amnesty International would – alongside Vluchtelingenwerk Nederland, a key organization embodying a myriad of smaller NGOs dealing with refugee protection founded in 1979 – connect individual refugee cases to the human rights situation abroad. By presenting the results of their own fact-finding missions, these NGOs could substantiate the claim that an individual applicant had grounded reasons for 'a reasonable fear for persecution' in their home country.[87]

[84] 'Asielrechten zijn Mensenrechten' *NRC* 13 December 1988.

[85] Success should be read in a somewhat relative way here: the greatest success was often to get a case declared admissible.

[86] NL-HaNA, Buza/Code 1975–1984, 2.05.330, inv. nr. 6240, 'Memo 11 July 1983'.

[87] As required by the 1951 Convention relating to the status of refugees.

What these NGOs proposed was therefore a mirroring link between the Dutch foreign policy in the area of human rights and immigration policy. If the situation abroad was such that the Dutch government itself deemed human rights violations to take place there, then what could be a reason to send people away to that area?[88]

Amnesty and others tied into a growing public awareness on matters of asylum. A gradual affair, the beginning of this increased attention can be roughly traced to 1975, when an outcry of public attention was provoked after 175 Moroccan men who had worked in the Netherlands for years were to be expelled. In order to evade eviction, they sought refuge in a church. Ensuing attempts to remove them from the church resulted in plenty of media attention and public protests, such that ultimately the men were allowed to stay.[89] It proved the beginning of campaigns against expulsions.

Crucially, these campaigns were increasingly framed in rights talk. After a case was brought before the Court on behalf of an asylum seeker for the first time in 1975, the topic would only continue to grow.[90] Migration became a topic of rights, not solely in courtrooms but also in discourse, revolving around family reunification and equal treatment in particular.[91] This meant that the developments in migration law cannot be seen in isolation from the developments as they emerged in family law. After all, Article 8 of the Convention became a central tool in the context of immigration. With the key position of family reunification, and the prohibition against expelling someone should that result in a violation of family life, one had to know when 'family life' existed. With the active position of the Hoge Raad on this topic in the realm of family law, it was no coincidence that activists and academics turned to that area of law to find support for pushing a similar liberal approach in the realm of family reunification.[92]

[88] NL-HaNA, Buza/Code 1975–1984, 2.05.330, inv. nr. 6240, 'Memo 11 July 1983.

[89] Archief Willem van Bellekom, International Institute for Social History, ARCH03190, inv. nr. 15, 'interview'; See also Reurs and Stronks, *Pioniers in het Vreemdelingenrecht*, pp. 49–50.

[90] Willem van Bellekom, IISH, inv. nr. 15, 'interview'.

[91] Bonjour, *Grens en Gezin*, p. 198.

[92] See for an overview S. K. van Walsum, '*Family Life* in de schaduw van de Grens' *NJCM Bulletin* Vol. 26 Nr. 6 (2001), pp. 731–740.

It were individual activists who led the charge in firmly establishing the practice of immigration as a field of law. People like Willem van Bennekom and Arie van Driel became known as 'pioneers of immigration law' and had a lasting impact on the field as such.[93] Key in their work was how they used (and in doing so, also expanded) the legal framework surrounding migration. This was legal engagement on the absolute microlevel. It is illustrative that in his work as immigration lawyer, Van Driel founded the 'Jusbus', an actual bus which he drove past the asylum seekers' centres in order to provide legal aid for the inhabitants.[94] In doing so, a situation was created which was comparable with the legal aid movement that had developed some time earlier: 'know your rights' began a slogan which shaped the law in question, also in the realm of immigration.

However, it was not plain sailing for this very new field of law, with little to no guidance or precedents at hand. Lawyers often drew on their own expertise and figured out the technicalities as they went along (and in doing so *became* the experts on the topic). Again, academia was vitally important, and the first academics and first lawyers in the field of immigration law had close connections. People like Kees Groenendijk, but perhaps most of all the young scholar Bert Swart, became crucial figures in the interlinkage between practice and academia. Swart's dissertation *De toelating en uitzetting van vreemdelingen* of 1978, and later his *Nederlandse uitleveringsrecht* of 1986, became the quintessential handbook for the field.[95]

Crucially, Swart firmly connected the Dutch legal framework to the international legal dimension, and in particular to human rights frameworks. In doing so, he not just innovated the academic field, he also presented the practicing lawyers with new input to test in court. As one commentator put it: 'Swart provided immigration law with a human rights dimension'.[96] This innovation was distinctively not kept in the ivory tower of academia. Like Alkema and others before him who were instrumental in getting the first cases into Strasbourg, these academics in the field of migration law were

[93] Reurs and Stronks, *Pioniers in het vreemdelingenrecht*, pp. 15–45.

[94] The 'legal aid buses' were something of a global phenomenon in the late 1970s and 1980s.

[95] A. H. J. Swart, *Nederlands Uitleveringsrecht* (Zwolle: Tjeenk Willink, 1986).

[96] A. H. Klip, 'In Memoriam A. H. J. Swart, 1941–2011', *Delict en Delikwent* Nr. 4 (2011), pp. 327–334.

active in reaching out to legal practice. Swart, for instance, stood in close contact with some of these early immigration lawyers, sharing insights into niche legal developments which could prove handy in immigration cases. 'You could call them day and night for advice', one lawyer recalled.[97]

Clearly, as had happened elsewhere, the lawyers who started to invoke European human rights were initially up against some stiff opposition from the judiciary. One time, the presiding judge in a lower court indignantly interrupted the pleading of a lawyer who pleaded for a violation of Article 8 ECHR, exclaiming, 'so you wish to argue the state is violating its treaty obligations? You will take that back!'[98] This judicial attitude was not surprising: little European jurisprudence in this area existed, and in a realm traditionally perceived as mostly a political affair in which the government had wide room for manoeuvre, judicial activism was not to be expected.[99] Throughout the governmental and judicial bodies, therefore, there persisted a firm belief that the Convention was not in any way relevant to migration law.[100]

The question caused quite some legal confusion. In line with the early restrictive approach, the Hoge Raad first settled on a cautious approach. In 1983, it made clear how it would not check those cases against the requirements of the ECHR, confirming its reluctant approach to human rights in the realm of migration.

In that context, Strasbourg in fact offered a promising way forward for the lawyers dealing with these cases. Just as the lawyers in the case of *Engel* had noted, the European system offered an additional venue to pursue justice, particularly in light of the limited potential of success at home. This meant that, roughly from the beginning of the 1980s, complaints in the field of immigration law ended up in Strasbourg and were brought before the commission.[101] Although not all cases were declared admissible, in due course the Commission, and the Convention with it, started to get involved in Dutch immigration policy, which truly became

[97] Reurs and Stronks, *Pioniers in het Vreemdelingenrecht*, p. 48.

[98] Reurs and Stronks, *Pioniers in het Vreemdelingenrecht*, pp. 114–115.

[99] In a string of cases this seemed to be confirmed: HR 12-04-1983, ECLI:NL:PHR:1983:, *NJ* 1983, 670; HR 06-12-1983, ECLI:NL:PHR:1983:AB9592, *NJ* 1984, 492.

[100] Bonjour, *Grens en gezin*, p. 189.

[101] Swart, *Bronnen van het Uitleveringsrecht*, p. 83.

evident around 1984/1985. In a combination of friendly settlements and declarations of admissibility of cases which in the Dutch legal context had been deemed perfectly in line with the Convention, questions were being raised as to the compatibility of Dutch practices with European demands. An important case on the meaning of family life in the context of migration (*Berrehab* v. *Netherlands*) was declared admissible by the Commission[102], but in the case *Abdulaziz* v. *UK.* the European Court also established Article 8 to be of relevance in immigration law.[103]

It should be noted that these were modest steps in terms of the actual demands which were made of the states. In matters of migration, the Court never doubted the prerogative of the state to set limits on migration and remained hesitant to find any violations.[104] Rather, the findings in Abdulaziz in fact entailed a 'reversal': the starting point in migration law would be not the right of an individual, as it usually is in human rights law, but the right of states to regulate the entrance into their jurisdiction.[105] Yet the case also entailed an affirmation that migration was in fact connected to the European Convention. That, as such, was a step into more extensive protection for human rights. For years, the Dutch judiciary had been convinced the ECHR did not play a role in immigration law. Faced with a ruling to the contrary, this position could no longer be defended.

And so, confronted with these European shifts, the Dutch judiciary began to move.[106] A first step was taken when the Hoge Raad declared that an expulsion to Turkey constituted a violation of Article 6 of the Convention in 1984. Although in principle the Netherlands was held to trust the human rights standards of the states with which it had signed an extradition treaty, this did not mean that human rights violations could

[102] *Berrehab* v. *The Netherlands*, EComHR 8 March 1985, Application nr. 10730/84.

[103] *Abdulaziz, Cabales and Balkandali* v. *the United Kingdom*, 28 May 1985, Series A no. 94.

[104] A. H. J. Swart, 'Het recht op gezinsleven in het Europees Verdrag en het vreemdelingenrecht (preadvies)' in *Handelingen Nederlandse Juristen-Vereniging 1990-I*, pp. 185–262, 188.

[105] See Dembour, *When Humans Become Migrants*, but also Bas Schotel, *On the Right of Exclusion: Law, Ethics and Immigration Policy* (London: Routledge, 2012).

[106] Groenendijk has noted how this development was the result of 'pressure from above, rather than pressure from below'. C. A. Groenendijk, 'mensenrechten tussen retoriek en praktijk: gebruik van het klachtrecht in Straatsburg en de bescherming van vreemdelingen' in L. Heyde, J. Leijten and Th. Mertens en B. P. Vermeulen (eds.), *Begrensde Vrijheid Opstellen over mensenrechten aangebonden aan Prof. Dr D. F. Scheltens bij zijn afscheid als hoogleraar aan de katholieke universiteit Nijmegen* (Zwolle, 1989), pp. 191–203.

be left aside, and there were grounded reasons to fear the absence of a fair trial in Turkey.[107] Matters progressed from there. At the end of 1986, for the first time, the Hoge Raad found another expulsion to be in violation of Article 8 of the Convention, relying on the findings in case law of the Commission and the Court in *Abdulaziz*.[108]

The most immediate impact, however, was when the case of *Berrehab* was decided by the European Court. *Berrehab* concerned the expulsion of a Moroccan man who had married a Dutch woman in 1977. In light of this marriage, he received a residence permit 'for the sole purpose of enabling him to live with his Dutch wife', but he got divorced right before the birth of their daughter in 1979. No longer married, the Dutch authorities sought to expel Mr Berrehab, even though he remained in close contact with his daughter and visited her four times a week.[109]

Faced with this situation, the divorced couple sought legal aid and turned to the Convention. The turn to the Convention in this situation was once again the result of the close interaction between academia and practice: given the dismissive attitude of his direct colleagues, Mr Berrehab's lawyer was only convinced to use the ECHR from working with academics who had knowledge of the Convention system and aimed at improving it.[110]

The question which emerged was whether or not the expulsion of Berrehab constituted an unjustifiable violation of family life in the meaning of Article 8 of the Convention. In a ground-breaking judgement, the European Court did find the expulsion to be a violation of the Convention. Crucially, it specified that 'family life' existed from the moment of the child's birth in a marriage and by the very fact of it, there existed between him and his parents a bond amounting to 'family life', even if the parents were no longer living together. Although – and this was an important nuance – subsequent events *could* have broken that chain, that was not the case in this situation.[111]

[107] HR 27-03-1984, ECLI:NL:PHR:1984:AC8362, *NJ* 1984, 611.

[108] HR 12-12-1986, ECLI:NL:PHR:1986:AC2777, *NJ* 1988, 188.

[109] *Berrehab* v. *the Netherlands*, 21 June 1988, Series A no. 138.

[110] Erik Larson, Wibo van Rossum and Patrick Schmidt, 'The Dutch Confession: Compliance, Leadership and National Identity in the Human Rights Order' *Utrecht Law Review* Vol. 10 Nr. 1 (2014), pp. 96–112, 104.

[111] *Berrehab* v. *the Netherlands*.

Berrehab definitively signalled how legal claims upon the Convention could be successful in the context of migration and expulsion on the basis of family law. Yet its relevance went beyond the individual case. It stood at the beginning of a surge in litigation on the basis of human rights in that realm. Drawing upon this initial success, Article 8 became the centrepiece in the campaigns of, or on behalf of, parents who were being denied family life with their children in the Netherlands. Here, the NGOs made their mark, as for example, the Clara Wichmann Institute was highly active in bringing cases to court in order to improve the situation of migrant women. Litigation on the basis of the Convention became the primary strategy to counter these situations.[112] Even though the European Court was by no means a guaranteed route of success, and complaints were consistently declared not admissible, this remained the go to strategy for parents and children in the years to come.[113]

Part of the reason why litigation remained so popular as a strategy in the context of migration was because of the limited potential for change at the political level. As immigration requirements became increasingly harsh over the course of the decade, the courts seemed to offer more potential than the law itself.[114] As such, the seeds for the later political conflict on human rights within the context of migration were laid.

Berrehab therefore stands for much more than the story of the late beginnings of European human rights in the context of migration. As much as it marked the beginning of legal activism in what came to be a core area of European human rights law, the case was also a conclusion of a movement which had started roughly a decade earlier, which had actively sought to make the Convention relevant in this context. Via a combination of top-down and bottom-up engagement, European human rights were made relevant not only in the domestic context, but also on the European level.

112 Sarah van Walsum, *The Family and the Nation: Dutch Family Migration Policies in the Context of Changing Family Norms* (Newcastle: Cambridge Scholars Publishers, 2008), pp. 241–242.

113 Walsum, *The Family and the Nation*, p. 242.

114 Something also foreseen by Swart in his pre-advice of 1990.

5.2.4 INTEGRATING EFFECTS: THE CONVENTION IN THE KINGDOM. These developments did not remain confined to the Netherlands. The legal revolution of the 1980s also brought the Convention into the picture in the Dutch Antilles and Aruba. But in contrast to the situation in the Netherlands, grassroots movements or engaged lawyers had never truly turned to the Convention as a solution on the Caribbean islands. Combined with the judicial restraint, which also reigned on the islands, the Convention didn't add much in legal procedure. Whereas engaged lawyers in the Netherlands tried to evade this situation by going directly to Strasbourg, such initiatives were rare to non-existent in the Antilles. As Alkema noted when he visited the islands in 1984, such a step had never been successfully attempted from the Antilles.[115]

In the absence of strong legal engagement from below, in the Antilles, the Convention was made relevant in a more top-down, court-centred way. The position of the Hoge Raad was highly important in this regard. As the supreme instance in the *Kingdom* in the realm of civil and penal law, its case law was also leading in the Antilles. Moreover, although the local 'staatsregeling' of the Antilles put fundamental rights at the centre of the legal order, some important rights were not included. This turned the provisions of the Convention into additional instruments of rights protection by the courts.[116] This all entailed the shifts in demeanour of the Hoge Raad, which above all entailed a growing willingness to test formal legislation against those Convention standards, were particularly impactful in the Antilles. Two consequences stand out in particular: on the one hand, the European norms came to serve as integrational tools in laying a shared minimum of fundamental rights protection in the Kingdom. On the other hand, in a broader context, the legal shifts of the 1980s entangled the Convention and the domestic legal orders in an ever-closer intertwinement.

As for the integrational effect of human rights, for example, in criminal law, the Convention was increasingly used to uniform diverging

[115] Evert Alkema, 'Wat betekenen de Europese mensenrechten voor de Antilliaanse rechtspraktijk?' *Tijdschrift voor Antilliaans Recht* Vol. 5 Nr. 1 (1984), pp. 1–12.

[116] Arjen van Rijn, 'De bescherming van de grondrechten in de Nederlandse Antillen' *NJCM Bulletin* Vol. 17 Nr. 2 (1992), pp. 131–149. See Van Rijn, Handboek Caribisch Staatsrecht (Den Haag Boom, 2019), p. 330.

standards of fundamental rights protection in the Kingdom by adding missing elements. In the Antilles, certain procedural safeguards such as the principle of *nemo tenetur* or the 'caution', were notoriously absent from the Antillean criminal code. Under the impact of the Convention, however, it became possible to 'read' these into the general requirements of a fair trial with reference to Article 6. As demands for changes in the Antillean criminal procedure grew, inspiration would be drawn from the requirements of the Convention.[117] When the European Court later confirmed how these principles were indeed part of the scope of Article 6, the safeguards in the criminal procedure in the Kingdom were also formally brought in line.[118] Comparable developments took place in administrative law, where the *Benthem* case left its mark when a legal venue in the Antilles comparable to the 'Kroonberoep' had to be adjusted in light of the judgement.[119]

The distinctive way in which the Convention was made relevant in the Antilles was therefore through a 'top down' approach, driven by the courts. Individual complaints based on the Convention were laid in front of the local judges, but were not pursued into Strasbourg. This was not surprising in itself, as knowledge and expertise on how to begin a procedure in Strasbourg were simply less present with the Bar or legislature on the islands. For individual plaintiffs on the Antilles, the European Court remained literally far away and the Bar was hesitant in pursuing complaints in Strasbourg. It took a long time, was expensive and the procedure was little known. The first complaint only came in the beginning of the 1980s. It was filed by a proponent of the independence of Aruba, Betico Croes, yet the complaint was declared inadmissible due to a non-exhaustion of local remedies.[120] Complaints filed from the Antilles or Aruba have remained extremely rare ever since.[121]

[117] F. J. M. Hoogenboom, 'Het verdrag van Rome en het Gerechtelijk Vooronderzoek' *TAR* Vol. 4 Nr. 1 (1983), pp. 9–13.

[118] *Funke* v. *France*, 25 February 1993, Series A no. 256-A; Johanna Diana den Hartog, *De Doorwerking van Artikel 6 EVRM in het Antilliaanse en Arubaanse Strafrecht* (Deventer: Gouda Quint, 1998).

[119] The 'gang naar de Gouverneur', basically a mirrored provision of the 'Kroonberoep'. Van Rijn, *Handboek Caribisch Staatsrecht*, p. 354.

[120] Van Rijn, *Handboek Caribisch Staatsrecht*, p. 314.

[121] Ibid.

This may not be surprising. For in the relatively small governments of the islands, it was not always possible to access the support and expertise of specialized civil servants in order to keep track of the demands laid down by European developments.[122] As a consequence, it was noted how the legislature on occasion lagged behind in formally updating – for example – penal law.[123] Combined with the strong position of the Convention, the judiciary was almost bound to step in when the inevitable gaps between domestic levels of protection and European minimum requirements emerged.

This had several implications. On the one hand, it created a risk. By relying so heavily on the courts (European and domestic) the local 'ownership' of the Convention remained relatively limited. This was indeed one of the feelings evoked by the changes in family law which were, in a way, 'dropped' on the islands, and prompted one commentator to note how the Convention 'can cause major legal uncertainty for a tiny country such as ours'.[124] Most clearly, though, its application in the Antilles ensured the entanglement of the Convention with the legal order of the *entire* Kingdom. As the local courts became increasingly tangled with demands on fundamental rights, with different reasons in different contexts, the Convention emerged as the prime source of those fundamental rights. For although human rights at large were primarily seen as export products, when it came to human rights *law*, they had unmistakably become domesticated.[125] This ensured European legal developments no longer seemed far away and irrelevant for the domestic lawyers. As ever more areas were drawn in the realm of European human rights law, combined with spill over effects into other areas of law (as we have seen in the links between migration law and family law), the Convention turned into a more visible part of national law.

[122] Illustrative is the finding how legal support would consist of fifteen civil servants, which in practice was much less; NL-HaNA, Buza/Code 1975–1984, 2.05.330 inv. nr. 6252.

[123] Cf. Hoogenboom, 'Het verdrag van Rome en het Gerechtelijk Vooronderzoek' *TAR* Vol. 4 Nr. 1, pp. 9–13; Alkema, 'Wat betekenen de Europese mensenrechten voor de Antilliaanse rechtspraktijk', pp. 1–12.

[124] For other illustrations of how the courts put forward fundamental rights in family life, see Van Rijn, *Handboek Caribisch staatsrecht*, p. 330.

[125] This could mean raising standards (think of prison conditions in the Antilles) or – curiously – *lowering* standards.

5.3 THE EMERGENCE OF CRITIQUE

One final result of this legal revolution was that human rights demands were increasingly *felt* in the realm of politics. The (European) case law and legal change brought about by the Convention in the 1960s or 1970s had been very little or about – relatively – niche fields: the treatment of the mentally ill, or the rights of soldiers. For decades, human rights simply had not been much of a threat to actual political decision-making, either because it was kept at bay or because of judicial deference to the government. But in the 1980s, human rights ceased to be 'all bark and no bite' as precisely the more politically salient areas of law had come under the spell of human rights: criminal, family and migration law. First emerging in academic circles, it also caused a first open rift between governmental political desires and fundamental rights protection. As such, a substantial pushback emerged against what was perceived as a human rights overreach.[126]

From the outset, it's important to note a key feature of the debate of the 1980s. In line with how the Convention came to matter (i.e., via an interplay between domestic and European courts), the debate revolved primarily around the new *domestic* application of European human rights norms. Did this mean the European Court was shielded from critique? Far from it, yet the pushback on the European level took on a slightly different form.

This domestic application began as topic of the debate in the academic community. Most praised the new activity of the courts, which was not surprising as these commentators had helped create this breakthrough in the first place. Yet aside from the active supporters, some other commentators were more cautious. Already in response to the *Marxck* judgement certain reactions were shocked. In the Dutch context, one prominent lawyer lashed out, stating how 'Dutch family law should be determined by the Dutch legislator, and this cannot be the task of

[126] For claims the Convention only became a topic of debate in recent years, see Martin Kuier, 'Guaranteeing International Human Rights Standards in the Netherlands: The Parliamentary Dimension' in M. Hunt, H. J. Hooper and P. Yowell (eds.), *Parliaments and Human Rights. Redressing the Democratic Deficit* (Oxford: Oxford University Press, 2015), pp. 295–305.

[...] a bunch of foreigners in Strasbourg'.[127] On the Antilles, other concerns were raised. The *Marxck* judgement was deemed to have major consequences in the local context due to the relatively large number of extramarital children in that society, raising the question of whether the impact of the European Court's reasoning might be too intrusive. As one commentator put it:

> This can cause major legal uncertainty for a tiny country such as ours [...] We would need to carefully think about the consequences of our submission to treaties. Do we need to carelessly join Treaties the Netherlands signs, do we need to let these prevail over our domestic laws, or should we see them, and the judgements based on those treaties, more as guidelines?[128]

Also the liberal usage of Article 8 by the Hoge Raad caused some consternation, as it was seen to take up a 'quasi-legislative task'.[129]

The key tension here was no longer between Article 8 of the Convention and private law, but between the usage of Articles 8 of the Convention and 94 of the Dutch Constitution. According to Article 94, legal provisions need be set aside if these are incompatible with directly applicable provisions of international law. Such a power sat uneasily with the principle of legal certainty and the prerogatives of the legislator, which for decades had been the defining points of view in dealing with judicial review. If the Hoge Raad could predict the European demands on its own account, what would be the role of the legislator?[130]

Also, the *content* of the choices of the Hoge Raad in determining what the ECHR entailed was criticized. Going beyond minimum requirements was one thing in light of separation of powers, yet *how* the Hoge Raad did so was not necessarily neutral either. From feminist corners, the judgement in which the father was given a *de jure* right to visit was

[127] Minkenhof, 'Inzake het Marxck arrest' *WPNR* 5618/19 (1980).

[128] M. van der Plank, 'Hoe het Europese Hof het Antiliaanse natuurlijke kind (meer) rechten verleent' *TAR* Vol. 4 Nr. 3 (1983), pp. 71–75.

[129] Evert Alkema, 'The Effects of the European Convention on Human Rights and Other International Human Rights Instruments on the Netherlands Legal Order' in R. Lawson and M. Blois (eds.), *The Dynamics of Human Rights Protection in Europe, Essays in Honour of Henry Schermers* (Dordrecht: Nijhoff, 1994), pp. 1–15, 5.

[130] See the annotation of Alkema and Luyten in *NJ* 1986, 588.

seen as a 'victory for men' which had the potential of keeping women trapped in contact with said men who subsequently could continue to exercise power over the family.[131] Again, the push towards the human rights system could have unintended consequences.

5.3.1 'AN EXCESSIVE RELIANCE ON RIGHTS': THE POLITICAL PUSHBACK. Such academic critique did not remain isolated. Soon after, politics became involved in voicing the same unease. Such political critique was new and related to the impact of human rights in areas which had become salient political topics. Most prominently in penal law and in migration law, areas where the impact of fundamental rights was being felt, political attitudes shifted in the 1980s in favour of more governmental power and restrictive activity. As the 'abolitionist' penal law movement of the 1970s, the calls for a 'humane' penal law system were increasingly replaced by calls for harsher punishments.[132] Alongside these calls, policies attempting to combat crime and seeking to ease the job of the public prosecutor were introduced. Instruments like undercover agents and phone taps were increasingly deployed, and the use of anonymous witnesses became more widely accepted and used.[133] When the courts subsequently stepped in and forbade certain interrogation techniques or set suspects free because of technical errors in the procedure, public discontent and pushback on 'soft' judgements began to grow.[134] Now precisely in the realm of those perceived technicalities, the Convention had begun to play a role: with the call for harsher punishments, the fundamental rights protection also came under scrutiny.

Simultaneously, the debate around migration shifted in the mid- to late-1980s. This new dynamic is usually described as starting with the arrival of Tamils coming from Sri Lanka into the Netherlands. The

[131] De Boer and Wijers, *Vrouw en Recht: De beweging, de mensen, de issues*, p. 82.

[132] Smits, *Strafrechtshervormers en Hemelbestormers*, p. 8.

[133] For a small overview of the measures introduced to combat crime, see 'Redactioneel Commentaar: Conventie-oneel Denken' *NJCM Bulletin* Vol.12 Nr.3 (1987), pp. 195–196.

[134] Leny de Groot-van Leeuwen, 'Rechters onder vuur: Kritiek op rechters in andere en deze tijden' in *Levend Strafrecht, Strafrechtelijke vernieuwingen in een maatschappelijke context. liber amicorum Ybo Buruma* (Deventer: Wolters Kluwer, 2011), pp. 225–237, 237.

group was met with a new dynamic in migration procedure: alongside the economic crisis of the 1980s, immigration requirements and asylum requirements became ever stricter.[135] Facilities were more and more aimed at 'deterring' immigration by providing nothing more than very basic provisions, and in the space of a couple of years, a restrictive regime replaced the previously relatively liberal refugee regime.[136] Also in this realm, the newly found legal protections in migration law increasingly conflicted with this new political preference.

In this increasingly challenging environment, it was the Prime Minister Ruud Lubbers himself who opened the political discussion on the limits of human rights protection and the perceived overreach of the courts. Lubbers took aim at what he saw as an excessive reliance of citizens on their 'rights', and the zeal of lawyers and judges to grant them these. Lubbers had no love for legal activism and spoke of an 'overkill of alerting people to their rights'.[137] To make matters worse, the judicial activism was mostly based on 'treaties which the Netherlands had signed merely for reasons of political symbolism'.[138] In particular this usage of international law posed problems for the legislature: those treaties could not simply be set aside or altered. As Lubbers would note, in the 1980s 'judges had become less restricted in reviewing [...] in fact, one almost fell short as a judge if you did not review against an international treaty'.[139] He was not wrong in this sense: the judiciary *had* increasingly turned to international law.

Instead, the reliance on 'rights' in societal settings would have to be rebalanced against the language of civic 'duties', or so was his idea. In that light he launched a campaign in 1987 for harsher punishments, stronger fines, and fewer consequences for technical errors in the criminal procedure.[140] Lubbers would continue his insistence on excessive

135 Bonjour, *Grens en Gezin*, pp. 192–196; Leo and Jan Lucassen, *Vijf Eeuwen Migratie* pp. 188–196.

136 Tycho Walaardt, 'Patience and Perseverance: The Asylum Procedure of Tamils and Iranians in the Netherlands in the Mid-1980's' *tijdschrift voor sociale en economische geschiedenis* Vol. 8 Nr. 3 (2011), pp. 2–31.

137 'Lubbers voert in Nijmegen zelf oppositie aan' *NRC* 5-09-1990.

138 Theo Brinkel, *Haagse jaren: de politieke memoires van Ruud Lubbers* (Amsterdam: Ambo Anthos, 2020), p. 273.

139 As quoted in a speech before NVR, *NRC* 26-11-1990.

140 Brinkel, *Haagse jaren*, p. 279.

rights claims in the years to come, becoming the face of this critique of the role of the judiciary. It was new for a leading Dutch politician to express himself in such critical terms on fundamental rights. Frank Kuitenbrouwer, who, as we have seen, was a leading voice in propagating human rights in the Dutch journal NRC, came to note that Lubbers' proposals to increase the powers of the criminal investigators constituted 'an assault on the rule of law'.[141] Some judges too were uncomfortable with the apparent pressure which was being put on their shoulders, even though the president of the Hoge Raad set aside the criticism of the Prime Minister as 'merely one of the factors in the scales'[142]

Yet even though one among many, it was a factor nonetheless, precisely because the discomfort with the increasing judicial interventions was not reserved solely for the Prime Minster. It was a feeling shared more broadly in the political system. In 1990, a committee consisting of almost all party leaders in Parliament, the Committee Deetman, presented this discomfort in a report on constitutional and governmental renewal. The report was noted how the 'balance' in the trias politica had been disturbed. The judiciary felt the consequences of this disturbance: as legislation became increasingly diffuse and members of Parliament became difficult to discern from their governing parties, the demands on the judiciary had changed. It now found itself in a somewhat curious position in which it also – among other things – had to 'maintain the trust of citizens in the democratic rule of law'.[143]

As a solution, Lubbers and his Minister of Justice, Ernst Hirsch Ballin, had one clear idea in mind to counter the problems arising from the review against international treaties: constitutional review. As Lubbers noted, formally, the Parliament had the last word on fundamental rights protection, yet in practice the judiciary had taken up this role as the most important rights had been laid down in international law.[144] Constitutional review would bring the discussion closer to home and could replace reliance on the international norms by the 'own' constitution. However, the

[141] Ibid.

[142] 'Lubbers rekent af met de jaren tachtig', *NRC* 26-11-1990.

[143] The Committee Deetman, Report available at https://kennisopenbaarbestuur.nl/Tentoonstellingen/1990Vraagpunten.html (Last accessed 18-10-2022).

[144] Brinkel, *Haagse Jaren*, p. 276.

proposal did not come to fruition: parliament declined to take up the idea, and it has remained an open, but relative stagnant discussion ever since.[145] The result was that the judiciary remained tied to international law when it came to fundamental rights protection: as the domestic solution was declined, international norms took the main stage in the legal review of legislation when it came to human rights.

5.3.2 THE CONSEQUENCES AT HOME: ECHR-IZATION AND SETTLING FOR THE MINIMUM. If left at that, the entire episode of discontent would have been no more than a blimp of political and academic irritation on the domestic application of international law. Yet after the political pushback, the domestic courts *did* alter their engagement with international human rights norms. The zeal of the mid-1980s was abandoned, and the judiciary instead settled on a more traditional approach. Although it is impossible to find a direct causal link between the critique and the new approach to the Convention by the domestic courts, it seems plausible the shift in attitude was at least partially influenced by the growing unrest surrounding judicial review as the courts reverted back to their more traditional position.

The step back of the judiciary was most articulately spelled out in the response of the Hoge Raad to the *Berrehab* ruling of the European Court. The Dutch judiciary had creatively used Article 8 in the realm of family law and read a specific meaning in the article which had not yet been established by the European instances. In *Berrehab*, however, the European Court had given detailed insight into the position of a biological father and his relation to family life. Crucially, it presented a finding which was more limited than the Dutch position. Instead of a *de jure* right to family life of the biological father, the European Court had opted for a more factual check, in which family life could also be lost if developments pointed into that direction.[146]

[145] E. M. H. Hirsch Ballin, 'Constitutionele toetsing van wetten als bijdrage aan de rechtsontwikkeling', in Willem Konijnenbelt (ed.), *Rechter en wetgever* (Den Haag: Raad van State, 2001), pp. 47–69, 49–51.

[146] In Berrehab the Court set out the standard for children born from a legal and serious marriage which could be broken by later developments. Therefore, it turned on a factual question, rather than a biological one.

In response, the Dutch judiciary was left with a burning question. Would its own interpretation, which went beyond this minimum of the Convention laid down by the Court, still stand? The Hoge Raad answered this question in a judgement in the realm of family law, and took the step of lowering the level of fundamental rights protection that it had previously awarded.[147] The Berrehab case 'urged a revision', the Hoge Raad noted. Following the European Court, it rejected its own doctrine, which had presented the biological father with a quite strong level of protection under Article 8, and instead introduced a more factual approach, as endorsed by the European Court.[148]

In doing so, it not only lowered the applicable human rights standard, but also created a rule for itself: the national judiciary would not be allowed to give a more far-reaching explanation to the Convention on its own account, or to review legislation against that standard. Rather, it would follow the interpretation given by the European Court. A higher standard of human rights protection would therefore still be possible, but not via actions of the judge: this was a task left to the legislator. This line was swiftly followed in other areas: in criminal law too, domestic courts that went beyond the European minimum were corrected by the Hoge Raad. As Myjer summarized the move: 'the Hoge Raad indicated that the domestic judge should not walk too independently ahead of Strasbourg…'.[149]

The year 1989 therefore saw the settlement of a question which had dominated much of the decade, namely how the Dutch judiciary would position itself with regard to using the Convention. After a remarkable period of legal activism, and ensuing critique on its usage of international law, it took a distinct step back. Lubbers himself was rather pleased with this development. 'The judiciary has become a bit

[147] HR 10-11-1989, ECLI:NL:PHR:1989:AC1692, *NJ* 1990,628.

[148] Ibid, as emphasized in the annotation of Alkema, *NJ* 1990, 628.

[149] Egbert Myjer, 'The European Dimension; More than a Non-commital Ornament/Notes on the Consequences of the ECHR for the Administration of Dutch Criminal Justice' in E. A. Alkema, T. L. Bellekom, A. Z. Drzemezewski, J. G. C. Schokkenbroek (eds.), *The Domestic Implementation of the European Convention on Human Rights in Eastern and Western Europe: Proceedings of the Seminar Held in Leiden, 24–26 October* 1991 (Strasbourg: Va. Engel, 1993), pp. 195–213.

more careful', he noted approvingly, and even though that turnaround could not be attributed entirely to his actions (something Lubbers certainly claimed), he was not wrong in finding the judiciary had settled down a little.[150]

The result was an 'ECHR-ization' of fundamental rights protection. This meant that human rights standards in the Netherlands to a large extent became synonymous with the demands flowing from the European Convention.[151] What was left for the national judge was a passive role: it could mirror the level set out by the European Court but would not go beyond the defined European standard: that was up to the legislator.[152] As such, the European Court was placed in the driver's seat when it came to determining the material requirements of the Convention in the Netherlands. This 'ECHR-ization' can be observed in a variety of contexts. Not only in the actions of the domestic judiciary, which settled on the material standards set by the Court, but also in the drafting of legislation, the ECHR became the leading benchmark for determining the fundamental rights degree of a proposed law.[153]

This had three consequences. The first main one was there was a settlement on a minimalist conception of human rights. As the Convention became established as the leading benchmark, combined with the constitutional prohibition of reviewing legislation against the constitution, it turned the European *minimum* requirements into a de facto national *maximum*.[154] It was a remarkable shift. From a highly active judicial engagement, the choice was made to settle on a – very – minimalist conception of fundamental rights protection.

[150] Brinkel, *Haagse jaren*, p. 277.

[151] Janneke Gerards en Carla Sieburgh (ed.), *De invloed van fundamentele rechten op het materiele recht* (Deventer: Kluwer, 2013), pp. 544.

[152] For the mirror analogy, see Janneke Gerards and Jozeph Fleuren, *Implementatie van het EVRM en de uitspraken van het EHRM in de nationale rechtspraak: Een rechtsvergelijkend onderzoek* (Nijmegen: WODC, 2013), pp. 51–52.

[153] A. H. J. Swart, 'het recht op gezinsleven in het Europees Verdrag en het vreemdelingenrecht', *Handelingen NJV*, pp. 187–262.

[154] Aernout Nieuwenhuis and Laurens Dragstra, 'Van minimum, tekort en meerwaarde Een vergelijking tussen de grondwettelijke bescherming van grondrechten en de bescherming op grond van het EVRM' *Preadviezen Vereniging voor de vergelijkende studie van het Recht*, Vol. 1 (2008), pp. 11–74.

This minimalist conception was reflected in the contents of human rights protection. After all, the case law of the European Court, even though it clearly went far beyond what was envisioned in the 1950s, was still characterized by a significant level of reluctance and 'state-friendliness'.[155] Although higher than before, admissibility numbers remained relatively low, and, for example, in the field of migration, the state was awarded a firm margin of appreciation. Moreover, in areas where the European Court was hesitant to intervene, such as socio-economic rights or contentious issues such as abortion on which no European consensus existed, human rights law would not provide any answers. This was to become even more acute as elsewhere, for example, in the Treaty of Maastricht, specific economic choices of the more neoliberal kind *were* being enshrined.[156] As a result, human rights law was left ill-equipped to deal with issues of socio-economic inequalities. This was a topic of particular importance, for example, when it came to the situation on the Caribbean islands: although human rights law served to provide a shared minimum of fundamental rights in, for example, criminal law, the absence of socio-economic rights would leave this topic simply outside the scope of the judiciary.

The second consequence of the 'ECHR-ization' of fundamental rights was that it entailed a narrowing of human rights protection into the realm of legal expertise. It may be surprising for the age of human rights mainstreaming to have ended in a somewhat paradoxical narrowing of knowledge and engagement. However, the increased turn to human rights in legal terms had been an important element of the trajectory in the 1980s, and was further strengthened by the choice for Europe, and the international framework to a slightly lesser extent. Increasingly, the public debate on human rights was a debate of, and between, legal experts. Whereas the domestic constitution,

[155] See in particular the analysis of Dembour in this sense, just as Thomas Spijkerboer has noted the curious situation that in Europe migration is seen not necessarily from a human rights framework, but from the lens of the *state* which has the right to limit access to its territory. Thomas Spijkerboer, 'Coloniality and recent European migration case law' in Stijn Smet and Vladislava Stoyanova (eds.), *Migrants' Rights, Populism and Legal Resilience in Europe* (Cambridge: Cambridge University Press, 2022), pp. 117–138.

[156] Resulting in a constitutionalization of policy choices of the economic kind.

for example, remained celebrated and discussed in formal historical education, dissemination of knowledge on the way more important Convention remained confined to those studying law.[157] As such, European developments which had become central in determining the human rights standards applicable 'at home', were ultimately relatively detached from the domestic public debate or scrutiny, resulting in a lack of public attention for the European dimension of fundamental rights protection.[158]

This was ultimately a somewhat paradoxical outcome to the decade in which human rights found their way into all aspects of society. Although this created common ground between government, NGOs and lawyers, it also entailed a narrowing of the focus, and ultimately a confinement of human rights agency to an increasingly specialized legal crowd.

To some, this came as a surprise after the remarkably active years of fundamental rights protection and it seemed like a step back in rights protection. Yet in retrospect, the devised strategy to follow the European Court fits in a broader historical engagement.[159] The period in which the judiciary used the Convention as a tool to open up the Dutch legal system was by all means new and remarkable, precisely because it did not fit easily with the traditional hesitancy with regard to human rights protection. For decades, the prerogative of fundamental rights protection *had* been left to the legislator. Under the pressure of domestic activism, which believed the legislature did not move (fast) enough, and through the increase of stringent procedures, courts were pressured into a more active role, however this '*prealable legislative*' never truly disappeared. Seen in a broader context, the 1980s were therefore a brief period of a brief and stormy love affair, before the judiciary settled on a more traditional, reserved role division.

[157] Oomen, Barbara 'Het vergeten geweten. Het EHRM als goed bewaard juristengeheim'. In Ashley Terlouw and Janneke Gerards (eds.), *Amici Curiae, adviezen aan het Europese hof voor de rechten van de mens* (Nijmegen: Wolf Legal Publishers, 2012), pp. 207–216.

[158] Oomen, 'Het vergeten geweten', pp. 207–216.

[159] Also because the Netherlands isn't the only country embracing this position: see Gerards and Fleuren *Implementatie van het EVRM en de rechtspraak van het EHRM in nationale rechtspraak*, pp. 19–64.

The third effect of this outsourcing of fundamental rights protection was how the national judiciary isolated itself as well to an extent from political critique. The critique as it emerged in the 1980s was directed at the application of fundamental rights by the *national* judges. As they subsequently placed the emphasis on the European instances, it was no longer the national, but the European Court which became central in the procedure, and was therefore at the forefront of any later critique on fundamental rights expansionism. In the 1980s, the political frustration with fundamental rights could mostly be delivered at the domestic judiciary, in the domestic public debate, and with a domestic political solution. With the choice for Europe, the debate and policy options were subsequently moved there as well.

That move created a new problem, however. The traditional domestic alternative for the government to act upon disagreement with judgements – simply changing the law – did not provide solace on the international level where one would have to alter a treaty altogether. Such was not problematic in a situation where judgements were primarily directed against other countries. The political preference for a strong, legalized system was pervasive, and the European Court was considered a minimalistic Court with high authority. Yet this could, and ultimately *would*, create the conditions for the political discomfort with the European Court as it would materialize again roughly fifteen years later.

5.4 INTO EUROPE: CHALLENGING, SAFEGUARDING AND REFORMING THE SYSTEM

When it came to the European sphere, the 1980s were the years in which the European Court decisively started to make its mark. Already in 1978, the president of the Court had perceived the increased activity of the institution, noting how

> since 1974, more and more cases have been referred to the Court, not only by the Commission but also by the states concerned. This development, which is to be welcomed, reached such a stage in 1977 that the Court can be stated to have entered a new phase in its existence: the Court

> is at last beginning to perform fully the role conferred on it by the drafters of the Convention...[160]

Now clearly what the Court envisioned, an active Court dealing with questions with implications for all states, was a rather creative rebranding of its history. Still, the increase in self-confidence is telling. Only a bit of wishful thinking was involved when, three years later, Wiarda himself would note how 'in my opinion it can justifiably be maintained that the [ECHR] and the institutions established under it for the protection of rights have become firmly implanted in the minds of our fellow citizens'.[161]

Such a strong role for the Court was something that the Netherlands had supported, and even helped to instigate through its campaign to activate the Court in the past decade. But the increased activity of the Court was increasingly met with caution. Where the European jurisprudence had a galvanizing effect on scholars, lawyers and judges on the domestic level, the government began to express doubts as to the direction of the system, and hesitation crept into the system as the decade went along.[162] So why had caution entered the thinking of Dutch officials? There were several reasons.

First, the system of the Convention itself had come under pressure. The Commission and Court were being put under strain by an increasing workload without proper backing. Membership of the Commission remained a part-time job, whereas the number of complaints was steadily rising and procedures easily took years to finish. In that light, any initiatives to expand the Convention, or initiatives which could result in even more working pressure, needed to be examined critically in order not to overburden the system.[163]

Second, the new zeal of the Court seemed to threaten precisely what was deemed important. For the Netherlands, the priority in the Strasbourg system was the proper functioning of the system, being the

160 NL-HaNA, Buza/Code 1975–1984, 2.05.330, inv. nr. 22149, 'Report 12 August 1978'.

161 Quoted in Bates, *The Evolution of the European Convention*, p. 381.

162 Bates, *The Evolution of the European Convention*, p. 428.

163 The option to simply expand the staff at the Council of Europe (or pay them more) remained even more contentious.

Commission and the Court. This support had only increased in light of the emergence of human rights talk throughout the world, and the reputational gains the European system brought with it. 'In light of all the drivel on human rights, which can be heard in all sorts of political areas, the system of the Council of Europe is unique in its hard and unescapable legal core. This is a major advantage for countries in the West who appeal to human rights with regard to others', the analysis went.[164] Yet this 'hard and unescapable' legal core needed to be carefully safeguarded. In a memorandum from the Ministry of Foreign Affairs in 1981, an urgent appeal was made to 'maintain and consolidate what has been reached since 1951, and to prevent a weakening of the system'.[165]

What was there to maintain? The strength of the Convention was seen as a generally accepted minimum standard of human rights throughout Europe. This was essential to consolidate, because only when this 'common floor' of human rights protection was protected the jurisprudence of Commission and Court could have the same impact in all signatory states. Here, the government showed that it was quite aware of the legal revolution in Strasbourg and acted accordingly. In itself, the jurisprudence of the Court was something to be welcomed. However, and this was the other side of the coin, it was also noted how *precisely* the activities of Court and Commission could lead to problems for the Convention. In particular, the Dutch government proved sensitive to the critique from other states on the Court. Wary of leading them to a point where they could ultimately hamper the system as a whole, a more restrictive policy was pursued. In a range of initiatives, from reforms to interstate complaints, the Dutch embraced a more cautious position within the Council of Europe.

What those initiatives show is how the legal revolution of the ECtHR did not go unnoticed. Instead of garnering tacit silent acceptance from governments, the Court caused debate and approval, and, most importantly, had an impact on political decisions with regard to the Convention. Part of the consequence of the case law of the Court was

164 NL-HaNA, Buza/Code 1975–1984, 2.05.330, inv. nr. 21825, '3 June 1981, advies Van der Wal'.

165 NL-HaNA, Buza/Code 1975–1984, 2.05.330, inv. nr. 22198, 'Memo 5 October 1981'.

how governments reacted accordingly in the Council of Europe to minimize the impact of the Convention. From the start, Strasbourg was not isolated from reaction from the capitals: political discussions surrounding the functioning of the Court and its impact on the system as a whole have indeed shaped the system throughout the years.

5.4.1 BETWEEN INDIVIDUAL HUMAN RIGHTS AND 'BURDENSOME SIDE EFFECTS': THE INTERSTATE COMPLAINT AGAINST TURKEY. The first instance in which this caution made its mark was in the Dutch response to the 1980 coup in Turkey. In many ways this was a situation comparable to that in Greece of roughly a decade earlier: the coup was followed by the detention of citizens and a crackdown on civil liberties. Not long afterwards, an interstate complaint was filed in 1982 by the same states as in the Greek case, the Scandinavian countries and the Netherlands, this time also joined by France.[166] When the news of the dire human rights situation in Turkey broke, the Dutch government was in fact an early proponent of such a move. With Max van der Stoel as Minister, combined with a unanimous motion from Parliament to the same end, it would seem there was a very clear consensus over using the European system to put pressure on the Turkish state.[167] Illustrative of the close link between the human rights activism and governmental practice was how the complaint to a large extent was based on the reports of human rights NGOs such as Amnesty International and the International Commission of Jurists. Their fact-finding missions produced hard evidence of human rights violations.[168]

But on the European level the outset had changed. Already in 1977, commenting on the conflict between Cyprus and Turkey, which was addressed in an interstate procedure, the outlook from the Dutch government was not optimistic. A Dutch memorandum noted how politics prevailed over the legal findings of the committee, to the detriment

166 Peter Baehr, Monique Castermans-Holleman and Fred Grunfeld, *Human Rights in the Foreign Policy of the Netherlands* (Antwerp: Intersentia, 2002), pp. 107–111. See *Denmark, France, Norway, Sweden & the Netherlands* v. *Turkey* 9940/82 & 9944/82.

167 NL-HaNA, Buza/Code 1975–1984, 2.05.330, inv. nr. 22105, 'Memo 26 June 1982, from chef DEU'.

168 Ibid, 'Note to M from Van der Wal, 18 January 1982'.

of the broader status of that body as such.[169] This was a broader problem within the Council of Europe: 'Although there is still barely a member state willing to openly criticize the findings of the European Commission, there is a growing tendency not to follow those conclusions on a political level'.[170]

This political dimension became clear as the complaint against Turkey proceeded. The Commission was keenly aware of the vulnerable position it was in: consistently delaying any planned visits to prisons in Turkey out of fear of further worsening relations with Turkey, it asked the governments to make clear what room there could be for a friendly settlement.[171]

It was clear Turkey wanted to get rid of the procedure as soon as possible, which, as its Minister of Foreign Affairs put it, put the country in a 'position blessée et frustrée'.[172] Moreover, the procedure hampered its ongoing talks with the EEC. There, the interstate complaint was increasingly felt as burdening the Turks in their conversations with the relevant parties. Even though the European Commission (not the human rights one, that is) had helped them in certain regards, for example, by postponing talks with the European Parliament until elections had taken place, such tricks could not go on indefinitely, and the longer the complaint dragged on, the more difficult these conversations would be.[173]

As for the states that had filed the complaint, a compromise was most welcome. Even though the allegations of torture were credible and under investigation by the Commission, the Dutch ambassador in Ankara urged his government to rethink the state of affairs, noting that moving on with the complaints would only harness Turkish disappointment and that 'surely, the Convention did not mean to produce such burdensome side effects'.[174] After elections in the Netherlands, and a new Minister of Foreign Affairs took over from Van der Stoel, this 'realist' position

[169] NL-HaNA, Buza/Code 1975–1984, 2.05.330, inv. nr. 2115, 'Memo 30th September 1977'.
[170] Ibid.
[171] NL-HaNA, Buza/Code 1975–1984, 2.05.330, inv. nr. 22108, 'Letter to DEU, 29 May 1984'.
[172] Ibid, 'Memo from Embassy in Ankara to the Hague, 6 March 1984'.
[173] Ibid.
[174] Ibid, 'Letter from Ankara to the Hague, 5 December 1984'.

was increasingly more welcome. As such, the governments came up with five key points Turkey would need to include for the complaint to be dropped. These included the ending of torture, amnesty for persons convicted or imprisoned for their political beliefs, just satisfaction for those whose rights had been violated, and a timetable to return to a state in conformity with Convention laws.[175]

Moving towards a compromise, Turkey promised to produce more clarity on limiting martial law, explained why it was particularly difficult to enact amnesty, and accepted a form of external oversight on the issue of torture in the form of a reporting duty to the European Commission.[176] This was hailed as a solid basis for a friendly settlement. On the issue of torture, Turkey was left with a duty to report to the Commission on the measures it had taken to ensure respect for Article 3 ECHR in legislature and practice. Ultimately, this was deemed sufficient, and the complaint was quietly put to rest.[177] One lasting consequence of the friendly settlement was the requirement of Turkey to accept the right of individual petition, opening the European system for Turkish citizens as well.[178]

It was a remarkably silent end to the procedure: especially when compared to the earlier Greek case, which famously ended in Greece leaving the Council of Europe with slamming doors, the friendly settlement was a bemused end to one of the more serious breaches the Convention experienced in the 1980s. Moreover, the Dutch position was of a very different preposition than that of the Greek case, which had ultimately revolved around the 'individual rights of man'. In the Turkish case, 'burdensome political side effects' won out.

Such came as a major surprise to the NGOs involved. No convincing changes would be made to alter the situation on the ground, and it would seem a compromise was made even on what appeared to be

[175] Ibid.

[176] NL-HaNA, Buza/Code 1975–1984, 2.05.330, inv. nr. 22108 'Memo from embassy Ankara to the Hague, 5 Dec 1984'.

[177] Report of the Commission in *France, Norway, Denmark, Sweden, Netherlands* v. *Turkey*, paras 37.

[178] Helen Keller, Magdalena Forowicz and Lorenz Engi, *Friendly Settlement before the European Court of Human Rights: Theory and Practice* (Oxford: Oxford University Press, 2010) p. 74.

non-negotiable rights. But it was also a sign of the changed tactics: the altered character of the protests, with the solidarity marches for Greece giving way to the more professional letters from NGOs, had the effect of keeping the situation in Turkey out of the headlines of domestic newspapers and shifted it into more closed arenas of policymaking, granting the government more leeway to act. As letters from human rights NGOs such as the NJCM came in pressuring the government to not too easily compromise on a friendly settlement, these could be set aside relatively easily with reference to the confidentiality of the procedure. Pressure from below was simply less pervasive when put forward in that format.[179]

5.4.2 SETTLING FOR THE MINIMUM LEGAL CORE. The preference for a political solution over legal ones was pervasive in other areas as well, in particular as the functioning of the Court became a topic of debate in Strasbourg. In several cases, the Court had stepped on the toes of states, and the United Kingdom in particular had been annoyed with the string of cases in which it found Strasbourg to rule against its interests.[180] In his resignation speech, the UK permanent representative, Donald Cape, had expressed his doubts on the evolution of the case law of the Court. Moreover, behind closed doors, the West German government too had wondered whether the Court had not gone too far in the case of *Luedicke* v. *Germany*, in which it was ruled that Germany violated the right to a fair trial by demanding convicted persons to pay for the costs of an interpreter. Confronted with a judgement which would seem to require costly changes in legislation, tempers flared in the Committee of Ministers on the limits of Article 54.[181] Openly, the Germans wondered 'whether or not the case law of the Court had reached a stadium in

179 NL-HaNA, Buza/Code 1975–1984, 2.05.330, inv. nr 22108, 'Letter NJCM 8 October 1984'.

180 See the analysis of Ed Bates on the position of the UK in the cases of Golder and Sunday Times; Bates, *The Evolution of the European Convention*, pp. 171–267.

181 *Luedicke, Belkacem and Koç* v. *Germany*, 28 November 1978, Series A no. 29. The question at hand was how the supervision and follow up of the judgement of the Court should be overseen. Germany pleaded flexibility, the directorate of human rights a more rigid legal change.

which the required change of national legislation was not excessive and difficult'.[182]

Clearly, hesitation with regard to case law of the Court may not have been new in the system of the Convention. Belgium had fought the *Belgian Linguistic* case every step of the road, for example. However, the Dutch noted a certain threat to the very system of the Convention. By now also the big member states had become critical. More than once, the United Kingdom and Germany had uttered how these judgements could have an impact on their acceptance of the right of individual complaint. Acceptance of this right had remained optional, usually to be extended every five years, meaning it could be used as a way to pressure the system: acceptance of the system was always conditional. The UK had already once used this as a tool to show their discontent, and it was feared the next step would be the removal of the provision altogether.

These threats alarmed Dutch officials. When in the *Luedicke* case, a way out of the interpretational conflict of Article 54 was proposed, namely a question to the Court, this was perfectly in line with the route the Dutch had always supported. Yet as the political resistance of the 'big three' (France, the United Kingdom and West Germany) was harsh, with the British embassy engaging in diplomatic moves to counter the move, the Dutch were scared off by this pressure. Foreign Affairs decided 'to not further strengthen the growing resistance against the implications of the Convention and the right of individual complaint'.[183] Faced with the choice to either push for an increased

[182] The case set off a heated debate in the Committee of Ministers on the meaning of article 54 of the Convention, which dealt with the follow up of cases and the implementation to remove the conflict between domestic law and Convention standards. Supervision on the follow up was left in the hands of the Committee of Ministers. Germany noted in the case of *Luedicke* no additional research was needed for new general measures, that is, legislation. The director of human rights thought differently, however, kicking off a heated discussion on the level of 'legal requirements' in the follow up procedure. Proposed was to ask a question to the Court on how to interpret the Convention, which was ultimately – after firm opposition of the United Kingdom – shot down to be resolved diplomatically. Key was to keep a certain level of diplomatic flexibility in the follow up of judgements, and not be 'straightjacketed' by firm legal requirements.

[183] NL-HaNA, Buza/Code 1975–1984, 2.05.330, inv. nr. 22199, 'Memo 6 May 1983, Van der Wal to the Hague'.

role of the 'legal core' of the Convention, or compromise and accept the doubts of the other states, safety was preferred. In order to safeguard the legal core, caution was advised.

This became the key strategy of the Dutch government over the course of the decade: to refrain from new initiatives which would enlarge the role of the Court and instead settle for an approach which would safeguard its role. Since that was already under pressure, now was not the time for legal experiments.

This became very clear in the follow-up to the 1978 declaration of the Committee of Ministers, who set out to 'give priority to the work undertaken in the Council of Europe of exploring the possibility of extending the lists of rights of the individual, notably rights in the social, economic and cultural fields'. In doing so, an active part would be played in the 'further realization of human rights and fundamental freedoms including [...] those in the social, economic and cultural fields...'[184]

In itself, this seemed a harmless call to merely 'explore' possibilities of socio-economic rights in the Council of Europe framework. However, it served as a starting point for a very concrete call to action which carried on into the 1980s, leading to the draft of a potential 'seventh protocol' incorporating social and economic rights into the system of human rights protection. As a follow-up, Austria launched an initiative for this new protocol and found support in the Norwegian delegation, the Secretary General of the Council of Europe, and Director of Human Rights, Peter Leuprecht.[185] After all, human rights were dynamic concepts, they held, and as such, the time was right to expand the Convention. If successful, this would mean a fundamental shift in the set-up of the Convention to move beyond the focus on liberal freedoms.

That was something to firmly oppose. For the Netherlands it was clear from the start that any step in the direction of legally enforceable socio-economic rights was undesirable. Socio-economic rights were seen as non-justiciable, even in the national context, let alone by

[184] Council of Europe, Declaration Committee of Ministers, 27 April 1978, 62nd session.
[185] NL-HaNA, Buza/Code 1975–1984, 2.05.330, inv. nr. 22198, '27 April 1978, vision JURA'.

a supranational court.[186] The responses to the proposal were therefore negative. Yet the government's motivation for opposing this 'seventh protocol' was more revealing than the denial itself. In its dismissal, the government not only voiced the principled opposition against socio-economic rights as enforceable human rights, but also reflected upon the nature and challenges of the Convention.

The Austrian initiative was seen as divisive, as it had been commonplace to agree that socio-economic rights were both less universal than liberal freedom rights as well as that supranational legal control over those rights was highly controversial.[187] The criticism focused on the nature of the Convention. 'Before all else, the Convention needs to be and remain a generally accepted minimum standard', the Dutch held.[188] Should such a protocol be drafted, it was not expected that all member states would sign up to it, causing an unequal field of human rights protection. Such developments needed to be avoided. The controversial nature of socio-economic rights would threaten that core aspect, and in turn, the strength of the Court's jurisprudence.

Said jurisprudence was the second reason why the initiative should be dismissed. It was noted how in case law, the Convention already accepted some elements of socio-economic and cultural rights. In the *Airey* v. *Ireland* case, in which Ireland was held to provide effective access to justice, the Court held that even though the Convention was aimed at civil and political rights, these could have firm implications for socio-economic rights. As there existed no 'watertight division' between civil and socio-economic rights, the Court could indeed have a say on those as well.[189] The *Airey* case was a perfect example of the new role of

[186] They were left out of the Constitutional reforms of 1983, for example.

[187] From the beginning it was clear such a proposal would not resonate with the U.K. for example, who would shun further oversight.

[188] NL-HaNA, Buza/Code 1975–1984, 2.05.330, inv. nr. 22198, 'Memo 27 April 1981'.

[189] As the Court set out in Airey, paragraph 26: 'The Court is aware that the further realization of social and economic rights is largely dependent on the situation – notably financial – reigning in the State in question. On the other hand, the Convention must be interpreted in the light of present-day conditions (above-mentioned Marckx judegment, p. 19, paragraph 41) and it is designed to safeguard the individual in a real and practical way as regards those areas with which it deals (see paragraph 24). Whilst the Convention sets forth what are essentially civil and political rights, many of them have

the Strasbourg Court, finding individual justice in a rather creative, but most certainly dynamic and progressive way.

Yet this new role also was noted by the states. The *Airey* case was explicitly mentioned in the context of the Austrian initiative as both a reason to pursue and as a reason to doubt the expansion of the Convention. Those in favour of the inclusion of socio-economic rights saw *Airey* as an argument in favour of the seventh protocol. The Court had already urged Ireland to provide a system of legal aid, in itself a socio-economic implication of a political right. The road was therefore open to move forward in that way, and institutionalize the shift in a protocol.[190]

The other way to interpret *Airey* was as a warning *not* to provide the Court with even more rights to interpret. 'Some states', the analysis went, 'have trouble accepting the legal system of control of the Convention [...] What plays a role here is the sometimes *very* dynamic jurisprudence of the Strasbourg organs, which has confronted the member states with obligations they could not have foreseen when they ratified the Convention: therefore, they have become a bit more cautious'.[191] The initiative therefore threatened to upset precisely that most valuable achievement: a stable minimum core. Here, the Dutch decided that, if they wanted to safeguard the legal supervision of the Convention, caution was necessary.

In that light, the inclusion of a new protocol was not seen as the best way to protect socio-economic rights. The United Kingdom, for example, noted the legal supervision of socio-economic rights as a political problem, whereas the Netherlands saw in the Court's supervision of these rights the danger of an 'excessive hold of the Commission and Court on legislation in member states'.[192] In the end, resistance from the states, in particular the 'big three', sealed the fate of the

implications of a social or economic nature. The Court therefore considers, like the Commission, that the mere fact that an interpretation of the Convention may extend into the sphere of social and economic rights should not be a decisive factor against such an interpretation; there is no water-tight division separating that sphere from the field covered by the Convention', *Airey* v. *Ireland*, 9 October 1979, § 26, Series A no. 32.

190 NL-HaNA, Buza/Code 1975–1984, 2.05.330, inv. nr. 22198, 'vision JURA, 27 April 1981'.

191 NL-HaNA, Buza/Code 1975–1984, 2.05.330, inv. nr. 22198, 'Memo 5 October 1981'. Emphasis in original.

192 NL-HaNA, Buza/Code 1975–1984, 2.05.330, inv. nr. 22198, 'Vision JURA, 27 April 1981'.

push towards social rights. In the commission of experts, where the proposal was discussed, it soon became clear it was a hopeless affair. Even a watered-down version, focused mainly on equal pay for men and women, was deemed undesirable to include in the Convention. Rather, all these rights should be moved to the Social Charter, where supervision was not binding.[193]

Now socio-economic rights may have been a controversial topic to begin with, with little chance of success from the start. Principled objections stood in the way of its acceptance, just as they had earlier in the drafting process of the Convention. Yet it was striking that in the late 1970s, some of the initial fears, such as an overtly intrusive Court, were now being explicitly spelled out with references to case law. This did result in vocal opposition from some states, with concrete results as to the set-up of the human rights system.

5.4.3 REFRAINING FROM ACTION: THE 'MERGER INITIATIVE' GRINDS INTO DEADLOCK. Still, even the policy of keeping the Convention as it was brought challenges of its own. This became particularly acute when, due to the explosive growth of applications, the system itself was put under strain. With the route to Strasbourg increasingly common in the domestic contexts, the amount of complaints which found their way to the institutions skyrocketed.[194] The resulting backlog swiftly became (in)famous. As it would take years for cases to be decided, a radical solution was proposed from several sides: the system should be fundamentally overhauled to set up a permanent Court. This Court would need to be the result of a merger between the Commission and Court. Instead of the two-tier stepped system which led to time-consuming procedures, a single court would be able to deal with the complaints much more efficiently. But precisely the radical character of the proposal swiftly turned the discussion in a great example of how the states would *not* support further meddling in the system.

In 1986, a summit of experts formally kicked off the initiative. In Neuchatel, the potential merger of Commission and Court was the topic

[193] NL-HaNA, Buza/Code 1975–1984, 2.05.330, inv. nr. 21804, 'Memo 26 November 1984'.

[194] Bates, *The Evolution of the European Convention*, pp. 391–431.

of a high-stakes conference. There, the Dutch participants had been remarkably positive about this solution. The national experts, Pieter van Dijk and Evert Alkema, supported the idea of a merger, with van Dijk noting how the merger was 'the only realistic and effective ultimate answer to the present stagnation of the supervisory machinery of the Convention'.[195] Wiarda too, in his capacity of judge at the European Court, supported a merger but also noted the risks of such a step. It would risk creating an ivory tower, with the judges being cut off from their national roots. This might cause them to lose contact with the domestic realities which for them constituted 'elements of appreciation of the utmost importance'.[196]

Wiarda came to this conclusion as he was firmly aware of the peculiar position which the Court occupied, between domestic sensitivities and effective European fundamental rights protection, which required constant balancing.[197] A linkage to the domestic social, cultural and political realities would be vital to maintain that sense of awareness, particularly in an area as sensitive as human rights protection. Wiarda had been on the bench for a long time and experienced the period in which the authority of the Court was very much in the balance, and he therefore believed that the process had to be treated with the utmost care. It would be one of his last public statements about the future of the Court. He had stepped down as a judge in 1986, having served almost a staggering twenty years, and would pass away two years later, a central figure in the cementing of the Convention in the Netherlands.

The 1986 conference became the clearest illustration of the growing difference between the position of the government and of the Dutch academic experts. Wiarda may have been cautiously in favour of a merger, but other academics embraced the idea with zeal. The government, however, was adamantly opposed to such an idea. At first sight, this may seem remarkable. The Dutch government had supported a strong legalization

195 The proceedings can be found in *Human Rights Law Journal*, Vol. 8, part 1 (1987), pp. 1–223, 'Merger of the European Commission and European Court of Human Rights: Second Seminar on International Law and European Law at the University of Neuchatel', 14–15 March 1986, pp. 5–212.

196 Ibid.

197 G. J. Wiarda, *Rechterlijke voortvarendheid en rechterlijke terughoudendheid bij de toepassing van de Europese Conventie ter bescherming van de rechten van de mens* (Utrecht, 1986).

of the procedure and built a reputation as a 'human rights friendly' nation, for instance, taking up a highly active position in the UN human rights protection system. However, when it came to the *European* system, the Dutch government expressed no desire 'to further give up sovereignty' to a renewed European Court.[198]

In Neuchatel, the Dutch governmental expert member of the Steering Committee was in fact absent altogether. For the British, this absence was enough to claim the Dutch were part of their rather conservative camp. The British speakers were dismissive of any plans for reform, with one of them, Paul Fifoot, having a long history of critical engagement with the Court.[199] In line with this tradition, he delivered a strong statement on the risks related to the merger, provided his support of the political elements of the Convention, and took a stance against the strengthening of the legal character of the regime. The British Permanent Representative, Cristopher Lush, drew the Netherlands explicitly into this 'group of resistance' by noting that both states opposed the merger in principle.[200]

It was the strongest sign yet that the Dutch had put the ambitions for a strong legalized European human rights system on hold. But it wasn't alone in that stance: rather, the Dutch caution should be seen as a sign of the times. In the late 1980s, the mood surrounding the Court and its interpretation of the Convention had taken a distinctly negative turn. The Dutch hesitation was but one tune in a growing chorus expressing concern with the route European human rights protection was taking, which was perceived to have 'moved too far too fast'.[201] As the European human rights system reached the end of the 1980s, these critical voices grew increasingly louder.

British discontent with the ongoing innovations from Strasbourg, for example, was widely known, with critical voices raised after the *Brogan* judgement, in which the Court put limits on pretrial detention period of a suspected terrorist in Northern Ireland, harshly criticizing the Court

[198] As Alkema noted at the conference in *NJCM Bulletin* Vol. 10 Nr. 5 (1985), pp. 420–442.

[199] Fifoot was the one warning the Court over its interpretation in the case of *Golder* v. *UK*; Bates, *The Evolution*, p. 294.

[200] *Human Rights Law Journal* Vol. 8, part 1 (1987), pp. 138–141.

[201] Bates, *The Evolution*, p. 430.

for putting the safety of the UK at risk.[202] However, voices of discomfort were also heard elsewhere. Switzerland had reacted badly to the *Belilos* judgement in which the Court had taken the revolutionary step of overruling an earlier – albeit quite broadly framed – reservation of the Swiss with regard to Article 6.[203] This was the clearest example of how the Court was comfortable in setting aside political sensitivities in favour of a more effective individual human rights protection. The Swiss Parliament only narrowly rejected a motion to withdraw from the Convention altogether in response.[204]

This had its impact on policies in Strasbourg. Behind the screens, an attempt was made to turn this criticism into a reality, as governmental experts worked on a new addition to Article 6. This addition aimed to limit the scope open to the Court in applying Article 6 ECHR, relating to the right to a fair trial, barring the realm of administrative procedures from review.[205] It was no surprise that the choice to reign in the Court fell on Article 6 ECHR. After all, precisely on the basis of that article, most member states were being confronted with the dynamic interpretation of the Court. As such, it was a clear answer of states to scale back the influence of the Court.[206]

These concerns made the quest to find a solution for the ever-increasing case load a difficult affair. In particular, the radical idea of a permanent Court did not fly well in this more hesitant political context. Attempts at reforms moved ahead slowly, but remained confined to changes *within* the system. The eighth protocol, for instance, foresaw minor changes in the setup of the commission, which allowed it to

[202] ECtHR, 29-11-1989, App. No. 11209/84; 11234/8411266/84; 11386/85, *Brogan and Others* v. *U.K.*

[203] Susan Marks 'Reservations Unhinged: The Belilos Case before the European Court of Human Rights' *The International and Comparative Law Quarterly* Vol. 39 Nr. 2 (1990) pp. 300–327.

[204] The editorial of the *NJCM Bulletin* was, in that sense, very pessimistic in tone: 'Editorial' *NJCM Bulletin* Vol. 14 Nr. 1 (1989).

[205] Ibid.

[206] Although the initiative was later retracted as it 'would be against the entire idea of the Convention and authority of the Court', that was not so evident in the late 1980s. Ministerie Buitenlandse Zaken, Jura/Ara Nr. access 3200 217 inv. nr. 00571, 'discussion deputies, 18 June 2000'.

work far more flexibly and therefore decide on cases more frequently.[207] Subsequently, the tenth protocol was drafted with an eye on reducing the period it took for cases to be decided in the Committee of Ministers. There, the required two-thirds majority would have to be scaled down to a simple majority, not only to let the process in the committee move ahead faster, but also with the aim of preventing as much as possible so-called 'non-decisions', which could frustrate the system.[208]

Yet these moves remained, in a way, tinkering around the edges, as fundamental changes were unforeseeable in the political context of the late 1980s. As a result, the initiative launched after Neuchatel to provide a template of what such a merger towards a permanent Court could look like, moved into a standstill. The governmental experts, tasked with providing a template for a potential merger, could not agree on the desirability of such a protocol and due to the lack of political desire to make a choice, by 1987 an impasse had been reached.[209]

Such a stalemate did not mean that the issue was not a topic of debate. In the Netherlands, the question of reforming the supervisory mechanism was – contrary to how discussion on the European sphere unfolded, and the governmental disposition therein – very much alive in the academic and non-governmental world. In the journals and action groups, the standstill on the European level was predominantly seen as an invitation to a call for action, a fact which they kept reminding the relevant actors in Parliament and government. The NJCM, for example, would provide unsolicited advice to the government on how to reform the system and campaign to set up one permanent Court.[210]

Simultaneously, the problems which the merger was supposed to solve did not disappear by not engaging with them. Despite the bickering governments, the number of complaints kept rising and was expected to continue to grow. Every member state of the Council of Europe had

[207] 8th protocol ECHR.

[208] 10th protocol ECHR.

[209] Andrew Drzemczewski, 'A Major Overhaul of the ECHR Control Mechanism: Protocol 11', in Academy of Europe Law (ed.), *Collected Courses of the Academy of European Law* (The Hague: Martinus Nijhoff Publishers, 1995) Vol. VI Bk. 2, pp. 127–243, 144–145.

[210] The discussion between the NCJM and the Adviescommissie can be revisited in P. van Dijk, R. Hermann and Y. S. Klerk, 'Gewogen en te licht bevonden: maar is de weegschaal wel geijkt?' *NJCM Bulletin* Vol. 15 Nr. 5 (1990), pp. 630–634.

recognized the right of individual complaint by 1988, and as greater numbers of citizens and lawyers explored the potential of the European human rights system, the very real danger existed that the European institutions would collapse under the influx of complaints.

These were the reasons which prompted the Dutch government to ask for advice from the Advice Committee on human rights. With an eye on the Dutch chairmanship of the Committee of Ministers of the Council of Europe of 1989, the Dutch Minister of Foreign Affairs, Hans van den Broek, believed that the debate could use a fresh impetus. On 21 December 1988, van den Broek asked the Advice Committee to come up with measures which could be taken in the short and long term to ensure a better and more streamlined procedure at the European instances.[211] But the hope for reform would remain limited: unless something radical happened, the deadlock seemed destined to remain in place.

Therefore, as the Convention approached the end of the decade, it was in a peculiar position. Flowing from a combination of top-down jurisprudence of the Court as well as bottom-up engagement with the Convention, European human rights were firmly nested in the domestic legal system. No longer distant and inactive, the decade had seen the mainstreaming of human rights law in the Netherlands. Yet there was a different side of the coin: the member states had grown increasingly wary of the jurisprudence of the Court, which had triggered a pervasive caution in the system. As ever more states expressed critique of the course of the Court, ambitious reforms were set aside in favour of protecting the system as a whole. Coming into 1989, few would have expected the 1990s to become a decade of fundamental reform: rather, the system was under strong and persistent pressure, criticized by states who had seemingly run out of patience with the highly active European Court. In that setting, any ideas of moving towards a permanent Court seemed highly preliminary. Only a radical change in circumstances could alter those dispositions.

[211] The details of the report will be treated in Chapter 6.

CHAPTER 6

1989–2022

From Permissive Consensus to Persistent Critique

On 29 May 2010, then Dutch Prime Minister Jan Peter Balkenende presented the European Court of Human Rights with the prestigious '4 freedoms award'. In his speech, Balkenende heaped praise on the institution, stating that 'over the last 50 years, the European Court of Human Rights has ruled on thousands of cases. It has ensured access to justice for every person in our vast and ancient continent. It has brought security and stability to our society. It has fully earned the respect and support of the member states of the Council of Europe'.[1]

It was all the more remarkable, then, when less than a year later, the Netherlands joined a growing chorus of critique on the European Court. In the same year, UK Prime Minister David Cameron noted that a judgement of the Court made him 'physically ill', while a series of intergovernmental summits was kicked off in the Council of Europe, which aimed at strengthening the place of states in the European system of human rights protection.[2] The Netherlands emerged as one of the supporters of such a rebalancing of the system.[3] It would seem the Court had not, in fact, *fully* earned the support of the member states of the Council of Europe after all.

So where did this turnaround come from?[4] Often, it has been noted that the Court stepped into deeply political matters, prompting strong

[1] The speech is accessible via www.omroepzeeland.nl/nieuws/zld54907/four-freedoms-awards-uitgereikt-in-middelburg.

[2] Cameron referred to the *Hirst* case in this context, relating to the voting rights of prisoners.

[3] Glas, 'From Interlaken to Copenhagen', pp. 121–124.

[4] A question which has vexed literature for some time: Mikael Rask Madsen, 'From boom to backlash? The European Court of Human Rights and the Transformation of

and emotional responses from the states.[5] The Court's case law has included topics such as migration,[6] abortion,[7] or the voting rights of prisoners,[8] all of which have been taken as examples of such a contentious area of 'mega-politics'.[9] Still, the focus on the Court obscures the multifaceted reasons for backlash. For although it is clear that political pushback can more readily be expected if the Court engages in controversial topics or 'mega-politics', societal issues are not inherently politically sensitive. Rather, they are *made* into hornets' nests by relevant political actors in – mostly – domestic political debates which define how the interference of the Court is evaluated.[10]

The Dutch case is illustrative of precisely these dynamics. The Court found itself the target of national criticism after 2010, mostly due to its case law in the realm of migration and amidst a wider contestation of international (human rights) institutions. Now clearly, rules and limits to governmental freedom to act on migration in the Netherlands had been consistently been set by the European Court ever since the late 1980s. Still, no one discussed this as a matter of 'mega-politics': it only

Europe' in Aust and Demir-Gürsel (eds.), *The European Court of Human Rights*, pp. 21–42; Spyridon Flogaitis, Tom Zwart and Julie Fraser (eds.), *The Court of Human Rights and Its Discontents: Turning Criticism into Strength* (Cheltenham: Edward Elgar, 2013); Patricia Popelier, Sarah Lambrecht and Koen Lemmens (eds.), *Criticism of the European Court of Human Rights – Shifting the Convention System: Counter-Dynamics at the National Level* (Antwerp: Intersentia, 2016); Øyvind Stiansen, Erik Voeten, 'Backlash and Judicial Restraint: Evidence from the European Court of Human Rights' *International Studies Quarterly* Vol. 64 Nr. 4 (2020), pp. 770–784.

5 Ran Hirschl, 'The Judicialization of Mega-Politics and the Rise of Political Courts' *Annual Review of Political Science* Vol. 11 (2008), pp. 93–118; for a wide overview of these issues, see Karen Alter and Mikael Rask Madsen, 'The International Adjudication of Mega Politics' *Law and Contemporary Problems* Vol. 84 Nr. 4 (2021), pp. 1–28.

6 *Hirsi Jamaa and Others* v. *Italy* [GC], no. 27765/09, ECHR 2012.

7 Consider *Vo* v. *France [GC]*, no. 53924/00, ECHR 2004-VIII and *A, B and C* v. *Ireland [GC]*, no. 25579/05, ECHR 2010.

8 *Hirst* v. *the United Kingdom (no. 2) [GC]*, no. 74025/01, ECHR 2005-IX.

9 Ximenia Soley and Silvia Steininger, 'Parting Ways or Lashing Back? Withdrawals, Backlash and the Inter-American Court of Human Rights' *International Journal of Law in Context* Vol. 14 Nr. 2 (2018), pp. 237–257.

10 Alter and Madsen, 'The International Adjudication of Mega-Politics', *Law and Contemporary Problems* pp. 1–28; Başak Çali, et al., 'The Legitimacy of Human Rights Courts: A Grounded Interpretivist Analysis of the European Court of Human Rights' *Human Rights Quarterly* Vol. 35 Nr. 4 (2013), pp. 955–984.

became a topic of relevance much later, after 2010. In fact, one of the crucial questions is why – if political concerns were not new and if the main reason for concern, migration, had been an area of law under the ECHR's influence for a very long time – the open critique of the Court in the Netherlands emerged so *late*. The Dutch case can hence serve to explain how and why the critique on the European Court emerged in the form and period as it did, and in doing so, shed light on the underlying reasons for the backlash.

In order to understand that, we need to take into account the trajectory of the Convention since the caution had seeped into the system in the late 1980s. For the fundamental transformation it went through afterwards was deeply connected to the role it currently plays.[11] As the supervisory mechanism was fully 'legalized', the potential for political 'voice' seemed to have been pushed to external summits.[12] But still, the political concerns did not suddenly leave the system: in many ways, the current situation the Convention finds itself in is but a re-emergence of earlier discussions.

6.1 TOWARDS A PERMANENT COURT

The institutional renewal of the Convention's system was rather surprising. After all, early in 1989, no one within the Council of Europe would have guessed the next decade would see the institution taking on a leading role in European integration with a permanent Court of human rights as the crown jewel thereof. Looking back on the tempestuous developments of human rights protection and international institutions as they were established in the 1990s, it is easy to forget how remarkable those feats in

[11] Andrew Drzemczewski, 'A Major Overhaul of the ECHR Control Mechanism: Protocol 11', *Collected Courses of the Academy of European Law*, pp. 127–243.

[12] Silvia Steininger, 'Creating Loyalty: Communication Practices in the European and Inter-American Human Rights Regimes' *Global Constitutionalism* Vol. 11 Nr. 2 (2022), pp. 161–196; Smekal, H., and Tsereteli, N. 'Reforming to Please: A Comprehensive Explanation for Non-Exit from the European Court of Human Rights' *European Constitutional Law Review* Vol. 17 Nr. 4 (2021), pp. 664–687; Mikael Rask Madsen, 'The Challenging Authority', *Law and Contemporary Problems*, p. 143 on the shift to institutional autonomy.

fact were. For instance, in 1998, when the European Court was installed as a permanent body, supervising human rights throughout what once had been a divided continent, no one seemed to remember how widespread the criticism of the Court had been in the decade before. Still in 1990, leading academics Pieter van Dijk and Fried van Hoof expressed their concern about the future of the European human rights system in the third edition of their handbook. Breaking with the hopeful final chapters of the earlier editions, which had expressed the wish for continuing progressive integration in the field of human rights, there now existed a 'tendency of diminishing acceptation', the authors held.[13]

As they noted, discontent with the perceived judicial activism of the Court had led to dissatisfaction, and even obstruction. This placed the key factor for the success of the Convention, the living instrument doctrine, in jeopardy. The optimism regarding the European system of human rights protection, so pervasive in earlier editions of the handbook, was gone. With political criticism increasing, the future of the system as a whole was now an open question. After all, the authors noted, the success or failure of the Convention was, in the end, dependent on the political will of the states involved.[14]

Yet eight years later, those very states had embraced a revolutionary option and put forward a permanent institution, which merged the Court and Commission into one body. Moreover, the states removed their own engagement from the individual complaint procedure, as the Committee of Ministers was no longer part of deciding cases, hence firmly 'legalizing' the procedure.[15] It was a remarkable turnaround.

6.1.1 HUMAN RIGHTS AFTER THE COLD WAR. All these developments had been inconceivable if not for the end of the Cold War. This had an immediate and lasting impact on the central tenets of thinking about international governance, and provided the key impetus

[13] van Dijk and van Hoof, *De Europese Conventie in Theorie en praktijk* (Nijmegen: Ars Aequi Libri, 1990), p. 677.

[14] van Dijk and van Hoof, *De Europese Conventie*, p. 678.

[15] By 'legalizing' is meant the removal of the governmental/openly political element in the procedure, characterized by the dual step of removing the Committee of Ministers altogether, and the introduction of a permanent acceptance of jurisdiction of the Court.

for the European Court to achieve its permanent position. For one of the defining elements of the early post-Cold War world order was the sincere belief in the benefits of the international legal order which would expand these universal liberal values over the world.[16] As the Berlin Wall came down, one vision remained; the liberal democratic world order with human rights as guiding ideals.[17]

Now when it came to human rights, clearly, these did not emerge out of thin air. As we have seen, human rights found themselves in the mainstream for a while. Still before the end of the Cold War, a search for a new modus vivendi, largely based around human rights, was already under way. One illustration of this already existing search was when, on 6 July 1989, Mikhail Gorbachev was welcomed in the Parliamentary Assembly of the Council of Europe.[18] In his speech, Gorbachev sought to lay out his vision of a 'common European home': a part of a broader vision on international coexistence of East and West based around shared values and cooperation.[19] The shared values around which this home would be built were cross-border elements such as environmentalism and – importantly – human rights. 'A world where military arsenals would be reduced but where human rights would be violated would not be a safe place', the leader of the Soviet Union remarked. Gorbachev's speech was a testimony to earlier commitment to the Helsinki agreements and willingness to make this into a common European endeavour. Human rights hence had already emerged in the late 1980s as concepts which could form the basis of new cooperation in Europe.[20]

[16] Illustrative is for instance, S. Huntington, who spoke in 1991 of the third wave of democratization, heralding a triumph of democracies and liberal rights, leading to democratization everywhere.

[17] Or at least, that would seem so, leading Francis Fukuyama to ponder the meaning of man at this 'end of history'.

[18] The Consultative Assembly changed its name into the 'Parliamentary Assembly'; A. Grachev, 'From the common European home to European confederation: François Mitterrand and Mikhail Gorbachev in search of the road to a greater Europe' in F. Bozo, M-P Rey, N. Piers Ludlow and L. Nuti (eds.), *Europe and the End of the Cold War: A Reappraisal* (London: Routledge, 2008), pp. 207–220.

[19] Malcolm, Neil, 'The "Common European Home" and Soviet European Policy' *International Affairs* Vol. 65 Nr. 4 (1989), pp. 659–676.

[20] Sarah B. Snyder, *Human Rights Activism and the End of the Cold War: A Transnational History of the Helsinki Network* (Cambridge: Cambridge University Press, 2011).

The end of the Cold War entailed an acceleration of this existing trend, but now proceeded largely *without* input from the former communist states, resulting in a singular perspective on liberal freedom rights going on to dominate the discourse. Even though Gorbachev's proposed common European home failed to materialize, notions of international human rights as common concerns requiring protection proved more durable, most visibly when George H. W. Bush unfolded his own idea of a 'new world order', embracing international institutions, democracy and human rights as key tenets thereof, to be enforced by the only remaining superpower, the United States.[21] This was an attempt to provide clarity on what was next in terms of ideology. In the curious vacuum of world views left by the demise of the Soviet Union, human rights and democracy were among the most prominent placeholders of grand political visions.[22]

Throughout the 1990s, therefore, human rights surged to absolute prominence in international (legal) thinking. As states would – at least rhetorically – claim to be democratic in nature, so too would human rights come to serve as the main tools for international justice.[23] International law, human rights, and their institutional framework – revolving around international courts – were presented as elements *and* drivers of this 'real new world order'.[24] As such, human rights functioned more prominently than ever before as an international language which could support surprisingly many different goals. Their uses ranged from providing reasons to engage in international humanitarian intervention, forming a rallying call for the International Criminal Court which would 'end impunity', to being used to celebrate 'anti-imperialist resistance', as in the 'Muamar Al Gadaffi international prize for human rights', sponsored and paid

[21] On the acceleration of human rights thinking in Europe: Sarah B. Snyder, 'Beyond Containment? The First Bush Administration's Skeptical Approach to the CSCE' *Cold War History* Vol. 13 Nr. 4 (2013), pp. 463–484.

[22] Cf. Moyn, *The Last Utopia*, pp. 140–175. The 'grand' political vision human rights offer is debated, however: to many, they don't seem to offer a vision at all, something we'll return to later in this chapter.

[23] Todd Landman, *Human Rights and Democracy* (London: Bloomsbury, 2013), pp. 46–59.

[24] Slaughter, A. -M., 'The Real New World Order' *Foreign Affairs* Vol. 76 Nr. 5 (1997), pp. 183–197.

for by the Libyan dictator.[25] Perhaps most illustrative of how commonplace human rights had become, was how even the fictional archetype of a desirable bachelor, Mr Darcy, was reinvented from aristocratic estate owner in the classic novel by Jane Austen, into a 'human rights barrister' in the popular 2001 movie *Bridget Jones's Diary* –a profession that had existed for barely twenty years.

Subsequently, human rights and the political thought which reached its zenith in the 1990s went very well together. Continuing on the trajectory started in the mid-1980s, a socialist free market economy promised a 'third way' forward, and political struggles were replaced with an increased managerial and 'pragmatist' attitude.[26] This was a kind of politics 'without adversary'.[27] Exemplarily in this regard were the Dutch governments of the time, consisting of classical ideological opponents from the Labour and Liberal parties, led by Prime Minister Wim Kok, who proudly proclaimed in 1995 that his Labour party had 'shed its ideological feathers'. Problems were there to be *solved*, aided along by neutral experts who would ultimately produce a correct outcome. Human rights, in their minimalistic and depoliticized form as had been established in the 1970s and 1980s, worked exceedingly well in this context. The aspiration, that human rights should serve as the moral floor beneath one could not drop, while leaving the ceiling wide open, was perfectly compatible with the new social free market, whilst in their neutral apolitical universalism version they fitted perfectly in an age where precisely those were deemed highly desirable qualities.[28] Paired with strong support for further European integration – the Dutch government put forward a federalist design in the lead up to Maastricht in 1991 – internationalism, Europe and human rights were relatively unquestioned concepts in the Netherlands.

[25] Recipients include, inter alia Nelson Mandela, Fidel Castro and Recep Tayyip Erdogan.

[26] Sociologist Hans Boutelier has described how in the 1990s a 'pragmacracy' was installed: Hans Boutelier, *Het Nieuwe Westen: de identitaire strijd om de sociale verbeelding* (Amsterdam: Van Gennep, 2021), pp. 17–30.

[27] Chantal Mouffe, *The Democratic Paradox* (London: Verso Books, 2000), pp. 108–129.

[28] For critical voices on this non-threatening existence, see Susan Marks, *A False Tree of Liberty: Human Rights in Radical Thought* (Oxford: Oxford University Press, 2019); Samuel Moyn, *Not Enough*. On the depolitization of politics, and the links thereof to law, see Tony Judt, *Ill Fares the Land* (London: Penguin, 2010), pp. 81–137 'on the unbearable lightness of politics'.

'Relatively', because this did not mean everyone supported the emerging European-human rights consensus. In the Netherlands, one critical voice when it came to this reigning political consensus came in the figure of Frits Bolkestein of the liberal VVD party. Bolkestein was distinctively dismissive of these two truisms of the 1990s: the direction of European integration and, more subtly, the universalist human rights ambition. In contrast, he focused on the nation state as ideal type for politics and society.[29]

In his political outlook, Bolkestein insisted on 'shared cultural values' as basis for integration, be it European or the integration of minorities. In a curious liberal reappraisal of Christianity as the true source of Western enlightenment, Bolkestein noted in 1994 how value-neutral liberalism could not cope with minorities and the possible accession of Turkey to the EU. Christianity, however, could serve as a shared moral foundation.[30] He was also the first to take a critical stance regarding the European human rights system in light of its potential consequences for migration policy: in the early 1990s, Bolkestein warned that a case before the Court concerning family unification of a second wife of a Muslim man could lead to the an 'influx of brides for polygamous Muslim men'.

But it was no persistent critique and was not directed at the Court as such. As the Court also never issued such a ruling, Bolkestein's attention and critique of this issue was isolated and quickly ebbed away.[31] Moreover, this was absolutely a minority point of view. Bolkestein stood out precisely because of the fact that the vast majority of academics, politicians and public opinion were firmly in favour of both European integration and international human rights protection. It was, however a prelude of things to come from 2010 onwards, precisely where they related to migration and culture.

6.1.2 THE COUNCIL OF EUROPE AS ENTRY TICKET INTO 'THE WEST'. The developments in the Council of Europe followed these trends. After the Cold War, a new dynamic was unleashed when it came to the politics in the Council of Europe. The increasingly critical mood which had

[29] Captured in the phrase of Paul Scheffer 'without a "we" things do not work out'.

[30] 'VVD-Fractieleider Frits Bolkestein, gymnasiast in de politiek', *NRC* 3 May 1994.

[31] 'Fantasie Bolkestein over veelwijverij', *Het Parool* (23 May 1992).

characterized politics in the Council of Europe in the 1980s was replaced by one of hope and excitement. It was a fundamental turnaround. As one Dutch civil servant in Strasbourg remembered, 'we truly had the idea the project would come to fruition and be of benefit to Eastern Europe'.[32] The new zeal was reflected in the energy and enthusiasm devoted to the Convention. Critique of the institutions aimed at protecting those values which were now universally praised, was dampened. Human rights were believed to have been instrumental in winning the Cold War: now was not the time to debate or criticize their guardians.[33]

In particular, the Council of Europe opened up to the newly independent European states. Driven by its Secretary General, Catherine Lalumière, the scene was set for integration of these states into the Council of Europe.[34] Human rights formed a key element of these talks. Almost acutely after 1989, the option had been raised by various academics and even certain diplomats to allow the Eastern European countries to accede to the European Convention in order to provide international human rights protection, even if they were not yet part of the Council of Europe.[35] Although this proposal was rejected due to the fundamental changes to the system it would entail, it was telling of the great value which was attached to the Convention in this process. A compromise was found, in that as of 1990, effective acceptance of the Convention, including the right of individual petition, had been made a requirement for membership of the Council of Europe.[36] Doing so made human rights essential elements for the integration of these states in the European framework.

An influx of applications for membership ensued from these newly independent states. First in line was Hungary, which applied for membership in 1989, swiftly followed by Poland, Yugoslavia, Bulgaria, Romania and Czechoslovakia in 1990.[37] As the line of states wanting to sign up

[32] Wassenaar, Interview civil servant, 8-11-2021.

[33] For a discussion of the idea of human rights as ending the Cold War, see Snyder, *Human Rights Activism and the End of the Cold War*, pp. 232–243.

[34] Wassenberg, *History of the Council of Europe*, pp. 131–142.

[35] Ministerie van Buitenlandse Zaken, JURA/ARA, 02442, inv. nr. 167, 'Letter from JURA to Minister 5 January 1990'.

[36] Ibid and Wassenberg, *History of the Council of Europe*, p. 133.

[37] Wassenberg, *History of the Council of Europe*, pp. 140–149.

to the European system grew, the status and prestige of the Convention were simultaneously enhanced. The prestige was only increased when the Copenhagen criteria laid down how a state had to show institutional safeguards for human rights protection as a requirement to accede to the EU: what better way to show one fulfilled that criterion than acceding to the ECHR? Adhering to the European Convention came to serve as the benchmark for modern European states. A symbol of independence was hence found in embracing limitations on the newly founded state.[38]

Integration into the human rights framework was actively supported by the Western states as well. From 1990, the so-called 'Demosthenes-program' was set up, which aimed at facilitating a smooth integration of the Central and Eastern European states into the Council of Europe. Expertise was provided, primarily in the legal realm, as training and assistance on rule of law and human rights were provided by leading Western European experts in the field.[39] It was not just the language of liberal individualism which was now being exported into the former Soviet states, but also the institutional set-up, tied to its international and supranational organizations.

Within this context, a new impetus was given to the longstanding discussion on institutional reform of the Convention. The Court and Commission remained burdened by their workload, and the quest for reform had been stalled in the late eighties. This new push for reform coincided with the advice of the 'Adviescommissie Mensenrechten'. Asked for by the Minister in 1988, the advice – drafted by van Dijk – was delivered right in the midst of these fundamental changes and proposed a new way of moving forward. Instead of striving for a merger, it

[38] Krastev and Holmes have noted how this, in the long term, led to a detachment: the strong liberal new constitutions did not fit well with the nationalism which formed part and parcel of the move towards independence. 'Liberal elites continued to speak the language of universal rights, their nationalistic counterparts incorporated the national symbols and narrative', Ivan Krastev and Stephen Holmes, *Falend Licht: Hoe het Westen de Koude Oorlog won maar de vrede verloor* (Amsterdam: Atlas Contact, 2019), pp. 75–77.

[39] It was a wide ranging state of affairs, ranging from the setting up of human rights libraries (ensuing a certain common literacy on human rights) to the organization of seminars for NGOs, lawyers and judges. Ministerie van Buitenlandse Zaken, DRW/ARA/00757, inv. nr. 16884 'Memo 18 November 1991'.

proposed to maintain a two-tier system of Commission and Court, and foresaw a streamlining of the procedure, creating permanent institutions and removing the Committee of Ministers.[40]

But what to *do* with the advice remained unclear for a while. Initially, the response from Minister of Foreign Affairs Van den Broek was cautiously positive, lauding the effort, but also noting some drawbacks of the advice.[41] Key therein was a central aspect of the advice, namely to strive towards a proper 'legalized' procedure. This, however, entailed getting rid of the influence of the Committee of Ministers.

That was a sensitive topic. After all, it had been a tenet of Dutch policy throughout the 1980s to maintain a role for the state in the Committee of Ministers in order to make sure the sometimes zealous jurisprudence of the Court would not undermine the political will required to safeguard the minimum core of the Convention. As such, the Committee itself provided a much desired 'balance between the demands of the state and the interests of the individual'.[42] In that sense, the advice was considered radical: as civil servants noted, this had not as such been brought forward in the Council of Europe. Also, the Minister himself initially noted in January 1990 how he considered this to be a 'bad idea' and called to preserve the political element of the Committee of Ministers in the procedure.[43] Still, some months later, he had second thoughts and would wholeheartedly embrace the advice as Dutch policy in the Council of Europe.

This turnaround had to do with the accession of new states. For the inclusion of the Eastern European states was not only cheered on, it also set off alarm bells in the capitals of the member states. Denying membership was not truly feasible in the political constellation after the end of the Cold War, which favoured expansion. Apart from the risk this entailed of watering down the requirements of membership, another issue was the impact this could have on an already stretched system of supervision. In particular, it was to be expected that this influx of new states that had all taken the – compulsory step of accepting the right of individual

[40] Klerk, *Het ECRM Toezichtmechanisme*, pp. 524–525.

[41] Ibid, p. 526.

[42] Ministerie van Buitenlandse Zaken, JUA/ArA/02442, inv. nr. 167, 'letter from Jura to Minister, 5 January 1990'.

[43] Ibid, 'draft letter from M. to Van Dijk, 19 January 1990'.

petition, would lead to an even further increase of complaints. Moreover, with more Ministers, more discussions could be expected, which would undoubtedly hamper the efficiency of the Committee of Ministers. To counter that, something had to happen. One member of the civil service even went so far as to note how, 'due to the changes in Eastern Europe, in my view the only outcome is that solely a permanent court [...] will be able to take over the protection of human rights sufficiently'.[44]

The ensuing debate on how to keep the system manageable in light of this expansion resulted in the Dutch embracing a fully legalized procedure. The new European human rights system would have to be a predominantly judicial one when it came to the individual complaints procedure. As the Minister wrote to van Dijk in response to his advice, the Netherlands now supported the removal of that institution in deciding individual cases, 'so that the supervisory mechanism could grow into a fully grown legal procedure'.[45] By removing the role of the Committee of Ministers, not only could the procedure be streamlined (on occasion, the Ministers had frustrated the handling of cases the Commission had sent it), but also the risks of internal division when it came to individual complaints were minimized.[46]

6.1.3 CHOOSING BETWEEN SYSTEMS: MERGER OR TWO-TIER. With the Dutch proposal on the table (where it coincided with a Swedish initiative, which by and large revolved around the same set-up), three options dominated the discussion. One was to strive for a merger which would create one, permanent human rights Court: the original Neuchatel idea. The second option was the Dutch–Swedish proposal to keep the existing system, but to grant the possibility of appeal to the European Court and remove the role of the Committee of Minsters. The

[44] Ibid, 'Memo Jura to DRW, 7 June 1990'.

[45] Letter 21 December 1990, cited in Klerk, *Het ECRM- Toezichtmechanisme*, p. 526.

[46] Concern over the accession of many states to the Committee of Ministers itself was due to a fear it would turn it into an unruly institution, a point prevalent in previous discussions on acceding states. Nl-Ha Na 2.05.330. Inv. Nr. 2178 on the accession of Liechtenstein, for instance. For a broader discussion on the practice of admissibility in the Council of Europe, see Kushtrim Istrefi, 'Kosovo's Quest for Council of Europe Membership' *Review of Central and East European Law* Vol. 43 Nr. 3 (2018), pp. 255–273.

final option was to simply do nothing, yet this was increasingly sidelined due to pressure from the accession of the new member states. From 16 to 20 March 1992, the relevant Committee of Experts (DH-PR) discussed the differences, similarities and benefits of the proposed ideas.[47] The hope, at least from the Dutch side, was that its proposal would be accepted by a clear majority, opening up the momentum to reinvigorate the discussions which had gone nowhere for years.

The first two proposals shared some similarities. First of all, both ideas noted the pressing *need* for change: it was clear things could not continue in the same way, and a quick solution had to be found. Second, both ideas aimed to reinforce the legalized character of the proceedings by abandoning the Committee of Ministers' power of decision with respect to individual applications. As the Netherlands had withdrawn their support of the institution in the procedure, the United Kingdom, the most vocal state when it came to preserving the role of the Ministers, was left increasingly isolated.[48] The defining difference between the two ideas was the existence of an appeals procedure. No such mechanism was envisaged in the 'Single Court' alternative.[49]

As the options were put on the table, Dutch hopes for a clear majority were dashed. In a 'tour de table' in which the representatives of the states were asked their opinions, little seemed to have changed. Fourteen experts, including those from the UK, were in favour of the Dutch–Swedish proposal, while nine experts, including the Germans and Austrians, were in favour of the merger. Of those favouring the two-tier system, France, Turkey and the UK were also willing to simply keep the present system in place.[50]

[47] The discussions can be found in *Human Rights Law Journal* Vol. 14 Nr. 1–2 (1993).

[48] The Brits used the Committee of Ministers also in their resistance against the ninth protocol, granting individuals the right to appeal to the European Court. It would, in their view, change the role of the Court into a straightforward court of appeal, which was never the original intention of the Convention, and 'would reduce the role of the Committee of Ministers in favour of the Court, which would risk upsetting the balance … between political and judicial elements'. Ministry of Foreign Affairs, inv. nr. 167, JUA/ArA/02442, 'Memo from British Embassy to Dutch Perm. Rep. 3 October 1990'.

[49] Klerk, *Het ECRM-toezichtmechanisme*, pp. 532–540.

[50] Ministry of Foreign Affairs, DG Europese Samenwerking inv. nr. 16885, 'Memo 23 March 1992 from Ass. Jura to The Hague'.

For the Netherlands, this persisting division had immediate consequences for the way it approached the discussion. As the Permanent Representation noted, 'it is wise to deal with the notion that structural changes in the Strasbourg procedure are for now derailed. Even though virtually everyone agrees on the necessity of (rather drastic) changes in the system, no consensus can be reached on the how this should be done[...]'.[51] In light of the clear and present danger to the system, from March 1992 onwards the Dutch government began to search for a compromise and focused on measures which could be taken on short-term notice. As such, it did not campaign for the two-tier system as strongly as perhaps one might have expected. Instead, the need for consensus trumped the perceived benefits of the proposal. This disposition became evident in the lead up to the next key meeting of the process, the 91st meeting of the Committee of Ministers on 5 November, where the political balance was tipped in favour of the single court.[52]

As a starting point, the time pressure became increasingly acute as a European summit of heads of state had been scheduled in October 1993 in Vienna. This summit had been Mitterrand's idea, launched in May 1992 in a speech before the Parliamentary Assembly, and was aimed at showing the new role of the Council of Europe in the newly integrated Europe. The summit put the politicians under a new kind of pressure. Summits require results, and it so happened the institutional reform of the Convention was put on the agenda in Vienna. That was no mere coincidence. After Mitterrand had proclaimed his desire for a summit, the French had kindly requested that Austria – the country chairing the Committee of Ministers for the second half of 1993 – should host the summit. This had come on the back of some pushback from Germany, and it appeared to the Dutch diplomats as though the French made a bargain: in exchange for holding the summit in Vienna, Austria and Germany, both proponents of the single Court, would together be able to set the agenda.[53]

[51] Ibid.

[52] Drzemczewski, 'A Major Overhaul of the ECHR Control Mechanism: Protocol 11', p. 158.

[53] Ministerie Buitenlandse Zaken, JURA/ARA/02353, DDO6 inv. nr. 267, 'Memo from DRW to JURA, 2 October 1992'.

The move alarmed the Dutch diplomats. For in the meantime, the Secretariat of the Council of Europe had also declared itself a proponent of a merger, a message forcefully carried out by its Secretary General, Lalumière. She put additional pressure on the governments to find a swift solution, advocating that 'radical solutions' – meaning a merger – were now needed.[54] Combined with the agenda-setting power of the Austrians and Germans, this would ensure that the proponents of a merger were in a powerful position to put forward their initiatives. 'The easier to achieve Dutch-Swedish modernization, which is supported by roughly two-thirds of the Member States, may be circumvented by a forceful French–German bulldozer, with Austrian support and under the supervision of the Secretariat', the diplomats expressed their fear.[55]

In the lead up to the meeting on 5 November, a compromise, drafted by the Swedish delegation, was proposed, consisting of a two-step decision, with a solution for the short term and one for the long one. The short-term solution would consist of moving forward with what the two initiatives shared, namely, as soon as possible, to abolish the Committee of Ministers' role in the individual complaints. In the long term, the Netherlands and Sweden would accept the notion to draw up a protocol for a possible merger, with a view to allowing the Committee of Ministers to take a decision at the earliest possible moment.[56]

Opinions on that compromise also remained divided, however. In preparation for the next meeting, it was noted how Germany and Switzerland, active proponents of a merger, would not support such a dual strategy, whereas the UK, noting how the two-tier system could count on the support of a majority of states, thought it was too early to come up with compromises.[57] The divisions could not easily be overcome. The outcome, on paper at least, was that the Committee of Ministers noted

[54] C. Lalumière, Human Rights in Europe: Challenges for the Next Millennium, in R. Macdonald, F. Matscher and H. Petzold (eds.), *The European System for the Protection of Human Rights* (Dordrecht: Nijhoff, 1993), xv–xxi.

[55] Ministerie Buitenlandse Zaken, JURA/ARA/02353, DDO6, inv. nr. 267, 'Memo 2 October 1992'.

[56] Ibid, 'Memo from Jura to Minister, speaking points for sitting 5-11-1992, 2 November 1992'.

[57] Ibid.

the technical background had been completed and now a political decision was needed, 'at the Vienna convention at the latest'.[58] This was more of a decision to set a deadline, instead of a decision on the content, but did add to the growing urgency of finding common ground.

During that meeting, a subtle trend could be discerned in balance in favour of the single court. For although the Dutch and Swedes had forcefully defended the two-tier system, the two states' expressed willingness to accept the drafting of a protocol which would foresee a merger was a massive step in the direction of that particular outcome. The Dutch justification for doing so may have been somewhat naïve (it was hoped that this would lead proponents of the merger to see the potential downsides of such an endeavour), but the step itself showed a merger was acceptable, even to the most active supporters of the two-tier system (the United Kingdom aside).[59]

The shifting panels were reflected in the new 'tour de table': now, fourteen states were in favour of a two-tier system, yet thirteen were in favour of a merger. Crucially, if not unsurprising with an eye on the summit coming up, France now indicated a preference for the merger, whereas it had been previously neutral on the matter.[60] Combined with unanimous support of the Parliamentary Assembly for the idea of a merger, the two-thirds majority in Commission and Court favouring the two-tier system could not prevent the idea of a merger from gathering steam. By expressing a willingness to join a protocol which would revolve around the merger, in that sense the Dutch had undermined their own proposal. As the states in favour of the merger had done no such a thing with regard to their proposition, the idea of a singular court was left as the clear route forward.[61]

Afterwards, the Dutch Parliament piled additional pressure onto the Dutch government to change its outlook by declaring itself unequivocally supportive of the merger. In a moment illustrative of the consensus on European integration, international institutionalism, and human rights,

[58] Ibid, 'Memo from Perm. Rep to DRW, 9 November 1992'.

[59] Ibid.

[60] Drzemczewski, 'A Major Overhaul of the ECHR Control Mechanism: Protocol 11', p. 150.

[61] Although some expressed willingness to compromise, this was not reflected in an acceptance of the two-tier system the way the Netherlands had done.

the issue was framed as an opposition between either being in favour of Europe, or against it. In a hearing concerning the Dutch position in the Council of Europe on 11 December 1992, the government was pressed by Parliamentarians on its support of the two-tier system. A remarkably broad coalition pushed for a shift towards accepting the merger proposal. Both the Christian Democrats and the Social Democrats, the governing parties at the time, asked the Minister to reconsider the Dutch preference for the two-tier system.[62]

Here, the influence of the campaign of the secretariat of the Council of Europe became evident. Christian Democrat Van der Linden attached great value to the stance of 'the Council of Europe itself', as both the secretariat and Assembly were pushing for a merger and asked the government to join the European 'mainstream'.[63] Van der Linden did not understand why the Netherlands continued to pursue a two-tier system and urged them to retract the Dutch initiative. His colleague Stoffelen of the Labour party, even threatened to table a motion if the Netherlands did not aim to achieve consensus on the merger proposal.[64] For him, the only solution to the increase in complaints was to set up a single court within a foreseeable timeframe. As these two parties had a majority in Parliament, to come up with motion was a very clear sign that the governmental strategy ideally would have to be reconsidered.

The message to the Minister was clear: it was better to strive for consensus in the form of a merger than to persist in the chosen two-tier system.[65] With the summit in Vienna coming up, to be a 'constructive European' was deemed to be of greater importance. In reply, the Minister submitted that the Netherlands 'did not have a principled preference for any kind of system, if only a model would be chosen on which consensus could be reached'. It was another step away from the initial position and towards a flexible mood when it came to the ultimate political decision.[66]

Afterwards, in the first months of 1993, the discussion went back to the lower level of experts and the Ministers' deputies in Strasbourg. As new

[62] *Kamerstukken II* 1992–1993, 22 800 V. Nr 52.

[63] Ibid.

[64] Ibid.

[65] Ibid.

[66] Ibid.

proposals came in, with a large group of twelve states submitting a proposal in favour of a merger in March 1993, the support for the two-tier system dwindled even further. Only the Netherlands, Sweden, Denmark and the UK now put forward a proposal in favour of the two-tier system.[67] Yet as we have seen, the political support for these initiatives was diminishing.

Personal changes mattered here as well. Minister Van den Broek, who had been a staunch proponent of the two-tier system, had stepped down in January 1993, to be replaced by professor of international law, Pieter Kooijmans, who had a background in human rights activism. Kooijmans was, in fact one of the first proponents of active engagement with the Convention, being involved in the Greek Case of 1969. His views on the matter proved more lenient than Van den Broek's, and as discussions grew increasingly politicized, in the lead up to a special meeting of the Ministers on 28 May 1993, the need for consensus trumped the feeling of being right.

During that meeting, the choice was ultimately made for one single, permanent Court and the Ministers opted to set up what was to become the eleventh protocol. Therein, traces of the Dutch–Swedish proposals can still be discerned As a gesture towards the proposal, the defining element thereof, the possibility for an appeal, had to be 'internalized' in the single Court. How to shape this counterintuitive combination was left to the experts. Over the course of the negotiations, conducted in a 'pressure cooker' of a meeting, their task was, in the words of the Dutch expert, to find a solution for how to square a circle.[68] The solution, a venue for internal appeal, was ultimately found in a distinct chamber system, with important cases or appeal cases to appear before the 'Grand Chamber', a finding of the Dutch expert, Karel de Vey Mestdagh.

6.1.4 THE NEW SYSTEM: LEGALIZED, BUT AT WHAT EXPENSE?. The proposed system was revolutionary in its character. A defining aspect in its set up was its removal of the Committee of Ministers from the procedure. In addition, the Commission, which had long served as a more diplomatically inclined filter mechanism, was replaced by the

[67] Ministry of Foreign Affairs, DVE/RvE/Verdragen, inv. nr. 01021, 'Report on Committee of Ministers, 3 May 1993'.

[68] Wassenaar, interview civil servant 8 November 2021.

Court itself, which in many ways was 'pushed into the Commission'. Such removals firmly limited the potential of 'political pressure' in the system. This was furthered by the mandatory acceptance of the right of individual petition: before, this had been an optional and renewable right which had granted the states the possibility of using threats of discontinuing their acceptance thereof as a tool to express discontent.[69]

Precisely this new, legalized character of the procedure remained difficult to accept for the most critical of all states, the UK. Throughout the negotiations, the UK had refrained from providing support for an option which would enhance the powers of the Strasbourg system. As a last resort, in the latest stages of the negotiation it proposed to alter the final set-up. On 6 April 1993, the British set out their concerns.

> The Court is accountable to no-one, yet has the power to make binding decisions. This is an enormous responsibility. My Government feels very strongly that the opportunity to review the Court's performance periodically and make a conscious decision to renew the right of petition is right and proper as a democratic safeguard and it therefore regards maintaining the status quo as absolutely essential.[70]

This was a final attempt to maintain the longstanding and cherished possibility of political pressure on the Court within the system. The British move should not come as a surprise. To safeguard the political elements in the system had been a constant disposition in its stance vis-à-vis the Strasbourg institutions, which had not changed after the end of the Cold War. Moreover, they had never been alone in voicing these concerns. Similar points of view had been brought up by other states in previous settings, not in the least by the Netherlands a mere couple of years before. The most remarkable aspect, therefore, was not the British resistance: it was the UK's isolation in resisting the permanent Court.[71]

[69] Mikael Rask Madsen, 'Legal Diplomacy – Law, Politics and the Genesis of Postwar European Human Rights', in SL Hoffmann (ed.), *Human Rights in the Twentieth Century: A Critical History* (Cambridge: Cambridge University Press, 2010), pp. 62–81, 65–66.

[70] Ministry of Foreign Affairs, DVE/RVE Verdragen, 115, inv. nr. 01021, 'Memo from Jura to DVE, 6 April 1994'.

[71] Although Turkey and Italy also had some concerns, but on different grounds. Turkey opposed the new role of the Court in interstate complaints where the state concerned has not recognized the mandatory jurisdiction of the Court.

For as the negotiations on the protocol had proceeded, the choice for legalization had already been made when the compromise proposal had been put forward. The Dutch, for instance, had altered their stance under pressure from Parliament and formed a distinct desire to indeed solve the problem of an ever increasing caseload. From there, the legalization of the system had been a core element in any discussion. The British attempt to save the governmental element was, at this stage of the proceedings, too little and above all, too late. As such, it was not of great concern to the Dutch negotiator. 'It is fully expected they will get into line before the deadline', he noted on the British proposal.[72] Indeed, they ultimately would. Without resistance from the UK, the new Court, a result of tense political negotiations, would ultimately kick off its journey in 1998.

The legacy was a fully legalized system in which the traditional venue for statal interference, the Committee of Ministers, was left to supervise the execution of judgements. This was the outcome of a distinct wish of the states themselves, and had been present in both options discussed. Yet it also entailed a change in how the political voice could be heard. After all, such a set-up was fine as long as the Court treaded relatively carefully and experienced a great sense of authority. Should that situation come under pressure one day, the States would find the room to voice their dissent diminished to more formal venues, such as protocols, or informal ones, such as open critique.

6.2 THE PERSISTENCE OF POLITICAL DOUBTS: HOW CONCERNS OVER THE POWER OF THE EUROPEAN COURT NEVER DISAPPEARED

For despite the move to institutional reform, concerns over an all-too-active Court lingered on in the – attempted – development of subsequent protocols and reforms to the Convention. As more and more states joined the European system, a wide variety of instruments were employed to further the human rights situation. Yet this should not be

[72] Ministry of Foreign Affairs, DVE/RVE verdragen, 115, inv. nr. 01021, 'Memo from Jura to DVE, 6 April 1994'.

seen as a full break with past attitudes towards the way in which European human rights protection functioned.[73] Even though the enthusiasm for human rights was tangible, the end of the Cold War did not mean the Court was no longer under scrutiny.

One difference, however, was that this caution was being met by a new dynamic, namely the wish to provide additions to the European human rights system which could be meaningful those Central and Eastern European states. In particular, the latter element was a new, vibrant element when it came to the Council of Europe. Dutch human rights policy had always thrived when it came to setting the standards for other states, such as in the UN, yet Dutch actors had acted more conservatively when those standards had to apply to themselves.[74] This tension was now also introduced in the Council of Europe, where, much more than before, a certain 'mission civilisatrice' of the Eastern European states had to be squared with how that would reflect on the own legal system.

The new motivation coincided with several new initiatives to alter the Convention, which were launched with different degrees of success. Due to the tension between the desire to set standards for Eastern Europe while safeguarding their own sensitivities, some protocols went nowhere, while others experienced a final breakthrough because of it. But most of all, the discussions surrounding these negotiations show that even though the choice had been made for a permanent Court, that permanent Court was *not* given a free ride. The British observation that 'the Court was accountable to no one, yet has the power to make binding decisions' remained a recurring tension in the Council.

6.2.1 DETAINEES AND NON-DISCRIMINATION, BETWEEN CAUTION AND EXPANSIONISM. Traditional hesitation won out, for example, with regard to a proposed protocol to safeguard the rights of detainees. The protocol was the outcome of a colloquium on the

[73] Illustrative is how the Netherlands continuously held (and holds) off the ratification of the seventh protocol, relating to penal law requirements, due to fears of an extensive interpretation of the Court, and to show discomfort on what was perceived to be a 'stretch' of the Court's interpretation of article 6, which the Court although the article speaks of a 'criminal charge', also applied in administrative procedure.

[74] Oomen, *Rights for Others*, pp. 1–24.

Convention and an idea of the president of the Court, Rolv Ryssdal, who saw a lacuna when it came to this group.[75] Even though it was perceived to be of use to the new member states, the additional value to the 'old' states was doubted. The crucial point for the Dutch was precisely that this could have an impact on the domestic legal system. With the experts drafting a proposal, the Dutch legal expert foresaw a negative outcome when it came to the Dutch application. As he noted, 'Dutch politics could, confronted with the proposal, be inclined to *lower* the existing domestic norms and settle for the new Strasbourg standard'.[76]

Such was the result of the particular legal status the Convention had achieved in the domestic context. As we have seen, the legal choice in the domestic context to settle for a minimum protection, had turned the Convention into a de facto *maximum*, including in political initiatives. If this was allowed by the Convention, it meant the action or legislation was in compliance with human rights standards: even though the Convention allowed countries to exceed its standard, in Dutch policy the Convention standard increasingly became a synonym for 'the' human rights standard. That particular disposition in turn hampered the willingness of Foreign Affairs to sign up to initiatives which did not add anything significant to the Dutch legal order out of fear of indeed *lowering* the human rights standard on the domestic level. The draft protocol did not make it in the end, due to a broader resistance from member states (alongside the Netherlands, France and the UK were also not keen on the proposal, as it would not only further expand the reach of the Court, but also was perceived to not add anything of great substance to the Convention).[77]

Another discussion related to what would become Protocol 12, concerning the prohibition of discrimination. This was part of a long-standing discussion in the Council of Europe on the inclusion of sex discrimination. Here, the balance ultimately shifted in favour of the perceived added value for Eastern European states. In 1994, briefly after the first new states had joined the Council, the initiative to include a

[75] Ministerie van Buitenlandse Zaken, DJZ/VE/Ara. Nr. Access. 3200.217, inv. nr. 3204, 'Memo JURA to DRW 1993, summary expert meeting, 26–30 April 1993'.

[76] Ministerie van Buitenlandse Zaken, 3200.217, inv. nr. 'Memo JURA, 3 June 1993'.

[77] Ibid.

prohibition of discrimination on the basis of sex was relaunched. This particular protocol merits some further attention. Without going into all the details of its drafting history, which took roughly six years, it provides an insight into how the accession of the new states made its impact on the negotiations and, ultimately, trumped concerns about how the Court would deal with any new rights to protect.

The initial Dutch stance was again one of hesitation. A similar attempt had been launched in the 1980s, and then the Netherlands had taken an adopted a negative stance due to fears of overlapping with EU law. In this relaunch too, opinions were divided. Although Foreign Affairs was in favour of such a protocol, the Ministry of Justice was opposed. 'Even though it would be useful to provide a psychological and political signal for those states involved in the Convention, but which are not yet a member of the EU, for the Netherlands itself it would not be of much use', the diplomats held.[78]

Concerns about the domestic application, this time related to how the judiciary would deal with non-discrimination issues, proved vital in this initial caution. Any proposal on the topic reminded the government of how the domestic judiciary had extensively interpreted the principle when it came to social rights, kickstarting the lively discussion on judicial overreach in the late 1980s.[79] In light of that controversy, caution was a necessity out of democratic concerns. 'The legislator has lost all say over the matter once directly applicable norms have been ratified', the civil servants warned.[80] It was a sign of how the controversy from the late 1980s about the impact that human rights law could have had left its mark and the political scare that had sparked would not be so easy to overcome.

This hesitation was reflected on the European stage. Plenty of discussion ensued in the steering committee on the set-up of the protocol: was it not more desirable to have a broader frame, which included race and other elements? A general feeling existed that the limited scope would

[78] Ministerie Buitenlandse Zaken, 3200.217, inv. nr. 00569, 'Standpuntbepaling Minister on Protocol, 7 November 1997'.

[79] See Chapter 5.

[80] Ministerie Buitenlandse Zaken, 3200.217, inv. nr. 00569, 'Memo Social Affairs on Proposal, 16 June 1994'.

maybe not add sufficient protection. Moreover, several states, such as Germany, France and the UK, were for their part adamantly opposed to the protocol, with an eye on potential positive measures which the protocol could force them to take.[81]

A factor which did not help in creating an active discussion was the fact that the Eastern European states, for whom the Netherlands at least believed the protocol to be of the utmost importance, remained relatively quiet during the procedure. The Dutch expert noted that their strategy seemed to be, above all, 'to give the impression not to stand in the way of further development of human rights, and would rather join the majority than to follow their own conviction'.[82]

The divisions proved to be too deep to be overcome. In October 1996, after two years of discussions, the majority of experts in the steering committee, including the Dutch representative, rejected the draft protocol. The balance had shifted in favour of hesitation. 'Experts saw difficulties in drafting a protocol in this field due to the uncertainty regarding the way in which the European Court would interpret such open-ended provisions since for the first time, a large number of economic, social, and political rights would come under the control of the organs of the Convention'.[83]

6.2.2 MOVING TO A GENERAL NON-DISCRIMINATION PROTOCOL. This was *not* the end of the initiative, however. Although the initiative for a protocol on non-discrimination on the basis of sex was dismissed, the idea of a *broader* protocol, encompassing race, for example, was considered to be a more relevant topic on which to draw up a legally binding instrument, and for this, only the UK had expressed its opposition.[84] At first sight, this may seem counterintuitive: a broader set-up would grant the Court even wider discretion. Yet the Dutch considerations shed some light on the thinking behind this reasoning. In the meeting defining the Dutch standpoint, the motivation was laid out. Key in supporting the initiative was – also in light of surging nationalism in the

[81] Ibid, 'Summary of Meeting CDDH, from Perm Rep to the Hague 5 December 1994'.
[82] Ibid, 'Report Meeting DH-DEV on Protocol, 24 September 1996'.
[83] Ibid, 'Summary Dh- DEV, 15–18 October 1996'.
[84] Ibid, 'Memo from Strasbourg to the Hague, 2 May 1997'.

former Soviet states – 'the normative value of such a protocol, especially for the Central and Eastern European states [...] The protocol fills a gap in the Convention and will have clear added value in standard setting'.[85] Fears of extensive interpretation by the Court were understandable and justified, but did not outweigh that importance. This motivation remained constant throughout the rest of the drafting process: in explaining the situation in 1999, the Dutch expert noted the protocol would primarily 'set an example' for the relatively new states of the Council of Europe, and would actively campaign for it to become a reality.

A majority of states would be on board with this broader set-up and as the finalization approached in late 1999 and early 2000, the final matter to be resolved was the classic problem of how the Court would respond. The negotiations on the 12th protocol show explicitly how the states were expressing doubts over the power of the Court in such relatively sensitive national areas. Caution, or even distrust, was prevalent in the discussions. Germany sought to explicitly add a national margin of appreciation and joined the UK in pushing for more weight to be given to the national context 'against rules that might be applied by an international court in a manner which is not acceptable in the social and cultural context of a member state'.[86]

Even though some states noted that such a provision amounted to nothing more than a codification of existing case law and would therefore only hamper the freedom of the Court, France noted dryly that this was precisely the point. France 'did not share the optimism of certain delegations [...] since the substantial freedom of the Court meant its case law was liable to change'.[87] One expert took it even further and described how he 'had the feeling human rights' were gradually being supplanted by the notion of 'lawyers rights' with the latter making increasingly routine use of the Strasbourg system, and noted it might be wise to counteract this tendency.[88]

85 Ibid, 'Definitieve standpuntbepaling Min over protocol', 7 November 1997.

86 Ministerie Buitenlandse Zaken, 3200.217, inv. nr. 00571, 'Memo from Strasbourg to the Hague, 2 May 2000'.

87 Ibid, 'From Strasbourg to the Hague, Report on Discussion at Deputy Level, 18 June 2000'.

88 Ministerie Buitenlandse Zaken, 3200.217, inv. nr.00570, 'From Strasbourg to the Hague, Report Meeting Steering Committee, 18 November 1999'.

In response, the representative of the Directorate Human Rights felt the need to step in on the discussion. As he noted, the fact that states declared that they were apprehensive about 'the need to codify the court's case law' formed a 'disquieting tendency'. Codification stood in tension with 'the spirit of the Convention', carried forward by the freedom of the Court, and as such, initiatives such as these 'called for the greatest prudence'.[89]

What had emerged wasn't truly a battle over the spirit of the Convention, but rather a clash between the two needs, always present in that same spirit, which characterized the European system: the idea of an independent court protecting individual rights and the need to balance that with the interests of the states involved. The DG Human Rights was of the mind that the Court's judicial freedom was the essence of the Convention: the critical states were concerned about *precisely* that. Codification of principles would provide the states with a degree of certainty as to the direction of the Court.

The final result was reflective of this tension. A majority supported the protocol, and the final vote consisted of twenty-nine states in favour, including the Netherlands, with eight abstentions. The UK and France, for example, would not sign the final protocol out of discomfort with the direction of the protocol.[90] For the Netherlands, the added value of the protocol outweighed the burden of a potentially more active Court: the final signature can be seen as a victory for the Dutch campaign for this protocol. The government had actively supported the protocol: the Dutch expert had chaired the meetings, and the final existence was to no small extent the result of the desire to create this document to provide the Convention with greater potency when it came to matters of discrimination, even though its motivation was to help the Eastern European states along in that regard.

Yet *equally* as important was the relatively strong opposition to the protocol which was voiced in the negotiation process. The criticism of

[89] Ministerie Buitenlandse Zaken, 3200.217, inv. nr 00571, 'Report on Discussion at Deputy Level, 18 June 2000'.

[90] Janneke Gerards, 'Gelijke Behandeling en het EVRM: Artikel 14 EVRM: van krachteloze waarborg naar "norm met tanden"?' *NJCM-Bulletin* Vol. 29 Nr. 2 (2004), pp. 176–198, 178.

the Court may have been somewhat more subdued after the fall of the Berlin Wall, but under the surface, the unease with regard to the position of the European Court lingered on. As the attention was in those years on the challenges facing the system at large, these political concerns would not disappear. Rather, they would resurface some ten years later, to the surprise of some, when a series of summits were held attempting to rebalance the system towards a more state-friendly orientation. Calls which were made during those meetings to codify the national margin of appreciation, the principle of subsidiarity, or broader discomfort with the Court being overly intrusive or expansive in its jurisprudence were a direct continuation of these earlier utterances.

The Dutch wouldn't follow that critical stance due to the strong political preference for European integration mixed with international human rights protection. The caution which had characterized the Dutch approach to the Convention was in the 1990s countered by a desire to raise the human rights standards in the Eastern and Central European states. As such, it was exemplary of the consensus of the decade, in which European integration and universal human rights protection were two sides of the same coin and, on occasion, rose above the hesitation of the previous decade when it came to expanding the Convention.

Yet it remained difficult to square the zeal for human rights 'elsewhere' with the desire to, in fact, keep human rights away from one's own domestic legal system. When a civil servant remarked how Moldova had ratified the seventh protocol of the ECHR with 'plenty of reservations', alluding to how this would not help with improving the human rights standard, it was pointed out by a colleague the Dutch had actually never ratified this protocol to begin with due to concerns it would have an impact on the Netherlands' criminal procedure. Hence, it was better to 'keep quiet on this point'.[91]

6.2.3 PROTOCOL 14: SAVING THE SYSTEM BY LIMITING ACCESS TO THE COURT. A final example of the continuation of concern can be found in the discussions leading up to Protocol 14,

[91] Nationaal Archief, Den Haag, Ministerie van Justitie/Afdeling Wetgeving; Tractatendossiers, nummer toegang 2.09.88, inventarisnummer 267, 'Memo 11 March 1998'.

which introduced new admissibility criteria. For the protocol was not just unequivocally 'supportive' of the Court, as it sometimes is framed.[92] Rather, the protocol was just as much the result of the desire to *limit* its power. The diplomatic discussions reveal the protocol emerged both from a desire to rescue the Court as well as a motivation to limit the activity of the Court as such.

The protocol itself developed out of dire necessity. After the reforms of the 1990s, the activities of the Court and governments in Strasbourg in the early 2000s were conducted in crisis mode. A number of troubles plagued the European system, from a rise in non-compliance throughout the system, with Italy and Turkey coping with a consistent backlog in similar cases. Also, the peculiar position of Russia in the Council of Europe, with its immense number of inhabitants and internal problems such as the war in Chechnya, put a strain on the Court.[93]

The most pressing issue was the relentlessly growing caseload before the Court and the delay this caused for individual plaintiffs. It was evident that the permanent Court, installed in 1998, was *not* ideally suited to deal with the problem it had been set up to solve. As it had to deal with a great number of applications from the member states, the pressure on the institution became untenable. With 65,000 applications pending before the Court at the end of 2003, the notion that the Court had become a 'victim of its own success' became something of a cliché, but was definitely true.[94]

Almost immediately after the creation of the permanent court in 1998, initiatives were employed to deal with the persisting problems, ultimately resulting in a proposal for the 14th protocol before the Committee of Ministers in 2003, which would allow the Court to deal more efficiently with the stream of applications.[95] The protocol foresaw a streamlining of

[92] Madsen, 'From Boom to Backlash?', p. 38.

[93] Ibid, pp. 32–38.

[94] Martin Eaton and Jeroen Schokkenbroek, 'Reforming the Human Rights Protection System Established by the European Convention on Human Rights: A New Protocol No. 14 to the Convention and Other Measures to Guarantee the Long-Term Effectiveness of the Convention System' *Human Rights Law Journal* Vol. 26 Nr. 1 (2005), pp. 1–17.

[95] For details, Christina G. Hioureas, 'Behind the Scenes of Protocol No. 14: Politics in Reforming the European Court of Human Rights' *Berkeley Journal of International Law* Vol. 24 Nr. 2 (2006), pp. 718–757.

the procedure, but also – and crucially – a new hurdle for admissibility, if the applicant had not suffered a significant disadvantage.

In its final activity report, the steering committee of experts, the CDDH, had not managed to reach agreement on all the proposals. In particular, there was disagreement on the proposed new admissibility criteria. There was a desire to square two distinct and, on the surface, contradictory objectives: the need for the Court to concentrate primarily on cases raising new and/or serious issues, while on the other hand maintaining the right of individuals to seek redress before the Court, the latter being the distinctive and unique achievement of the Convention system.[96] This had already been the topic of a heated debate, as it touched upon the very character of the Convention. Was this a tool for individual justice or rather a more 'constitutional' document, setting out general standards?[97]

For the Netherlands, the negotiations had been carried out in very clear parameters. The fully legalized system had to be kept in place, so a return to the previous two-tier system was not an option. Furthermore, the procedure for very similar cases should be simplified (taken up by the Court in the pilot-judgement system), and – above all – the backlog of cases was a much greater evil than a new admissibility criterion. Justice delayed was, to the view of the Dutch negotiators, justice denied. An excessive focus on individual justice would, in the long run, lead to the end of the system itself.[98] This resulted in strong support for a new hurdle for complaints to be declared admissible, in order to save the system from collapsing altogether. The new hurdle envisioned was set out in general terms: 'if the applicant has not suffered a significant disadvantage and if the case raises neither a serious question affecting the interpretation or application of the Convention or the Protocols thereto, nor a serious issue of general importance', the case would be declared inadmissible.[99]

[96] Eaton and Schokkenbroek, 'Reforming the Human Rights Protection System established by the European Convention on Human Rights', pp. 1–16.

[97] For an overview, see S. Greer and L. Wildhaber, 'Revisiting the Debate about "constitutionalising" the European Court of Human Rights' *Human Rights Law Review* Vol. 12 Nr. 4 (2012), pp. 655–687.

[98] Ministerie Buitenlandse Zaken, DJZ/VE, toegang 3200.380, inv. nr. 00114, 'Letter from Perm. Rep. to the Hague, 8 March 2004'.

[99] See for the details Eaton and Schokkenbroek, 'Reforming the Human Rights Protection System Established by the European Convention on Human Rights', pp. 1–16.

In supporting the introduction of this criterion, the Netherlands found itself in the company of a comfortable majority of states, including the UK and France, as well as roughly two-thirds of the Court.[100] But their motivations differed. Had the Netherlands been spurred on by a desire to keep the system afloat, for the UK and France, the fact that limits on applicability would simply reduce the activity of the Court was *in itself* desirable.[101]

One peculiar new phenomenon which came to fruition in the 1990s and 2000s was the expanding audience the states had to deal with, with a large contingent of NGOs making their presence and influence felt in the process.[102] States could no longer voice their opinions and only take into account their own domestic policy preference or that of other states: rather, a cohort of professional organizations was involved as well.[103] Their preference was clear: individual justice – by and large the raison d'être of these organizations – had to be safeguarded. The 'activist' side of the negotiations were hence firmly against the institution of limits on individual access to justice. Their position was shared by a minority, but committed group of states: Belgium, Finland, Austria, Hungary, Latvia and Luxembourg. Of that group, Belgium was most adamant about keeping the access to individuals as open as possible.

It proved the beginning of a tense political negotiation. At the summit approached during which a final decision had to be made, the resistance had not subsided. For the Dutch representative, a successful summit was 'crucial for the continued existence of the Court' and therein, the admissibility procedure was of vital importance.[104] The Belgians were

[100] Ministry of Foreign Affairs, DJZ/VE, NR. Access 3200.380, inv. nr. 00114, 'Memo from DJZ to Minister, 9 March 2004'.

[101] Ministry of Foreign Affairs, DJZ/VE, NR. Access 3200.380, inv. nr. 00114, 'Memo 29 March 2004'.

[102] Hioureas, 'Behind the Scenes of Protocol No. 14', p. 733.

[103] It is one of the reasons why, when the pushback indeed *reaches* the formal venue, much of the claims tend to get watered down. No, solely because the discussion often turns technical, after which instruments to achieve more subsidiarity usually turn out to be already in place, but also because a different cohort of usually critical or human rights inclined voices are encountered there. See to this end also Madsen, 'Two-level Politics and the Backlash against International Courts', pp. 736–738.

[104] Ministerie Buitenlandse Zaken, DJZ/VE, Nr. toegang 3200.380, inv. nr. 00114, 'Memo from DJZ to Minister, 9 March 2004'.

resistant for two reasons: a certain distrust in how the Court would apply the provision, and the personal convictions of their Minister of Foreign Affairs, Louis Michel, who was rigid in his convictions to maintain full access of individuals to the Court. The Dutch civil servants understood that this had to do with the desire to show how the Belgian government, with elections coming up, stood firm for international human rights – even though they had a hard time believing this could be a relevant theme in the political context.[105]

As the summit drew near, the continued resistance of the group meant some form of compromise had to be found, but also that these further negotiations were taking place under increasing political pressure. As the other states reminded the group of the need for consensus, the Dutch Minister called his Belgian counterpart, while a registrar of the Court spoke of 'a wrong war, against the wrong enemy at the wrong moment'.[106] For one of the first times, the dynamics of European integration and expansion more broadly were also distinctly part of the process. The fact member states were bound in the EU began to have its effects, simply by virtue of that togetherness, and this became visible when the Irish Minister of Foreign Affairs went so far as to use his seat of the presidency of the EU to remind the bickering states, most of them EU Member States or newly admitted, of their exemplary position to the rest of Europe.[107] Dutch civil servants too feared the continued disunity of the EU member states would do harm to the image of the EU in the eyes of the non-member states.[108] A solution was required, if only to prevent further reputational damage.

In a series of informal meetings, the issue was further discussed. The Belgian representative served as the spokesperson for the group and proposed adding the phrase 'and provided that no case may be rejected on this ground which has not been considered by a tribunal applying the

105 Ministerie Buitenlandse Zaken, 3200.380, inv. nr. 4489, box 1166836, 'Memo from Perm Rep. to Civil Servants, 4 May 2004'.

106 Ministerie Buitenlandse Zaken, 3200.380, inv. nr. 00114, 'Memo from DJZ to Minister, 9 March 2004'.

107 Ministerie Buitenlandse Zaken, 3200.380, inv. nr. 4489, box 1166836, 'Letter from Brian Cowen to EU Member States, 1 March 2004'.

108 Ibid, 'Memo from DGES to Minister, 6 April 2004'.

Convention and its case law'. Such offered ground for further discussion. In a gesture towards addressing the concerns of those worried about the position of the individual, the final compromise text read that an application would be declared inadmissible if 'the applicant has not suffered a significant disadvantage, unless respect for human rights as defined in the Convention and the Protocols thereto requires an examination of the application on the merits and provided that no case may be rejected on this ground which has not been duly considered by a domestic tribunal'.[109]

'Duly considered' therefore replaced the more stringent requirement of actual applications of the Convention on the domestic level, leaving a bit more leniency for the Court to determine when this was the case. It was a concession to the minority, making the hurdle somewhat less steep than originally desired, but maintaining the hurdle as such.

The discussion around the admissibility requirement shed light on two broader trends. First of all, it made explicit that the national context, in principle, took centre ground when it came to the protection of European human rights, reaffirming the 'embeddedness' of the Convention in national contexts.[110] Taking a closer look, it was just as much a limitation of the Court. The important element of the 14th protocol was how the Court and its fiercest criticaster the UK – *bien étonnés de se trouver ensemble* – in fact agreed on the necessity of posing limits on individual access. Both agreed on the need to cut back the number of complaints reaching the Court, yet this was never a question of British support for the Court at large.[111]

For the Court, supported by the Netherlands, the protocol dealt with the existential question of safeguarding its own future. For the more critical states, however, the idea of the Court receiving fewer domestic complaints was *in itself* desirable. Criticism of, and support for, the system therefore coalesced into a coalition aimed at reducing the number of people able to find their way to Strasbourg. The two aims, installing

109 Protocol 14 ECHR, article 12 b.

110 Laurence R. Helfer, 'Redesigning the European Court of Human Rights: Embeddedness as a Deep Structural Principle of the European Human Rights Regime' *European Journal of International Law* Vol. 19 Nr. 1 (2008), pp. 125–159, 142.

111 Ministerie Buitenlandse Zaken, 3200.380, inv. nr. 4489, map 00113, '4 May 2004 from Perm. Rep. to the Hague'.

an obstruction in order to maintain the freedom of the Court, could therefore garner support from both sides, but were ultimately driven by different motivations. It is a reminder how the renewed attention to rebalancing the equilibrium in favour of the national 'margin of appreciation' did not come from nowhere in 2010, but rather was a continuum of *one* motivation which was prevalent in the 14th protocol as well.

6.3 THE NATIONAL PUSHBACK

Far away from these sometimes fiery debates in Strasbourg, the Convention experienced a much more peaceful existence on the domestic level. When it came to the Netherlands, the general attitude towards the Convention in these years could be described as 'not knowing much, and not caring much either'.[112] Rather, the Convention was a self-evident part of the Dutch legal order, possessing a constitutional character as the leading fundamental rights instrument. Yet that character was beginning to be put under strain. For however self-evident the Convention or human rights in general may have been, the consensus of which they were part started to come under pressure. Despite their high-ranging promises, the internationalist human rights friendly 1990s, characterized by a pervasive depoliticization, internationalism and pragmatism carried the seeds for its own discontent, turning into a reaffirmation of the nation.

This disposition related directly to European human rights. After all, the Convention was part of this human rights-friendly outlook. For even though European human rights became increasingly present in the national context, critique was only seldom heard. This increased involvement primarily derived from the Court itself, which enjoyed a spark of renewed activity in the 1990s and beyond. Having seen its own authority tremendously enhanced, by 1994 it was housed in a futuristic new building, also visibly dragging the Court into the modern era.[113] The Court moved forward in its active human rights protection, and in the case of *Loizidou v. Turkey* in 1995, the Convention was described as a 'Constitutional

[112] Oomen, 'A Serious Case of Strasbourg Bashing', pp. 413–414.

[113] Arold Lorenz, Nina-Louisa, Xavier Groussot and Gunnar Thor Petursson, *The European Human Rights Culture – a Paradox of Human Rights Protection in Europe?* (Leiden: Nijhoff, 2013), pp. 60–61.

instrument' which aimed to achieve greater unity in the maintenance and further realization of human rights. In doing so, it not only took the symbolic step of claiming for itself a 'constitutional' role, but also put its dynamic interpretation to the question of enforcement, overruling a territorial exception of the Turkish state, reasoning that this stood in the way of the effectiveness of Conventional human rights protection.[114]

The increased activity on the European level was matched by its ever-growing normality on the domestic level. The Convention had, as we have seen in Chapter 5, moved into the mainstream of the Dutch legal order by the end of the 1980s. By the early 2000s, a little more than a decade later, this was perceived to be a completely self-evident state of affairs. The two developments, the mainstreaming on the national level and the increased activity of the European Court, mutually reinforced one another. With expanding European jurisprudence flowing from the rise in complaints from the domestic level, it became easier for domestic judges and lawyers to refer to the Convention, as the material demands were increasingly coloured in. As the Dutch constitutional rights are relatively lacking in such material criteria, the Conventional rights were simply much easier to use.[115] Hence, the active position of the Court reinforced the domestic position of the Convention as well. The legacy of the debates in the 1980s carried onwards however: the Dutch judiciary would closely follow Strasbourg, but was not keen to go beyond it. The choice of the Strasbourg minimum, and a certain hesitation of Dutch courts to move beyond that, have been constant factors in the Dutch legal order ever since.

Both in academic as well as public debate, the consensus around the desirability of the role of the European Court was strong: the emergence of critique in the eighties had subsided again in the nineties.[116] Even though the Convention made a notable impact in the Dutch legal order

[114] *Loizidou* v. *Turkey* (Preliminary Objections) ECHR (1995) Series A. No. 310, para. 75 Reports of Judgments and Decisions 1996-VI.

[115] Gerhard van der Schyff, 'De beperkingssystematiek van de Nederlandse grondrechten: Kanttekeningen bij het rapport van de Staatscommissie Grondwet', *Tijdschrift voor Constitutioneel Recht*, Vol. 2 Nr. 1 (2011), pp. 186–194, 187.

[116] Based on a survey of the relevant journals, no Dutch debate about the *position* of the Court had truly taken off. The manner of interpretation was another, but even there, the balance would seem to be more in favour of 'missed opportunities' rather than 'going too far'.

in these years and touched upon sensitive issues, its legitimacy was never in doubt. For instance, debates surrounding migration remained firmly disconnected from discussions on the Convention or Court at large. The early concern of Bolkestein had not been followed up. Even though the domestic migration policy was deeply influenced by the demands the Convention placed on Dutch law (Swart even spoke of an 'invasion' of Article 8 ECHR in the procedures surrounding migration), the Court's influence over what would become such a salient issue later on was not part of any political debate.[117] Cases with immediate implications in, for instance, the criminal procedure by requiring a lawyer to be present during a hearing,[118] or even a violation of Article 2 after the Amsterdam police had not followed up upon its duties to review a fatal shooting,[119] were all sensitive issues which passed without much political ado.[120]

Even though some academics expressed hesitation as to the direction of the Court, like when Pieter van Dijk, who served as the first Dutch judge in the 'new' Court, noted how 'only lip service seemed to be paid to the national margin of appreciation', a persistent idea of pushing back or rejecting the Court was non-existent.[121] Such wasn't necessarily surprising: the leading voices in Dutch human rights academia either had a personal history in the human rights activism of the 1970s, where the aim had been to *activate* the Court, were involved in the institutional set-up of the Court or Commission themselves, or both.[122]

The situation was not much different in the governmental circles, where a highly loyal stance to the demands of the Convention was adopted. This was partly the result of personal influences, as expertise

[117] A. H. J. Swart, 'Het recht op gezinsleven in het Europees Verdrag en het vreemdelingenrecht', *Handelingen NJV*, pp. 187–262.

[118] Flowing from the requirements of the case of *Salduz* v. *Turkey [GC]*, no. 36391/02, ECHR 2008.

[119] *Ramsahai and Others* v. *the Netherlands [GC]*, no. 52391/99, ECHR 2007-II.

[120] Oomen, 'A serious case of Strasbourg Bashing', p. 413.

[121] Pieter van Dijk 'Het "nieuwe Hof" Tien Jaar; Tel Uw Zegeningen' *NJCM-Bulletin* Vol. 33 Nr. 7 (2008), pp. 927–929, 927.

[122] Egbert Myjer was one of the first members of the NJCM and went on to become a judge, H. G. Schermers was a member of the Commission, Evert Alkema stood at the basis of involving the Court and went on to become a member of the Commission, Fried van Hooff was a strong proponent of human rights protection, just as Pieter van Dijk, who would become judge at the European Court.

in the human rights framework entailed a certain disposition with regard to the framework. As one former civil servant explained: 'there were all around the relevant departments lawyers with a history in the NJCM'. This had its bearing on the general attitude of the departments, which was reinforced by a self-image of the leading department, Foreign Affairs, as the 'guardian of the international rule of law', and the Convention took up an important position in the post-Cold War era, when there was a genuine and strong belief in the benefits of international law.[123] In a similar vein, the Convention wasn't a topic of deep political debate in Parliament either, but rather something to be clearly accepted. In Parliament, it 'seemed the Court could do no wrong'.[124]

As such, the Convention and the Court were embraced as inherently desirable and self-evident. One illustration of this was how, when an attempt was made to introduce the potential for constitutional revision in the early 2000s, dismissive voices noted it would be redundant, since we 'already had the Convention'.[125]

However, this self-evident character of European human rights protection came under pressure, as discontent with the international-legal tradition of which it was a part grew. The managerial politics of the 1990s, characterized by 'reasonableness', left little room for fundamental political differences of opinion.[126] The celebrated internationalism was swiftly confronted with horrors in Rwanda and the former Yugoslavia, leading to a new attempt at reframing the state of affairs. Samuel Huntington, writing partly in response to Fukuyama's ideas, offered a new vision of 'clashing civilizations', turning to irreconcilable differences of culture and identity as explanatory elements for the new world order. The turn to identity as a key element of attention would form the main element in the political debates flowing from this discontent.

123 Wassenaar, interview civil servant, 8 November 2021.

124 M. Kuijer, 'Guaranteeing International Human Rights Standards in the Netherlands: The Parliamentary Dimension' in M. Hunt, H. J. Hooper and P. Yowell (eds.), *Parliaments and Human Rights: Redressing the Democratic Deficit* (Oxford: Hart Publishing, 2015), pp. 295–305.

125 G. Boogaard and J. Uzman, 'Wie zijn zij, dat zij dit mogen doen? Over de Legitimatie van de Straatsburgse Rechtspraak' *Preadvies voor de staatsrechtdag voor jonge juristen 2012* (Leiden, 2012), p. 6.

126 Boutelier, 'Het nieuwe Westen', pp. 9–17.

For this reaffirmation of identity was a cultural enterprise just as much as a political one. In this backlash against internationalist universalism, the search for a 'home' was increasingly found in the own nation state.[127] In political theory, it has been noted how the 1990s saw a marriage between liberalism and democracy: democracy turned into a distinctive *liberal* democracy, focused primarily on defending human rights, placing limits on popular sovereignty. In response, precisely that popular sovereignty was neglected and would re-emerge with a vengeance in the 2000s.[128] Both needs – for identity and popular sovereignty – came together in the search for who this 'populus' actually was. In particular from the early 2000s onwards, when a populist revolt shook up the established Dutch political system, the search for a new 'we' became increasingly prevalent in the public and political debate.[129]

This search for a new national 'we' had a peculiar relation to human rights. On first sight, human rights seem ill-suited to fit a desire for a national story. They seek, by their very nature, to remove the division between 'us' and 'them' and force us to overcome that division by seeing the other in ourselves. And yet, that is what happened in the Dutch context. In the backlash against global governance in the Netherlands, human rights were presented as elements of the country's own national culture, and whereas an image of the Netherlands as champion of legal internationalism was no stranger in nationalist discourse, the way human rights were now being employed started to be used to delineate a very specific other against which to define the national identity. This, in turn, was also one of the main reasons why the pushback in the Netherlands against human rights emerged relatively *late.*

For a long time, the precise direction of the pushback remained unclear and multifaceted, but the connotation with culture and identity was a constant factor. This became most visible in the Dutch pushback

[127] J. W. Duivendak, *Thuis, Het Drama van een Sentimentele Samenleving* (Amsterdam: Amsterdam University Press, 2017).

[128] Mouffe, *The Democratic Paradox*, p. 4.

[129] Illustrated by the desire to build a 'national historic museum' from the early 2000s, which kicked off in earnest in 2006. Even *more* illustrative is how discussions surrounding the museum were subsequently plagued by disagreements, before it was decided to simply *not* found the museum at all.

against the 1990s pragmatist consensus, which came to revolve primarily around 'multiculturalism'. At this time, the status of minorities in society and integration became a prominent political and identarian battleground. Increasingly, the nation became presented in conservative outlets as the result of a 'Judeo-Christian' culture, a discourse which would truly kick off after the attack on the World Trade Centre in 2001 and the murder of two criticasters of Muslim migration, Pim Fortuyn in 2002 and Theo van Gogh in 2004.[130] In particular, Islam was increasingly perceived as the external threat to Dutch culture and values, and as a principal obstacle to the integration of Muslim migrants.[131]

This would seep through into human rights thinking. There, the first pushback on the self-evident character of human rights protection came from the liberal corner as well. Connected to the VVD by virtue of being chair of the Telders-stichting, the party's scientific bureau, Paul Cliteur became one of the first prominent academic voices who expressed criticism and caution about all too expansive human rights proliferation. In his work, Cliteur, noting the special character of human rights which would supersede 'regular' law, advocated 'legislative and judicial restraint'.[132] This in itself was a relative novelty in the Dutch academic human rights debate. The leading voices therein were by and large supportive of the European Court and its interpretation.[133]

Yet human rights also came to play a distinct role when Cliteur connected them to the debate around multiculturalism. Writing on the challenges thereof, Cliteur noted how a radical or postmodern variant of multiculturalism and an excessive reliance by individuals on, for

[130] Leo Lucassen and Jan Lucassen, 'The Strange Death of Dutch Tolerance: The Timing and Nature of the Pessimist Turn in the Dutch Migration Debate' *The Journal of Modern History* Vol. 87 Nr. 1 (2015), pp. 72–101.

[131] Conny Roggeband and Rens Vliegenthart, 'Divergent Framing: The Public Debate on Migration in the Dutch Parliament and Media, 1995–2004' *West European Politics* Vol. 30 Nr. 3 (2007), pp. 524–548.

[132] Paul Cliteur, *De filosofie van de mensenrechten*, (Nijmegen: Ars Aequi, 1997), pp. 86–89.

[133] A lot of the leading academic voices in Dutch human rights thinking had, for instance, been part of the first names putting up the NJCM, and had later on become professors, or were directly involved in the system themselves. Even the more conservative voices, who warned against excessive overreach such as Donner or Alkema, would not question the need for extensive interpretation as such.

instance, their freedom of religion, could threaten the social cohesion in European states, as 'societies without a shared corpus of values [...] would lose their very cement'.[134] In light of this perceived threat, Cliteur found precisely the secular Western state to hold the answer. Rejecting cultural relativism, he noted how 'the human rights regime of these states proved to be the best safeguard for multiculturalism'.[135]

A more radical position was prevalent in the work of fellow professor in Leiden, Afshin Ellian. Ellian, a refugee from the dictatorial regime in Iran, embraced human rights in his 2006 oration as values to be defended and praised, but particularly in light of threats coming from (radical) Islamic quarters. Ellian proposed that a new course on 'human rights' had to be introduced in Dutch primary schools in order to teach young Muslims these values. As he noted, 'the true meaning of integration of Muslims in Europe lies in the recognition of rights by Muslims. The predecessors of Islam, Christianity and Judaism have already gone through this process of recognition: the Europeanization of Muslims isn't a racial or nationalistic movement, it is a human rights movement'.[136] What took place here was an alignment between human rights (universal in nature) and the Western state (particular in nature). The 'Judeo-Christian' elements of society were presented as the status quo: the Muslims had to integrate, or indeed 'learn' human rights.

As the debate on multiculturalism went on, by accounts such as those sketched above, human rights were drawn into the image of what constituted the national 'we'. Cementing the link between human rights and identity, Bolkestein aptly observed how 'using the universal declaration as benchmark, we can rank different cultures'. The resulting outcome was that 'Islamic culture' had become 'objectively' less desirable than the Western one. Respect for human rights had turned into a key element of what made 'us' – human rights-friendly Westerners – better than 'them' – oppressive bearded men who beheaded those who disagreed.[137]

[134] Cliteur, *De filosofie van de mensenrechten* (Nijmegen: Ars Aequi, 1999), p. 76.

[135] Cliteur, *De filosofie van de Mensenrechten,* pp. 74–76.

[136] A. Ellian, *Sociale Cohesie en Islamitisch Terrorisme* (Oratie: Leiden, 2006).

[137] Cf. Bolkestein who approvingly cites Cliteur 'one side wears the pen, the other side beheads' Frits Bolkestein, *De Intellectuele Verleiding: Gevaarlijke Ideeën in de Politiek* (Amsterdam: Bert Bakker, 2011), p. 267

These usages of human rights in political and academic discourse form an example of 'the conservative embrace of progressive values'.[138] In response to the multicultural society and the political discussion on national identity, conservative voices now turned to progressive values they had previously shunned or opposed. For the Netherlands, these were mostly the rights of women and 'gays', which were being presented as defining elements of our culture, which needed to be protected in light of the threat from Islamic influences.[139] Human rights were used to a similar end, as they became part of a set of values which were presented as belonging quite naturally to one culture, and something to aspire to for the other. As such, it was a subtle different take on way human rights had been presented in the 1990s, namely, legalized claims to be protected by international institutions.

The link of human rights to 'Western culture' had a somewhat paradoxical outcome when it came to the Convention, as such a disposition helped reduce potential critique of the European Court. For throughout this period, the Court was more busy with the human rights situation in Turkey then with other Western European member states.[140] In a way, some of the most prominent European case law of the early 2000s, which allowed Turkey to enact a ban on headscarves in public education centres or to ban an Islamist political party, was even seen as *confirming* the narrative of the conservative pushback.[141] Human rights, it would seem, were on the side of liberal democracy and offered the tools to *defend* that society against – Islamic – threats. Combined with the Court-friendly disposition arising from the 'permissive consensus'[142] around European

[138] Merijn Oudenampsen, *De Conservatieve Revolte: Een Ideeëngeschiedenis van de Fortuynopstand* (Nijmegen: Vantilt, 2018).

[139] Oudenampsen, *De Conservatieve Revolte*, pp. 187–223.

[140] Bar Italy, which continues to this day to have a dire problem of execution of judgements.

[141] *Leyla Şahin* v. *Turkey [GC]*, no. 44774/98, ECHR 2005-XI; *Refah Partisi (The Welfare Party) and Others* v. *Turkey [GC]*, nos. 41340/98 and 3 others, ECHR 2003-II.

[142] A theme used in the European integration literature focused on the EU, but some key elements, such as a focus on output legitimacy and elites embracing the project, but keeping the broader public out, can be transposed into the area of European human rights as well. Critique on European integration as such became more prevalent, particular after the Treaty of Maastricht. See also Hooghe, L. and Marks, G. 'A Postfunctionalist Theory of European Integration: From Permissive Consensus to Constraining Dissensus' *British Journal of Political Science* Vol. 39 Nr. 1 (2009), pp. 1–23.

integration and human rights protection, the Court as such, was no sustained feature in the domestic debate, let alone criticized.[143]

6.3.1 BREAKING WITH TRUISM AND THE EMERGENCE OF POLITICAL PRESSURE. In order for a change in disposition to occur, first a break had to be forced in this self-evident acceptance of international human rights protection, especially relating to the European Court. Both academically and politically speaking, the fact that the Court was there to protect human rights was deemed to be a valuable asset in itself.[144] It was precisely this idea which came under attack from 2010 onwards. In Leiden, Thierry Baudet, then a PhD candidate of Paul Cliteur and sharing some of his supervisor's doubts on the proliferation of rights, launched an attack on the European court, labelling it, in a widely read opinion piece in Dutch newspaper *NRC*, a 'threat to national democracy' and an 'illegitimate monster'.[145] The reasoning behind these strong words was the idea that it was only in the national context that democratically legitimate rules could be established. The European Court, in essence, was a foreign invader in the precious national legal order. This was a principled point in part, but the later impact of the piece lies as much in the examples of the European case law in the Dutch context which Baudet put forward: both related to migration.[146]

One explanation for academic consternation the piece provoked was the fact that Baudet definitively broke with the – until then unchallenged idea – that international human rights protection *as such* was desirable. Baudet latched on to the earlier British critique and transplanted the peculiar British idea of absolute Parliamentary Sovereignty into the

143 In particular after enlargement, the complaints were distributed very asymmetrical. Nearly half the Court's judgments between its establishment in 1959 and 2011 concern four states: Turkey (2,747), Italy (2,166), Russia (1,212) and Poland (945). See Greer and Wildhaber, 'revisiting the debate about Constitutionalism', p. 655.

144 As illustrated by the handbook of van Dijk and van Hoof, explicitly praising the living instrument doctrine as it allowed for more human rights protection.

145 Thierry Baudet, 'Het Europees Hof voor de Rechten van de Mens vormt een ernstige inbreuk op de democratie', *NRC Handelsblad*, 13 November 2010.

146 Baudet explicitly referred to the cases, *Salah Sheekh* v. *the Netherlands*, no. 1948/04,11 January 2007, and *A.* v. *the Netherlands*, No. 4900/06, 20 July 2010.

Dutch context.[147] The Court, according to this reasoning, became the prime threat to domestic rule making. As it was an illusion that human rights would not require interpretation, the Court would always need to make political judgements. This, according to Baudet, had the result of putting European human rights over national prerogatives, thereby fostering 'intolerance and a constriction of cultural diversity'.[148]

As debate ensued, a position was put forward which was distinctively new to the Dutch context: an embrace of the nation state which dismissed any international influence. The piece could have remained just that: an opinion in a newspaper which kicked off a heated academic debate in legal journals, had it not been it was picked up by politicians who felt the need they 'had to do something' with this scathing critique.[149] This urge to 'do something' had to do with a new political reality. For while Baudet took an extreme position of dismissing the legitimacy of the Court altogether, not supported by any single party, his examples on migration fitted a political constellation which grew increasingly concerned by the limits set by the Court.

This new critique was brought to the fore by the influence of a permanent political party to the right side of the VVD on the political spectrum. Such was a novelty. Throughout parliamentary history, the 'right' side of the spectrum had been traditionally occupied by the VVD. With the Fortuyn revolution, this had briefly changed, but Fortuyn's party, the LPF, was not a lasting force in Dutch politics and swiftly disintegrated. The PVV, however, founded by former VVD Parliamentarian (and aide to Bolkestein), Geert Wilders, was there to stay. The party was set up in 2006, and after their clear election victory in 2010, it was clear they had come to occupy a permanent and popular position in the Dutch political landscape. This led the liberals to reflect on their own position. What set the PVV apart, apart from its general dismissal of European integration and its forceful resistance to Islam, was a strong opinion on migration.

[147] T. Baudet, 'Brits Verzet tegen Europees Hof is terecht', *NRC Handelsblad*, 14 februari 2011.

[148] A remarkable break with the secularist venue of Cliteur, the piece embraced cultural relativism, noting universal rights would always have to be adapted to national cultural peculiarities.

[149] H. Ede Botje and M. Cohen, *Mijn meningen zijn feiten, de wording van Thierry Baudet* (Amsterdam: Atlas Contact, 2020), pp. 88–93.

The VVD, fearful of losing further ground, responded to the populist challenge by embracing calls for a stricter migration policy itself.[150] This was only enhanced by the fact that after 2010, the VVD and CDA formed a minority government which was supported by the PVV. The situation granted the far-right a major influence on the discussion, particularly when it came to matters of migration, something it would continue to exercise well after the fall of the government two years later.

Yet precisely in that realm, for decades the limits on Dutch policy had been consistently set by the European Court. Never a topic of political debate, with a permanent populist voice calling for ever stronger migration policies, and attention in the public debate focused on the European Court, political parties pushing for stronger limits on migration now found a target which stood in the way of that ambition. When it comes to the Dutch case, it is therefore no coincidence the open political pushback came on the wave of an explosive rise of interim measures by the Court in the context of migration.[151]

The Netherlands encountered this instrument, for instance, in 2007, in the case of *Salah Sheekh*, a Somalian asylum seeker who could not be deported due to the unsafe situation in his country of origin.[152] The success of this legal action bred further activity. Dutch migration lawyers turned to the Court with requests for interim measures, noting how Iraq and Afghanistan, the most prominent lands of origin for asylum seekers were, in fact, not safe. And with success: the expulsion of Iraqi asylum seekers was halted *tout court* for a brief period by the European Court. For a while, no single Iraqi could be deported, before the Court reversed the systematic ban and promised to investigate individual cases.[153] This situation had created a more acute political incentive to bring forward the simmering caution of judicial overreach of the Court, which had already been brewing for a while.

[150] Sjoerdje van Heerden, Sarah L. de Lange, Wouter van der Brug and Meindert Fennema (2014) 'The Immigration and Integration Debate in the Netherlands: Discursive and Programmatic Reactions to the Rise of Anti-Immigration Parties' *Journal of Ethnic and Migration Studies* Vol. 40 Nr. 1 (2014), pp. 119–136.

[151] *Al Sadoon & Mufti* v *the U.K.*, No. 61498/08, 30 June 2009.

[152] *Salah Sheekh* v *Netherlands*, No. 1984/04, 11 January 2007.

[153] Letter ECHR to the Netherlands, 22 October 2010, available at Migratieweb *ve10001892*.

VVD politicians Dijkhoff and Blok took on these controversies with an opinion piece of their own. In the text, they expressed the reasons for their concern quite clearly: the European Court had to be 'reigned in', as precisely in its decisions in the realms of migration (they mentioned the MSS case as an example, in which the Court had found conditions in the Greek refugee camps to be so horrid that one could not be sent there) and social security, the Court reached 'too deeply' into the nationally democratic prerogative.[154] A similar concern about the sudden overreach of the Court was echoed by members of the CDA, who drafted a motion calling upon the government to intervene more often in cases to send the signal to the Court to provide a larger margin of appreciation for states to safeguard their 'national peculiarity'.[155]

This critique was swiftly translated into governmental policy itself, which found its expression in the Dutch position in a series of intergovernmental summits. When the president of the Court invited states to an intergovernmental summit in Interlaken to discuss the backlog and other challenges to the European system, the states seized on the opportunity to address a more fundamental question: had the Court gone too far in its fundamental rights protection? Additional summits in Izmir (2011), Brighton (2012), Oslo, Brussels and Copenhagen (2018) continued to reflect upon that question. In particular, the question of subsidiarity became a central tenet throughout these summits: the Court, it was believed, had overstepped its boundaries and should leave more room for the national sensitivities of Member States.[156]

The Dutch position with regard to the summit in Izmir was therefore characterized by a shift away from its previous supportive position to a more critical one.[157] Surprise was tangible in the Dutch public and academic debate when the Dutch government openly joined the critique on the Court, calling for a reaffirmation of the principle of

[154] S. Blok, K. Dijkhoff, 'leg het Europees Hof aan banden' *De Volkskrant* 7 April 2011. However, taking into account that the Court had not found the Netherlands in any violation when it came to social security for over 10 years, the main reason for concern seems to indeed have been migration.

[155] *Kamerstukken II*, 32 500 VI Nr. 29.

[156] Lize Glas, 'From Interlaken to Copenhagen', pp. 121–124.

[157] *Kamerstukken II* 32 735, Nr. 32.

subsidiarity, expressed support for increasing the role of the Committee of Ministers, and noting the need to further regulate the measure of interim measures.[158]

At first sight, there seemed to be relatively little acute reason for these measures. As the government itself acknowledged, the vast majority of cases were declared manifestly ill-founded, and in the last four years the Netherlands had been convicted in a mere ten cases.[159] Two things stand out here, aside the general call for increased subsidiarity, as they are illustrative of the more general discontent: the call for 'a more active position of the Committee of Ministers' on the one hand, and the expressive discontent with the instrument of interim measures on the other, which the Court applied to prevent irreparable harm from occurring. The former related to a desire to reinforce the more political element of the system, something which had lost out in the reforms surrounding the 11th protocol, whereas the latter formed the most tangible element of the Court's perceived intrusiveness.[160] It was the beginning of a series of summits which revolved more or less around calls for subsidiarity and attempts to get the Court to change its practice.[161]

6.3.2 THE QUEST FOR SUBSIDIARITY. Following the domestic consternation when it came to the Court's limit on expulsion, it should not come as a surprise that for the Netherlands, the topic of interim measures was placed on the agenda. The Netherlands therefore began the Izmir summit in a relatively strong position, noting the instrument of the interim measures 'should be further regulated'. The desire to cut back on the instrument was reflected in the outcome of the summit, in which an 'expectation was voiced on a significant reduction in the number of interim measures granted by the Court, and [...] the speedy

[158] For an overview see, J. H. Gerards, 'Waar gaat het debat over het Europees Hof voor de Rechten van de Mens nu eigenlijk over?' *NJB* 518 Nr. 10 (2011), pp. 608–612; T. P. Spijkerboer, 'het debat over het Europese Hof voor de Rechten van de Mens' *NJB* 242 Nr. 4. (2012), pp. 254–262.

[159] *Kamerstukken II 32 735* Nr. 32.

[160] Lize Glas, 'From Interlaken to Copenhagen', pp. 139–142.

[161] Mikael Rask Madsen, 'The Narrowing of the European Court of Human Rights? Legal Diplomacy, Situational Self-Restraint, and the New Vision for the Court' *European Convention on Human Rights Law Review* Vol. 1 Nr. 2 (2021), pp. 180–208.

resolution of those applications'.[162] This desire was later reiterated after the Brighton summit, which called upon the Committee of Ministers to assess both whether there had been a significant reduction in their numbers and whether applications in which interim measures were applied were now dealt with speedily and to propose any necessary action.

The discussions in those working groups shed light on the value which was attached to the topic, but also on how the formal discussion, when it came to actual measures concerning interim measures, proved less threatening to the system then some people had feared. For the Netherlands, two more practical elements formed the essence of the discussion, namely to make sure lawyers would not demand an interim measure (an admissibility hurdle) without the consent of their client, and second, the wish to engage with the Court in dialogue *before* an interim measure would be granted, not afterwards.[163]

Even though, for instance, the UK entered the roundtable with a stronger position proclaiming the desire that systemic bans on expulsions would be a thing of the past and that the 'Court would not again use the interim measure, as had been previously the case when it came to Iraq and Somalia', it did not take the step of proposing limits to the Court's capacity to *apply* interim measures.[164] A reason for not taking this step to institutional reform was the fact that the Court itself, in fact, actively went along with this discussion. The institution was not content with the measure: interim measures took up a considerable chunk of already scarce time, and as such, the Court and the States agreed that numbers had to be brought down. In response to the rise of procedures and subsequent critique from the states, the Court responded swiftly. It acknowledged that the use of the instrument had risen explosively, from fewer than 1,000 times in 2006 to 3,775 times in 2010, mostly due to cases relating to migration. Noting the dissatisfaction with, in particular, the

[162] See for the instance of the UK on this element the report of Alice Donald, Jane Gordon and Philip Leach 'The UK and the ECHR' in *Equality and Human Rights Research Report 83* (2012).

[163] Ministerie Buitenlandse Zaken, DJZ/IR nr. toegang. 26498, inv. nr. 03101, 'CDDH Report on Interim Measures Under Rule 39 of the Rules of Court, 2 February 2013'.

[164] Buitenlandse Zaken, 26498.7 inv. nr. 03101, 'Report on Meeting Follow Up Brighton, 12–14 December 2012'.

'quasi-systemic way' in which the interim measures had been applied, it reassured states that 'the Court is resolved to do everything so that such situations do not recur'.[165]

The Court's president afterwards took the remarkable step of issuing a statement recalling that the role of the Court was not to be a court of appeal and warned against overloading the Court with requests for interim measures. In doing so, the Court took seriously the concerns of the states and *changed* its demeanour. Exemplary of how the Court in fact, took on board the feedback from the states in its practice, the number of interim measures went down significantly in the post-Brighton period, something for which 'the Court should be lauded', also the CDDH noted. The final report was again watered down and asked the Court primarily to specify reasons for which it would apply the interim measure – something which has not been taken up quite prominently in its case law, however.[166]

What stands out here is how the impact of the Interlaken process may arguably best be measured not by its institutional impact, but by the changes it made to the practice of the Court.[167] The source of discontent lay not as much in the potential of interim measures, but rather in how these were applied. The pushback, brought forward by a concern on behalf of the states, was an example of how the political voice had taken shape in the system in a form of external, open pressure, instead of the more internal means by which discontent was expressed previously.

6.3.2.1 THE 15TH AND 16TH PROTOCOLS. While the concerns surrounding migration and interim measures could be – relatively – easily fixed by a change in practice of the Court, the broader wish for more attention to the principle of subsidiarity resulted in two

[165] Buitenlandse Zaken, 26498, inv. nr. 03101, CDDH Report on Interim Measures under Rule 39 of the Rules of Court, 2 February 2013.

[166] Something later reiterated in the Brussels declaration. See further Philip Leach, 'Urgency at the European Court of Human Rights: New Directions and Future Prospects for the Interim Measures Mechanism?' in Eva Rieter and Karin Zwaan (eds.), *Urgency and Human Rights: The Protective Potential and Legitimacy of Interim Measures* (The Hague: T. M. C. Asser Press, 2021), pp. 198–220.

[167] Madsen, 'The Narrowing of the European Court of Human Rights?,' pp. 180–208.

protocols: the 15th, containing some new limits on admissibility, and the 16th, introducing the potential for national courts to ask the European Court for advice. This was an echo of the idea already propagated in the fifties by the Dutch judge in the European Court, van Asbeck.[168] The 16th protocol appealed to a need for increasing discussion between the domestic legal contexts and the European system: it was envisioned to not merely serve as a testimony to the subsidiary character of the Court, but also to move its character in a more 'constitutional' direction.[169]

The 15th protocol in particular contained a novelty, namely an addition to the preamble including the margin of appreciation doctrine. This came out of the Brighton summit, which in its final declaration called upon the Committee of Ministers to make sure 'a reference to the principle of subsidiarity and the doctrine of the margin of appreciation as developed in the Court's case law should be included in the Preamble to the Convention'.[170]

Such was an already watered down version of a debate in Brighton, where initially the conversation had revolved around amending the substantive articles of the Convention itself.[171] By expressively including the Margin of Appreciation in the preamble, however, the states still brought forward the value they attached to the principle of subsidiarity, which had been the topic of quite some consternation. Key in the debates was the position of the Court in defining that margin of appreciation, with states questioning whether there should be a reference to the Court with regard to the principle. In other words, was it something the states possessed or something dependent on the leniency of the Court?

On this point, the domestic debate became influential in the Dutch position, as this time the Netherlands came out in support of the Court. After the critical position the government had taken, the Dutch Senate

168 See Chapter 3.

169 ECHR, 'Opinion of the Court on Draft Protocol No. 16 to the Convention Extending its Competence to Give Advisory Opinions on the Interpretation of the Convention', 6 May 2013.

170 Brighton Declaration, article 12 B.

171 Buitenlandse Zaken, 3200.380, inv. nr. 15957 piece no. 1201024015, 'Letter from Dean Spielman to Steering Committee, 23 November 2012'.

had stepped in to defend the Court from overtly zealous positions.[172] In the remarkably fierce debate, the senators had pushed back strongly against the governmental position and forced a return to the 'classic' position of support of the Court.[173]

In light of that debate, the Dutch position in the debates had subsequently softened as well. In the discussion surrounding the Margin of Appreciation, the choice was therefore made to push for the inclusion of the Court as the institution defining those margins, to show broader support for the system.[174] In doing so, the Netherlands was brought into a diametrically opposed position to that of the UK, which was adamantly opposed to any mention of the Court.[175] The British took issue with the original reading of the text, which, when it came to the Margin of Appreciation read: 'which the Court defines'. This formulation placed control over the provision squarely in the hands of the Court, although British resistance meant the phrase was put between brackets. The Committee ultimately seemed to settle on a more neutral phrasing, 'subject to the supervisory jurisdiction of the European Court…'

Such a wording attracted the concern of the Court itself. Dean Spielman, president of the Court, wrote to the Steering Committee that the Margin of Appreciation doctrine was a complex one and 'the Court had difficulty in seeing the need for, or the wisdom of, attempting to legislate for it in the Convention, any more than for the many other tools of interpretation which have been developed by the Court in carrying out the judicial role entrusted to it'.[176] In contrast, the Court proposed to add the phrase 'as developed in the Court's case law', which would again place the Court's jurisprudence centrally.

172 E. Myjer, *Het leest als een boek: Over opmerkelijke daden van een rechter, mensenrechten die vooral voor andere landen zouden zijn bedoeld, perifere zaken en wolfisering* (Nijmegen: Wolf Legal Publishing, 2011).

173 *Kamerstukken I* 2011/2012, nr. 22, item 3, pp. 3–50. For a similar mechanism, see Madsen, 'Two-level Politics and the Backlash against International Courts' pp. 728–738.

174 Buitenlandse Zaken, 3200.380, inv. nr. 15957, 'Report Meeting on Reform Process Court, 8 November 2012'.

175 Ministerie Buitenlandse Zaken, DJZ, Nr. Access 3200.180, inv. nr. 10578 (map 03096) 'Internal report DJZ, 24 October 2012'.

176 Buitenlandse Zaken, 3200.380, inv. nr. 15957 piece no. 1201024015, 'Letter from Dean Spielman to Steering Committee, 23 November 2012'.

It was therefore – once again – about the struggle between the two competing visions on the Convention: that of the independent Court and its jurisprudence as progressively moving forward, or that of 'democratic rights of states' as prime guardians of their own interpretation of human rights. What ultimately won out was a compromise: one which neither fully embraced the Court's position, nor the British rejection of any mention of the Court whatsoever. It turned into a more convoluted phrasing, notably: 'Affirming that the High Contracting Parties, in accordance with the principle of subsidiarity, have the primary responsibility to secure the rights and freedoms defined in this Convention and the Protocols thereto, and that in doing so they enjoy a margin of appreciation, subject to the supervisory jurisdiction of the European Court of Human Rights established by this Convention'.[177]

In the end, this was largely a symbolic gesture: the legal value of inserting the principle into the preamble was, after all limited.[178] But symbols are not devoid of value, and this was a very clear sign of the political pushback of states against a direction of the Convention they did not fully agree with. Seen from a longer perspective, it was also a reaffirmation of the strongly felt need for a political voice in this trajectory. After this had been taken out of the Convention in the 1990s, the *desire* for a certain influence had never truly disappeared. Therefore, what the series of summits above all stand for is how this urge, caused by a different set of motivations, not just erupted, but in fact, re-emerged.

Finally, what these deliberations show is how when the pushback ultimately reached the formal venues, the occasional inflammatory rhetoric was swiftly tuned down when the need arose to engage with more technical elements. At that stage, it turned out the desired increase of subsidiary was either already part of the system or could be achieved with existing instruments, resulting in – relatively – limited institutional reforms.[179] Moreover, the political pressure was itself dependent on the domestic context. In the Dutch case, the pushback was carried forward

[177] 15th protocol ECHR.

[178] Janneke Gerards, 'De Brighton-Verklaring en de Toekomstbestendigheid van het EHRM' *NTM* Vol. 38 Nr. 5 (2013), pp. 609–625, 616.

[179] This substantiates the argument of Madsen, 'Two-level Politics', p. 728.

by the political relevance of the PVV. When that party subsequently disappeared from the position of power it had occupied and the public debate subsided somewhat, it also entailed the end of a rather unique period in which the Convention was topic of conversation. As one Dutch civil servant in Strasbourg concluded after these tempestuous years, things had reverted once again to the more welcoming state of 'peace and quiet' which had characterized Dutch engagement with the Convention for years.[180]

6.3.3 PERSISTENT STRUGGLES: GETTING THE KINGDOM IN LINE. With the plea for more subsidiarity, which has sounded increasingly since 2010, the domestic level was placed centre stage. Yet precisely that also caused problems for the Netherlands. After all, the Convention served as a benchmark and source of legal renewal throughout the *entire* Kingdom. Human rights therefore served as an integrational tool, bringing the legal regimes of the Caribbean and European parts of the Kingdom closer in line, as had happened in the realms of penal and administrative law. Yet integrational effects increasingly produced internal tension in the Kingdom as well. When it comes to human rights in the Kingdom, therefore, calls for subsidiarity led to an internal discussion on who was in fact able and willing to protect human rights in that sometimes difficult internal constellation.

These tensions are the result of the shared responsibility which exists in the Kingdom when it comes to fundamental rights protection. As the 'Statuut' of the Kingdom puts forward, each country in the Kingdom has a duty of care when it comes to the effectuation of fundamental rights standards. However, safeguarding fundamental rights is also a matter of the Kingdom as a whole.[181] This means that fundamental rights standards are a continuous topic of conversation between the different parts of the Kingdom. Yet as such, it is also a contentious topic. The government of the Netherlands is not keen on intervening in the Caribbean

[180] Buitenlandse Zaken, 3200.380 inv. nr. 15957 (04752-map) Map 1201024015 'Prot 15, from Perm. Rep. to The Hague, 18 September 2013'.

[181] This flows from article Art. 43 statuut: Art. 2 'Het waarborgen van deze rechten, vrijheden, rechtszekerheid en deugdelijkheid van bestuur is aangelegenheid van het Koninkrijk'.

parts of the Kingdom, whereas the limited resources or political set-up occasionally render the governments in the Caribbean quite simply unable, or sometimes unwilling, to comply with human right standards. Intervention from the Kingdom, moreover, is only possible when there are 'structural' issues which need to be addressed.[182]

In light of that situation, the courts at both local and European levels have proven key players in pressing for change. A recent example of how local courts can act if the domestic governments remain inactive can be seen when the local court declared in 2021 that Curaçao should introduce legislation on the politically sensitive topic of legalizing gay marriage. Even though a fundamental right in the European part of the Kingdom, Curaçao had long held off the possibility and crucially, also failed to provide viable alternatives. After the political initiative had failed, the Court took it upon itself to force the issue, even though the political follow up remains open.[183]

In doing so, court cases have also served as reminders that situations in the Caribbean parts of the Kingdom are not just isolated incidents but can have a direct impact on human rights protection in the European part of the Netherlands as well. In that regard, the European Court has played an active part in reminding the Kingdom of its shared responsibility. For when it comes to fundamental rights protection in the Kingdom, the major topic of shared concern and conversation relates to detention conditions in the Caribbean.

These have been below-par for a long period of time, most specifically relating to the 'Koraal Specht' prison on Curaçao.[184] Built in the late sixties to host a maximum of 300 detainees, it was swiftly overcrowded with more than 550 people in 1993, with dire consequences for hygiene and social safety. With no flowing water in the cells, cockroaches and rats lived among the inmates. Criminal gangs ruled much of its interior,

[182] Gregory Bakhuys, *Autonomie, toezicht en interventie in de Caribische Landen van het Koninkrijk* (Rotterdam, 2020), pp. 117–133.

[183] ECLI:NL:OGEAC:2021:160 – Gerecht in eerste aanleg van Curaçao, 13-09-2021. For background, see D. J. Misiedjan and H. Palm, 'Papaja's met peren vergelijken: Hoe de Nederlandse wetgever onderscheid maakt tussen Caribisch en Europees Nederland aan de hand van artikel 1 lid 2 statuut' *Caribisch Juristenblad* Vol.2 Nr. 1 (2012), pp. 19–29.

[184] Nowadays known as 'Sentro di Detenshon i Korekshon Korsou'.

and disciplinary measures, such as naked confinement to isolation cells, in total darkness, on a diet of water and bread, were commonplace. It gained the nickname of 'the hell of the Kingdom' for good reason.[185]

As early as 1993, a local judge on Curaçao ruled the practice of solitary confinement of two weeks or less in a dark cell without running water to constitute a violation of Article 3 of the Convention, as it amounted to inhumane treatment.[186] In 1996, the CPT (the Committee for the Prevention of Torture), an agency of the Council of Europe, would provide a scathing report on the prison, noting how 'the Koraal Specht Prison displayed a pernicious combination of overcrowding, a regime which offered very few activities and a poor level of cleanliness and hygiene'. These three problems were compounded by the generally run down state of the establishment. To subject prisoners to such conditions of detention amounted, in the CPT's opinion, to inhuman and degrading treatment.[187] Yet in the decade that followed, little improvement could be discerned. Collective punishments and corporal punishments remained part of the disciplinary regime.[188] Subsequent lawsuits were brought and won, for instance in 1997, when local courts banned the use of collective and corporal punishments.[189]

Yet the first engagement of the European Court with these issues did not emerge until much later, in 2005. This quite late engagement points to an important element of the Strasbourg system in the Caribbean parts of the Kingdom: it is far removed from daily legal life. The Court is quite literally far away, and with its lengthy and costly proceedings, it is not a self-evident option for the domestic Bar. Such a

[185] A picture of the sensitive politics surrounding the matter emerges from the report of two journalists, Louis Cornelisse and Hans Goslinga, 'Het geduld van De Vries is op/ Koraal Specht' *Trouw* 28 January 1999.

[186] Arjen van Rijn, 'De bescherming van de grondrechten in de Nederlandse Antillen' *NJCM Bulletin*, p. 148.

[187] Council of Europe, *Report to the authorities of the Kingdom of the Netherlands on the visit to the Netherlands Antilles carried out by the CPT from 26 to 30 June 1994* (Strasbourg, 18 January 1996), CPT/Inf (96) 1.

[188] 'Daar zit Nederland natuurlijk achter: Antilliaanse minister boos over uitlekken EU-rapport Koraal Specht' *Trouw* 12 December 1998.

[189] Floris van Laanen, 'Levenslange gevangenisstraf en artikel 3 EVRM' *NJCM-Bulletin* Vol. 31 Nr. 7 (2006), pp. 970–983.

disposition has historically grown. Ever since the first moments of being involved in the European human rights system, the Antillean countries have expressed little desire to be fully bound by the Strasbourg system, and have only been persuaded to do so in order to prevent Dutch interference.[190]

In this light, it has often been noted how remarkably few complaints have arrived in Strasbourg from Curaçao, Aruba and Sint Maarten.[191] To this day, hesitation in taking a case to Strasbourg is pervasive in those states, also in for instance present-day challenges surrounding the hosting conditions of Venezuelan refugees.[192] With the local government declining to put protection into law, but rather keeping asylum a matter of the Minister himself, uncertainty remains high for those appealing on the Convention.[193] As one local lawyer put it, the time-consuming element of the procedure plays an important factor here: in light of the uncertain outcome and costly aspect thereof, it is not a self-evident step to be made.[194]

The European Court's engagement with the topic of detention conditions in the Kingdom kicked off when, in the case of *Mathew* v. *Netherlands,* the Court found a violation of Article 3.[195] Mr Mathew, a violent criminal, had severe disciplinary issues and was detained in a harsh system. He was kept for at least seven months in a cell on Aruba in which there was a large opening in the roof 'through which the rain penetrated'.[196]

The Court, aside from noting how these conditions amounted to inhumane treatment, noted further how this was *not* an issue to be resolved only by Aruba. As the Court pointed out, the fact that even

190 See Chapters 3 and 4.

191 Van Rijn, *Handboek Caribisch Staatsrecht,* p. 314.

192 M. den Heijer, 'Haal ons uit ons isolement: Over Venezolaanse vluchtelingen op Curaçao' *NJB* Nr. 17 (2019), pp. 1246–1251.

193 Ibid.

194 See for further information the damning report of Amnesty International, *Nog Steeds Niet Veilig* (2021).

195 These cases were also more *prone* to end up in Strasbourg, as the clients themselves were also in jail for a long period of time, having in that sense little to 'lose' from a lengthy procedure.

196 *Mathew* v. *the Netherlands,* no. 24919/03, § 210, ECHR 2005-IX.

though accommodation suitable for Mr Mathew's needs did not exist in Aruba at the time, there also had been no attempt of transportation of Mathew to a place where he could have received the care he needed:

> [...], it is not Aruba but the Kingdom of the Netherlands which is the Party responsible under the Convention for ensuring compliance with its standards. Judicial orders given in one of the three countries of the Kingdom – the Realm in Europe, the Netherlands Antilles and Aruba – can be executed throughout the Kingdom. The Court is concerned to find that, despite a request to that effect from the applicant, no attempt appears to have been made to find a place of detention appropriate to the applicant in one of the other two countries of the Kingdom.[197]

As such, the Court reminded the Netherlands of the shared responsibility of *all* countries within the Kingdom to safeguard fundamental rights. It set the stage for a comparable follow up case in which, again, the necessary conditions for psychiatric treatment (TBS) were not available in Aruba, where the case originated. On the island, there existed no facilities or expertise which could offer such specialized care. Yet the prison did hold detainees who should ideally receive psychiatric treatment. In the absence of those facilities and in face of the Dutch rejection to take on those – costly – treatments, the detainees with special psychiatric or psychological needs were left in a highly unsatisfactory position.

This formed part of the complaint of *Murray v Netherlands*, which dealt with a convicted murderer who, despite his psychiatric needs, never received aid, simply because there were no facilities available. He served a life sentence, and any plea for release was, precisely because of the absence of treatment and hence lack of improvement of his condition, hopeless to begin with. As a result, Mr Murray served a life sentence without any hope of ever getting out of jail. The Murray case was picked up and subsequently brought to Strasbourg by two Dutch lawyers, after which the Court found a violation of Article 3.[198] In complete absence

[197] Ibid, § 204.

[198] One being a former professor of penal law, who was in fact well versed in the potential the ECHR could offer in this situation. It is a reflection also of the very small scale of the islands and the available legal expertise.

of any real chance of release, the life sentence had been a case of inhumane treatment.[199]

The case had two direct implications: for Aruba, it became clear a form of TBS treatment had to be installed, a requirement which obviously entailed a financial commitment as well. But, and this was a key reminder of the integrational dynamics of human rights in the Kingdom, it also forced the Netherlands to change its policy on life sentences. The Dutch life sentences were famously harsh, as life sentences were literally for life, with possibilities for release limited and dependent on the personal discretion of the Minister. Here, the situation in Aruba *also* entailed the Netherlands altering its policy in order to fit the minimum requirements which applied to the entire Kingdom. Hence, the question also came up whether, should a detainee be transferred to the Netherlands, the Netherlands *themselves* would be in conformity with the standard of the Court? It seemed unlikely. It was therefore no surprise how after *Murray*, a change in policy has been set in motion to alter the Dutch practice in order to provide the prisoner with a legitimate sense of hope of release.[200]

Politically, however, the Dutch government immediately noted how the case 'changed nothing' in the internal set-up of the Kingdom. The acting Minister told Parliament explicitly that no detainees serving life sentences would be transferred to the Netherlands.[201] Moreover, the Minister made very clear that ideally *no* detainees requiring TBS treatment should be transferred into the Netherlands. The responsibility for dealing with – even costly – Strasbourg requirements was put squarely back in the Court of Aruba and Curaçao.

This line of cases is illustrative of the sometimes tricky relation between the different countries in the Kingdom flowing from a shared commitment to human rights. The European Court has served in that regard as an active reminder of the responsibility of the *entire* Kingdom

[199] *Murray* v. *the Netherlands* [GC], no. 10511/10, 26 April 2016.

[200] Pauline Jacobs, 'Licht aan het eind van de tunnel? De door de staatssecretaris voorgestelde en reeds doorgevoerde wijzigingen in de tenuitvoerlegging van de levenslange gevangenisstraf beschouwd in het licht van artikel 3 EVRM' *NJCM Bulletin* Vol. 42 Nr. 2 (2017), pp. 188–204.

[201] Bakhuys, *Autonomie, toezicht en interventie in de Caribische Landen van het Koninkrijk*, p. 118.

for the effectuation thereof. But its pleas remain relatively meaningless if the internal discussion does not follow up in effectuating judgements, and therein the real problem lies, as the different countries of the Kingdom exhibit different attitudes. In light of an – understandable – Dutch unwillingness to engage in the internal affairs of the other states, and Caribbean financial limitations or political unwillingness, individual cases can potentially be left in deeply unsatisfactory conditions. Ultimately, this is a political discussion to be had in the Kingdom: the courts, domestic and European, serve as continuous reminders of the constitutional ties, where it is often forgotten how situations in each country can affect *all* the other ones.

Conclusion

SPEAKING IN FRANKFURT IN 1980, Gerard Wiarda, the newly elected president of the Court, looked back in wonder. Theoretically, the Convention had occupied a unique position in Europe ever since it was signed in 1950, with its promise to safeguard human rights for all Europeans and to serve as a bulwark against totalitarianism. Yet people appeared to be ignorant of its existence, and the Convention was deemed hardly relevant to legal practice. In 1980, however, Wiarda saw a change in the situation, and perceived a recent trend, namely that the Convention had become 'firmly embedded in the minds of our fellow citizens'.[1] Even though that particular fact was an important step itself, the future trajectory of the Convention remained wide open. 'Historians will have to judge someday whether, and the extent to which, the Strasbourg system has [...] succeeded in contributing to the creation of a European system of fundamental rights'.[2]

Since then, over forty years have passed. If historians nowadays had to judge whether a European system of fundamental rights had been created, the answer would likely be a resounding 'yes'. But they would differ in their analysis as to how and why exactly that result emerged. For was it truly the Strasbourg system itself which created this system?

In this book, I have argued for a different narrative, and presented a story in which the character of the Convention was always open to contestation. Three elements are of particular importance therein: the role of empire and decolonization, the need to focus on how a multitude of

[1] Quoted in Bates, *The Evolution of the European Convention*, p. 380.
[2] Ibid.

actors altered the meaning of the Convention over time and finally, the need to see the story of the Convention as one of constant interaction between the national and European sphere. All in all, instead of a top-down development by the Court, the trajectory of the Convention was a contingent and open history.

As to the first point, the reception of the Convention in the Netherlands was never just a question solely for the metropole, but always one which affected the Kingdom as a whole. This resulted in tensions which have remained present from its drafting through the course of its history until now. For the drafting of the Convention was not exactly the result of a pervasive liberal thinking which sought to protect the individual, but also of conservative views relating to European integration. Human rights were deemed 'serious business' which entailed that those deemed 'emotional', such as women and inhabitants of the 'overseas territories', were placed in a disadvantaged position from the beginning. As notions of 'Europeanness' were being defined in the set up of the Convention, it mattered who was defined as Europeans worthy of protection. Clearly, this did not refer to all subjects of the Kingdom.

The link between human rights and Empire entailed several consequences. First of all, the scope of the Convention's application was limited in order to exclude colonial subjects, something which the Dutch government defended with reference to the perceived backwardness and 'emotional nature' of the people living there. But this was never a given: alternatives were tried and tested, and the final choice for a closed system was not self-evident. Moreover, distrust went both ways. The European character of the Convention and its connection to the Council of Europe, wherein the 'plan Strasbourg' envisioned an economic connection to maintain a highly unequal relation, were for Henri Pos of Suriname, for instance, reasons to be wary of participating. Only after reassurances that the impact would be minimal was Suriname convinced to drop its resistance.

Now the hesitance of European states to open up human rights protection beyond Europe is relatively well known. Yet one aspect peculiar to the Dutch context was how the right of individual petition was quite swiftly extended to the Netherlands' 'overseas territories', namely in 1964 to Suriname and in 1974 to the Antilles and Aruba. This allowed complaints from beyond the metropole to reach the Strasbourg system. Motivations for accepting this right differed. Where for Suriname, this was a sign of the territory's own capacity to make decisions and bind itself to international institutions, the Antilles and Aruba accepted the right of individual petition precisely to *maintain* the close connection with the Kingdom by tying themselves to a shared institution.

Despite the symbolic importance which this step entailed, as it moved the Convention from a 'European' treaty more in the direction of a human rights document, the practical value in Suriname and the Caribbean remained rather limited. Very few complaints ever reached Strasbourg from the overseas territories, as expertise, time, and money were not always available, and these limits have continued to hamper the flow of cases from Curaçao, Sint Maarten, and Aruba. Even though pertinent injustices persist, Strasbourg is rarely called upon. The venue may seem to be equal on paper, but in reality, the potential for plaintiffs in the Netherlands to bring a complaint to Strasbourg is very different from that in the Caribbean parts of the Kingdom.

As a result of these different historical trajectories, human rights continue to form a consistent source of contention within the Kingdom, as the demands placed upon the Kingdom serve as a constant reminder of a shared responsibility for the protection of the rights of each individual therein. However, this requires solutions which are politically, constitutionally, and historically sensitive.

Moreover, the legacy of imperialism did not suddenly disappear from the European system as a whole, but would continue to cast its shadow over decisions decades later. The initial choice of a closed system of human rights protection 'for Europeans only' was, after all, a choice which could well have been different. Initiatives to open up the system did emerge, yet were disregarded out of fear of 'incompetent judges' from the newly independent states.

Also, the colonial context entailed the Convention was sometimes deliberately kept at bay. Migration is a key element in this regard: the Dutch government went to lengths to keep the fourth protocol on free movement out of the Kingdom. Faced with potential consequences on their own internal set up, support for the European human rights system lost out to the desire to limit migration into the metropole.

As to the second main element, it is remarkable how fluid the meaning of the Convention was as it went through different phases. To be clear, the boundaries between those phases were not clear cut. Instead, old and new interpretations coexisted and continue to collide. Still, when applied to the Convention, it becomes clear why the initial conservatism which characterized engagement with the Convention gave way to a more dynamic interpretation of what the Convention entailed. That particular interpretation became solidified as the mainstream, which was maintained without much disagreement from roughly the 1980s until the present-day, when some basic tenets of that image came under pressure.

For the idea that the Convention simply 'did not matter' in the early years is misleading. Instead, it entered the Dutch legal order following a heated debate on its legal value, which only seemed to end as the Hoge Raad smothered alternative, further-reaching interpretations. The limited legal value was combined with the fact that the government did not accept the right of individual petition out of fears of an overly intrusive European Court. Backed by early key academic interpreters such as Leo Beaufort and Willem Riphagen, who had been involved in the drafting process and supported a restrictive reading of the Convention, these circumstances led to the idea the Convention would be of little added value, with appeals on the Convention in the national courts being almost always unsuccessful.

Yet this was always a contested image. International lawyers such as Frederik van Asbeck and Bert Röling wrote tirelessly in support of a more dynamic reading, and were supported in this view by civil servants from the Ministry of Foreign Affairs and non-governmental activists propagating a strong stance in favour of European integration, yet to little direct avail.

This conservative phase carried on until the late 1960s. In order to explain the change which occurred afterwards, the interstate complaint against Greece of 1967 proved a key moment, as it heralded the beginning of a new engagement with the Convention. The case not only tied the government to upholding a specific interpretation of the Convention as being about the right of the individual, it also galvanized grassroots support for human rights, which became established as a shared language to address the suffering of others. Its legal implications were not immediately visible: in domestic courts, those initiatives were less successful.

But from this grassroots activism grew a durable legacy. One of the main results thereof was how distinct 'human rights scholars' emerged from the intersection with activism. This group would take over the main bulk of activity on the Convention from those working more on European integration. As the latter focused their attention on the European Communities, the Convention and the Council of Europe became the realm of human rights activism. Most prominently, it was from this group of early human rights scholars that the idea of the Convention as something which protected individual rights *also* in the domestic context became established as 'the' interpretation of the Convention. Outlets such as the NJCM Bulletin and the first Dutch handbook on the Convention helped enshrine this message. Combined with the firm stance of the government in favour of a more dynamic reading, the 1970s entailed a 'perfect storm of support' for the Convention as a veritable tool for human rights protection. Crucially, this interpretative revolution predated the legal revolution on both the European and the national levels. The Convention was already a 'living instrument' to key national interpreters well before the European Court ruled it to be so.

Still, the 'mainstreaming' of the Convention in law and society was something which only truly took place in the 1980s. This was also the time when the Convention acquired its 'self-evident' status within Dutch legal order, and following a period of intense debate, the domestic courts settled on an embrace of the Strasbourg minimum as the Dutch standard. But this mainstreaming went hand in hand with the return of caution into governmental policy with regard to the European system.

Concerned with the new direction and zeal of the Court, a variety of more ambitious reforms were shut down by the states. Critique was more prevalent than support at the end of the 1980s: contentious judgements had important member states expressing their discontent with Strasbourg, and it would take the end of the Cold War and the immediate flow of accessions from the former Soviet bloc to revitalize the system. However, although the eleventh protocol fundamentally altered the system in favour of the Strasbourg institutions vis-à-vis governmental influence in the procedure, the 'legalization' that this entailed should also not be overestimated. Political discussions and discontent never left the system, but rather emerged out in the open.

In turn, the self-evident character of the Convention in the Dutch legal order, which had been pervasive for roughly twenty years, has come under pressure in recent years. Human rights were caught up in the 'conservative revolt' calling for a reaffirmation of the national. European human rights were presented by a group of politicians as a threat to national democracy, in particular when it came to the demands they placed on politically sensitive topics – migration being the crucial factor above all.

This brings us to the final element this book has challenged: the top-down narrative of how it was the European Court itself which brought forward change throughout Europe. Rather, as the Convention was taken up by a variety of actors in the national context, the results of their reception also fed back into the European level.

First of all, the state, via its diplomats and ministerial experts, played a key role in this process. The fact that the state can restrain the European institutions has been obvious since the early days when limits on the Convention were set, up until present-day discussions and reforms of the system that have put more emphasis on the principle of subsidiarity.

But, and this point tends to occasionally be overlooked, the state also had a major role in *supporting* the system. One often forgotten but important element in the 'activation' of the Court was the campaign to get the Commission to refer more cases to the Court. The reason for this break with previous policy, which embraced the more diplomatic character of dispute settlement under the Convention, was political conflict. This was a fundamental shift in policy. Instead of a threat to national sovereignty, the Court emerged as a neutral and depoliticized solution for conflict. Another example of strong governmental support can be found in the 1990s, when the system was overhauled to institute a permanent Court in a legalized system, even though the critique in the 1980s was so pervasive that stakeholders doubted the viability of the project.

Second, individual actors take on a crucial role in this regard. 'Double hatting' is equally relevant in this interactive process as individuals move not just between different roles within the national context, but also move back and forth between the national and European level. The

Dutch judge van Asbeck, for instance, not only attempted to energize the Court in which he found himself on the European level, but actively lobbied at the domestic level in order to achieve the same. Later in the 1980s, Wiarda used his stature built over many years in the national legal context to explain the importance for the Dutch system of the European cases which he presided over as President of the Court. He thereby 'normalized' the Convention, also in areas long considered out of its reach.

Moreover, the interpretative revolution as it took place in the 1970s did not remain confined to the national legal order. Some scholars not just wrote about what the Convention should mean, but also attempted to make it a reality. Evert Alkema, for instance, was closely involved with activists who put forward some of the first cases decided against the Netherlands by the European Court. This was no accident. Alkema worked to get strategic cases to the European level, both in order to activate the system and to change the reluctance of Dutch courts to apply the Convention. A similar tactic, albeit more focused on legal advice, was employed during the 1980s in the area of migration law, where pioneering scholars were happy to help practising lawyers in using the potential of Strasbourg. Crucial here is the fact that these experts did not passively wait for cases to emerge. Instead of merely passively responding to European case law, they actively steered, advised, and directed cases towards Strasbourg, thereby fuelling not just domestic, but also European developments.

This new narrative entails several consequences for how we see, understand, and frame the place of the Convention in the present-day. The history of the Convention is distinctively not an elaborate heist, in which the Court jumped on unexpecting states with new human rights demands. Instead, governments have been involved every step of the way in that process. From supporting it in the mid-1970s to contesting it in the decades afterwards, they have enacted a constant influence on the shape of the Convention. As governments declined alternatives or sought to reign in the Court, the history of the Convention is one of continuous interaction between the Court and the states. The search for a balance between individual rights protection and the prerogatives of states, which the drafters found so precious, has never left the system, regardless of the far-reaching institutional reforms from the 1990s. To persist in the narrative of how the Court made the Convention against the wishes of the states into something they never desired is hence not fully convincing.

This finding goes both ways, though. Aiming for a purely legalized European system free from political pressure would be equally unconvincing. After all, if governments speak critically of the Convention this in itself is no cause for concern, nor is it a bad thing per se. Concern from the national capitals with regard to the way European human rights develop has, after all, been a consistent element of the system ever since its inception.

Instead, we would do well to see the development of the Convention as one carried forward by a great multitude of actors, in continuous co-creation. Its meaning is not solely dependent on what a single Court makes of it. It also depends on academics, commentators and individual plaintiffs perceiving injustices. The consequence of this is how the history of the Convention was, and remains, distinctively open. From the content of the Convention to the way the institutions function, many aspects could very well have been otherwise. Perhaps seen at face value, that statement seems like a blatant truism: of course things could have been different. Still, that insight contains a valuable basic insight.

Many initiatives and readings failed, but some gained traction and were made a reality. The fact that the Court nowadays routinely rules against states is a reminder of precisely that notion. Some other initiatives came very close to realization: socio-economic rights were the topic of debate on several occasions and were very seriously considered to be taken up in the early 1980s. Other elements of the system now taken for granted, such as legalization brought forward by the eleventh protocol, had been absolutely inconceivable only years before they were a reality.

These insights from Dutch history can therefore serve a broader goal: they can break open the 'prison of the present'. European human rights are not as fixed as they would seem: they have been made to matter, or not matter, in various fields and differed over time. That is a message which can inspire or frighten. The Convention is no common destiny: states can opt in or be forced to leave the Council of Europe, as happened with Greece and Russia. New rights claims have been shown to suddenly come up and thrive as if they always belonged to the common legal heritage. In the present-day climate crisis, that thought offers hope to an increasing number of people.[3]

With the open past of the Convention therefore comes an open future, in which multiple paths lay open. In deciding which ones to pursue, this choice is not solely up to the European Court, but to a wide variety of actors. In other words, the past, but also the future of the Convention, *c'est nous.*

[3] At the time of writing, the Court has held that climate change is indeed a human rights issue covered by the Convention: *Verein KlimaSeniorinnen Schweiz and Others* v. *Switzerland [GC] app. no 53600/20* (ECtHR 9 April 2024). On climate change cases and the Convention, see Helen Keller and Corina Heri, 'The Future Is Now: Climate Cases before the ECtHR', *Nordic Journal of Human Rights* (2022), pp. 1–23.

Bibliography

ARCHIVAL COLLECTIONS

INTERNATIONAL INSTITUTE SOCIAL HISTORY

Collectie Comité Vrij Griekenland, ARCH00314
Archief Coornhert Liga, ARCH03001
Archief Vereniging voor Dienstplichtige Militairen, ARCH01547
Archief Willem van Bellekom, ARCH03190
Archief Peter Baehr, ARCH03439
Archief Amnesty International Nederland, ARCH01331
Archief Liga voor de Rechten van de Mens, ARCH03094

HISTORISCH DOCUMENTATIECENTRUM VOOR HET NEDERLANDS PROTESTANTISME (1800-HEDEN), VU

W.F. De Gaay Fortman, Collectienummer 338

NATIONAL ARCHIVES, THE HAGUE

Ministerraad, nummer toegang 2.02.05.02
Tweede Kamer der Staten-Generaal, nummer toegang 2.02.28
Ministeries voor Algemeene Oorlogvoering van het Koninkrijk (AOK) en van Algemene Zaken (AZ): Kabinet van de Minister-President (KMP), nummer toegang 2.03.01
Ministerie van Binnenlandse Zaken: Bureau Juridisch Adviseur, nummer toegang 2.04.63
Ministerie van Buitenlandse Zaken: Code-archief 1945-1954, nummer toegang 2.05.117
Ministerie van Buitenlandse Zaken: Code-archief 1955-1964, nummer toegang 2.05.118
Ministerie van Buitenlandse Zaken: Code-archief 1965-1974, nummer toegang 2.05.313
Nederlandse Permanente Vertegenwoordiging bij de Verenigde Naties te New York, nummer toegang 2.05.273

Nederlandse Permanente Vertegenwoordiging bij de Raad van Europa te Straatsburg, nummer toegang 2.05.278
Ministerie van Justitie: Afdeling Wetgeving m.b.t. de Internationale Organisaties, nummer toegang 2.09.84
Ministerie van Justitie/Afdeling Wetgeving; Tractatendossiers, nummer toegang 2.09.88
Kabinet van de Vice-Minister-President en Kabinet voor Surinaamse en Nederlands-Antilliaanse Zaken, nummer toegang 2.10.41
Ministerie van Koloniën en opvolgers: Dossierarchief, nummer toegang 2.10.54
Digitaal Duplicaat: Gouverneur van Suriname, Kabinet, nummer toegang 2.10.26
Europese Beweging in Nederland en Voorgangers, nummer toegang 2.19.109
Ministerie van Cultuur, Recreatie en Maatschappelijk Werk, nummer toegang 2.27.19
Collectie 451 van Asbeck, nummer toegang 2.21.183.03
Collectie 544 B.V.A. Röling, 1915-1985, nummer toegang 2.21.273
Ministerie Buitenlandse Zaken, DJZ, nummer toegang 3200.180
Ministerie Buitenlandse zaken, DJZ/VE, nummer toegang 3200.380
Ministerie van Buitenlandse Zaken, DJZ/VE/Ara, nummer toegang. 3200.217

NJCM

Notulen bestuur
Ingekomen post 1975
Correspondentie met ICJ

BIBLIOGRAPHY

Alfaro, Ricardo Alfaro, Frederik Marie van Asbeck, and Leo Beaufort (eds.), *Varia juris Gentium: Liber Amicorum aangeboden aan Jean Pierre Francois ter gelegenheid van zijn 70ste verjaardag* (Leiden: Slijthoff, 1959).
Alkema, Evert, *Studies over Europese Grondrechten* (Deventer: Kluwer, 1978).
Alkema, Evert, 'Advocaat en mensenrechten: vuistregels en vooruitzichten' *Advocatenblad* Vol. 61 Nr. 15 (1981), pp. 298–322.
Alkema, Evert, 'Wat betekenen de Europese mensenrechten voor de Antilliaanse rechtspraktijk' *Tijdschrift voor Antilliaans Recht* Vol. 5 Nr. 1. (1984), pp. 1–12.
Alkema, Evert, 'The Effects of the European Convention on Human Rights and Other International Human Rights Instruments on the Netherlands Legal Order' in R. Lawson and M. Blois (eds.), *The Dynamics of Human Rights Protection in Europe, Essays in Honour of Henry Schermers* (Dordrecht: Nijhoff, 1994), pp. 1–15.
Alkema, Evert, *Over implementatie van internationaal recht: De internationale rechtsorde is de onze nog niet* (Leiden: Faculty of Law, Leiden University, 2005).

Alter, Karen, *Establishing the Supremacy of European Law: The Making of an International Rule of Law in Europe* (Oxford: Oxford University Press, 2001).

Alter, Karen, Mikael Rask Madsen and Laurence Helfer (eds.), *International Court Authority* (Oxford: Oxford University Press, 2018).

Alter, Karen and Mikael Rask Madsen, 'The International Adjudication of Mega Politics' *Law and Contemporary Problems* Vol. 84 Nr. 4 (2021), pp. 1–28.

Andrén, Mats and Ettore Costa, 'Transnationalism in the 1950s Europe, Ideas, Debates and Politics' *History of European Ideas* Vol. 46 Nr. 1 (2020), pp. 1–12.

Asbeck, F. M. van, J. Tinbergen, and J. H. W. Verzijl (eds.), *Bouwstof voor de oplossing van Na-Oorlogsche Vraagstukken* (Den Haag: Nijhoff, 1946).

Aukes, Nico, *Nederland en het Griekse Kolonelsregime* (Leiden: Instituut voor Internationale Studiën, 1984).

Aust, Helmut and Esra Demir-Gürsel (eds.), *The European Court of Human Rights: Current Challenges in Historical Perspective* (Cheltenham: Edward Elgar, 2021).

Baauw, Peter, 'Advocaat en mensenrechten: strafrechtspleging en straatsburg' *Advocatenblad* Vol. 61 Nr. 15 (1981), pp. 322–347.

Baehr, Peter, 'Trials and Errors: The Netherlands and Human Rights' in David P. Forsythe (ed.), *Human Rights and Comparative Foreign Policy* (New York: United Nations University, 2000).

Baehr, Peter, Monique Castermans-Holleman and Fred Grunfeld, *Human Rights in the Foreign Policy of the Netherlands* (Antwerp: Intersentia, 2002).

Bakhuys, Gregory, *Autonomie, toezicht en interventie in de Caribische Landen van het Koninkrijk* (Rotterdam: Erasmus University Rotterdam, 2020).

Balsem, Rubiah (ed.), *De Amsterdamse Rechtswinkels in beeld: 40 jaar sociale rechtshulp in beeld: 1970–2010* (Amsterdam: Nederlandse Orde van Advocaten, 2010).

Barkhuysen, Tom (ed.), *De Nederlandse Grondwet geëvalueerd: Anker of verdwijnpunt?* (Alphen aan den Rijn: Kluwer, 2009).

Bates, (ed.), *The Evolution of the European Convention on Human Rights: From its Inception to the Creation of a Permanent Court of Human Rights* (Oxford: Oxford University Press, 2010).

Baudet, Han, Nederland en de rang van Denemarken. *BMGN – Low Countries Historical Review* Vol. 90 Nr. 3 (1975), pp. 430–443.

Baudet, Floribert and Peter Malcontent, 'The Dutchman's Burden? Nederland en de internationale rechtsorde in de twintigste eeuw' in B. de Graaff, D. Hellema and B. van der Zwan (eds.), *De Nederlandse Buitenlandse Politiek in de twintigste eeuw* (Amsterdam: Boom, 2003), pp. 69–104.

Baudet, Floribert, 'The Ideological Equivalent of the Atomic Bomb'. The Netherlands, Atlanticism, and Human Rights in the Early Cold War' *Journal of Transatlantic Studies* Vol. 9 Nr. 4 (2011), pp. 269–281.

Beaufort, L. J. C. M., *Van anarchie naar Rechtsgemeenschap: Rede uitgesproken bij de aanvaarding van buitengewoon hoogleraar in het volkenrecht aan de R.K. Universiteit te Nijmegen op maandag 15 maart 1948* (Nijmegen: Dekker and Van de Vegt, 1948).

Bederman, David, 'Foreign Office International Legal History' in Matthew Craven, Malgosia Fitzmaurice and Maria Vogiatzi (eds.), *Time, History and International Law* (Leiden: Brill, 2007), pp. 43–63.

Beerens, Hans and Marc Broere, *De Bewogen Beweging: Een halve eeuw mondiale solidariteit* (Amsterdam: KIT Publishers, 2004).

Benvenisti, Eyal and Doreen Lustig, 'Monopolizing War: Codifying the Laws of War to Reassert Governmental Authority, 1856–1874' *European Journal of International Law* Vol. 31 Nr. 1 (2020), pp. 127–169.

Berg, Ester M. van den, *The Influence of Domestic NGOs on Dutch Human Rights Policy: Case Studies on South Africa, Namibia, Indonesia and East Timor* (Groningen: Intersentia, 2001).

Bonino, Pauline, *La France face á le Convention européene des droits de l'Homme (1949–1981)* (Paris: Université de Cergy-Pontoise, 2016).

Botje, Harm Ede and Mischa Cohen, *Mijn meningen zijn feiten, de wording van Thierry Baudet* (Amsterdam: Atlas Contact, 2020).

Bhuta, Nehal, *IILJ Working Paper* 2022/1. A Thousand Flowers Blooming, or the Desert of the Real? International Law and Its Many Problems of History, available at www.iilj.org/wp-content/uploads/2022/06/Bhuta-IILJ-WP-HTIL-2022.pdf.

Biesen, Phon von, 'Sociale advocatuur en mensenrechten' in Tom van Hoogenboom (ed.), *Sociale Advocatuur en de rechten van de mens: Congresverslag Maastricht* (Nijmegen: Ars Aequi Libri, 1989), pp. 1–8.

Bleich, Anet, *De Stille Diplomaat: Max van der Stoel, 1924–2011* (Amsterdam: Balans, 2018).

Boer, Margreet de and Marjan Wijers, *Vrouw en Recht: De beweging, de mensen, de issues* (Amsterdam: Amsterdam University Press, 2009).

Bolkestein, Frits, *De Intellectuele Verleiding: Gevaarlijke Ideeën in de Politiek* (Amsterdam: Bert Bakker, 2011).

Bonjour, Saskia, *Grens en gezin. Beleidsvorming inzake gezinsmigratie in Nederland, 1955–2004* (Amsterdam: Aksant, 2014).

Boogaard, Geerten and Jerfi Uzman, 'Wie zijn zij, dat zij dit mogen doen? Over de Legitimatie van de Straatsburgse Rechtspraak', in *Preadvies voor de staatsrechtdag voor jonge juristen* (2012).

Boutelier, Hans, *Het Nieuwe Westen: De identitaire strijd om de sociale verbeelding* (Amsterdam: Van Gennep, 2021).

Bouwman, Bastiaan, 'Outraged, Yet Moderate and Impartial: The Rise of Amnesty International in the Netherlands in the 1960's and 1970's' *BMGN-Low Countries Historical Review* Vol. 132 Nr. 4 (2017), pp. 53–74.

Bouwman, Bastiaan, 'From Religious Freedom to Social Justice: The Human Rights Engagement of the Ecumenical Movement from the 1940s to the 1970s' *Journal of Global History* Vol. 13 Nr. 2 (2018), pp. 252–273.

Brathagen, Kjersti, 'Competition or Complement to Universal Human Rights? The Norwegian Position on a European Convention on Human Rights,

1949–51' in Rasmus Mariager, Karl Molin and Kjersti Brathagen (eds.), *Human Rights in Europe during the Cold War* (New York: Routledge, 2014), pp. 15–26.

Brinkel, Theo, *Haagse jaren: de politieke memoires van Ruud Lubbers* (Amsterdam: Ambo Anthos, 2020).

Brown, Megan, *The Seventh Member State: Algeria, France and the European Community* (Cambridge: Harvard University Press, 2022).

Brown, Wendy, *Undoing the Demos. Neoliberalism's Stealth Revolution* (New York: Zone Books, 2015).

Brugmans, Hendrik, 'Het Personalisme Leeft Voort' *De Gids* Vol. 154 Nr.8 (1991), pp. 607–614.

Bruin, Robin de, *Elastisch Europa. De integratie van Europa en de Nederlandse politiek, 1947–1968* (Amsterdam: Wereldbibliotheek, 2014).

Buruma, Ybo, 'Wat is een goede rechter? Een mentaliteitsgeschiedenis (1900–2020)' (Inaugural lecture Nijmegen, 2016).

Çalı, Başak, et al., 'The Legitimacy of Human Rights Courts: A Grounded Interpretivist Analysis of the European Court of Human Rights' *Human Rights Quarterly* Vol. 35 Nr. 4 (2013), pp. 955–984.

Castermans-Holleman, Monique, *Het Nederlandse mensenrechtenbeleid in de Verenigde Naties* (Den Haag: TMC Asser Instituut, 1992).

Christiaens, Kim, 'Communists Are No Beasts: European Solidarity Campaigns on Behalf of Democracy and Human Rights in Greece and East-West Détente in the 1960s and Early 1970s' *Contemporary European History* Vol. 26 Nr. 4 (2017), pp. 621–646.

Daalder, Hans and Jelte Gaemers, *Premier en elder statesman; Willem Drees 1886–1988, de jaren 1948–1988* (Amsterdam: Balans, 2014).

Dam, Peter van, *Staat van Verzuiling: over een Nederlandse mythe* (Amsterdam: Wereldbibliotheek, 2011).

Davies, Bill, *Resisting the European Court of Justice: West Germany's Confrontation with European Law, 1949–1979* (Cambridge: Cambridge University Press, 2012).

Davies, Bill and Morten Rasmussen, 'Towards a New History of European Law' *Contemporary European History* Vol. 21 Nr. 3 (2012), pp. 305–318.

Dehm, Julia, 'Highlighting Inequalities in the Histories of Human Rights' *Leiden Journal of International Law* Vol. 31 Nr. 4 (2018), pp. 871–895.

Dembour, Marie-Bénédicte, *When Humans Become Migrants: Study of the European Court of Human Rights with an Inter-American Counterpoint* (Oxford: Oxford University Press, 2015).

Dezalay, Yves and Bryant G. Garth, *Dealing in Virtue: International Commercial Arbitration and the Construction of a Transnational Legal Order* (Chicago: University of Chicago Press, 1996).

Dezalay, Yves and Mikael Rask Madsen, 'The Force of Law and Lawyers: Pierre Bourdieu and the Reflexive Sociology of Law' *Annual Review of Law and Social Science* Vol. 8 (2012), pp. 433–452.

Dijk, Boyd van, *Preparing for War: The Making of the 1949 Geneva Conventions* (Oxford: Oxford University Press, 2022).

Dijk, Pieter van and Fried van Hoof, *De Europese Conventie in Theorie en Praktijk* (Nijmegen: Ars Aequi, 1979).

Dijk, Pieter van, 'Domestic Status of Human Rights Treaties and the Attitude of the Judiciary, the Dutch Case' in Mannfred Nowak, Dorothea Steurer and Hannes Tretter (eds.), *Progress in the Spirit of Human Rights: Festschrift Für Felix Ermacora* (Kehl, 1988a), pp. 631–649.

Dijk, Pieter van, 'De houding van de Hoge Raad jegens de verdragen inzake de rechten van de mens' in B. Baardman (ed.), *De plaats van de Hoge Raad in het huidige staatsbestel. De veranderingen in de rol van de Hoge Raad als rechtsvormer*, (Zwolle: W.E.J. Tjeenk Willink, 1988b), pp. 173–209.

Dijk, Pieter van, R. Hermann and Yvonne. S. Klerk, 'Gewogen en te licht bevonden: maar is de weegschaal wel geijkt?' *NJCM Bulletin* Vol. 15 Nr. 5 (1990), pp. 630–634.

Dijk, Pieter van, 'Het 'nieuwe Hof 'Tien Jaar; Tel Uw Zegeningen' *NJCM-Bulletin* Vol. 33 Nr. 7 (2008), pp. 927–929.

Dijk, Ruud van, Samuel Kruizinga, Vincent Kuitenbrouwer and Rimko van der Maar (eds.), *Shaping the International Relations of the Netherlands 1815–2000: A small Country on the Global Scene* (Oxford: Routledge, 2018).

Donert, Celia, 'Women's Rights in Cold War Europe: Disentangling Feminist Histories' *Past and Present* Vol. 218 supplement 8 (2013), pp. 180–202.

Doolan, Brian, *Lawless v Ireland: The first Case before the European Court of Human Rights: An International Miscarriage of Justice?* (Aldershot: Ashgate, 2001).

Dotan, Shai, *International Judicial Review: When Should Courts Intervene* (Cambridge: Cambridge University Press, 2020).

Dubow, Saul, 'Smuts, the United Nations and the Rhetoric of Race and Rights' *Journal of Contemporary History* Vol. 43 Nr. 1 (2008), pp. 45–74.

Drooglever, Pieter, *Een Daad van Vrije Keuze: De Papoea's van Westelijk Nieuw Guinea en de grenzen van het Zelfbeschikkingsrecht* (Amsterdam: Boom, 2005).

Drzemczewski, Andrew, 'A Major Overhaul of the ECHR Control Mechanism: Protocol 11' in Academy of Europe Law (ed.), *Collected Courses of the Academy of European Law* (The Hague: Martinus Nijhoff Publishers, 1995) Vol. VI Bk. 2, pp. 127–243.

Duivendak, Jan Willem, *Thuis, Het Drama van een Sentimentele Samenleving* (Amsterdam: Amsterdam University Press, 2017).

Duranti, Marco, *The Conservative Human Rights Revolution: European Identity, Transnational Politics, and the Origins of the European Convention* (Oxford: Oxford University Press, 2017).

Duve, Thomas, *Entanglements in Legal History: Conceptual Approaches* (Frankfurt: Max Planck Institute, 2014).

Eaton, Martin and Jeroen Schokkenbroek, 'Reforming the Human Rights Protection System established by the European Convention on Human

Rights: A new Protocol No. 14 to the Convention and other Measures to Guarantee the Long-Term Effectiveness of the Convention System' *Human Rights Law Journal* Vol. 26 Nr. 1 (2005), pp. 1–17.

Eckel, Jan, *Die Ambivalenz des Guten: Menschenrechten in der Internationale Politiek seit den 1940ern* (Göttingen: Vandenhoeck & Ruprecht, 2015).

Eckel, Jan and Samuel Moyn (eds.), *The Breakthrough: Human Rights in the 1970s* (Philadelphia: University of Pennsylvania Press, 2015).

Ellian, Afshin, *Sociale Cohesie en Islamitisch Terrorisme* (Oration, Leiden, 2006)

Elzinga, W. 'Ontwikkelingen in het Nederlandse familierecht in het licht van EVRM en BUPO' in Tom van Hoogenboom (ed.), *Sociale Advocatuur en de rechten van de mens: Congresverslag Maastricht* (Nijmegen: Ars Aequi Libri, 1989), pp. 91–101.

Emde Boas, Menno van, 'The Impact of the European Convention of Human Rights and Fundamental Freedoms on the Legal Order of the Netherlands' *Nederlands Tijdschrift voor Internationaal Recht* Vol. 13 Nr. 4 & Vol. 14 Nr. 1. (1966–1967), pp. 337–330.

Epp, Charles, *The Rights Evolution: Lawyers, Activists, and Supreme Courts in Comparative Perspective* (Chicago: University of Chicago Press, 1998).

Erades, Lambertus, 'De Proeve 1966 en de artikelen 60–67 van de Grondwet', *NJB* Nr. 26 (1966), pp. 603–610.

Erpelding, Michel, 'Juristes internationalistes, juristes mixtes, Euro-Lawyers: l'apport de l'expérience semi-coloniale à l'émergence d'un droit supranational', Clio@Themis [online journal], Vol. 22 (2022).

Etinson, Adam, (eds.), *Human Rights: Moral or Political* (Oxford: Oxford University Press, 2018).

Fernandes Mendes, Hugo, *Onafhankelijkheid en Parlementair Stelsel in Suriname: Hoofdlijnen van een nieuw en democratisch staatsbestel* (Zwolle: Tjeenk Willink, 1989).

Flogaitis, Spyridon, Tom Zwart and Julie Fraser (eds.), *The Court of Human Rights and Its Discontents: Turning Criticism into Strength* (Cheltenham: Edward Elgar, 2013).

Frazer, Arvonne S., 'Becoming Human: The Origins and Development of Women's Human Rights', *Human Rights Quarterly* Vol. 21 Nr. 4. (1999), pp. 853–906.

Galligan, Denis, *Law in Modern Society* (Oxford: Oxford University Press, 2007).

Gammeltoft-Hansen Thomas and Mikael Rask Madsen, 'Regime Entanglement in the Emergence of Interstitial Legal Fields: Denmark and the Uneasy Marriage of Human Rights and Migration Law' *Nordiques* [Online], Vol. 40 (2021), pp. 1–18.

Gerards, Janneke, 'Gelijke Behandeling en het EVRM: Artikel 14 EVRM: van krachteloze waarborg naar "norm met tanden"?' *NJCM-Bulletin* Vol. 29 Nr. 2 (2004), pp. 176–198.

Gerards, Janneke, 'Waar gaat het debat over het Europees Hof voor de Rechten van de Mens nu eigenlijk over?' *NJB* Vol. 518 Nr. 10 (2011), pp. 608–612.

Gerards, Janneke, 'De Brighton-Verklaring en de Toekomstbestendigheid van het EHRM' *NTM* Vol. 38 Nr. 5 (2013), pp. 609–625.

Gerards, Janneke and Carla Sieburgh (eds.), *De invloed van Fundamentele rechten op het materiele recht* (Deventer: Kluwer, 2013).

Gerards, Janneke and Jozeph Fleuren, *Implementatie van het EVRM en de uitspraken van het EHRM in de nationale rechtspraak: Een rechtsvergelijkend onderzoek* (Nijmegen: WODC, 2013).

Guieu, Jean-Michel and Christophe Le Dreu (eds.), *Le Congrès de l'Europe à La Haye (1948–2008)* (Brussels: Peter Lang, 2009).

Glas, Lize, 'From Interlaken to Copenhagen: What Has Become of the Proposals Aiming to Reform the Functioning of the European Court of Human Rights?' *Human Rights Law Review* Vol. 20 Nr. 1 (2020), pp. 121–151.

Grachev, Andrei, 'From the Common European Home to European Confederation: François Mitterrand and Mikhail Gorbachev in Search of the Road to a Greater Europe' in Frederic Bozo, Marie-Pierre Rey, N. Piers Ludlow and Leopoldo Nuti (eds.), *Europe and the End of the Cold War: A reappraisal* (London: Routledge, 2008), pp. 207–220.

Greer, Steven and Luzius Wildhaber, 'Revisiting the Debate About "Constitutionalising" the European Court of Human Rights' *Human Rights Law Review* Vol. 12 Nr. 4 (2012), pp. 655–687.

Groenendijk, Cees, 'mensenrechten tussen retoriek en praktijk: gebruik van het klachtrecht in Straatsburg en de bescherming van vreemdelingen' in Ludwig Heyde, Jan Leijten, Thomas Mertens en Ben P. Vermeulen (reds.), *Begrensde Vrijheid: Opstellen over mensenrechten aangebonden aan prof. Dr. D.F. Scheltens bij zijn afscheid als hoogleraar aan de Katholieke Universiteit Nijmegen* (Zwolle: Tjeenk Willink, 1989), pp. 191–203.

Groot-van Leeuwen, Leny de, 'Rechters onder vuur: Kritiek op rechters in andere en deze tijden' in *Levend Strafrecht, Strafrechtelijke vernieuwingen in een maatschappelijke context. liber amicorum Ybo Buruma* (Deventer: Wolters Kluwer, 2011), pp. 225–237.

Halliday, Simon and Patrick Schmidt (eds.), *Human Rights Brought Home: Socio-Legal Perspectives on Human Rights in the National Context* (London: Bloomsbury, 2004).

Hansen Peo and Stefan Johnson, *Eurafrica: The Untold History of European Integration and Colonialism* (London: Bloomsbury, 2014).

Hartog den Diane, *De Doorwerking van Artikel 6 EVRM in het Antilliaanse en Arubaanse Strafrecht* (Deventer: Gouda Quint, 1998).

Harmsen Robert, 'The Reform of the Convention System: Institutional Restructuring and the (Geo-) Politics of Human Rights' in Jonas Christoffersen and Mikael Rask Madsen (eds.), *The European Court of Human Rights Between Law and Politics* (Oxford: Oxford University Press, 2011), pp. 119–143.

Harris, David and John Darcy, *The European Social Charter* (New York: Transnational Publishers, 2001).

Havinga, Tetty and Leny de Groot-van Leeuwen, 'Onder de microscoop en door de verrekijker: 25 jaar rechtssociologie in Nijmegen' in Paul Minderhoud (ed.), *De Januskop van het Recht* (Nijmegen: Wolf, 2007).

Heerden, Sjoerdje van, Sarah L. de Lange, Wouter van der Brug and Meindert Fennema, 'The Immigration and Integration Debate in the Netherlands: Discursive and Programmatic Reactions to the Rise of Anti-Immigration Parties' *Journal of Ethnic and Migration Studies* Vol. 40 Nr. 1 (2014), pp. 119–136.

Heerikhuizen, Annemarie van, *Pioniers van een Verenigd Europa: Bovennationaal denken in het Nederlandse Parlement (1946–1951)* (Amsterdam, Dissertation University of Amsterdam, 1998).

Heerikhuizen, Annemarie van, 'Europe: A "Common Interest?" The Netherlands at the Congress of Europe, May 1948' in Jean-Michel Guieu and Christophe Le Dreu (eds.), *Le Congrès de l'Europe à La Haye* (2009), pp. 199–211.

Heijer, Maarten den, 'Haal ons uit ons isolement: Over Venezolaanse vluchtelingen op Curaçao' *NJB* Nr. 17 (2019), pp. 1246–1251.

Helfer, Laurence, 'Redesigning the European Court of Human Rights: Embeddedness as a Deep Structural Principle of the European Human Rights Regime' *European Journal of International Law* Vol. 19 Nr. 1 (2008), pp. 125–159.

Helfer, Laurence and Erik Voeten, 'Walking Back Human Rights in Europe?' *European Journal of International Law* Vol. 31 Nr. 3 (2020), pp. 797–827.

Hellema, Duco, *Nederland en de jaren zeventig* (Amsterdam: Boom, 2012).

Hennette-Vauchez, Stéphanie, 'Constitutional v International? When Unified Reformatory Rationales Mismatch the Plural Paths of Legitimacy of ECHR Law' in Jonas Christofferson and Mikael Rask Madsen (eds.), *The European Court between Law and Politics* (Oxford: Oxford University Press, 2011), pp. 144–163.

Hennette-Vauchez, Stéphanie, 'The ECHR and the Birth of (European) Human Rights Law as an Academic Discipline' in Antoine Vauchez and Bruno de Witte (eds.), *Lawyering Europe: European Law as a Transnational Social Field* (Oxford: Oxford University Press, 2013), pp. 117–137.

Hioureas, Christina G., 'Behind the Scenes of Protocol No. 14: Politics in Reforming the European Court of Human Rights' *Berkeley Journal of International Law* Vol. 24 Nr. 2. (2006), pp. 718–757.

Hirsch Balllin, Ernst, *'Tot welke wijzigingen in het Nederlandse Recht dienen de beginselen van behoorlijke rechtspraak, neergelegd in het Europees Verdrag tot Bescherming van de Rechten van de Mens en de Fundamentele Vrijheden, alsmede in het Internationaal Verdrag, aanleiding te geven?' Preadviezen NJV, Handelingen NJV* (Deventer: Kluwer, 1983).

Hirsch Ballin, Ernst, 'Constitutionele toetsing van wetten als bijdrage aan de rechtsontwikkeling' in Willem Konijnenbelt (ed.), *Rechter en wetgever* (Den Haag: Raad van State, 2001), pp. 47–69.

Hirschl, Ran, 'The Judicialization of Mega-Politics and the Rise of Political Courts' *Annual Review of Political Science* Vol. 11 (2008), pp. 93–118.

Hoek, Anne-Lot, *De Strijd om Bali: Imperialisme, Verzet en Onafhankelijkheid 1846–1950* (Amsterdam: De Bezige Bij, 2021).

Hollander, Jieskje, *Constitutionalizing Europe: Reactions to an Incoming Tide (1948–2005)* (Amsterdam: Europa Law Publishing, 2013).

Hommes, Wiebe, 'Het NJCM: Een schets van de geschiedenis' *NTM* Vol. 42 Nr. 4 (2017), pp. 577–583.

Hoogenboom, Fred Hoogenboom, 'Het verdrag van Rome en het Gerechtelijk Vooronderzoek' *TAR* Vol. 4 Nr. 1 (1983), pp. 9–13.

Hoogenboom, Tom van (ed.), *Sociale Advocatuur en de rechten van de mens: Congresverslag Maastricht* (Nijmegen: Ars Aequi Libri, 1989).

Hoogers, Gerard and Gohar Karapetian, 'Hoe grondrechten in het Koninkrijk zoek raakten: een beschouwing over de binding van koninkrijksorganen aan grondrechten' *Tijdschrift voor Constitutioneel Recht* Vol. 8 Nr. 1 (2017), pp. 4–36.

Hooghe, Liesbet and Gary Marks, 'A Postfunctionalist Theory of European Integration: From Permissive Consensus to Constraining Dissensus' *British Journal of Politic Science* Vol. 39 Nr. 1 (2009), pp. 1–23.

Huyghe, François Bernard and Pierre Barbes, *La Soft-Idéology* (Paris: Laffont, 1987).

Ignatieff, Michael, *The Rights Revolution* (Toronto: Anansi, 2000).

Istrefi, Kushtrim, 'Kosovo's Quest for Council of Europe Membership' *Review of Central and East European Law* Vol. 43 Nr. 3 (2018), pp. 255–273.

Jacobs, Pauline, 'Licht aan het eind van de tunnel? De door de staatssecretaris voorgestelde en reeds doorgevoerde wijzigingen in de tenuitvoerlegging van de levenslange gevangenisstraf beschouwd in het licht van artikel 3 EVRM' *NJCM Bulletin* Vol. 42 Nr. 2 (2017), pp. 188–204.

Janse, Ronald, 'The Evolution of the Political Criteria for Accession to the European Community, 1957–1973' *European Law Journal* Vol. 24 Nr. 1 (2018), pp. 57–76.

Jasanoff, Sheila, (ed.), *States of Knowledge: The Co-Production of Science and the Social Order* (London: Routledge, 2004).

Johnston-White, Rachel, 'A Moral Language for Our Time? Human Rights and Christianity in Historical Perspective', *Contemporary European History* Vol. 31 Nr.1 (2022), pp. 155–166.

Judt, Tony, *Postwar: A History of Europe since 1945* (New York: Vintage, 2006).

Judt, Tony, *Ill Fares the Land* (London: Penguin, 2010).

Kaiser, Wolfram, *Christian Democracy and the Origins of European Union* (Cambridge: Cambridge University Press, 2007).

Keck, Margaret and Kathryn Sikkink, *Activists Beyond Borders: Advocacy Networks in International Politics* (New York: Cornell University Press, 1998).

Keller, Helen and Alec Stone Sweet (eds.), *A Europe of Rights: The Impact of the ECHR on National Legal Systems* (Oxford: Oxford University Press, 2008).

Keller, Helen, Magdalena Forowicz and Lorenz Engi, *Friendly Settlement before the European Court of Human Rights: Theory and Practice* (Oxford: Oxford University Press, 2010).

Kelk, Constantijn, De historie van het Willem Pompe instituut in W. M. J. Bekkers and e.a. (eds.), *Rechten in Utrecht* (Deventer: Kluwer, 2002), pp. 45–77.

Kennedy, James, *Nieuw Babylon in Aanbouw: Nederland in de Jaren zestig* (Amsterdam: Boom, 2017).

Keys, Barbara, 'Anti-Torture Politics: Amnesty International, the Greek Junta, and the Origins of the Human Rights 'Boom' in the United States' in Akira Iriye, Petra William Goedde and William Hitchcock (eds.), *The Human Rights Revolution: An International History* (Oxford: Oxford University Press, 2012), pp. 201–214.

Klerk, Yvonne and Bart van Poelgeest, 'Ratificatie à contre coeur: de reserves van de Nederlandse regering jegens het Europees Verdrag voor de Rechten van de Mens en het individueel klachtrecht' *RM Themis* (1991), pp. 220–246.

Klerk, Yvonne, *Het ECRM Toezicht-Mechanisme; Verleden, Heden, Toekomst* (Nijmegen: Ars Aequi Libri, 1995).

Klos, Felix, *Winston Churchill, Vader van Europa* (Amsterdam: Hollands Diep, 2016).

Kuijer, Martin, 'Guaranteeing International Human Rights Standards in the Netherlands: The Parliamentary Dimension' in Murray Hunt, Hayley J. Hooper and Paul Yowell (eds.), *Parliaments and Human Rights. Redressing the Democratic Deficit* (Oxford: Oxford University Press, 2015), pp. 295–306.

Kuitenbrouwer, Maarten and Marij Leenders (eds.), *Geschiedenis van de Mensenrechten: Bouwstenen voor een interdisciplinaire benadering* (Hilversum: Verloren, 1995).

Kuitenbrouwer, Vincent, 'Beyond the Trauma of Decolonization: Dutch Cultural Diplomacy during the West New Guinea Question, 1950–1962' *The Journal of Imperial and Commonwealth History* Vol. 44 Nr. 2 (2016), pp. 306–327.

Laanen, Floris van, 'Levenslange gevangenisstraf en artikel 3 EVRM', *NJCM-Bulletin* Vol. 31 Nr. 7 (2006), pp. 970–983.

Landman, Todd, *Human Rights and Democracy* (London: Bloomsbury, 2013).

Langen, M. de, 'De betekenis van artikel 8 EVRM voor het familierecht' in *Handelingen Nederlandse Juristen Vereniging, 1990 I* (Zwolle: Tjeenk Willink, 1990), pp. 85–185.

Larson, Erik, Wibo van Rossum and Patrick Schmidt, 'The Dutch Confession: Compliance, Leadership and National Identity in the Human Rights Order' *Utrecht Law Review* Vol. 10 Nr. 1 (2014), pp. 96–112.

Lavrysen, Laurens, 'Strasbourg was Something New, It was an Adventure: A History of the Belgian Cases before the European Court of Human Rights in the 1960s, 1970s and 1980s' *TVRG* Vol. 86. Nr. 3–4 (2018), pp. 482–527.

Lawson, Rick and Egbert Myjer, (eds.), *50 jaar EVRM, vijftig jaar Europees Verdrag voor de Rechten van de Mens* (Leiden: NJCM, 2000).

Leach, Philip, 'Urgency at the European Court of Human Rights: New Directions and Future Prospects for the Interim Measures Mechanism?' in Eva Rieter and Karin Zwaan (eds.), *Urgency and Human Rights: The Protective Potential and Legitimacy of Interim Measures* (The Hague: T.M.C. Asser Press, 2021), pp. 198–220.

Leeuwen, Karin van, *Uit het spoor van Thorbecke: Grondwetsherziening en Staatsvernieuwing in Naoorlogs Nederland (1945–1983)* (Amsterdam: Boom, 2013).

Leeuwen, Karin van, 'Paving the Road to "legal revolution": The Dutch Origins of the First Preliminary References in European Law (1957–1963)' *European Law Journal* Vol. 24 Nr. 6 (2018), pp. 408–421.

Leeuwen, Karin van, *Rights for Others, Firing Back?: Decolonization and Human Rights in Dutch Constitutional History, VerfBlog,* 2022/1/27, https://verfassungsblog.de/rights-for-others-firing-back/.

Liagre Böhl, Herman de., 'Consensus en Polarisatie spanningen in de verzorgingsstaat, 1950–1990' in R. Aerts (ed.), *Land van kleine gebaren: een politieke geschiedenis van Nederland 1780–1990* (Nijmegen: Boom, 2007).

Lijphart, Arend, *The Trauma of Decolonization, The Dutch and West New Guinea* (New Haven: Yale University Press, 1966).

Lorenz Arold, Nina-Louisa, Xavier Groussot, and Gunnar Thor Petursson, *The European Human Rights Culture – A Paradox of Human Rights Protection in Europe?* (Leiden: Nijhoff, 2013).

Lorenzi, Sara, Umberto Tulli and Illaria Zamburlini (eds.), *The Human Rights Breakthrough of the 1970s: The European Community and International Relations* (London: Bloomsbury, 2022).

Lowe, Keith, *The Fear and the Freedom: How the Second World War Changed Us* (New York: Picador, 2017).

Lucassen, Leo and Jan Lucassen, 'The Strange Death of Dutch Tolerance: The Timing and Nature of the Pessimist Turn in the Dutch Migration Debate' *The Journal of Modern History* Vol. 87 Nr. 1 (2015), pp. 72–101.

Lucassen, Leo and Jan Lucassen, *5 eeuwen migratie: Een verhaal van winnaars en verliezers* (Amsterdam: Atlas Contact, 2018).

Macdonald, Ronald, Franz Matscher and Herbert Petzold (eds.), *The European System for the Protection of Human Rights* (Dordrecht: Nijhoff, 1993).

Madsen, Mikael Rask, *La Genèse de l'Europe des droits de l'homme: enjeux juridiques et stratégies d'état (France, Grande-Bretagne et pays scandinaves, 1945–1970)* (Strasbourg: Presse Universitaires de Strasbourg, 2010a).

Madsen, Mikael Rask, 'Legal Diplomacy – Law, Politics and the Genesis of Postwar European Human Rights', in S. L. Hoffmann (ed.), *Human Rights in the Twentieth Century: A Critical History* (Cambridge: Cambridge University Press, 2010b), pp. 62–81.

Madsen, Mikael Rask, 'The Protracted Institutionalization of the Strasbourg Court: From Legal Diplomacy to Integrationist Jurisprudence' in Jonas Cristoffersen and Mikael Rask Madsen (eds.), *The European Court of Human Rights between Law and Politics* (Oxford: Oxford University Press, 2011), pp. 43–61.

Madsen, Mikael Rask, 'The Legitimatization Strategies of International Justices: The Case of the European Court of Human Rights' in Michal Bobek (ed.), *Selecting Europe's Judges: A Critical Review of the Appointment Procedures to the European Courts* (Oxford: Oxford University Press, 2015), pp. 259–278.

Madsen, Mikael Rask, 'The Challenging Authority of the European Court of Human Rights: From Cold War Legal Diplomacy to the Brighton Declaration and Backlash' *Law and Contemporary Problems* Vol. 79 Nr. 1 (2016), pp. 141–178.

Madsen, Mikael Rask, 'Two-Level Politics and the Backlash against International Courts: Evidence from the Politicization of the European Court of Human Rights' *The British Journal of Politics and International Relations* Vol. 22 Nr. 4 (2020), pp. 728–738.

Madsen, Mikael Rask, 'From Boom to Backlash? The European Court of Human Rights and the Transformation of Europe' in Helmut Aust and Esra Demir Esra (eds.), *The European Court of Human Rights: Current Challenges in Historical and Comparative Perspective* (Cheltenham: Edward Elgar, 2021a), pp. 21–42.

Madsen, Mikael Rask, 'The Narrowing of the European Court of Human Rights? Legal Diplomacy, Situational Self-Restraint, and the New Vision for the Court' *European Convention on Human Rights Law Review* Vol. 1 Nr. 2 (2021b), pp. 180–208.

Majone, Giandomenico, 'The Rise of the Regulatory State in Europe' *West European Politics* Vol. 17 Nr. 3 (1994), pp. 77–101.

Majone, Giandomenico, 'From the Positive to the Regulatory State: Causes and Consequences of Changes in the Mode of Governance' *Journal of Public Policy* Vol. 17 Nr. 2. (1997), pp. 139–167.

Malcontent, Peter, *Op Kruistocht in de Derde Wereld: de Reacties van de Nederlandse regering op ernstige en stelselmatige schendingen van fundamentele mensenrechten in ontwikkelingslanden 1973–1981* (Hilversum: Verloren, 1998).

Margry, Peter Jan, *Teedere quasties: Religieuze rituelen in conflict : confrontaties tussen katholieken en protestanten rond de processiecultuur in 19e-eeuws Nederland* (Hilversum: Verloren, 2000).

Marks, Susan, 'Reservations Unhinged: The Belilos Case before the European Court of Human Rights' *The International and Comparative Law Quarterly* Vol. 39 Nr. 2 (1990), pp. 300–327.

Marks, Susan, *A False Tree of Liberty: Human Rights in Radical Thought* (Oxford: Oxford University Press, 2019).

Mourik, Martin Jan A. van, 'Ouderlijke macht buiten huwelijk' *Ars Aequi*, Vol. 35 Nr. 9 (1986), pp. 554–558.

Mazower, Mark, 'The Strange Triumph of Human Rights, 1933–1950' *The Historical Journal* Vol. 47 Nr. 2 (2004), pp. 379–398.

Mazower, Mark, *No Enchanted Palace: The End of Empire and the Ideological Origins of the United Nations* (Princeton: Princeton University Press, 2009).

Mazower, Mark, *Governing the World: The History of an Idea* (London: Penguin Press, 2012).

Meuwissen, Damiaan, *De Europese Conventie en het Nederlandse Recht* (Leiden: Sijthoff, 1968).

Meurs, Wim van, (eds.), *Europa in alle staten: Zestig jaar geschiedenis van de Europese Integratie* (Nijmegen: Vantilt, 2013).

Middelaar, Luuk van, *Politicide; De moord op de politiek in de Franse filosofie* (Groningen: Historische Uitgevrij, 2011).

Misiedjan, Daphina J. and Hanneke Palm, 'Papaja's met peren vergelijken: Hoe de Nederlandse wetgever onderscheid maakt tussen Caribisch en Europees Nederland aan de hand van artikel 1 lid 2 statuut' *Caribisch Juristenblad* Vol. 2 Nr. 1 (2012), pp. 19–29.

Mooij, Remko, 'Een niet geringe zaak: Nederland en het nieuwe mensenrechtenstelsel, 1948–1957' *Tijdschrift voor Geschiedenis* Vol. 132 Nr. 3 (2019), pp. 445–465.

Moor, Louise and Brian Simpson, 'Ghosts of Colonialism in the European Convention on Human Rights' *British Yearbook of International Law* (2005), pp. 121–193.

Moravcsik, Andrew, 'The Origins of Human Rights Regimes: Democratic Delegation in Postwar Europe' *International Organization* Vol. 54 Nr. 2 (2000) pp. 217–252.

Mouffe, Chantal, *The Democratic Paradox* (London: Verso Books, 2000).

Moyn, Samuel, *The Last Utopia: Human Rights in History* (Cambridge: Harvard University Press, 2010).

Moyn, Samuel, *Human Rights and the Uses of History* (New York: Verso Books, 2014).

Moyn, Samuel, *Christian Human Rights* (Philadelphia: University of Pennsylvania Press, 2015).

Moyn, Samuel, 'The End of Human Rights History' *Past & Present* Vol. 233 Nr. 1, (2016) pp. 307–322.

Moyn, Samuel, *Not Enough: Human Rights in an Unequal World* (Cambridge: Harvard University Press, 2018).

Müller, Jan Werner, *Contesting Democracy: Political Ideas in Twentieth Century Europe* (New Haven: Yale University Press, 2013).

Myjer, Egbert, 'overzicht rechtspraak' *NJCM Bulletin* Vol. 5 Nr. 3 (1980), pp. 148–150.

Myjer, Egbert, 'Dutch Interpretation of the European Convention: A Double System?, in Franz Matscher and Herbert Petzold (eds.), *Protecting Human Rights: The European Dimension. Studies in Honour of Gérard J. Wiarda'* (Köln: Heymanns, 1988), pp. 421–430.

Myjer, Egbert, 'over hoe het EVRM verzeild raakte in de Nederlandse strafrechtspleging en wie dat valt toe te rekenen' in Aalt Willem Heringa, Jeroen Schokkenbroek (eds.), *40 jaar EVRM* (Leiden: NJCM, 1990), pp. 271–296.

Myjer, Egbert, 'The European Dimension; More than a Non-commital Ornament/Notes on the Consequences of the ECHR for the Administration of Dutch Criminal Justice' in Evert A. Alkema, Theo L. Bellekom, Andrew Z. Drzemezewski and Jeroen G. C. Schokkenbroek (eds.), *The domestic implementation of the European Convention on Human Rights in Eastern and Western Europe: proceedings of the Seminar Held in Leiden, 24–26 October 1991* (Strasbourg: Va. Engel, 1993), pp. 195–213.

Myjer, Egbert, 'The Plain Meaning of the Word "promptly"', in P. Mahoney e.a. (eds.), *Protecting Human Rights: The European Perspective – Studies in memory of Rolv Ryssdal* (Heidelberg: Carl Heymanns Verlag, 2000a), pp. 975–992.

Myjer, Egbert, *Bij een Vijftigste Verjaardag: aantekeningen over het Europees Verdrag tot bescherming van de rechten van de mens en de fundamentele vrijheden en de Nederlandse strafrechtspleging* (Oration, Amsterdam, 2000b).

Myjer, Egbert, *Het leest als een boek: Over opmerkelijke daden van een rechter, mensenrechten die vooral voor andere landen zouden zijn bedoeld, perifere zaken en wolfisering* (Nijmegen: Wolf Legal Publishing, 2011).

Neil, Malcolm, 'The "Common European Home" and Soviet European Policy' *International Affairs* Vol. 65 Nr. 4 (1989), pp. 659–676.

Nieuwenhuis, Aernout and Laurens Dragstra, 'Van minimum, tekort en meerwaarde Een vergelijking tussen de grondwettelijke bescherming van grondrechten en de bescherming op grond van het EVRM' *Preadviezen Vereniging voor de vergelijkende studie van het Recht* Vol. 1 (2008), pp. 11–74.

Nijman, Janne, 'Marked Absences: Locating Gender and Race in International Legal History' *European Journal of International Law* Vol. 31 Nr. 3 (2020), pp. 1025–1050.

Normand, Roger and Sarah Zaidi, *Human Rights at the UN: The Political History of Universal Justice* (New York: Indiana University Press, 2008).

Oomen, Barbara, 'Het vergeten geweten. Het EHRM als goed bewaard juristengeheim' in Ashley Terlouw and Janneke Gerards (eds.), *Amici Curiae, adviezen aan het Europese hof voor de rechten van de mens* (Nijmegen: Wolf Legal Publishers, 2012), pp. 207–216.

Oomen, Barbara, *Rights for Others: The Slow Home-Coming of Human Rights in the Netherlands* (Cambridge: Cambridge University Press, 2014).

Oomen, Barbara, 'A Serious Case of Strasbourg-Bashing? An Evaluation of the Debates on the Legitimacy of the European Court of Human Rights in the Netherlands' *The International Journal of Human Rights* Vol. 20 Nr. 3 (2016), pp. 407–425.

Oomen, Barbara and Alexandra Timmer, 'Four or Fewer Freedoms: Justice Contested and Codified between 1941 and 1957' In Trudie Knijn and Dorota Lepianka (eds.), *Justice and Vulnerability in Europe: An Interdisciplinary Approach* (Cheltenham: Edward Elgar, 2020), pp. 73–89.

Oostiendie, Gert and Inge Klinkers, *Knellende Koninkrijksbanden: Het Nederlandse dekolonisatiebeleid in de Caraiben, 1940–2000 –deel 1, 1940–1954* (Amsterdam: Amsterdam University Press, 2001).

Orford, Anne, *International Law and the Politics of History* (Cambridge: Cambridge University Press, 2021).

Oudenampsen, Merijn, *De Conservatieve Revolte: Een Ideeëngeschiedenis van de Fortuynopstand* (Nijmegen: Vantilt, 2018).

Panhuys, van Haro, *Het Verdrag van Rome, de reclame en de commerciële televisie* (Uitgave Onafhankelijke Televisie Exploitatie Maatschappij, 1962).

Pas, Niek, *Aan de wieg van het nieuwe Nederland: Nederland en de Algerijnse oorlog 1954–1962* (Amsterdam: Wereldbibliotheek, 2008).

Patel, Kiran Klaus *Project Europe: A History* (Cambridge: Cambridge University Press, 2020).

Patel, Ian Sanjay, *We're Here because You Were There: Immigration and the End of Empire* (London: Verso, 2021).

Pavone, Tomasso, 'From Marx to Market: Lawyers, European Law, and the Contentious Transformation of the Port of Genoa' *Law & Society Review* Vol. 53 Nr. 3 (2019), pp. 851–888.

Pijpers, Alfred, 'Dekolonisatie, compensatiedrang en de normalisering van de Nederlandse buitenlandse politiek' in N. C. F. van Sas (eds.), *De Kracht van Nederland. Internationale positie en Buitenlands beleid* (Haarlem: Becht, 1991), pp. 204–218.

Plender, Richard, 'European Commission of Human Rights: Decision on Admissibility of Applications by East African Asians Against United Kingdom', *International Legal Materials* Vol. 10 Nr. 1 (1971), pp. 6–55.

Popelier, Patricia, Van de Heyning and Van Nuffel (eds.), *Human Rights Protection in the European Legal Order: The Interaction between the European and the National Courts* (Cambridge: Cambridge University Press, 2011).

Popelier, Patricia, Sarah Lambrecht and Koen Lemmens (eds.), *Criticism of the European Court of Human Rights – Shifting the Convention System: Counter-Dynamics at the National Level* (Antwerp: Intersentia, 2016).

Rajkovic, Nikolas, Aalberts, Tanja and Gammeltoft-Hansen, Thomas (eds.), *The Power of Legality: Practices of International Law and their Politics* (Cambridge: Cambridge University Press, 2016).

Reiding, Hilde, *The Netherlands and the Development of International Human Rights Instruments* (Antwerp: Intersentia, 2007).

Reiding, Hilde, 'The Netherlands Gradually Changing Views on International Economic and Social Rights Protection' *Human Rights Quarterly* Vol. 34 Nr. 1 (2012), pp. 113–140.

Reinisch, Jessica, 'Introduction: Agents of Internationalism' *Contemporary European History* Vol. 25 Nr. 2 (2016), pp. 195–205.

Reurs, Marcel and Martijn Stronks, *Pioniers in het vreemdelingenrecht* (Utrecht: SDU Uitgevers, 2011).

Richard, Anne-Isabelle, 'The Limits of Solidarity: Europeanism, Anti-colonialism and Socialism at the Congress of the Peoples of Europe, Asia and Africa in Puteaux, 1948' *European Review of History: Revue européenne d'histoire* Vol. 21 Nr. 4 (2014), pp. 519–537.

Richard, Anne-Isabelle, *The European Convention of Human Rights' Colonial Clause and the End of Empire*, *VerfBlog*, 2022/1/26, https://verfassungsblog.de/the-european-convention-of-human-rights-colonial-clause-and-the-end-of-empire/.

Rijn, Arjen van, 'De bescherming van de grondrechten in de Nederlandse Antillen' *NJCM Bulletin* Vol. 17 Nr. 2 (1992), pp. 131–149.

Rijn, Arjen van, *Handboek Caribisch Staatsrecht* (Den Haag: Boom, 2019).

Roggeband, Conny and Rens Vliegenthart, 'Divergent Framing: The Public Debate on Migration in the Dutch Parliament and Media, 1995–2004' *West European Politics* Vol. 30 Nr. 3 (2007), pp. 524–548.

Röling, Bert, 'Het individuele klachtrecht in de Europese Conventie voor de mensenrechten' *Nederlands Juristenblad* Nr. 13 (1956), pp. 293–315.

Römkens, Renée, 'Bestemd Voor Binnenlands Gebruik: De Invloed van de Vrouwen- En Mensenrechtenbeweging Op Het Debat En de Aanpak van Gendergerelateerd Geweld' *Tijdschrift Sociologie* Vol. 12 Nr. 3 (2016), pp. 295–319.

Rorty, Richard, 'Human Rights, Rationality and Sentimentality' in Stephen Shute and Susan Hurley (eds.), *On Human Rights: The Oxford Amnesty Lectures 1993* (Oxford: Oxford University Press, 1994), pp. 111–134.

Rossum, Wibo van, 'The Roots of Dutch Strategic Human Rights Litigation: Comparing "Engel" to "SGP"' in Marjolein van den Brink, Susanne Burri and Jenny Goldschmidt (eds.), *Equality and Human Rights: Nothing but Trouble? Liber amicorum Titia Loenen* (Utrecht: SIM, 2015), pp. 387–401.

Schabas, William, 'Ireland, the European Convention of Human Rights and the Personal Contribution of Sean MacBride' in John Morison, Kieran McEvoy and Gordon Anthony (eds.), *Judges, Transition and Human Rights* (Oxford: Oxford University Press, 2007), pp. 252–274.

Schermers, Henry, *Het Europese Verdrag tot Bescherming van de Rechten van de Mens en de Fundamentele Vrijheden* (Zwolle: Tjeenk Willink, 1964).

Schermers, Henry (ed.), *The Influence of the European Commission of Human Rights* (The Hague: TMC Asser Instituut, 1992).

Schyff, Gerhard van der, 'De beperkingssystematiek van de Nederlandse grondrechten: Kanttekeningen bij het rapport van de Staatscommissie Grondwet' *Tijdschrift voor Constitutioneel Recht* Vol. 2 Nr. 1 (2011), pp. 186–194.

Schotel, Bas, *On the Right of Exclusion: Law, Ethics and Immigration Policy* (London: Routledge, 2012).

Schrijver, Nico, 'A Portrait of Judge P. H. Kooijmans' *Leiden Journal of International Law* Vol. 27 Nr. 4 (2014), pp. 839–858.

Segers, Matthieu, *Reis naar het continent: Nederland en de Europese integratie, 1950 tot heden* (Amsterdam: Prometheus, 2019).

Simpson, A. W. Brian, *Human Rights and the End of Empire: Britain and the Genesis of the European Convention* (Oxford: Oxford University Press, 2004).

Slaughter, Anne Marie, 'The Real New World Order' *Foreign Affairs* Vol. 76 Nr. 5 (1997), pp. 183–119.

Smekal, Hubert and Tsereteli, Nino, 'Reforming to Please: A Comprehensive Explanation for Non-Exit from the European Court of Human Rights' *European Constitutional Law Review* Vol. 17 Nr. 4 (2021), pp. 664–687.

Smits, Hans, *Strafrechthervormers en Hemelbestormers: opkomst en ondergang van de Coornhert-Liga* (Amsterdam: Amsterdam University Press, 2009).

Snyder, Sarah, *Human Rights Activism and the End of the Cold War: A Transnational History of the Helsinki Network* (Cambridge: Cambridge University Press, 2011).

Snyder, Sarah, 'Beyond Containment? The First Bush Administration's Skeptical Approach to the CSCE' *Cold War History* Vol. 13 Nr. 4 (2013), pp. 463–484.

Soeharno, Jonathan, 'From Guardian of the *Rechtsstaat* to Ruler in the Rule of Law: An Inquiry into the Increased Role of the Judiciary' in A. van Hoek, A. M. Hol, O. J. D. L. M. Jansen, P. Rijpkema and R. J. G. M. Riddershoven (eds.), *Multilevel Governance in Adjudication and Enforcement* (Antwerp: Intersentia, 2006), pp. 157–178.

Soley, Ximena and Silvia Steininger, 'Parting Ways or Lashing Back? Withdrawals, Backlash and the Inter-American Court of Human Rights' *International Journal of Law in Context* Vol. 14 Nr. 2 (2018), pp. 237–257.

Sørensen, Max, 'Les experiences personelles de la Convention. L'experience d'un membre de la Commission' *Revue des droits de l'Homme* (1975) Vol. 3, pp. 329–342.

Spano, Robert, 'Universality or Diversity of Human Rights? Strasbourg in the Age of Subsidiarity' *Human Rights Law Review* Vol. 14 Nr. 3 (2014), pp. 487–502.

Spijkerboer, Thomas, 'het debat over het Europese Hof voor de Rechten van de Mens' *Nederlands Juristenblad* Nr. 4. (2012), pp. 254–262.

Spijkerboer, Thomas, 'Coloniality and Recent European Migration Case Law' in Stijn Smet and Vladislava Stoyanova (eds.), *Migrants' Rights, Populism and Legal Resilience in Europe* (Cambridge: Cambridge University Press, 2022), pp. 117–138.

Stappert, Nora, 'Practice Theory and Change in International Law: Theorizing the Development of Legal Meaning through the Interpretive Practices of International Criminal Courts' *International Theory* Vol. 12 Nr. 1 (2020), pp. 33–58.

Steenhoff, Gerrit Jan Willem and René Johan Quirin Klomp, *G.J. Wiarda: Schets van Leven en Werk* (Utrecht: G.J. Wiarda Instituut, 1998).

Steininger, Silvia, 'Creating Loyalty: Communication Practices in the European and Inter-American Human Rights Regimes' *Global Constitutionalism* Vol. 11 Nr. 2 (2022), pp. 161–196.

Stiansen, Øyvind and Erik Voeten, 'Backlash and Judicial Restraint: Evidence from the European Court of Human Rights' *International Studies Quarterly* Vol. 64 Nr. 4 (2020), pp. 770–784.

Stoffel, Simon Henri, *De Massa-mensch en zijn toekomst* (Amsterdam: Uitgeverij Vrij Nederland, 1946).

Swaan, Abraham de, *Zorg en Staat: Welzijn, onderwijs en Gezondheidszorg in Europa en de Verenigde Staten in de Nieuwe tijd* (Amsterdam: Bert Bakker, 1989).

Swart, Bert, *Nederlands Uitleveringsrecht* (Zwolle: Tjeenk Willink, 1986).

Swart, Bert, 'Het recht op gezinsleven in het Europees Verdrag en het vreemdelingenrecht (preadvies)' in *Handelingen Nederlandse Juristen-Vereniging 1990–I* (1990), pp. 185–262.

Swirc, Maurice, *De Indische Doofpot: Waarom Nederlandse Oorlogsmisdaden in Indonesië nooit zijn vervolgd* (Amsterdam: Arbeiderspers, 2022).

Thomas, Martin, Bob Moore and Larry Butler, *Crises of Empire: Decolonization and Europe's Imperial States* (London: Bloomsbury, 2015).

Tolley, Howard, *The International Commission of Jurists: Global Advocates for Human Rights* (Philadelphia: Pennsylvania University Press, 1994).

Vauchez, Antoine and Bruno de Witte (eds.), *Lawyering Europe: European Law as a Transnational Social Field* (Oxford: Oxford University Press, 2013).

Vauchez, Antoine, *Brokering Europe: Euro-Lawyers and the Making of a Transnational Polity* (Cambridge: Cambridge University Press, 2015).

Veegens, Dirk Jacob, 'Het Europees Verdrag tot bescherming van de rechten van de mens en het nationale recht' *Mededelingen van de Nederlandse Vereniging voor Internationaal Recht* Nr. 43 (1960), pp. 42–82.

Venzke, Ingo, *How Interpretation Makes International Law: On Semantic Change and Normative Twists* (Oxford: Oxford University Press, 2016).

Vondraek, Th. J., 'The Netherlands-The Televizier Case: Two Conflicting Concepts of Freedom' *The American Journal of Comparative Law* Vol. 15 Nr. 3 (1966), pp. 537–546.

Vree, Frank van, *In de Schaduw van Auschwitz: Herinneringen beelden, geschiedenis* (Groningen: Historische Uitgeverij, 1995).

Waal, Tamar de, 'Liberal Democracy and the Judeo-Christian Tradition' *Netherlands Journal of Legal Philosophy* Nr. 1 (2020), pp. 7–21.

Walaardt, Tycho, 'Patience and Perseverance: The asylum procedure of Tamils and Iranians in the Netherlands in the mid-1980's' *Tijdschrift voor sociale en economische geschiedenis* Vol. 8 Nr. 3 (2011), pp. 2–31.

Walsum, Sarah van, '*Family Life* in de schaduw van de Grens' *NJCM Bulletin* Vol. 26 Nr. 6 (2001), pp. 731–740.

Walsum, Sarah van, *The Family and the Nation: Dutch Family Migration Policies in the Context of Changing Family Norms* (Newcastle: Cambridge Scholars Publishers, 2008).

Wassenberg, Birte, *History of the Council of Europe* (Strasbourg: Council of Europe, 2013).

Westerveld, Mies et al., (eds.), *35 jaar sociale advocatuur* (Den Haag: SDU Uitgevers, 2010).

Whyte, Jessica, *The Morals of the Market: Human Rights and the Rise of Neoliberalism* (New York: Verso, 2019).

Wiarda, Gerard, 'de betekenis van art. 6 lid 1 van het Europese verdrag tot bescherming van de rechten van de mens voor de Nederlandse administratieve rechtsgangen' in Piet Abas and Nicolaas Joseph Pieter Giltay Veth (eds.), *Non sine causa (opstellen aangeboden aan prof. Mr. G.J. Scholten)* (Zwolle: Tjeenk Willink, 1979), pp. 459–474.

Wiarda, Gerard, *Rechterlijke voortvarendheid en rechterlijke terughoudendheid bij de toepassing van de Europese Conventie ter bescherming van de rechten van de mens* (oratie, Utrecht: Utrecht University, 1986).

Wilder, Gary, *Freedom Time: Negritude, Decolonization and the Future of the World* (Durham: Duke, 2015).

Wit, Joke de, *Artikel 94 Grondwet Toegepast: Een onderzoek naar de betekenis, de bedoeling en de toepassing van de woorden 'vinden geen toepassing' in artikel 94 Grondwet* (Rotterdam: Doctoral Thesis, 2012).

Zwaak, Leo, 'A Friendly Settlement in the European Inter-State Complaints against Turkey' *SIM Newsletter* Nr. 13 (1986), pp. 44–48.

Zwaak, Leo, 'Netherlands' in Robert Blackburn and Jörg Polakiewicz (eds.), *Fundamental Rights in Europe: The ECHR and Its Member States, 1950–2000* (Oxford: Oxford University Press, 2001), pp. 595–624.

Zwart, Faas P., 'De invloed van artikel 26 van het IVBPR en artikel 14 van het EVRM op de rechtspraak van de Centrale Raad van Beroep' in Ronald Maria Van Male, Herman Bolt e.a. (eds.), *Centrale Raad van Beroep 1903–2003* (Den Haag: SDU Uitgevers, 2003).

Index

www.ingramcontent.com/pod-product-compliance
Lightning Source LLC
LaVergne TN
LVHW011702200926
848484LV00004B/1045

* 9 7 8 1 0 0 9 6 7 6 8 1 6 *